For Nelson –

With love and gratitude for our decades-long friendship.

December 2022

PASQUALE

TALES OF A BROOKLYN GROCER'S SON

I hope you enjoy the saga of the Franzese clan!

Merry Christmas!

Peter M. Franzese

PETER M. FRANZESE

MINDSTIR MEDIA

Pasquale: Tales of a Brooklyn Grocer's Son
Copyright © 2022 by Peter M. Franzese. All rights reserved.

No part of this book may be used or reproduced in any manner whatsoever without written permission, except in the case of brief quotations embodied in critical articles and reviews. For more information, e-mail all inquiries to info@mindstirmedia.com.

Published by Mindstir Media, LLC
45 Lafayette Rd | Suite 181| North Hampton, NH 03862 | USA
1.800.767.0531 | www.mindstirmedia.com

Printed in the United States of America
ISBN: 979-8-9863201-3-7 (paperback)
ISBN: 978-1-9587295-6-4 (hardcover)

Other Books
_____

Nettie: Tales of a Brooklyn Nana

"I had a good life. It was a roller coaster. My life was a roller coaster. Sometimes it was up and sometimes it was down."

—**Pat Franzese**
November 30, 2019

Contents

Acknowledgements ix
Foreword xvii
Prologue xxi

Chapter 1   The Franzese Family of Palma Campania 1
Chapter 2   The Grocer 7
Chapter 3   The Grocer's Son 19
Chapter 4   The Franzese Boys Go Off to War 51
Chapter 5   Romance on Richardson Street 103
Chapter 6   The Portis and The Cilibrasis 115
Chapter 7   A Coney Island Courtship 139
Chapter 8   Jackson Street 157
Chapter 9   In Sickness and in Health 183
Chapter 10 Life After Rose 201
Chapter 11 In Search of Rose 223
Chapter 12 Finding Grandpa Pat 261
Chapter 13 Victoria's Pa Pat 287
Chapter 14 Life Without Grandpa Pat 351

Acknowledgements

While it became an ambition of mine to write a book about my paternal grandmother, Rose Porti Franzese, based on the family history project I had worked on back when I was in the seventh-grade honors English class of Lynn Simmons in 1991, the creation of this book really began while sitting with my grandfather, Pat Franzese, sipping Carlo Rossi Burgundy wine at his kitchen table on an afternoon in February of 2006. That afternoon became the springboard of countless more visits and experiences with him that found me sitting with a notebook, a tape recorder, and a camera, as he reached back into the past to begin linking the stories of his early life, which he loved to share, to the ones about the few, short years that he knew my grandmother, Rose. Over time, I was so enthralled by the stories of his early youth that the real focus of my book became more about him than about her. From 2006 until 2019, the telling and retelling of these stories, whether at kitchen tables or on long car rides, transported me back in time on the journey of the Italian grocer and his wife through their early years in the New World, seen through the eyes of the youngest of their seven children.

Although he did not live to see the ending of this project, I am eternally grateful to my Grandpa Pat for sharing with me the stories of his early years with his parents and for the connection we made over his last twenty-five years of his life.

I am deeply grateful to my wife, Vanessa, and my daughter, Victoria, who were always patient and supportive as I spent countless hours talking on the phone, researching, transcribing my grandfather's interviews, and writing this book. They are the stars of my love story, as I wrote the story of his.

Also, I am so incredibly grateful to my parents, Peter and AnnMarie, who knew from when I was a young boy that I was fascinated by this beautiful young woman in a wedding picture who was my Grandma Rose and the hunger I had for knowledge about her. When I was just on the cusp of becoming a teenager, they would drive me to churches to get certificates, drove past houses where she lived, drove me to cemeteries to visit ancestors, and bringing me to visit with living relatives of the older generations. They helped me so incredibly much as I began this journey, and it is my gift, especially to my father, to share with him the story of his parents, who he never really knew. I am also grateful to my brother, Robert, who listened to me share and retell these stories to him over and over again, as I wanted to instill their importance in him as well.

While my Franzese family are all about honoring and remembering their family, they are not deeply invested in the ancestors they did not know, so it took a great deal of sleuthing to uncover who the forefathers and foremothers were of our clan. The late Sal Abramo, his brother, my Uncle Charlie Abramo, and later Sal's son, James Abramo, of the now defunct Abramo Funeral Home, were the first people to help me begin to uncover my ancestors in 1991. Then, in 2000, I met a long-lost distant Franzese cousin, the late Suzanne Nunziata Ciechalski, who spent long hours intensely studying the microfilms at the Church of Jesus Christ of Latter-Day Saints in Plainview, New York, and later that year made a pilgrimage to Palma Campania, Italy, to find out the story of the original Franzeses. She was insistent that I had to uncover the past of the name that I bore and to make the family proud. When I graduated from college, Suzanne gave me a leather-bound family journal and a Franzese family crest before her death in 2002. She insisted that one day I would uncover the family history and fill it with my findings. Years later, I made another connection with a distant Franzese cousin,

Chris Milmerstadt, who has made my Franzese family tree grow and flourish more than any single person in the thirty years that I have been conducting family research. Then, through Ancestry.com, I made the acquaintance of yet another distant cousin, Anna Ferrara Giunta, whose ancestor was the sister of Grandpa Pat's beloved grandmother, Angelina Fama Nunziata. It was due to her incredible generosity that Angelina's family tree was fully shared and explained to me as well.

Besides my grandfather letting me copy photographs from his collection for this book, I am forever indebted to my cousin, James Glynn, for letting me make copies of the photos that he inherited from his mother, once belonging to my great-grandparents, Pete and Lorenzina Franzese. Because of his willingness and generosity, I am able to tell this story visually from the moment when the Franzeses arrived in Brooklyn until the present day. I am also indebted to my cousin, the late Joe Pisano, his wife, Mary, and their daughter, Joni Pisano Roderka, who also let me make copies of the photos that they inherited once belonging to Joe's grandmother, Virginia Franzese Spizio.

I wish to thank my Aunt Susan Boniface for her tremendous and unfailing support and belief in this project and in every single project that I undertake. Like my parents, she took an active role in assisting me in my research in the years before I was of age to do it independently. There is no aunt and godmother who is more loving and supportive, with no questions asked or criticism ever expressed, in the world. She is a shining light in our lives and is at your side with only a moment's notice. Besides my mother, Aunt Sue is the greatest gift that my Boniface grandparents ever gave us in this life.

Although they are no longer with us, two special women in the life of my Grandma Rose, through their stories, helped make the woman in the black and white wedding photo a vivid and excitingly alive young woman. They are my grandmother's sister, the late Theresa Porti Accardi, and my grandmother's cousin, the late Rose Raia Suglia. Aunt Theresa would say about her late sister, "to know her was to love her," and Cousin Rose would say, "I see her in your twinkling eyes." It was because of them that I could now see Rose and love her as they did.

There are many other people who have helped me with my research over the years with this story. Special thanks to the following:

Jack Calabrese
The Late Betty Scala Ciambrone
Margaret Dalto
John D'Arienzo
Rita DiCanio
The Late Margaret Keller Formato
The late Carmine Franzese
Paul & Victoria Franzese
The late Millie Franzese Glynn
Steven Goddard
Dr. Hope Franzese Jordan
Rosalie Accardi Kinstel
Kristine Okpych Marks

Mary Lodato McCarthy
Maria Suglia Mobus
Michael & Tina Morena
Carol Ann Torre Napolitano
Carmela Nunziato
Patricia Raia Ochs
Joanna Pasquale
Rhea Nunziato Passarella
Leonard Peters
The Late Peter Porti
Steve & Diana Porti
Jennie Franzese Ramos
Theresa Caliendo Taormina

The late Mary Ann Dalia Carlo

Also, special thanks to Maryann Arlia, the administrative assistant of Divine Mercy Parish in Brooklyn who helped me uncover the Franzese records at the Parish of St. Francis de Paola RC Church.

Authors always strive to have that one incredible best friend who is more their soul brother than their best friend, who inspires them and encourages them by bringing out the best in them and their God-given gift with words. It is the magic of their presence in the author's life that sometimes helps the author to enlighten the page in the same way their best friend has enlightened their soul. Jack Kerouac had Neal Cassady. F. Scott Fitzgerald had Ernest Hemingway. And in more recent years, Dorothea Benton Frank had the great *Prince of Tides* himself, Pat Conroy. My soul-brother and best friend, Eric Daniels, keeps me determined and from losing my focus while he continually inspires me in my steadfast commitment to seeing my projects through to the end. Eric's constant encouragement, example, and our shared incredible passion for storytelling helps us to inspire one another to tell and share our stories. The unlikely arrival of Eric in my life and the way he has impacted my journey and how

I see the world is a book in itself, and one I am sure will be told one day. Eric is a hero to me and the older brother God gave me at the age of forty-one. I am so incredibly blessed to have him in my life and have him become such a major part of my own story.

And, last, but far from least, I thank the woman who started me on my journey as a writer back in September of 1989. When I was eleven years old, my 6th grade English teacher, Rita Charney Alessi, told me that I was an author, as she inspired me to interview and write the life story of my Nana Nettie Boniface, which fifteen years later became my first book. She told me when I was only eleven that she would hold a book that I would write in her hands one day. Now, more than thirty years since then, her words made such an indelible mark on my soul that they continue to inspire me throughout my life. Had I not had the good fortune of having been her student at John F. Kennedy Intermediate School in Deer Park, New York, and been molded to believe in myself and discover my talent, this book would not exist without her. Without Rita Charney Alessi, there never would have been *Nettie: Tales of a Brooklyn Nana* or *Pasquale: Tales of the Brooklyn Grocer's Son*.

For My Beautiful Wife,
Vanessa Elizabeth Paula Kelsch Franzese
And My Adorable Daughter,
Victoria Rose Franzese,
The Stars of My Love Story

Foreword

My grandfather lived a grand total of ninety-two years, three months, and eleven days. In a matter of weeks, his eventful life came to a swift and somber closing. His life story was always about being surrounded by his family, which interestingly enough included family members born as far back as 1852 and as late as 2012. He didn't fade away, but just slipped away over the course of a few days after a hard, ten-week fight for survival. Grandpa remained sharp, funny, cantankerous when pushed, mischievous when given the opportunity, and passionate about everyday life until those last moments. There were always two spools of film playing in his head. One in vibrant color in which he could give perfect recall of all the events that had happened in his every-day life…and another…one in sepia tone, of him in pinstriped suits and fedoras, and driving his green 1946 Hudson around Coney Island and Bear Mountain Park. He was always living in the present, but had the gift of also being a time machine to take you on that ride with him in old fashioned cars back into more idealistic times.

This is not a definitive biography of Pat Franzese. I am not entirely sure that one could be written. Like the many facets of a diamond, each key person in his life story has a completely unique vision of who he was and an entire set of stories that they personally shared with him, which may have nothing in common with the person who had shared in another aspect and era of his life. I think back to his daughter-in-law Vicki's eulogy. Vicki, who was one of the very few people who knew most of the facets of Grandpa Pat best in this world, said it so succinctly when she said, "Pasquale, Pat, Papu, Grandpa, PaPat, Skinny Ginny, Daddy, Dad, Jack of All Trades-different persona for each unique role. Different relationship with each one of us. This is why we all have such varying memories of the impact he had on each of us individually."

This work is a compilation of the stories Grandpa Pat chose to share with me over those last thirteen years about how he saw his life back then in the scope of his life as a man in his eighties and then in his nineties. This is also the story of my connection to a grandfather that I only knew on the surface in my youth but did not really get to intimately know until those closing years. It is the development of a grandfather and a grandson going from casual acquaintances to dearest friends, and the repairing of broken bridges that seemed so long abandoned, that their brokenness was just accepted and no longer even noticed. The last thirteen years of my Grandpa Pat's life that I spent with him were more healing than anyone realized. Interviewing him was like sifting through sand at the beach and trying to find the seashells underneath. I had to go through a whole lot of granules to get to the prize. The prize was always worth all of the sifting, though. In the end, there was redemption and unification. It is the story that where there is life there is hope, hope can never be lost, and it is never too late to forgive and to try to build a new foundation on top of an old and broken one.

Grandpa Pat was younger than all of his six siblings, of which he knew five. He had two wives, of which my grandmother was the first, but their marriage was so short that to many she should merely be a footnote in the course of a lifespan of nearly a century. He definitely did not see her as merely a footnote, but as a bittersweet memory that transcended all those decades until the last one. He also spent his life with his second wife for nearly forty years, his true partner in life, and together they suffered great sacrifice to achieve a happiness and family life that had eluded him his first time around. He had three children, of which my father is the eldest, but the only one that he did not live with for any length of time. I am the oldest of his six grandchildren, who would become one of his most inti-

PASQUALE

mate people in his life at the end after I had become an adult. My daughter is his sole great-grandchild, who had his love completely and unreservedly from the moment she was placed before him the day after her birth, until she saw his casket being lowered on the day of his funeral. I do not tell the story of Pat Franzese that encompasses everyone's experience of him. If anyone feels that their story needs to be told, I encourage them to write and tell their unique story of the life of this incomparable and multi-faceted man. Each of the facets of him is just as vital and just as true, and there is enough of his animated stories to make the world smile, regardless of the era of his life. He was such an engaging and charismatic character. It is one of the greatest blessings of my life that we were given this time, this opportunity, and that both of our hearts were open to the possibility for this relationship to flourish and experience to happen. My life is forever blessed because of the adult friendship that I built with my grandfather, Pasquale "Pat" Franzese.

For better or for worse, this is the story of the Italian Brooklyn Grocer's Son that Grandpa Pat chose to share with me of who Pete the Grocer's son, Pat, was, and this is the story of the life and bond I shared with him as he lived in the present with me and shared the past. I hope that both threads of this story restore your faith in possibilities and inspiration for endurance and survival, as it has for me. For my father, this entire story is a gift that eluded him for all of his life. Dad, here is the story of the father and mother that God first gave you.

Peter Michael Franzese
North Babylon, New York
October 16, 2021

Prologue

The last apartment where Grandpa Pat lived, in the home of his youngest child, my Uncle Paul, with his wife, Vicki, in Baldwin Harbor, Long Island, was always a showcase to me of his life on display in a single room if you had to encompass his whole life into a snapshot. In his little kitchen area, Grandpa would make the most delicious meals based on those taught to him long ago by his mother, whether macaroni, meatballs and sausage with sauce, chicken cutlets with mashed potatoes and sautéed spinach, pork chops, or spaghetti with garlic and oil. When you put the fork to your mouth and savored the taste, you couldn't help but feel that he was the extension of welcoming you to his mother's long-ago kitchen table behind the long-ago grocery store in Brooklyn. Everything Grandpa Pat made was always with care, and always with the welcoming sight of two short cut-glass wineglasses for us to commune over with a glass of his trademark Carlo Rossi Burgundy as we shared what was in our souls.

The large room was a gallery of the history of our family. When you weren't sitting with him at the wooden kitchen table sharing a meal or a glass of wine, he was reclined in his overstuffed brown recliner with his slippered feet stretched out in front of him with the TV on. I never could pay attention to the television because the stories he shared and the frames surrounding us all around the room kept me captivated. The large room held his kitchen, living room, and washing machine and dryer. While he had been a widower for a quarter of a century, he could never feel alone with all of the faces of his family, past and present, smiling at him from dozens of frames. On tabletops, on bookshelves, on the walls, and from his refrigerator door, all of the people he ever loved were smiling at him. They ranged from the very young to the very old, vibrant colors, faded colors, sepias, and black and whites. There were his long-ago unsmiling grandparents in turn-of-the-century immigrant dress, his father dressed in a suit and his mother in perpetual black, all of his siblings, young and old. Photos of the young soldiers in his family who never came home. The two women who he loved and celebrated but who had long departed this life. His children as they grew, got married, and made him a grandparent. His half dozen grandchildren, spanning all different ages, and the one great-grandchild who had given him the unique title of "Pa Pat" on her own. He loved them all. He cherished each one. He celebrated them in his own way, in spite of complaining about the dusting of these frames. He had lived for ninety-two years, but they were the faces who had made their exciting entrances, and some their painful exits, in his life. These were the faces of the key players in the story of his long and storied life who had made his life story the "roller coaster" that he claimed it to be.

Grandpa Pat's story began with the people in the early pictures decorating his apartment. This story began not in Greenpoint, Brooklyn, but decades before his birth in the town of his father's birth, Palma Campania, in the Naples region of Italy. It began with the story of his immigrant forbearers who dared to dream of a life outside the only town they had known in his family for centuries. Unbeknownst to Grandpa, it began with the encouragement of his grandmother, who inspired the determined youth his father had been to aspire for a life better than the one she could give him on the soil where he was born. The young man his father had once been had made a journey based on nothing but prayer, without the ability to write his name, with a tongue that could not serve him the answer to an American dream, but forced him to overcome this with the tenacity to realize his dreams of a store as he sold his wares from a horse-drawn cart. It was the dreams of the father, who would make Grandpa Pat the Grocer's Son, that would one day be passed down by my father to me. It was this inheritance to continue the tradition of unwavering faith and determination, of devotion to family and to God, and the ability to never stop laughing in spite of sorrow, which I inherited from the long-ago ancestors to keep the family going and pass on these gifts to the generations to come. To understand, you must look back…from Long Island to Brooklyn…from Brooklyn to Palma Campania.

CHAPTER ONE

The Franzese Family of Palma Campania

1680-1908

Palma Campania, known until 1863 as Palma di Nola, is a municipality in the metropolitan city of Naples in the Campania region of Italy, located about fifteen and a half miles east of Naples. It was in this town where the earliest Franzese recorded was Domenico Franzese, who was born there in 1680. Domenico and his wife, whose name is unknown, bore a son, Sabatino in 1705. Sabatino was married to Carmina Cassese, and together they had six children. Domenico, the eldest of the six, was born there on March 31, 1724. He married his twenty-four-year-old wife, Anna Della Marca, on August 29, 1754. Their son, Francesco, was born in Palma di Nola in 1755. Francesco was the manager of a tavern, called in Italian a "bettoliere." Together, Francesco and his wife, Angela Prevete, had six children between 1791 and 1801. Their youngest son, Michele Natale, was born on Christmas Day in 1801, in Palma di Nola. Francesco's wife, Angela, died in her sixtieth year in Palma di Nola on February 2, 1822, when Michele Natale was twenty years old.

The year following Angela's death, the twenty-one-year-old Michele Natale was married on February 16, 1823, in Palma di Nola to the twenty-three-year-old Teresa Simonetti, also of Palma di Nola.

During the first six years of marriage between Michele Natale and Teresa Simonetti, the couple welcomed a succession of sons, Francesco on July 18, 1824, Pietro on June 28, 1827, and Antonio on August 15, 1829. Three months later, the Franzese patriarch, Francesco, died at the age of seventy-four, on November 20, 1829, seven years after the death of his beloved wife, Angela.

Michele Natale and Teresa welcomed their first daughter, Angela, on October 2, 1831, and another son, Antonio, on December 4, 1833. The previous son, Antonio, had died in infancy. Eight months following the birth of the second Antonio, tragedy struck the Franzese household when Teresa died on August 11, 1834, at the age of thirty-four. Michele Natale and Teresa had been married for eleven years, having had five children together.

Michele Natale, at the age of thirty-three, took a second wife six months after the death of his first. On February 9, 1835, he married the twenty-six-year-old Giuseppa Giannone. Together, they had a son, Felice, on October 29, 1837, and another son, Onofrio, on December 4, 1839. Onofrio died at the age of seven months on July 14, 1840, and another son was named Onofrio when he was born on September 3, 1841. This baby also died within his first three and a half years of life.

On October 10, 1842, Michele Natale and Giuseppa welcomed their fourth child together, his ninth, with the delivery of their son, Massimino. A third Onofrio was born on May 8, 1845, a daughter, Maria Teresa, on November 3, 1847, and their last child, Teresa, on March 18, 1850. In the end, Michele Natale was the father of nine sons and three daughters.

Massimino, at the age of twenty-nine, married the eighteen-year-old Michela Iovino, on April 11, 1872. Michela Iovino was born on June 4, 1853, in Palma di Nola, to Pasquale Iovino and Brigida Peluso. Her father, Pasquale, born to Michele Iovino and Brigida Majeia on April 8, 1821, in San Paolo Bel Sito, Italy, married the twenty-two-year-old Brigida Peluso in her birthplace of Palma di

PASQUALE

Nola, on January 3, 1850. While it is unknown for certain how many children Pasquale and Brigida had together, they did have at least one child in addition to Michela. Their son, Giuseppe, was born in 1868.

During the first decade of their marriage, Michela bore her first child, a daughter, Giuseppa, on April 25, 1874. There were no other recorded children born for another eight years until the birth of Michela's son, Pasquale, named for her father, on May 4, 1882. As Michela was to tell her son years later, in the season of the cherry blossom, she gave birth to her son named Pietro in Palma Campania, the new name of Palma di Nola, on June 2, 1887. Two days later, on his mother's thirty-fourth birthday, Pietro was baptized at the same baptismal font where she too had been baptized, at the Church of Saint Michael the Archangel in Palma Campania. Following Pietro's birth, Michela had her final child, Virgilia "Virginia," on July 27, 1889.

While there is little known about Massimino Franzese one hundred and eighty years after his birth, and no photos of him survive, the stories of the nefarious treatment he gave his kind and holy wife would survive down the generations and across the vast Atlantic Ocean. Years later, Pietro would relay stories to his family about his wicked father who was always miserable and equally abusive, especially to his wife. He was known for taking up with women of ill repute, much to the humiliation of Michela. He treated his wife as a servant, Pietro said, "like any other worker," and paid her a pittance as a laborer. He was also known for being brutal in his physical abuse to his children. Fearing for the safety of her children, Michela vowed to help them escape.

Michela's younger brother, Giuseppe "Joseph" Iovino, had married his wife, Rose, in Palma Campania, and had a son Pasquale, named after the Iovino patriarch, in 1889. Together, Joseph, Rose, and Pasquale came to the United States in 1896, and settled at 702 Lorimer Street in the Williamsburg section of Brooklyn, New York, where he worked as a shoemaker. They then had a daughter, Anna, in 1898, a son, Fred, in 1902, and a daughter, Maria, in 1903. Six years after Joseph's arrival in America, Michela sent her oldest son, Pasquale, to live with her brother in the "New World," where he would live and work alongside his cousin as a cooper, a barrel maker, in a barrel factory. According to his "Petition For Naturalization" form, Pasquale arrived in New York on his twentieth birthday, May 4, 1902, after eighteen days at sea aboard the Tartan Prince, which had set sail from Naples. Also, the form states that Pasquale had been married in Palma Campania to Grazia Simonetti, but that she was now deceased and they had no children. Pasquale, without a living spouse or children, was able to save enough money to send for his brother, Pietro, to next escape the tyranny of Massimino's household.

A few weeks shy of his sixteenth birthday, Pietro would leave his father's house and Palma Campania behind, never to set foot in either ever again. Sending him with a stick of salami and her prayers, Michela told Pietro that soon they would be reunited in the New World. The anxiety that must have filled the young Pietro to leave his mother and sisters behind defenseless in the home of his cruel father! On the day that Pietro set out for Naples, the town of his birth went into his history, as well as the father he despised, and would never see again. Pietro would tell his oldest son years later that he never knew what became of his father after they all left and did not care.

The SS Patria pulled into New York Harbor and landed at Ellis Island on April 21, 1903, and when that day came to an end, Pietro spent his first night in his newly adopted home in Brooklyn. While the sight of his older brother and his uncle must have filled him with much comfort, the anxiety of his mother left behind in Palma Campania was his unceasingly burning ambition to drive him to make enough money to bring her and his sisters over quickly. Practically as soon as he got to Brooklyn, Pietro, or Pete as he would be known in his newly adopted home, went to work with his brother, Pasquale, and cousin Patsy Iovino, in the barrel factory. At the turn of the Twentieth Century, there were barrel factories all over the neighborhoods of Greenpoint and Williamsburg in Brooklyn at that time. There was one at 80 Wythe Avenue, near the Williamsburg waterfront, which opened in 1901, but most likely they worked at one closer to where the Franzese brothers and their Iovino family members were living on Lorimer Street.

Nearly ninety years after his arrival, Pete's oldest son said that when the two brothers worked in the barrel factory, an Irish foreman was calling them guinea, wop, and dago. Being illiterate and only able to speak Italian, Pete was to learn very quickly the segregation that existed in the New World, as he came up against difficulties with other nationalities in the barrel factory. At first, not knowing what the Irishman was saying to them, the two brothers ignored these insults. One day, having enough of the foreman's insults, the brothers took one of the heavy barrels and threw it at him and quit the job on the spot, but not before saving the money to send for their mother and sisters. Michela and her youngest daughter, Virginia, came to settle in Brooklyn with the brothers. Their other sister, Giuseppa, was disgusted by the family life in Palma Campania and wished to part ways with the Franzeses permanently. She went on to Argentina, and despite efforts of Pasquale to look for her, was never heard from again.

The youngest sister, Virginia, was eighteen when she was given in marriage to Antonio Ospizio on August 22, 1907. Antonio, born on September 29, 1885, in the Piemonte region of Umbria, Italy, came to America aboard the SS Umbria on June 9, 1903. He settled with his uncle on Lorimer Street and there met his eighteen-year-old bride. A year later, they welcomed their first child, Vincenzo "Jimmy," on June 29, 1908, the first Franzese grandchild. The first roots of the Franzese family tree were now planted in the New World in the Greenpoint-Williamsburg section of Brooklyn, New York.

Pietro "Pete" Franzese, age 21, early 1909

Pete's mother, Michela Iovino Franzese

CHAPTER TWO

The Grocer

1908-1927

Pete, now owning his own horse and wagon, was a peddler of fruit and vegetables living at 49 Frost Street, when he spoke with Francesco Maiello, living at 72 Richardson Street, if he knew of a suitable wife for him. The parents of Francesco's wife, Lucia, were still in Palma Campania, but he was the acting guardian of their daughters in America. The two men arranged for Pete to marry the next eligible daughter, Carmela Nunziata, who was two years Pete's senior. They were married at the Italian Church of Our Lady of Mount Carmel, located at the corner of North Eighth Street and Union Avenue in Williamsburg, Brooklyn, on April 9, 1908. Their witnesses were Gennaro Duca and Pete's sister, Virginia. During their eight-month marriage, it is believed that Carmela was expecting a child. Only four months into the marriage, Carmela took ill and was placed under the care of Doctor Nacciarone. After careful examination, Doctor Nacciarone from 271 Union Street, diagnosed Pete's young bride with "aortic incompetency," which would claim her life at four in the morning in the bedroom of her Frost Street home on December 30, 1908. She was twenty-three-years-old. Pete turned to his uncle, Joseph Iovino, who led him to his neighbor, the 29-year old undertaker, Joseph Citro, at 703 Lorimer Street. From her home on Frost Street, the horse drawn carriage took the young bride to Our Lady of Mount Carmel for a funeral mass on the last day of the year, before the procession went over the Penny Bridge down Greenpoint Avenue, where she was laid to rest in the newly dug grave in Calvary Cemetery.

Carmela Nunziata Franzese

Pete, like his brother Pasquale had before him, mourned for his young bride for thirteen months, wearing a black mourning band on his arm, as was shown in the earliest known portrait of him taken in 1909. In January of 1910, when the year of mourning came to an end, Pete once again arranged with Francesco Maiello to remarry. This time the bride had not been as submissive to marry, in spite of not being given a choice. This next eligible Nunziata sister had an iron will of her own and had planned to become a nun, but Pete nonetheless obtained the marriage license to marry her on January 13, 1910. Iron will or not, she was told that she had to marry her brother-in-law, so on the day before her twenty-first birthday, Lorenzina Nunziata married Pete Franzese at Our Lady of Mount Carmel Church on February 6, 1910. Their witnesses were Pete's brother, Pasquale, and Armina Duca. Pete's brother, Pasquale, also remarried a month later to Anna Rollo on March 17, 1910, at Our Lady of Mount Carmel. Pasquale and Anna had a house built on Kingsland Avenue shortly after their marriage and then welcomed the birth of their only child, Michela, known as Margaret, on December 15, 1910. When the second Franzese grandchild of Michela Iovino Franzese was born, Lorenzina was five months pregnant with her first child.

Lorenzina Nunziata Franzese

Lorenzina went to live with Pete at the house he owned at 49 Frost Street, where her late sister, Carmela, had also lived with him. Pete's mother, Michela, had her own apartment in the same house. According to the United States Census taken that year on April 21, 1910, Pete is listed as a peddler of vegetables and Lorenzina as a salesman of groceries. Lorenzina proved to be an astute businesswoman and worked side by side with her husband in the grocery business. In the months following the census, Pete sold the house at 49 Frost Street and purchased a larger home at 224 Frost Street. It was there they were living when Lorenzina gave birth to her first child, Michela, who they called Margie, on April 26, 1911. On May 17, 1912, Dr. Simon Davis from 104 Marcy Avenue in Williamsburg was summoned to the Franzese household when Margie became seriously ill. Dr. Davis told Pete and Lorenzina that their year-old daughter was suffering from bronchial pneumonia. Over the next eight days, Margie failed to improve and developed pulmonary edema from the bronchial pneumonia. She died in Pete's arms at 11:30 in the evening on May 25, 1912 after only one year and twenty-nine days of life. Two days later, baby Margie was laid to rest in Calvary Cemetery in the same grave as Carmela. Lorenzina was five months pregnant with her second child at the time.

Four months later, Lorenzina would give birth to a son, Carmine, on September 8, 1912. Breaking from tradition and not naming his first son after his father, Massimino, it is believed that Pete named his first son in honor of Our Lady of Mount Carmel, as he was an active member of the Carmine Society. In spite of the strife and tragedy that befell Pete during his first years in the United States, he chose to place himself under the protection of Our Lady of Mount Carmel. It was her who he chose as his special patron and to her he gave credit for the better fortune he would have in the future. He was a leader in the Carmine Society, a male fraternal religious organization that existed in the parish of Our Lady of Mount Carmel in the early part of the twentieth century and graced his home with a two-foot high statue of his patron saint, in addition to wearing a ring on his finger of Our Lady of Mount Carmel.

According to the history of the parish written for its 100th anniversary in 1987, The Church of Our Lady of Mount Carmel, then on the corner of North 8th Street and Union Avenue, was built in 1887, the same year as Pete's birth, to serve the ever-growing Italian population of the Greenpoint-Williamsburg section of Brooklyn. Bishop John Loughlin, the first Bishop of Brooklyn, assigned Father Peter Saponara to establish the parish for the Italian community of Williamsburg. Saponara, who was pastor from 1887 to 1926, purchased the site of the original church for $5,000 at the corner of North 8th Street and Union Avenue. The cornerstone for the church was laid by Bishop Loughlin on July 31, 1887, and placed under the protection of Our Lady of Mount Carmel. To accommodate a larger congregation, for a still increasing parish, the original church where Pete married both Carmela in 1908 and Lorenzina in 1910, was torn down in 1920 and a larger church was built on the same site in 1930, only to have that church demolished in 1947 to make way for the construction of the Brooklyn-Queens Expressway, following the end of World War II. The current church of Our Lady of Mount Carmel was built in 1950 on the corner of North 8th and Havemeyer Streets, the site of the annual feast of Our Lady of Mount Carmel and Saint Paulinus that draws the descendants of these first immigrant founders back to the streets where their families began their American adventures.

Two years after the birth of Carmine, Lorenzina gave birth to another daughter, Michelina, also called Margie, on October 12, 1914. Living at 224 Frost Street with Pete and Lorenzina and their two small children was Pete's mother, Michela. The Franzese matriarch was a meek and quiet woman who was known for her innate kindness, in spite of the fact that she lived for so many years under the cruel treatment of her husband. Back in Italy, she had become accustomed to being given only what was at the bottom of the barrel for herself. One day, Pete saw his elderly mother sitting at the table cutting all of the rotten parts off of a piece of fruit so she could have something to eat. Giving her a fresh piece of fruit, Pete declared to his mother that she would never have to eat from a rotten piece of fruit ever again. He and his family took care of her lovingly for the rest of her days. On August 10, 1915, Pete first signed his Declaration of Intention to become a citizen of the United States. He was twenty-eight years old at the time and listed as a peddler. He was described as being 5'8" in height and 145 pounds, with a dark complexion, dark brown hair, and brown eyes. Since he was illiterate, Pete put an X in the place of his signature.

Two more children followed the birth of Margie, when Carmela, who they called Millie, named after Pete's first wife, was born on November 7, 1916, and Massimino, who they called Sammy, named after Pete's father, was delivered on February 23, 1919. On June 18, 1920, Pete was able to sign his name to the Petition for Naturalization. A neighbor, Virginia Ziccardi, a baker living at 230 Frost Street, and his brother-in-law, Lorenzo Nunziata, a candy maker, living at his same address, were listed as the witnesses to his signing the affidavit. Lorenzo, now home from serving in the US Army during World War I, was living in an apartment in Pete's house. Lorenzo had arrived with his father, Salvatore, from Palma Campania on November 30, 1912. His mother, Maria Angela Fama, known as Angelina, and his sister, Rose, had arrived six months before them on May 9, 1912.

Pete and Lorenzina welcomed a sixth child, Salvatore, named after Lorenzina's father, on April 25, 1921. Sometime between his renewal of his peddler's license in 1922 and when the census taker came on June 1, 1925, Pete sold 224 Frost Street to his brother-in-law, Lorenzo, and bought a grocery store at 501 Humboldt Street. According to the census, Pete became a United States citizen in 1920. He had Lorenzina, his five surviving children, and his mother living with him in the rooms behind the store. While only a few blocks away, they left behind much of the Nunziata family, whose last name changed from Nunziata to Nunziato, and Pete's sister's family, the Ospizio family, who now called themselves the Spizios, on Frost Street.

The Franzese Children in 1919 (l.-r.) Carmine, Sammy, Millie, & Margie

The father of Lorenzina and Carmela, Salvatore Nunziata, was born on October 8, 1852, in Palma di Nola, Italy. He was the son of Lorenzo Nunziata, born January 28, 1825, and Lucia Ferraro, born July 23, 1825, also in Palma di Nola. They were both twenty-six when they married in the city of their birth on October 2, 1851, and their son, Salvatore, arrived six days after their first wedding anniversary.

Lorenzina and Carmela's mother, Angelina, was born Maria Angela Fama, the daughter of Domenico Fama and Pasqua Serafino, on January 31, 1857, in Sant' Anastasia, Italy. Her father, Domenico Fama, was born on May 27, 1810, the son of Antonio Fama and Carmina Barone. Her mother, Pasqua Serafino, was born on April 6, 1817, the daughter of Antonio Serafino and Angela Rosa Di Manzo. Both of Angelina's parents were also born in Sant' Anastasia, where they were also married on June 6, 1833. Angelina was the youngest of Domenico and Pasqua's eight children. While the dates of death are unknown for Domenico and Pasqua, it is assumed that they both died when Angelina was still very young, and that Angelina went to live with her sister, Angela Carmela, who left Sant' Anastasia and moved to Palma Campania, following her marriage to Filippo Sorrentino on February 10, 1864, and subsequently had seven children with Fillipo between 1864 and 1877.

At the age of twenty-two, Angelina would leave Angela Carmela's home when she married Salvatore Nunziata in Palma Campania on November 23, 1879. Angela Carmela, who was seventeen years older than Angelina, would die two and a half years later on May 17, 1882, at the age of forty-one. The death of Angela Carmela was most likely more like the loss of a mother than a sister for Angelina.

While the exact number of children that Salvatore and Angelina had is unknown, they did have seven children who survived into adulthood: Lucia on December 3, 1880, Carmela in June of 1885, Lorenzina on February 7, 1889, Concetta on February 3, 1891, Philomena on December 16, 1893, Rose on August 25, 1897, and their only son, Lorenzo, on April 23, 1900.

Lucia, the eldest child, married Francesco Maiello, in Palma Campania in the late 1890's and had two children who died there in infancy. They came to the United States around 1903 and settled at 242 North Fifth Street in Williamsburg, Brooklyn, as the census taker recorded their address in 1905. Once settled in Brooklyn, Lucia and Francesco had a daughter, Anna, on November 15, 1904, and Francesco, called Frank once settled in America, sponsored his Nunziata in-laws in the United States. Carmela came over in 1904, then Lorenzina and Philomena came together on the SS Madonna, leaving from Naples on June 21, 1906, and arriving at Ellis Island on July 3rd. Carmela would marry Pete in 1908 and die in the same year. Concetta followed her sisters to America in 1910, the same year that Lorenzina and Pete married. Their mother, Angelina, and their sister, Rose, would arrive on May 9, 1912. The last to leave were their father, Salvatore, and the only brother, Lorenzo, when they boarded the SS Venezia in Naples on November 16, 1912, and after two weeks at sea, they had arrived at Ellis Island on November 30th. According to the ship's manifest, Salvatore was sixty years old and stood at 5'5", had brown hair, but was balding, had blue-gray eyes, and was carrying $16. Upon their arrival, the newly arrived Nunziata's went to live with the Maiello's on North 5th Street. In the months before Salvatore's arrival, his one-year-old granddaughter, Margie, had been laid to rest in May and his daughter, Concetta, married Bernardino Caliendo on July 14, 1912. The following year, Salvatore was there to marry off Philomena to Domenico Croce, a widower six years her senior with three motherless children, on July 31, 1913. Salvatore's youngest daughter, Rose, had hoped for a different husband than the one chosen for her and was devastated when at nineteen she was forced to marry Gennaro Annunziato instead on February 4, 1917.

In the meantime, Lorenzo served in the United States Army during World War I from May 22, 1917 until April 12, 1919. His brother-in-law, Gennaro, had told him to meet a certain ship coming into Ellis Island where a beautiful red-haired girl was due to arrive named Biondina "Maria" Peluso. Meet her he did and they were married on August 7, 1921. Salvatore and Angelina saw all of their children married off and all living within blocks of one another in Williamsburg, Brooklyn. The majority of the Nunziata family was living on Frost Street, where there are still some descendants living well over one hundred years later. The homestead of 224 Frost Street is still owned by the Nunziata family, whose last name at some point around World War I was changed to Nunziato. When coming to America, Salvatore worked in the city dump, interestingly enough as one of his grandsons and one of his great-grandsons would work together for the New York City Department of Sanitation in Greenpoint seventy years later. Angelina worked as a seamstress.

PASQUALE

Lorenzina's parents, Salvatore and Angelina (Fama)
Nunziata, with their youngest children, Rose and Lorenzo,
while still living in Palma Campania circa 1910

Salvatore & Angelina (Fama) Nunziata

The Nunziata family grew with the next generation, as Lucia would have eight children in Brooklyn, Lorenzina would have seven, Concetta had eleven, Philomena had six and three step-children, Rose had eight, and Lorenzo had eleven.

Pete's "Peddler-Horse and Wagon" license issued by the City of New York on May 31, 1922, survives and states that Pietro Franzese living at 224 Frost Street "in consideration of eight dollars, receipt of which is acknowledged, is hereby licensed to ENGAGE IN BUSINESS AS A PEDDLER WITH HORSE AND WAGON IN THE CITY OF NEW YORK." Once he purchased the store at 501 Humboldt Street, Lorenzina would sell predominantly from the store, while Pete peddled from the wagon. By 1926, Carmine would become the first child to graduate from the eighth grade in the family and head to high school that fall. The sisters, Margie and Millie, would both be enrolled at Public School 132 on Manhattan and Metropolitan Avenues, and Sammy would be enrolled at Public School 23 on Humboldt Street, where Carmine had just graduated from. It is unknown if the five-year-old Sal would have entered kindergarten yet at that time. Nonetheless, as the year of 1926 drew to a close, approaching her thirty-eighth birthday on February 7, 1927, Lorenzina was expecting her seventh child to arrive in September.

PASQUALE

Pete's Italian American Grocery Store, 501 Humboldt Street, Brooklyn

Pete's Our Lady of Mount Carmel Statue still
on display in his last home in 2018

CHAPTER THREE

The Grocer's Son

1927-1941

The eighty-degree heatwave of the first Friday in September had broken by the time that Lorenzina went into labor on Labor Day, September 5, 1927, with her seventh child. The fifty-six-year old midwife, Antonia "Antoinette" Menna, of 61 Skillman Avenue, had been sent for to come to Lorenzina's bedside at the Herbert Street entrance of 501 Humboldt Street. In that windowless bedroom, the midwife declared to Lorenzina that her seventh child was a boy.

With the birth of each son, Pete's brother, Pasquale, would always pester Lorenzina to name her newborn infant after him. As his wife, Anna, did not have any children after their only child, Margaret, in 1910, Pasquale longed to have a namesake. After having named their first three sons in honor of Our Lady of Mount Carmel and then both of their fathers, Lorenzina relented and named this infant son in honor of her husband's older brother. Pasquale rejoiced at the news of the birth of his namesake nephew. This infant Pasquale would hold a special place in his hard-boiled uncle's heart.

Lorenzina had changed her parish from the now overcrowded Italian Church of Our Lady of Mount Carmel to the new Italian church, Saint Francis de Paola, on Conselyea Street, which first opened its doors in 1918. The site of Saint Francis had been the home of the Old Bushwick Dutch Reformed Church from the 1660's, until it was disbanded in 1918, when the Diocese of Brooklyn purchased the old Dutch "Church on the Hill," as it was well known then. The diocese named Rev. Leo A. Arcese the first pastor of the parish, and placed it under the protection of Saint Francis de Paola, a fifteenth century friar from the Calabria region of Italy who, while never ordained a priest, founded the Order of Minims. He is the patron saint of Calabria, Italy. The first structure of Saint Francis utilized a chapel that was left over on the site from the Dutch Reformed Church on the corner of Old Woodpoint Road, until the first church was constructed. The church was built in the mission style, a bell tower stood next to the rectory. Father Carmelo Russo, the third pastor of Saint Francis, built a larger church, which was blessed and dedicated in June 1923 by the Third Bishop of Brooklyn, the Most Rev. Thomas E. Molloy. It was here in this newly constructed church that Lorenzina's youngest child was brought for his baptism, unlike his siblings who had all been baptized at Our Lady of Mount Carmel.

Well known throughout her family for ensuring that all of her children were baptized within days of their birth, Lorenzina sent the seventeen-day-old Pasquale to be baptized on September 22, 1927. In the presence of his godparents, his father's eldest nephew, Vincent "Jimmy" Spizio, and his mother's youngest sister, Rose Nunziata Annunziato, Father Carmelo Russo poured the waters of baptism over the infant Pasquale's head.

Patsy, or Pat, as the baby was known, came into the world in the back rooms behind the Franzese Italian-American grocery store that his father, Pete, had opened a few years before. While primarily a produce peddler with his horse and wagon in the years after leaving the barrel factory when he came to America in 1903, he supported his family selling his wares from his wagon. This wagon had supplied him the funds to purchase his first house at 49 Frost Street, later on 224 Frost Street, which he sold to his Nunziato in-laws, and now the large building of 501 Humboldt Street on the corner of Herbert Street. In addition to this, Pete also owned a plot of land in West Hempstead, Long Island, which had two houses on the property. West Hempstead was the family's summer haven.

Lorenzina holding Pat as a baby

"My father had a pretty big store," Pat remembered in 2018. "One side he had fruits and vegetables. On the other side he sold dry goods. He had cans of tomatoes and soups, macaroni, and a scale to weigh cookies. They had a rack with a glass front with cookies and sold cookies by the pound. They used to weigh them on the scale. He had six different kind of cookies. He also had cold cuts and made sandwiches. He had a refrigerator with prosciutto and salami. Olives, he only had in the can, and other stuff in cans. He sold bread. Toilet paper. He had a showcase where he sold cigarettes and he had a candy counter. He used to make and sell lemon ices and he used to make the wine. My father used to sell the grapes to the people who wanted to make it themselves. My brothers had the crates stacked all outside the store almost to the next floor on the sidewalk. When he used to make the wine, he made a barrel for us. He made a barrel of white wine and a couple of other barrels. He used to fill up the gallon bottles and sell them. He didn't have to tell me twice to go down and use the squeezer. Because there was a glass down there and you test it to make sure you have enough raisins in it. The raisins make the wine sweeter. He didn't make sweet wine, but if you make it just from the grapes, it is very bitter. He put a case of raisins into the barrel and I used to stand up there on a chair with a stick and I used to push the grapes into the grinder and my brothers used to grind the grapes into this great big barrel. It was a monster! I think it held three barrels and my father, he was pretty smart with that stuff, when he had to buy the barrels, used to buy barrels that had had whiskey in them and the inside of the barrel had alcohol in it because the wood soaks it in, so he used to buy them. When the grapes used to go into the squeezer, they used a barrel cut in half with a spout on it and all the wine would go in there when you squeezed the grapes. You used to have to taste it once in a while and that's why the glass was there. I used to take a swig as the wine came out of the spigot. I used to run like a thief in the night down the cellar stairs if my father told me to go taste the wine.

"Margie was in the store working sometimes too," Pat continued. "Once in a while, she would be in the store because I remember when the cops came in, my father used to give them a ham and cheese sandwich on a roll for fifteen cents. Everyone else paid a quarter. So, my sister was at the counter when the cop came in and she knew my father did this. Margie said to the cop, 'If you want the sandwich, it's a quarter.' The cop said, 'Your father sells it to me for fifteen cents.' She said, 'I'm not my father. You want me to make the sandwich, it's a quarter. If not, you go down to Tota's on Graham Avenue.' It was Tota, his wife, and two daughters working in his store and he used to charge thirty cents for a ham and cheese sandwich, so the cop would say, 'No, go ahead. Make the sandwich for a quarter.' She was a good businesswoman, my sister, Margie. Better than my father and better than Carmine."

While no stores were allowed to be open or operate in any fashion on Sundays in those days, Pete's grocery store was open from Monday until Saturday from six in the morning until eleven o'clock at night, six days a week. "You couldn't buy nothing on Sunday at that time," Pat said. "One time, my mother was sitting outside the store on Sunday and the cop came from across the street and said, 'You can sit here, but you gotta close that door.' My mother said to the cop, 'I got no lights on. I'm not selling nothing.' 'Regardless,' he said to her, 'you gotta close that door and lock it if you wanna sit here.' My mother got disgusted and went back in the house and locked the door."

On the whole though, the relationship between the Franzeses and the police officers at the 87th Precinct across the street was always a good one. "The captain used to come into the store and my father used to take him in the house and he used to give him a glass of wine," Pat said. "On his way out, there was a showcase with candy in it and the captain used to open up the showcase and take a piece of chocolate to kill the smell of the wine. My father got away with a lot, because one time, my father went to my Uncle Dominick Croce's bar by Saint Francis Church, who was his brother-in-law. He got drunk there one Saturday night into Sunday and the sergeant was riding in the police car and he had a driver. The sergeant spotted my father and I guess my father wasn't walking right. He told the cop, 'stop here, let me see.' He stopped my father and he said to his driver, 'I'll stand here and wait for you. Take him home. He lives across the street from the station.' So, my father got in the sergeant's seat and the cop took him home. Now on a Sunday morning, my father was always up and dressed in a suit and tie. In the meantime, I was twelve or thirteen at the time and I was looking out the window and I see a P.D. car pulling up to the house and I see my father sitting where the sergeant usually sat. My mother was sick. I think she had a cold or something and she was in bed. I was all dressed in a suit to go to church. And I went in my mother's room and said, 'Ma! Ma! Papa's coming out of a police car!' She just said, 'Go open the door and help him in. He's drunk. He was by your uncle. Open the door and help him in.' So, he come strolling in half stewed and I sat him on the chair and taking his shoes off and oh my God, he's kissing me and slobbering all over me. I had to wash my face before I went to church. I had to help him get undressed and into bed and then left for church."

Pete behind the counter of his grocery store in 1930 with his friend, August Formato. Sammy has his hands on young Pat's shoulders, while Rocky Formato stands a bit apart from them.

In Pat's early childhood, Pete was still peddling his wares on the streets while Lorenzina sold the wares in the store. "My father had a horse and wagon," Pat remembered. "He sold the stuff in the street. He sold fruit and vegetables." There was a garage on Frost Street where Pete used to keep his horse and wagon at night. After a day of peddling, Pete would place Pat atop of his horse and they would walk from Herbert Street to Frost Street. Lorenzina would admonish her husband not to keep Pat out too late because there was school in the morning. "I'll be right back," Pete would always reply. Pat would watch as his father removed his horse from the wagon and brush him down and feed him. Pete loved his horse dearly, in contrast to his brother who always beat his horse.

Pete's brother, Pasquale, who they called Uncle Patsy, had a horse and wagon from which he sold fish. One of his main customers was Vincent's Restaurant on Mott Street in Little Italy. Patsy owned a two-family house at 131 Kingsland Avenue, around the corner from his sister, Virginia, and the garage was on the bottom of the house, where he kept his horse and wagon. Pete and Patsy got into many fights because Patsy was so cruel to his horse. Pete and Virginia took after the even temperament of their mother, Michela. Patsy inherited the fiery temper of his abusive father, Massimino. One time, Patsy's horse kicked him in the leg and the injured leg remained raw and refused to heal, since he suffered badly from diabetes. "Uncle Patsy nearly lost his leg," Pat remembered.

Pete's brother, Pasquale "Patsy" Franzese

Back in Pete's living quarters behind the store, Patsy would come by with his wagon and fill the tub with some water so he could put a few eels in for young Pat to play with. Patsy loved his namesake and enjoyed seeing the delight in the little boy's face and his squeals of delight as the rubbery eels slipped through his small fingers. Patsy would pull a chair over to the tub so Pat could stand on it to reach the eels until Lorenzina would come in to admonish her brother-in-law, "He gets the water all over the floor!"

"Ah, the kid has got to play!" Patsy would say to his disgruntled sister-in-law.

While Patsy and Lorenzina would constantly argue over the eels, Lorenzina did love to eat them, so eventually she would calm down, skin them, cut them up and throw them into the frying pan. They would still be wiggling as they hissed on the pan.

As the 1920's drew to a close, the older generation of the family began to see the end of their days. Lorenzina's seventy-six-year-old father, Salvatore Nunziata, died at 11:30 in the morning on August 13, 1929, four days after falling ill from heart failure. The funeral took place three days later from his home of 224 Frost Street, where he had died, under the direction of Peter Cucurillo of Franzese and Cucurillo Funeral Directors on Havemeyer Street. After a funeral mass at St. Francis de Paola, Salvatore was laid to rest in Calvary Cemetery in a grave occupied by his two young grandsons who had been named after him, Salvatore Nunziato and Salvatore Annunziato. Two months later, the stock market would crash, and Christmas that year was far from a merry occasion. Already mourning the loss of Lorenzina's father, Pete's mother, Michela Iovino Franzese, suffered a cerebral thrombosis on Christmas Eve, 1929. As Dr. Feminella tried to treat the Franzese matriarch in her serious condition, she developed chronic myocarditis and chronic interstitial nephritis. Shortly after the new year of 1930 was ushered in, the seventy-six year old Michela Franzese died at 7:30 in the morning on January 18, 1930, twenty-five days after her stroke. She too was buried under the direction of Peter Cucurillo on January 21, 1930, in a newly dug grave in Calvary Cemetery, following a funeral mass at St. Francis de Paola.

The losses of both Michela Iovino Franzese, who also lived with Pete and Lorenzina, sharing her bed with Margie and Millie, as well as the loss of Salvatore Nunziata, left the Franzeses shaken. Pete had done all that he could for his mother in the new country to bring to her peace in her old age that had eluded her in the old country. Ninety years later, Pat had no recollection of these long-ago grandparents, as he was only two years old at the time of their losses.

On April 13, 1930, when the Census Bureau came to collect statistics, 501 Humboldt Street was valued at $11,000. Pete and Lorenzina were listed as salesman and saleslady of their own grocery. They had six children ranging in age from seventeen to two and a half. Pat's five older siblings were all still in school. Lorenzina would rise before the rest of the family at five in the morning to head for early morning mass at Saint Francis. As the mother of six living children and the wife of the proprietor of an Italian American grocery store, this was the only time Lorenzina had to herself, where she prayed for her family and communed with Jesus. After receiving the host on her tongue, she would make her way back home to make breakfast for all the children getting ready for school. For Pete, he looked forward to Lorenzina returning home with the warm, crusty sfogliatella, the clamshell-shaped Italian pastry native to the Campania region where he came from. When she returned home, the house was alive, as everyone had gotten up from their slumber and were busily preparing for school. After the breakfast dishes were cleared, the children gone off to school, and Pete in the store, Lorenzina began her daily tasks maintaining the apartment and the rest of the tenement house.

"You entered the apartment through the Herbert Street entrance into the kitchen," Pat said, "which was half-paneled walls on the lower portion and painted white on the top portion. There was the sink and the tub. There were beads hanging in the doorway to separate the kitchen from the parlor." The living quarters behind the store was a kitchen, small parlor where Carmine had a desk and later on the telephone sat on top of it, and three bedrooms. Pete and Lorenzina had a windowless room, as did the four boys, but the sisters, Margie and Millie, had two windows that led to the backyard in their room, where their mother had a shelf that held all of her saint statues and votive candles would be burning. "We weren't allowed in the bedroom other than to get dressed or to go to bed," Pat remembered. "You couldn't sit on the end of the bed, either. That's why the chair was there. Mama said that when you sit on the end of the bed, you smash the cushion. You make it flat. My mother had four beds to make a day and she spent one day a week washing them. The washing machine, you had to pull by the sink and fill it up with the hose. And it had a ringer on top. You needed two people to press the water out of them. Then she used to have to carry it to the back room and hang it all out on the clothesline and at the end of the day bring it all in. They worked from early morning until late at night."

The Franzese brothers attended Public School 23 on Humboldt Street. The property near the church of Saint Francis de Paola had been the site for schools since the year 1662. Originally, the Dutch Reform Church of Bushwick had the first schoolhouse, which was next to their church and was surrounded by the church's graveyard. Eventually, these buildings ceased to exist and the first Public School 23 was erected on Conselyea between Humboldt Street and Graham Avenue. The second Public School 23 was built on Humboldt and Conselyea directly across from the old Dutch church and faced its graveyard, with graves dating back to the 1700's. Around the time when Carmine was born in 1912, boys were taught in one building and girls in the other, but Pat's sisters, Margie and Millie, attended Public School 132 on Manhattan and Metropolitan Avenues during the 1920's. By the time that Pat would attend the school in 1933, the bodies in the graveyard had long been exhumed and moved and the old church was torn down to extend Conselyea Street one block. By the time that Pat was ready to attend school in 1933, the marble tower of Saint Cecilia's loomed over Humboldt Street, the bell from its tower reverberating down the block since 1891 until this very day. Lorenzina was told that it would be better to just send Pat to Saint Cecilia's School on Herbert Street, but she protested. "P.S. 23 was across from Saint Francis Church," Pat remembered. "It was a big three-story, old building. Carmine, Sammy and Sal had gone there. We lived on Herbert Street and I was supposed to go to Saint Cecilia's. My mother said, 'I work hard and I can't be walking him to school. His brothers walk him to school.' With all the work that had to be done between the living quarters, the tenants' hallways, and the store, how could she have the time to walk me to school? It would be so much easier if I could walk with Sal, who was already going to Public School 23." Lorenzina pled her case and Pat began the school where his brothers had attended before him, walking with Sal until he reached the age where he could walk there himself.

When Pat would return home from P.S. 23 each day, he would go down the basement and chop a bushel of wood and gather up two buckets of coal, placing it all in the kitchen for his mother. One day, a letter came home to Lorenzina that Pat was having trouble reading the blackboard, so Lorenzina asked Margie to take Pat to the eye doctor. "I ain't going!" Pat declared. Lorenzina went for a piece of the freshly chopped wood and spanked Pat on the behind. Then Pat said to Lorenzina, "I'm not going and I'm not going to chop wood for you anymore either!"

"What did you say?" Lorenzina's eyes grew dark. Pat repeated himself and Lorenzina hit her son with the wooden plank. "Say it again!" Lorenzina yelled at her son. He obliged and again his mother hit him. Eventually he relented and Margie brought her youngest brother for eyeglasses.

Another time when Pat was a student at P.S. 23, he didn't want to go to school and told his mother that he was sick. Holding his forehead against her chin, Lorenzina said "You got no fever." Pat then told her that his stomach bothered him and she said "All right, leave your pajamas on and go to bed." Pat crawled back into bed in his windowless room that only had a dresser to hold the clothes of the four boys and a chair for them to sit on to put their shoes on in the morning. Without even a radio to pass the time, he laid there and stared at the four walls of the darkened room alone, as Sal was gone for the day at school. The other bed where Carmine and Sammy slept was also empty. Lorenzina had gone in to make their bed when she told her young son how lucky he was to be able to read and write. All she could do was say the rosary to pass her time. When school let out that afternoon, Pat told his mother that he had recovered, but she insisted that he remain in bed for the rest of the day. He had learned his lesson. Pat would not play hooky ever again.

Ahead of his time, Pete was adamant that his children receive an education in this new country. Carmine was the first to receive a high school diploma in 1930 and go on to Saint John's College in Jamaica, Queens, New York, to study accounting. Margie graduated from Girls High School in 1933 and Millie right behind her in 1934. Very conscious of the fact that he was illiterate, Pete was not content to sign his name simply with a X for the rest of his life.

"My father taught himself how to write his name," Pat said. "It took him forever to write it, but he figured it out. Math, forget it. You give him numbers and he could do it right in his head and throw out the answer to you. Especially when he had the store. We weren't rich. We could have been rich, but a lot of people took advantage of my father. They didn't have the money and he would have a pen and paper and trust them that they would pay and they would run up a bill. A lot of them lived in the house and they didn't pay the rent.

Some owed him rent and moved out without paying. He lost a lot of money, my father." Having felt blessed for the fortune in the new country that he attributed to his protection from Our Lady of Mount Carmel, the losses did not seem to have a lasting effect on him. "He belonged to the [Carmine] Society at Our Lady of Mount Carmel," Pat remembered. Medals discovered in Pete's house in recent years reveal that he held a high office in the society. "He got out of it after a while because he didn't like what was going on with it. There was the feast and he used to walk through the streets with the band and they used to go from house to house and sing. He used to decorate the window in the store and he had a huge statue of Our Lady of Mount Carmel in the window. In fact, the ring he wore was from that society."

Holidays were spent together primarily with Pete's family, Patsy's family and Virginia's family, the Spizios. Patsy hosted Christmas Eve, Pete hosted New Year's Eve, and Virginia hosted Easter Sunday. Christmas Eve was a special time for the entire Franzese family to gather on Kingsland Avenue at Patsy's home. The three children of Michela Iovino Franzese continued the tradition long after her death in 1930 of staying together on this solemn and holy night. Called the "Precepio," Patsy would recreate the scene of the Nativity in the corner of his kitchen. Using rolled up newspapers that he painted with white paint, he constructed a mountainous region. Among the statues of the Holy Family, there were houses and other figures. The most memorable one for Pat was the Butcher statue who had a knife in his hand and standing at the counter. "He was really gifted for building that," Pat said. The precipio took Patsy three months to build before the Christmas season. All of the Franzese relatives gathered on that night at Patsy's and he would hand each person a long-tapered candle and everyone would sit around the perimeter of the kitchen wall. The candles would be lit and Patsy would go to the front room and open the window. He was hard of hearing, so he would put his ear outside to the cold night and wait for the chime of Saint Cecilia's bells to ring at the stroke of midnight in celebration of the Birth of Christ. For many years, until the birth of Patsy's granddaughter, Rita, in 1939, and Virginia's twin grandsons, Joseph and

PASQUALE

Anthony, in 1941, and then Patsy's grandson, Vincent, in 1945, Pat was the youngest in the family and given the special honor of carrying the statue of Baby Jesus. Patsy would drape a towel on Pat's head that would extend to his hands, with which he would carry the infant to each relative in the room. Every member of the family would then kiss the feet of the statue of the newborn Christ child. After everyone had done so, Patsy would then kiss the statue, take the statue from his namesake, then Pat would kiss it. At the end, Patsy would place the statue in the manger. Then everyone would play home-made instruments and sing songs together, all while there was endless food to eat and drinks to drink. Everyone would sing songs in Italian. Everyone had filled the table with trays of food and jugs of homemade wine. The children would parade and dance the tarantella on Kingsland Avenue. Decades after this tradition had ended, those who were still living still retained vivid memories of this annual tradition.

A week later, everyone would be gathered on Humboldt and Herbert and wait for the stroke of midnight when the gong from Saint Cecilia's bell tower would mark the advent of a new year. Pete would make homemade instruments for them to play as the wine flowed once again and everyone danced in celebration.

"When it was a holiday," Pat said, "my mother made her own raviolis with my sisters. They were big. She had one sheet that she just kept for the holiday and she put it on the bed and she'd roll out her own raviolis. They made the Easter pies too."

Easter Sunday was celebrated on Frost Street at the home of Virginia Franzese Spizio and her husband, Tony. Pete and Lorenzina would come with their six children, and Patsy and Anna with their daughter, Margaret, would join the Spizios and their four children to celebrate the resurrection of Christ.

When it was an ordinary night at home having supper, Pat always sat next to his father. Lorenzina would put the platter of macaroni and beans on the table and hand them each their dish. Pete would pick out the macaroni and give it to Pat, keeping the beans for himself. Pat would pick out the macaroni and give his father the beans. Their arrangement worked out to each other's benefit. Pete didn't like macaroni very much, so they would swap. It was the same when

Lorenzina made potatoes and macaroni. Pete would eat the potatoes and Pat the macaroni. Pat remembers the platters of peas with elbow macaroni, pasta e fagioli, steaks, and pork chops that would be on his mother's table. During dinner, Pat and Pete would poke each other to gales of laughter. When the family sat around the table for dinner, there were eight people at that table, and Pete's rule was "nobody moves from the table until everybody is finished eating." Pete's decree was respected and never challenged. Not that his children feared him, but the high regard they held for him made it painful to ever hurt or disappoint him. While he was not a tall man, unlike his sons, Pete was a large man with large hands, but he never used them to chastise his children and never raised a hand to his wife, which was common in many other homes during those days. While Pat listened to his father's decree, he always knew that he was sitting between his father and the wall and wasn't going anywhere, in spite of his friends poking their heads in the kitchen window on Herbert Street and calling for him to come out to play. "C'mon, Pat, we're playing ball!" Pat would sit there and try to be patient in spite of itching to get back out onto Herbert Street and play stickball. The bases were drawn onto the street with chalk and their bat was the handle of a discarded broomstick. Everything was handmade from discarded wares in the home. One time they constructed a wagon. Someone had thrown out a baby carriage and Pat took off the wheels and axels with his friends. Then he would get an empty wooden crate from his father's store, a wooden beam, and make a front piece, get a board and put a hole in it, drive a spike nail into it, and then they had the ability to steer the wagon. Then Pat would take an old clothesline, attach it to the axels of the two front wheels, and steer. "We made our own push mobiles and our own wagons," Pat said at the age of ninety-one in 2018. "Today, they get everything handed to them."

When it came time to play football in the street, Pat would get an empty burlap potato sack from his father's store, fold it like a bracciole, tie it with rope, and the football was created. The sewer plate took the place of the goal. When it came time to play hockey, Pat had skates that went over his shoes and locked with a key. They would grab their stick from stickball, get a block of wood to be a puck, and aim to get it over the plate.

The friends who joined Pat on his childhood adventures were Joey Frabasilio, who lived on Herbert Street near Graham Avenue, and Bobby Gentile, who lived next door on Humboldt Street. Eddie Briggs was another chum who also lived next door on Humboldt Street. Jimmy Mc Farland on Herbert Street, whose father, Raymond, was a patrolman, was the awe of the other kids. He had a real football and a football uniform.

Pete's eldest son, Carmine, on his graduation day from St. John's College 1934

In 1934, Pete realized his great American dream for his children when his eldest son, Carmine, received his bachelor's degree in accounting from Saint John's College. As a role model for the rest of the family, Carmine's portrait in his black cap and gown was framed in a place of honor and given out amongst his aunts and uncles. Following his graduation, Carmine went to work as an accountant for Mr. Niles, who lived up on the corner from where the Franzeses lived. Mr. Niles had a taxi cab business. Within a few months though, Carmine found himself disillusioned with his accounting career, and around this time, he met an older Jewish man named Bob Davis. Davis had the middle floor of a factory on Manhattan Avenue and Bayard Street. The owners of the building had the top floor and the basement. Carmine went into business with Davis, and in a few short years, he bought Davis' share of the company when he wanted to retire. With help from his father, Carmine became the sole owner of the business before the end of the 1930's. The company was called Brooklyn Box Toe, because in those days, they manufactured box toe shoes. Not only did Carmine buy out Bob Davis, he bought the entire building from the owners. Carmine ran Brooklyn Box Toe for over fifty years, closing the business and selling the building himself in 1988. When Carmine bought the business, he retained the long-time superintendent from the original owner, Frank Keller. "He handled all the payroll," Frank's daughter, Margie Keller Formato, remembered in 2019. While Pete dreamed of a wall full of high school and college diplomas to line the walls of Humboldt Street, it would be thirty-eight years after 1934 before another college diploma would be earned in the family.

During Pat's formative years, those summers of the 1930's were spent outside of the city once school had ended for his brothers and sisters. While Pete remained on Humboldt Street to run the store, Lorenzina would go with the children and her mother, Angelina Nunziata, to the summer home in West Hempstead, purchased sometime before Pat's birth in the 1920's. Pete had one house that the family used and a second one that was rented. Their neighbors across the street were the descendants of Thomas Adams, the man who invented chewing gum. Adams was an inventor who in 1869 found that the use of chicle could be used to make chewing gum. The chewing gum he created, *Chiclets*, is still manufactured today one hundred and fifty years later. The Adams Chewing Gum family lived primarily in Brooklyn, but had their summer home in West Hempstead, equipped with horses. One time before Pat was born, his sisters, Margie and Millie, had gone with their grandmother, Angelina, into the woods near the property. Somehow, they lost their grandmother along the way and she was discovered by one of the young girls in the Adams family while out riding her horse. The Adams girl returned the crying grandmother back to the house, where Lorenzina made the children sorry for losing and frightening her elderly mother.

During the summer months in West Hempstead, it was Pat's eldest sister, Margie, who took charge of his care. Margie would refer to Pat as "my baby" and walk up and down the sidewalk to push his carriage to lull her baby brother to sleep. One day, the Adams daughter emerged from their property with their large, rambling house in the distance atop her horse and rode up to take a peek at Pat in his carriage. Pat was drinking a bottle in the carriage and the Adams girl turned to Margie and said, "He's too big to be drinking a bottle!" Margie was flabbergasted. She turned the tables back on the rich young woman and said to her "Mind your business! You know about horses. I know how to take care of babies!" The Adams daughter rode off in a huff.

Pat would have a hard time sleeping out in the summer house as a baby, so Margie would cradle her baby brother and walk up and down with him all night long. One night, the windows were open and the full moon loomed large outside and there was a breeze blowing the trees. Pat was frightened by the shadow of the tree branch jostling up and down on his bedroom window. He couldn't keep his eyes off of the branch that looked like a withered arm approaching his bed and he screamed as Margie tried to comfort his night terrors.

Lorenzina's sister, Philomena, and her husband, Dominick Croce, came with their family to stay for the weekend a few times over the years in West Hempstead. Pete and his brother-in-law Dominick, who owned both a butcher shop and a bar and grill on Humboldt Street, would drink wine and play bocce ball. The women would cook and everyone would eat outside. Watermelons were consumed to refresh everyone in the heat. At the end of the night, the windows were kept open to help battle the ever-present stifling heat, and because of Uncle Dominick's snoring, Margie had to walk up and down all night holding Pat who couldn't sleep once again.

Another treasured companion of Pat while he was out in West Hempstead was the only grandparent he knew long enough to have bonded with, his grandmother, Angelina Nunziata. The tall, thin woman who had towered over her husband and wore stylish clothing of her own creation, was seventy by the time Pat was born in 1927. Following the death of her husband of fifty years in 1929, Grandma Nunziata was a constant companion for the Franzese children when those summers of the 1930's were highlighted with the trips to the house "in the country," West Hempstead. "We used to go to West Hempstead in the summertime," Pat said. When she wasn't sitting in the house in contemplative prayer while clutching her rosary beads, "my mother's mother used to take me by the hand across the street to the wooded area," Pat remembered. "There were blackberries there. We used to pick blackberries with her. There were apple trees too." With her young grandson, Grandma Angelina would gather up her apron in a pouch and the two of them would fill the pouch she made with berries to bring back to the house. It was an escape from the sweltering house, in spite of the windows always being open. The young boy and his elderly grandmother would enjoy the respite in the cooler wooded area, as well as the stream that ran nearby. "It could be ninety degrees outside and the water was pure, clear, and freezing cold as if it had come from a refrigerator," Pat remembered. "Sammy and Sal used to walk through the woods together to go to the movies when they were kids," while Pat remained back at the house with his grandmother.

On Easter Sunday, April 21, 1935, the thirty-five-year-old doctor, Geremia Rizzuti of 215 Franklin Avenue came to 224 Frost Street and diagnosed the seventy-eight-year-old Grandma Angelina with lobar pneumonia. When Pat, at the age of seven, heard of his grandmother's illness, he went to her bedside to bring her an orange because she wasn't well. Angelina was too weak and she explained to him that she couldn't eat it because she couldn't peel the fruit and to put it back in his father's store. "I remember her well," Pat remembered eighty-four years later. "I loved that lady. We respected people then. Nothing is the same today." Looking back, he regretted in his old age that he hadn't known better to bring her something she could have possibly eaten.

Grandma Angelina Fama Nunziata died at home four days later at four in the afternoon on Friday, April 26, 1935. Once again, Peter Cucurillo came from 18 Havemeyer Street to prepare for the three-day wake at 224 Frost Street as the matriarch was laid to rest. Her funeral took place on April 29th with a solemn requiem mass at St. Francis de Paola, followed by burial with her husband and grandchildren in Calvary Cemetery. Not yet eight years old and only days before his First Holy Communion down the same aisle that his grandmother's casket had been brought, all of Pat's grandparents were now deceased.

PASQUALE

Angelina Fama Nunziata in the mid-1930's

Young Pat with his older brothers, Sammy (l.) and Sal (r.) circa 1934

As the youngest child, Pat was looked after not only by his parents, but his five older siblings as well. It was not uncommon for Lorenzina to ask one of her older children to accompany Pat when he had to go somewhere. One time, she asked Sammy to take Pat to the dentist when he was about ten years old, and after waiting an eternity in the waiting room, Pat would take off out the door when his name was called. Margie also had an experience when Pat had his tonsils removed at Saint Catherine's Hospital on Humboldt Street. The doctor had to check him there at the small hospital and they were sitting on the bench waiting their turn. When they moved to the end of the bench and it was their turn, Pat spotted the doctor in the glass showcase. He had a big, round, silver circle on his head. Pat was frightened, looked at Margie, looked around the room, and bolted out the door. Margie was yelling at her mother, "I'm not taking him no place no more!" Sammy was disgusted when he had the same experience and refused to take his brother when he had to have a molar pulled out. Cousin Jimmy Spizio, Pat's godfather, was summoned to take his godchild and he said to Pat, "Goomba, don't worry! I go with you! If he hurts you, I'll pull his leg off of him!" Pat believed him, so he went. When the appointment was all over, Jimmy turned to him and said, "See! It didn't hurt!"

Jimmy was a constant presence in the Franzese house, especially on Sunday when Lorenzina made macaroni. Lorenzina would be standing at the stove and stirring her tomato sauce when Jimmy would rip off a piece of Italian bread from the loaf and stick it into the simmering "gravy," savoring the smooth and flavorful taste soaked into the bread. Then he would bring his aunt into his confidence when he would declare, 'Aunt Laura, don't say nothin', but you make a better gravy than my mother.' As the oldest nephew and clearly the most beloved member of the extended family, Lorenzina never admonished his dipping bread into her sauce with such loving declarations.

"I loved Cousin Jimmy Spizio," Pat said of his cousin and godfather. "He was close to all of us. He was rolling the barrels and dumping the coal down into the cellars for a living. He got the flu one time and got very sick and couldn't do it, so Carmine drove his truck for him and ran his business while Jimmy was sick. He knew how to roll the barrel. You gotta know how to roll the barrel because it's heavy stuff and you gotta get the corner a certain way to get it to where you have to dump it."

While Pat was close with his older siblings, he also looked up to his older cousins Jimmy Spizio and Jimmy's sister, Millie. When he asked Jimmy, who was his baptismal godfather, to stand up as his Confirmation sponsor, Pat asked Millie Spizio to come along with him to buy his confirmation suit.

Pat's propensity for taking off was not limited to only with his siblings. On Sundays, Lorenzina would take him by the hand and walk him over to Saint Francis de Paola for religious instruction to prepare for First Holy Communion in 1935, and later on, Confirmation, in 1938. As soon as Lorenzina left him at the church steps, Pat would sneak out and head for home by way of Graham Avenue, so they wouldn't cross paths on Humboldt Street. "I'm so stupid," Pat laughed eighty years later as he said, "I went to go sit on my stoop. My mother comes home and sees me sitting there on the steps. She stops short and looks and yelled, 'What are you doing? Come here!' and she grabbed me by the arm and dragged me back to Saint Francis." When it came time for his confession though, Pat was eager to get on line at the confessional of Father Caliendo, who was well known for going easy on the penances he doled out. "He had a clubbed foot," Pat said. "He was very nice."

Pat received his Confirmation at Saint Francis on April 30, 1938, by Bishop Raymond Augustine Kearney. The youngest auxiliary bishop of Brooklyn, Kearney had been ordained a priest at the Basilica of St. John Lateran in Rome on March 12, 1927, a mere six months before Pat's birth. He was twenty-four years old at the time. Only seven and a half years after being ordained, Kearney was appointed auxiliary bishop of Brooklyn by Pope Pius XI and received his episcopal consecration from Archbishop Thomas Edmund Molloy. At age thirty-two, Kearney was the youngest Catholic bishop in the world and the first born in the twentieth century. It was three years after his consecration that Bishop Kearney came to Saint Francis de Paola Church and conferred the sacrament of confirmation on Pat in presence of his sponsor, Cousin Jimmy Spizio. Pat took Vincent as his confirmation name because Jimmy's actual name was Vincent. Sammy had picked Jimmy as well for his confirmation sponsor in 1930.

Pat on his First Holy Communion in 1935 and with his Confirmation Sponsor, Jimmy Spizio, on his Confirmation Day in 1938

Across the street from the Franzese's Herbert Street entrance of their home was their neighbors and close friends, the Bonomo family, at 24 Herbert Street. The father, Pasquale Bonomo, was a very close friend of Pete's, in spite of being Pete's senior by fifteen years, and his wife, Maria, was a close friend of Lorenzina. They had originated from Sanza, Italy, before coming to Brooklyn, and were the parents of five children: Joseph born in 1896, Millie born in 1897, Angie born in 1906, Marie born in 1909, and Marion born in 1911. Joseph and his wife, Pauline, were the parents of Pasquale, known as Patrick, born in 1922, who went onto become a judge. Marion and her husband, Johnny Dalto, courted for five years before they married in 1934. Their only child, a daughter named Margaret, was born in 1936.

In 2019, at the age of eighty-three, Margaret remembered Pete by beginning, "my family were very good friends with Pete and all

PASQUALE

of the Franzeses. The whole family. My mother, Marion, lived in the Niles house and Pete had his grocery store. So, I used to go down there and my mother used to say, 'Margaret, go get some candy.' And I wasn't really a candy eater. 'Go ahead.' And she gave me two cents. Now, I was a little girl, so she gave me two cents and then she was talking with Pete's wife, Lorenzina. She and Lorenzina were very good friends. Their daughter, Margaret, was very good to me. She treated me so good as a young girl. She used to take me here. We used to go to the park. She was very good. So, I went to Pete and I told him that I wanted candy and I gave him the two cents. I wasn't a stupid kid! He showed me the five-cent ones and the two-cent ones. Naturally, I chose the five-cent one. Well, he said I can have that. Then when I go to leave, I said, 'Pete, I want change.' So, he said, 'What change?' So, he gave me the two cents back and my mother came back and said, 'Pete! What did you do?' He said, 'She wouldn't leave the store!' He would joke with my mother, 'Customers like her I don't need.' I was a little girl. So, she said, 'Don't do that when I give her the two cents.' He said, 'No, she's very good.' Every time I used to go there, he used to put his head down and say, 'I've got such a headache!' I used to go, 'Ma! Go upstairs and bring Pete aspirin.' My mother would say, 'Pete, don't do that all the time! I gotta make two flights of stairs.' But he used to take them, so he must have really had a headache. 'She's so good,' he used to say. 'Nobody worries about me. Only Margaret worries about me.'

"When my grandmother died," Margaret Dalto continued, "Lorenzina said to my mother, 'Don't worry about Margaret. She comes over by us.' And if it wasn't for Pete, we wouldn't have gotten the rooms on Humboldt Street. My mother was talking with him and she said, 'I've got a problem, Pete. I need rooms. Margaret is getting very sick. We need steam heat and you can't get steam heat around here.' He said, 'I know somebody on Humboldt Street and they want somebody to live there that they know. I'll recommend you.' So, my mother said, 'oh good!' So, we went to live in the Niles House. It was three rooms, but very big rooms.

"I remember when Carmine bought his mother a five-inch television set. They used to say on a Sunday, 'Margaret, come over to watch Ed Sullivan.' It was a small, black and white television set. One time, Pete asked my grandfather to come over to watch the boxing match. My grandfather got all prepared to go and goes over there and the guy gets knocked out in the first round." Pasquale Bonomo went home very disappointed.

Those summer days in the 1930's when Pat and his family were home in Brooklyn, instead of the summer home in West Hempstead, meant that he was looking for chores around the house so he could see his swashbuckling hero, Errol Flynn, perform great heroics as Robin Hood and a slew of other iconic roles. From Monday through Friday, the movie theater would give you a coupon and it was a nickel to get in to see two features and cartoons. On the weekend, admission was a dime. When he wasn't with his friends, Pat was enthralled by the darkened theater and being transported from Brooklyn to the far away and mysterious lands in the movies. Whenever Pat asked his mother for a nickel for admission, Lorenzina would pass off the broom for him to sweep the halls and the store. At that time, 501 Humboldt Street was a five-family building, including the living quarters behind the store where they lived. The apartments on the upper levels were two side by side apartments on each floor. To get money from Lorenzina, it had to be earned.

It was 1939 and *Dodge City* was on the screen starring Errol Flynn and Olivia De Havilland. The swashbuckling hero, Flynn, was Pat's hero and he couldn't wait to see him in his latest picture. Pat went to Lorenzina for the five cents and she told him that she was too busy. She was in the midst of making the four beds. "My mother," Pat remembered, "when you asked her for a nickel, you got a nickel. I do tip my hat to her though for making me the way that I am. That's why I was able to keep my head above water later on. She didn't think you should spend all your money." On that day when Pat wanted to go see *Dodge City*, Lorenzina told Pat that if he wanted the money that he should go into the store and ask his father for it. "I went to my father and said, 'Dad, can you give me a nickel?' He rang up 'No Sale' on the cash register and gave me a quarter. My father gave me the quarter with no ifs, ands or buts," Pat remembered.

"Papa, this is a quarter!" Pat told him in disbelief.

PASQUALE

"I know what I gave you," Pete told his son. "Maybe you want to buy yourself something." Pat would go between the three movie houses, The Grand on Grand Street, The Graham on Graham Avenue and the Winthrop Park Theater.

When Pat wasn't trying to get change from his mother or father, then he would turn to Sal. Although only the next oldest to Pat, Sal was six and a half years older and was described by Pat as "a handsome guy with wavy blond hair and I had blond hair too, but it was kinky like. The girls used to swarm around him like bees with honey. I'd go over to him and hit him up for money and he didn't want to look cheap in front of the girls, so he'd give me a nickel or a dime. Then he'd say, 'Get outta here now!' But he was always good to me. He liked me, my brother, Sal. Oh yeah."

The day of a 1930's Brooklyn summer would come to an end when the bells of Saint Cecilia's would gong at six o'clock and Pat would have to reluctantly say goodnight to his chums still playing in the street. Lorenzina's command was that was when Sal and Pat would go to bed. Sal never wanted to go to bed at that time. Lorenzina would say, "Oh, go lay down and you'll fall asleep and then you'll wake up." Although it was Sal who protested when they both went to bed, he would soon fall fast asleep while Pat would lay there wide awake and stare at the ceiling still full of life from the day's excitement.

By 1936, Sammy left Automotive High School to work full time in the grocery store with his father. While Pete was disappointed that Sammy did not want to graduate like Carmine and the girls had, he was happy that his son wanted to follow in his footsteps and take over the helm of the store. While Pete was still a presence in the store, he took more of a backseat role and let Sammy handle much of the operation. In the meantime, Sal was sixteen and still in high school during the day and working part-time for Western Union with his best friend from Humboldt Street, Jimmy Glynn. "They used to deliver Western Union telegrams and they wore a suit and they had leather leg-ins they wore so their pants didn't get caught in the chain and they wore a broken peaked cap," Pat said. "There was a two-car garage on Herbert Street and Sal used to keep his bicycle in there.

One side, Carmine kept the car. The other side, the guy around the corner kept his car in there. I asked Sal, 'Can I ride your bike?' Now Sal was tall. I used to go from one side of the pedal to the other because I was small. He said to me, 'No, you can't have the bike, Pat. I got a slow leak in the front tire and I need it for work.' So, he went out and the guy across the street was polishing his car in the garage, so the garage was open, so I said, 'Are you gonna be long?' He said, 'Yeah, I'm gonna be a few hours.' So, I took Sal's bike out. I'm going down Herbert Street toward Graham Avenue and a trolley car came and I didn't expect him to stop. I thought he was gonna keep going and he stopped and I hit the back part of the trolley car. I bent the wheel. 'Oh my God!' I thought to myself. 'What am I gonna do?' I had to roll the bike back to the garage and I put it away and I didn't say a word. Now, for some reason, Sal straightened out the wheel to go to work and he never said a word to me how the wheel got bent. Maybe he thought he bent it and didn't notice it or something."

By the end of 1938, Sal left high school after completing his junior year, left his job working for Western Union, and decided to go to work for his brother, Carmine, at Brooklyn Box Toe. Pete was once again disappointed that now a second son had chosen to not graduate when he himself put so much stock in getting his children their education. Once Sal hung up his Western Union uniform for the last time, he gave his bicycle to his kid brother, Pat.

When sitting on the seat and gripping the handlebars, Pat was filled with exhilaration as he felt the wind through his hair going down the streets of Greenpoint. One day, Lorenzina had run out of potatoes, so Pat gladly jumped on his bike to go over to Frost Street to Aunt Virginia and Uncle Tony Spizio's grocery store. Pete's sister had a small store and sold fruit, vegetables, and canned food. After his Uncle Tony filled a paper bag with potatoes, Pat jumped back on his bike to take off for home, when the bag ripped. All of the potatoes were rolling onto Frost Street. Uncle Tony was yelling at Pat as he knelt down to retrieve them.

"I was twelve years old," Pat said. "One of our tenants in West Hempstead had a son who was my age and he had an old, skinny-tired bicycle. I had my brother, Sal's bike that he used to use for

Western Union that he gave to me. We drove to West Hempstead to go to the movies. And in West Hempstead there was a bicycle store and there was an alleyway. And in the back the guy used to have a bike rack and the guy let us put our bikes back there. There were three or four bikes in the bike rack. Him and I put our bikes in there and went to the movies. When we came out of the movies, the only bike there was his. Mine was gone. And my father wouldn't buy me another bike. That's the last time I had a bike. I was twelve years old. Not that he was cheap, but he said because we were going back to the city. 'I don't want to see you get hit with a car,' he said. 'If we stay here, I'll buy you a pony.' I said, 'Papa, what am I gonna do with a pony? Everybody here's got bikes.' Then he says, 'Well, we're going back to the city, so I'm not gonna get you a bike.'"

Pat was crestfallen as his bike riding days came to an end. His brother, Sal, was going to get him a bike instead. He went to Tony Florio, who had a bicycle store. "He had a shitty bike and I think he wanted ten dollars for it. My brother, Sal, said the bike wasn't worth ten dollars. And I loved riding a bike. I used to ride it all the time. That's all we did when we were kids, riding bikes and playing ball in the street."

On September 1, 1939, Pat was enjoying his last weekend of summer vacation before beginning his last term at Public School 23 and celebrating his twelfth birthday when Nazi Germany, led by Adolf Hitler's Third Reich, launched its first "Blitzkrieg" and invaded Poland, triggering off the war in Europe. While the big black letters filled the covers of the newspapers across the neighborhood, it was the summer of blockbuster movies and the promise of the bright "World of Tomorrow" being highlighted a few miles away in Flushing Meadow Park during the 1939 World's Fair. Public School 23 brought Pat and his class by school bus to experience all that the World of Tomorrow had to offer. Walking with his classmates among the showcases of the world, Pat remembered eighty years later munching on a vinegar-soaked Heinz pickle that each child was given to taste. In June of 1940, Pat's days at Public School 23 came to an end, and unlike his brothers before him, he would be attending a separate junior high school.

Shortly after Labor Day, September 2, 1940, Pat was celebrating his thirteenth birthday and preparing to begin attending a new school. A mile and a half walk from his door on Herbert Street, just off the corner of Humboldt, Pat would set out for Graham Avenue. "I took Graham Avenue," Pat said. "It's on Graham Avenue. It's way up past Grand Street. In fact, it is near Girls High School on Bushwick Avenue. That building was only built four years before I went there. I went from P.S. 23 to P.S. 49-William Gaynor Junior High School. It was a long walk."

William J. Gaynor Junior High School, also known as Public School 49, was built in 1936 at a cost of $1.5 million to serve 3,700 students as part of the $12 million Williamsburg housing project to serve the 5,000 residents with children from kindergarten age through the ninth grade. The school was dedicated on May 10, 1937, and reported in the *New York Times* on that date under the headline "New Fount of Knowledge Tapped." Brooklyn Borough President Raymond V. Ingersoll presented the key to the new principal, James F. Smith, Jr., at a dedication exercise in the school auditorium with one thousand in attendance, including senior students, their parents, and delegations from civic societies. Ingersoll was quoted by the *New York Times* on that day as saying, "This is a center of enlightenment and sound Americanism." The purpose of the new school was a Public Works Administration project to create an integrated community center in which housing, education, health and recreation were being provided through the aid of government agencies. Located at Graham Avenue and Stagg Street, the main entrance to the building is 223 Graham Avenue, with a side entrance on Ten Eyck Walk.

The junior high school was named in honor of the late former Mayor of New York City, William Jay Gaynor. Gaynor, the 94th mayor of the City of New York from 1910 until 1913, and previously a New York Supreme Court Justice from 1893 until 1909, was known as a reformer who refused to take orders from the Tammany boss, Charles Francis Murphy. On August 9, 1910, only seven months into his term, Gaynor was shot in the throat by James J. Gallagher, a New York dock night watchman who had been discharged from his position three weeks before. Although Gaynor quickly recovered from the assassination attempt, the bullet remained lodged in his throat for the next three years. Gaynor died in office, aboard the RMS Baltic, 400 miles from the Irish Coast, on a deck chair from a heart attack on September 10, 1913, at the age of sixty-four. The body of the fallen mayor was returned to New York aboard the Lusitania from Liverpool, where he would lie in state at City Hall before being laid to rest in Brooklyn's Greenwood Cemetery. Gaynor's would-be assassin, Gallagher, died in prison the same year. Following the building of the school that would bear his name in 1936, a bronze bust of the late mayor was gifted to the school in 1937. When Pat first enrolled in the new school in 1940, U.S. presidential hopeful, Wendall Wilkie, made a political appearance at the school on his campaign tour through Brooklyn on October 5, 1940.

While Sal worked full time for Carmine at Brooklyn Box Toe by the end of 1938, Sammy, who had left school by the end of 1935, was becoming disillusioned by life running his father's grocery store. Opening up at six in the morning and not shutting the lights off until eleven every night, six days a week to just earn a living was arduous and left nothing for him to enjoy out of life. "Even on a Sunday," Pat said, "people would knock on the back door that they needed milk or something and he would have to go in the store, and he wasn't supposed to, but he used to go in the store and get the milk out or whatever they were short. It was long hours and he wasn't getting rich. He was just earning a living." Once Sal began working for Carmine, Sammy would watch his younger brother be able to freshen up and go out with his girlfriend, Nancy, once the dinner plates left the table. He decided the life of his father, the life of a grocer, was not for him. While Pete had retired, more or less, he kept his finger in the goings on at the store and still spent time there with Sammy. Much to Pete's disappointment, they decided to close the store by 1942 and Sammy went to work for Carmine.

Once the store closed, Pete made the decision to renovate the entire house of 501 Humboldt Street. "He was fixing up to get a contractor to redo the house, so we went to West Hempstead to live," Pat said. Pete got all of the tenants out of the apartments and packed up the whole family to go live at the summer house in West Hempstead until the renovations were complete. Carmine would drive everyone into the city every day for work and back in the evening. Pat was the only one left in school and did not want to transfer his school to West Hempstead, so he too went back and forth each day with his brothers and walked from Brooklyn Box Toe on Manhattan Avenue and Bayard Street to William Gaynor on Graham Avenue. After school was released for the afternoon, "I used to go to the shop and I used to do my homework," Pat said. "Then Frank Kellar gave me a little ax and scrap leather. When they cut a sole out of it, there was a piece like two inches, three inches thick out of it and I used to cut the excess off, throw the scrap in the scrap barrel, and the good pieces went into a clay box. The pieces we were gonna keep were used to cut lifts for the girls' shoes and that stuff. Frank gave me an ax and I used to chop and do that. Then I started working on Saturdays."

Then the whole world changed and the far away war in Europe came to affect the lives of every citizen of the United States of America when the Japanese led a surprise attack on the United States Naval Base at Pearl Harbor, Hawaii, at 7:53 A.M. on Sunday, December 7, 1941. The attack claimed the lives of 2,403 American military, 188 destroyed aircraft, and a crippled Pacific fleet that saw eight battleships damaged or destroyed, which included the U.S.S. Arizona, which sunk to its watery tomb, and the U.S.S. Oklahoma, which was capsized.

The next day, on the Feast of the Immaculate Conception, President Franklin Delano Roosevelt addressed Congress and was heard far and wide over the airways saying, "Yesterday, December 7, 1941—a date that will live in infamy—the United States of America was suddenly and deliberately attacked by naval and air forces of the Empire of Japan ... As Commander-in-Chief of the Army and Navy, I have directed that all measures be taken for our defense ... No matter how long it may take us to overcome this premeditated invasion, the American people in their righteousness will win through to absolute victory ... I ask that the Congress that since the unprovoked and dastardly attack by Japan on Sunday, December 7th, a state of war has existed between the United States and the Japanese empire." America was at war.

The Franzeses could not imagine what changes were in store for them that Christmas Eve of 1941 when they gathered on Kingsland Avenue at Uncle Patsy's Christmas Eve celebration. While there were new additions to the family with the birth the week before of Aunt Virginia Spizio's twin grandsons, Joseph and Anthony Pisano, the sons of her daughter, Margaret, and her husband, Mikey Pisano, on December 17th, some faces would not be there for the gathering on Christmas Eve 1942. The boys would soon be going off to war in far off places they never imagined going.

Pete & Lorenzina circa 1942

Uncle Patsy's house on Kingsland Avenue where the Franzese family spent Christmas Eve from 1910-1951. The house, built by Uncle Patsy in 1910, was torn down in 2022.

CHAPTER FOUR

The Franzese Boys Go Off to War

1942-1948

The neighborhood boys began to be called up to report for active duty early in 1942. Carmine, much to his disappointment because of his desire to serve his country, was a 4-F due to a heart arrhythmia and a perforated ear drum. The next Franzese brother in line was Sammy. On February 9, 1942, with his valise in his hand, Sammy said goodbye to his parents in their bedroom before first light. Besides his family, he was also leaving behind his girlfriend of a few months, Josephine Vizzari. Josie, as everyone called her, lived on Metropolitan Avenue and was the best friend of Sammy's cousin, Millie Croce, Lorenzina's sister, Philomena's daughter. When Millie married Cono Dalia on October 26, 1941, Josie had been her maid-of-honor. Millie had introduced her "best girlfriend" to her cousin, and although they had only been together for a few months, Josie promised to wait for Sammy to come home. She went to a portrait studio to have her picture taken for Sammy to take with him to remember her waiting for him back home. And wait for him she did. By day, she was a forelady at a powder puff factory and at night she would be writing to Sammy.

Sammy in his army uniform

    From Brooklyn, Sammy went to Fort Dix in New Jersey and was assigned to the Third Armored Division. Then from New Jersey, he was sent to Fort Polk in Louisiana for basic training. In July, the division was transferred to Camp Young, California, and from there, Sammy saw himself being taken with his division by train to the Mojave Desert where temperatures reached 130 degrees and the wind felt like a furnace.

    According to the Third Armored Division history, written at the time of the war that Sammy would eventually bring home with him, the time the soldiers spent in the Mojave Desert was not in vain. "Desert maneuvers of 1942 probably did more to toughen the 3rd and prepare it for ultimate combat than had all previous training." The maneuvers performed there were in preparation for the division's planned participation in the invasion of North Africa, which was not needed. He would remain there until November, when the division came back to Camp Pickett near Blackstone, Virginia. It was there that he would end the year of 1942.

Back home, Carmine was driving the family back and forth between Brooklyn and West Hempstead. Due to the war, the renovations of 501 Humboldt Street were put on hold because "you couldn't get materials," Pat said. "You couldn't do nothing. Carmine was the only driver. He used to go back to Brooklyn at night because he had a girlfriend I guess or something. He used to make the trip four times a day. So, my father seen him going back and forth and he didn't want him driving back and forth like that, so he says, 'I want you to get somebody to paint the apartment downstairs and we're moving back to Brooklyn.' So, he hired a couple of painters to paint the bottom floor and we moved back to Brooklyn into the back of the store again. We just cleaned it up and lived back there."

The Franzese's parish, Saint Francis de Paola, had been rebuilt and was dedicated on April 26, 1942. The pastor, Fr. Carmelo Russo, whose masses Sammy had served as an altar boy, died later that year. The new pastor, Fr. Gaetano Sabia, was appointed the following year and erected the main altar with marble imported from Carrara, Italy. One pew in the church was donated by Pete and Lorenzina and another was in memory of Salvatore and Angela Nunziata. Pete's sister, Virginia, lost her husband, Antonio "Tony" Ospizio on May 16, 1942, at the age of fifty-eight. Only five months after welcoming the births of their twin grandsons, Tony was laid to rest in Calvary Cemetery four days later. At Brooklyn Box Toe, Carmine and his foreman, Frank Keller, wistfully saw all of the young men going off to fight in the war and only the older, middle-aged men remained. Six months after Sammy was drafted, Sal too was called to report to Fort Jay on Governors Island on August 17, 1942. Like Sammy before him, Sal left behind his girlfriend, Nancy, as he too departed for basic training. They planned to marry when he returned home after the war. His best friend, Jimmy Glynn, and Margie's boyfriend, Al, also were off to fight the war. All of the young men of the neighborhood were off to see new worlds they never could have imagined outside the boundaries of Brooklyn, New York.

The Franzese Family in West Hempstead in 1942

While his brothers were off to fight in the war, Pat was still in junior high at William Gaynor and worrying about getting the attention of the girls down the block on Bushwick Avenue at the girl's junior high school. "At that time," Pat remembered, "across the street from the girl's junior high school, there was a cellar and they had the doors open and they had a screen so nobody could fall down there. They used to make soft pretzels there, two for a penny, and we used to go down there to buy them. They used to put two pretzels in a brown paper bag and hand them to us and we gave them a penny. The stores had the same pretzels on a rack on the counter and you would take the pretzels off the rack and you would pay a penny a piece. And it laid on the counter! So, we used to go down by the store. And then the girls were out and the boys used to break off pieces of their pretzels and throw them into the girls' hair. Now these pretzels, the dough would stick when it goes into the hair and they couldn't get the damned thing out. Well, the girls got disgusted and they spoiled it for us. Well, I can't blame them. So, what happened, they went and complained to their teachers and the teachers went to the principal. Their principal got in touch with our principal and he turned around and told our teachers, 'now, you tell your class anybody gets caught down by the school is gonna be expelled from the school. They are not allowed down there and when you go home, if you gotta go home that way, that's OK then. If not, you better not be near that place.'"

While it was a disappointment to be banned from going past the girls on the way home and the taste of the warm, soft pretzels, it was also a different era that Pat lived in and a teacher had no qualms about laying their hands on their students if they perceived them to have committed any infraction. While people constantly speak of the rough treatment of students by Catholic nuns and brothers at that time, Pat claimed that the same treatment took place with public school teachers.

"Mr. Banks taught us English," Pat said. "I hope they buried him upside down. He was a son of a bitch. We had to wear a tie to school. The teacher would pin a paper to your shirt collar with a paperclip if you forgot your tie. I forgot it once, but I never forgot it again. Anyway, they used to line us up by the blackboard. They were discharging us to go to another class and they used to line us up against the blackboard when we walked out. I was next to the tallest, so the guy behind me was taller than me. This big boy who was behind me pushed me, playing around. We were friends. They had gotten this girl, a very young and pretty girl, to be a teacher. All dressed up with high heels on. They must have gotten her fresh out of college. And Mr. Banks, Mr. Macho Man, was out in the hallway with her. She was young enough to be his granddaughter. She was standing next to Mr. Banks and the kids were all coming out. The whole hallway was full of kids going to different classes and this guy behind me picked up the eraser full of chalk and threw it and caught the girl teacher on the back part of her hip. I was the next one coming out and Mr. Banks grabbed me by the shoulder and pushed me into the classroom and smacked me up against the blackboard. I thought he broke my shoulder! He held onto the top of my shirt and said, 'I want you to apologize to her!' And I yelled, 'I'm not apologizing! I didn't throw it!' I had tears in my eyes. I was crying because my shoulder was hurting me. He grabbed me by the shirt and pulled me into the hallway and she said, 'leave him alone. It's only chalk. I can brush it off.' And she brushed it off. Then he let me go and I went to my next class. Today, he would have been in trouble for putting his hands on me. I hated him ever since that time."

Another teacher, Mr. McBean, had been a detective and he carried a gun. Another teacher, of whom Pat was very fond, was Mr. Hornstein. "He was a chubby guy and he wore glasses," Pat said. "He used to read us stories and he had a habit of playing with his fingers and he used to pinch you if you didn't clear your desks when he walked up and down. And I liked him because we didn't do no work with him. He used to tell us stories. But to make sure we was payin' attention, he'd say, what did I just say? What happened before that? To see that you were listening."

But pretzels in girls' hair and a roughhousing teacher paled in comparison to a fateful Friday morning in Pat's final year of junior high that would forever leave a mark on the young school's history and on all the three thousand students who attended that day.

On Friday, October 2, 1942, two former students of William J. Gaynor Junior High School dressed in zoot suits, sixteen-year-old reform school graduate, Neil Simonelli and his nineteen-year-old friend, Joseph Annunziata, wanted to cause trouble at the school where they had formerly attended. They arrived at the school shortly after the school day began at 9 a.m. and went to the second-floor boy's lavatory with the intent, "to have some fun with Mr. Goodman." According to the *New York Times*, "the maintenance of discipline in that part of the building was one of Mr. Goodman's duties." Irwin Goodman, the thirty-six-year-old math teacher who had been an educator at the school since 1938, was described as a small man of five feet three inches and weighing around 135 pounds, mild-mannered, and targeted by the two boys because of his size. The two boys were smoking in the bathroom and sent a younger student to go tell Mr. Goodman that there was someone smoking in the bathroom. Goodman entered the bathroom, where the former students insulted him and entered in a physical altercation with him that involved pushing and tie pulling. Goodman was able to bring both boys before the Assistant Principal, Rose Ray. Mrs. Ray later testified that Simonelli was using profanity and "acted like a mad man." She said that Annunziata tried to reason with Simonelli and that she in turn lectured both boys at length and ordered them to leave the premises. Mr. Goodman shook hands with Annunziata for bringing his friend under control and the three of them left the office. Mr. Goodman ended by saying that all he wanted was for the boys to stay away and not cause any trouble.

"I'll get even with that guy," Simonelli allegedly said to Annunziata, according to newspaper reports, outside of the school building. The two boys walked eight blocks to Simonelli's home on Metropolitan Avenue to retrieve a .32 caliber automatic pistol that Simonelli had claimed to have discovered in a vacant lot about two weeks before. They returned to the school an hour later, the pistol in Simonelli's pocket. Simonelli alone entered the school, walked past the principal's office and opened the door off Ten Eyck Walk for Annunziata, and the two boys headed for the stairwell.

Simonelli and Annunziata came up the staircase and saw Goodman with his back toward them at around 10:45 a.m. when Simonelli pointed the pistol at his former teacher's back and pulled the trigger. Nothing happened. He did it again. Nothing happened. Annunziata reportedly said to Simonelli, "Gimme that gun," and grabbed the pistol from Simonelli, because he said to police, "I got impatient," aimed the pistol and fired. The bullet entered the right side of Goodman's back and the teacher's lifeless body tumbled to the landing in between the first and second floor, where he was discovered a few minutes after the fatal shot was fired during the change of classes. The two assassins fled the building.

Principal James F. Smith summoned an ambulance from Saint Catherine's Hospital nearby. Due to the shortage of doctors with the war effort, there was only an attendant in the ambulance who was unable to pronounce the death of Mr. Goodman. Dr. A.H. Hangarter of 264 Graham Avenue was then summoned. At first it was believed Goodman had suffered a fatal heart attack, until the small bullet wound in his back was discovered by Hangarter. The police were summoned and Detective Captain John J. McGowan arrived from the Stagg Street station. The two boys were the immediate prime suspects.

Pat was a student of Mr. Goodman at the time of the shooting. Although all newspaper reports claim that Goodman was a math teacher, Pat, remembering that morning vividly seventy-seven years later, insisted that he had Goodman for science. That period, Pat said, "I was a monitor at the bathroom. I was sitting outside the bathroom on the chair. After I was done sitting by the bathroom, I was going to Mr. Goodman's class. He was a short man with a little mustache. I liked him. He was a nice teacher. He was a quiet, timid, tiny guy. I think I had him for science. My English teacher was the big guy, Mr. Banks. He was running around and he asked me was anybody in the bathroom. I said no. He went in anyway and came out. He said, 'leave here and go into the schoolyard.' So, I got off the chair and went into the schoolyard. The school was almost empty. They put all the kids in the schoolyard and closed the fence. The whole school was in there. All the teachers got the whole school emptied out and they put us in the school yard cause it's fenced in. They closed the gate and locked us all in there and we had to stay in there for a long time. I know that they said Mr. Goodman was shot and the teachers were all running around trying to find them. I don't even remember seeing cops. It was the teachers who were doing all the running around. When they caught the guys, they opened the gates of the schoolyard and told us to go home and come back in the morning. So, we went back in the morning. I don't know who took Mr. Goodman's place."

Detective McGowan discovered the pistol in a clothes hamper in Simonelli's home with one chamber empty. Simonelli was found at his job at the Meadow Gold Ice Cream Company to collect his weekly pay and brought into William J. Gaynor Junior High School for questioning. Immediately, Simonelli admitted to his part in the shooting. Once the two boys were apprehended, the 3,000 students who were evacuated from the school and squashed inside of the gate of the schoolyard were dismissed for the day after the tragedy at 1p.m.

By mid afternoon, Annunziata had been brought into the school as well. The boys were questioned both separately and together when about 5 p.m., Simonelli looked over at his accomplice and said, "Say, handsome, why don't you tell these people the truth?" It was then that the police learned that Annunziata had been the one who fired the fatal shot after Simonelli's two failed attempts. Annunziata replied, "All right—I did it. I killed that guy." They were questioned until 8:30 at night at the Stagg Street police station in Williamsburg, Brooklyn, where they also spent the night.

Irwin Goodman was laid to rest two days after his murder on Sunday, October 4, 1942, after a funeral service conducted by Rabbi Harry Halpern of the East Midwood Jewish Center at the Flatbush Memorial Chapel. Dying from an assassin's bullet during a time of war, Halpern said: "He perished for a cause he thought was right. May this keep us on the alert and aware of the problem that arises in time of war—a breakdown of character and morale that is bound to ensue." More than 1,000 people attended the funeral, including Dr. John E. Wade, Superintendent of Schools, who declared Goodman's devotion to duty would serve as an inspiration to his colleagues. Assistant Superintendent Elias Lieberman said: "The dangers he ran all teachers have to run who are courageous and fearless. The problem of the young hoodlum isn't one the schools alone can solve. It is a cooperative job that must be done by the home, the church, the social service settlement, the judges and the schools. Immediate thought must be given by the community to the whole problem of wholesome recreation for children and youths on a continuous basis throughout the day and evening hours, so that young people won't be driven to criminal associations through the fact that there is no other place for them to go. The boys who committed this murder are both far past junior high school age. They had time to get into bad company and learn criminal and vicious practices." Goodman left behind a wife, a four-year-old daughter, and a three-year-old son. He was laid to rest in Mount Zion Cemetery in Maspeth, Queens, New York.

Simonelli and Annunziata were sentenced by Judge Peter Brancato on November 20, 1942, to 50 years to life at Sing Sing for murder in the second degree. Had the verdict been first-degree murder, they would have been the youngest New Yorkers ever executed.

Christmas Eve of 1942 was a somber one with Sammy and Sal both away in basic training in the U.S. Army. Uncle Tony Spizio had died that year, so Aunt Virginia and her family were in mourning. Her twin grandsons, Joseph and Anthony Pisano had their first birthday the week before and Uncle Patsy's only grandchild, Rita Ann Lezza, was three-years-old. The family once again gathered on Kingsland Avenue to honor the birth of the Christ child and listen for the bells of Saint Cecilia's to gong at midnight. A week later, the year of 1942 would come to an end, and filled with anxiety of what the future would hold, the Franzese family looked toward 1943.

Sammy's unit transferred for training to Indiantown Gap, Pennsylvania, in January 1943. Over the next seven months, the training experience there prepared the soldiers for combat in northern Europe.

There would be more loss at home for the Franzese family when Uncle Patsy's wife, Anna Rollo Franzese, died at Greenpoint Hospital on February 18, 1943, eight days after a catastrophic fall at their home on Kingsland Avenue. Diabetes mellitus, in addition to a shattered femur as a result of the fall, were listed as the causes of death on her death certificate. She was laid to rest four days later with the Franzese matriarch, Michela Iovino Franzese, on February 22, 1943, in Calvary Cemetery. Anna was only six days shy of her fifty-sixth birthday on the date of her passing. In spite of her devastating loss, Uncle Patsy would continue the Christmas Eve tradition at his house for the rest of his life.

Pat and his ninth-grade class graduated from William J. Gaynor Junior High School the last week in June of 1943. "I had a suit on and it was hot as hell," Pat remembered, "and it faded onto my white shirt." With so many young men gone off to war, Pat worked all summer long at Brooklyn Box Toe.

On August 26th and 27th of 1943, the Third Armored Division was preparing to embark overseas and transferred to Camp Kilmer in New Jersey. During the last days of August, the soldiers were given 12 hour passes for a "last whack at the night spots of New York." Sammy got to come home to Brooklyn and see his family and Josie before being shipped to Europe. Sal wasn't granted a furlough, but snuck home for a few hours on a Saturday afternoon to see the family before he shipped out to India. It was the only chance the Franzese family had of seeing Sal in his army uniform.

At 8 p.m. on September 1, 1943, the "blackout" went into effect for the Third Armored Division. This was the alert that preceded movement to the port, usually coming within 48 hours of the actual move. During the interim, no one was allowed off the post, visitors were forbidden, and no wire or telephone calls could be made. Mail went out, but now each address bore the censor's stamp "In Care of Postmaster." On September 4th, the units left Kilmer and boarded trains for New York Harbor. On the pier, a few hours later, the long line of soldiers waited patiently. Each man carried the bulk of his equipment in a barracks bag and each had his helmet numbered in white chalk. The line moved slowly with each GI waiting until his last name was called. He answered with his first, and then struggled up the gangplank into the ship.

Sammy embarked from New York Harbor on Pat's sixteenth birthday, Sunday, September 5, 1943. According to the history of the Third Armored Division, "Over the stern, the Statue of Liberty grew indistinct in blue mist. GI's of the future first American 'Spearhead' were, for once, speechless. They tried to make conversation, failed: just stood there by the railing and watched Liberty until she was a shadow—until she was a dream in the distance." Across the water in a small church in Brooklyn, Lorenzina was in her pew at Saint Francis de Paola with her head bowed in prayer for her two boys off fighting for the country she had left her homeland of Italy for thirty-eight years before.

Ten days at sea aboard three ships, the Third Armored Division landed at Liverpool on September 15, 1943. "Upon disembarking, units were loaded in Britain's small 'Toonerville Trolley' trams and transported across country to the southwest counties of Somerset and Wiltshire for final training. At every stop, small English children collected a wealth of gum and candy, oranges, and C-rations. Hot tea was served by NAAFI units, for the first time to 3rd Armored Personnel. Most of the division elements reached their new camps in the deep night, struggled out of trucks and trudged in to find straw pallets in Nissen huts or barracks." The Third Armored Division would have further training in Britain throughout the rest of the year. Christmas Day 1943 was celebrated with English beer and an occasional bottle of scotch, with parties for British children, and with roast turkey and cranberry sauce in the old tradition, but not the tradition of the Franzeses. Sammy must have been thinking that as he drank the English beer and ate his turkey dinner of his family gathered at Uncle Patsy's on Kingsland Avenue surrounding the Precipio and of Josie back home in Brooklyn waiting for his return. Back at home that fall, Pat followed in Sammy's footsteps and began high school at Automotive High School.

Overlooking McCarren Park in Greenpoint at 50 Bedford Avenue, Automotive High School is the largest auto trade school in the nation. First opening the doors of its current building in 1937, Automotive specializes in training their students in the vocation of auto repair mechanics. Sammy attended the school first, but after completing two years, left at the age of 16 in 1935 and chose to work with his father in the grocery store instead. Having spent the summer at Brooklyn Box Toe, Pat had the taste of a working man's paycheck and yearned to return to the factory to the smell of freshly cut leather. He went home to Pete and told his father that he was quitting school to go work for Carmine. Pete was furious. "I used to fool with my father until the day I quit school," Pat said.

Whether it was days or weeks that Pat remained at Automotive, he was no longer sure after over seventy-five years. He did not complete the fall semester of 1943. The following day, Pat walked with his father to the school, where Pete very reluctantly signed his name, knowing that his son would not remain regardless of his remonstrations. All of his hopes and dreams for his youngest son were now dashed. During a very tense walk home from the school along the McCarren Park fence, Pete turned to his son and said, "You're gonna be a donkey for the rest of your life!" Once signed out, Pat was supposed to attend continuation schooling once a week for the rest of the school year, but he never returned. "My father was mad as hell," Pat said. "He knew what it meant to have an education and he told me, 'You're gonna be a donkey for the rest of your life,' and it was true."

For three days, Pete refused to speak to Pat. There was no more fooling or poking at the dinner table. The next day, Pat reported for his first day of full-time work at Brooklyn Box Toe. After three days, Pete walked to the factory and stood there watching Pat skiving leather. After a while, he walked over to his son and said, "so this is what you want to do for the rest of your life?" Pete, who wished that he could have had the opportunities that he made possible for his children, that so many of his friends and relatives did not choose or value for their children, was left baffled in addition to his anger and disappointment.

"I started on the floor downstairs with Frank Keller," Pat said. "There was a machine like a half a sole goes on the back of the shoe and it goes through the machine and the front of it takes the front down so when you step on it, you don't have that lump and the machine shoves them through and the pieces fall into a box in the back of it. I used to do that. I was on the buffer machine. It was a sanding machine that had two rollers on it. And we used to buff the stuff off of it. I did mostly floor work over there.

"I was only a teenager working seven days a week in Carmine's factory during the war. I had no teenage life. On Sunday, we were supposed to work half a day. You know what half a day was? Eight o'clock in the morning until two thirty or three o'clock in the afternoon. Frank Keller used to go to church and come in at nine o'clock after church on Sunday morning. It was Carmine and myself. One of our customers had a thing with the government. The thing that goes inside the peaked cap. It was a kind of stiff canvas. They used to cut them for the government for the hats that they wore. And we used to cut them on a Sunday. Carmine and I used to set up the settings. We used to put five of them high and then staple it. When Frank would come in, he would tack it on the back of the machine and cut it out on a table and we used to count them when we put them in a box and make it and seal it. Carmine knew where it had to go. We got done two thirty or three o'clock and then we'd come home. Sometimes I used to force myself to go see a movie just not to stick around the house, go to bed, and wake up and be back in Brooklyn Box Toe again."

With the shortage of men, Carmine was anxious to find men to run the machines to keep up with production. When he was unable to come up with a solution, Pat came up with the idea of hiring and training women to run the machines in the meantime. "I taught my sister, Millie, how to round," Pat said. "I said, 'Millie, watch me and I'll show you. You can't get hurt. You put your hand on the top of the machine and that machine will go around. The other hand is on the handle, so you can't get hurt.' I taught her that way. And then I taught my brother Sal's girlfriend, Nancy, and Irene Robinson. Irene was raising a son by herself. Her husband had died and I had three women on the rounding machine. They were just as good as the men. I was able to give the customers more work.

"My brother, Carmine, comes upstairs and he never used to come up. This one time he comes up and he sees the three women on the machine and his eyes got wide and he says 'What are you crazy?' I said, 'What do you mean, am I crazy?' He says, 'You got the girls working on the rounding machine?' I says, 'Yeah! And they're just as good as any man.' He goes, 'Well, you shouldn't have girls working on the machines,' I says, 'you don't want the women on the rounding machine? Then get me men to replace them.' I says, 'they're just as good as the men.' And they were. 'I got customers screaming at me,' I told Carmine. 'I'm not sending them enough work. What am I gonna do?' Which was true. We had to keep sending our help home and he keeps bringing in more customers. We got so busy he didn't even have to go out for customers. They used to come to us because through the channels our competitors got less out of the leather than we did and we gave them a good percentage and leather was expensive. We got more out of their leather than our competitors. Why? Because we taught the men that the leather has to be stretched from side to side, not front to back. If you cut it the wrong way, then 8 becomes 8 ½ after the person does it, so from side to side they would pull it to the last, so you have to cut, stretch it and then you put your die. Carmine turned around and went back downstairs."

Millie showed a propensity for the rounding machine, much to the surprise of Carmine, and kept at the job for the remainder of the war. Margie Keller Formato, the daughter of the Brooklyn Box Toe

Superintendent, Frank Keller, was also one of the women workers at that time. "I worked there with Sal's girlfriend, Nancy," Margie remembered at the age of ninety-three in 2019. "I liked her so much that I named my oldest daughter Nancy, like her. She was very nice. She took me under her wing. I was only sixteen. She was in her early twenties. That shop made the soles and heels for shoes. We didn't make the full shoe."

The year of 1943 came to an end with the youngest and oldest sons working together. For the first time in their lives, the two brothers separated by an age difference of fifteen years were holding the factory together, and in these unprecedented times, their sister was working there too. Pat worked as the skiver machine operator. He fed pieces of leather into the machine, which cut it to desired uniform thickness.

In the new year of 1944, a letter arrived at 501 Humboldt Street from Sal that he was driving a truck on the Burma Road, the 717 mile road through rough mountain country linking Burma with the southwest of China, delivering supplies to the men fighting at the front. "He said the road was so bad that it was hurting his back," Pat said, "and he wanted a heavier belt to put around him." On February 25, 1944, Sal was on an air-drop mission to deliver supplies over the Burma Hump, the eastern end of the Himalayas, in a cargo plane among nine soldiers from an airfield in Assam, India. The goal of these missions was to deliver thousands of tons of supplies from India over the Himalayas into China. On the ground below, the 5307th Composite Unit, known as Merrill's Marauders, began a 1000-mile march over the Patkai range, the hills on India's north-eastern border of Burma, and into the Burmese jungle behind Japanese lines. However, this strategic air lift came at a tremendous cost. In the process, 700 Allied planes crashed or were shot down and 1,200 soldiers were lost. In the middle of the mission, Japanese fighter planes shot down the plane that Sal was in, killing all nine soldiers on board. "There was an approximately one in three chance of being killed," historian Francis Pike wrote in his book, *Hirohito's War: The Pacific War, 1941-1945*.

A Western Union telegram arrived at 501 Humboldt Street to inform the Franzese family of Sal's death at the age of twenty-two. Pat remembers the whole family being baffled because they all thought that Sal was with his unit on land. By the time that his family received word of his passing, Sal's remains had been recovered from the crash site and buried in the American Military Cemetery at Kalaikunda in the Calcutta region of India. The cemetery was a temporary resting place until the time came that his remains could be sent back home to Brooklyn.

Sal in his army uniform in 1943

With all of her hopes and dreams for a life with Sal after the war now over, his girlfriend, Nancy, decided to leave her work at Brooklyn Box Toe. She found it too overwhelming to be reminded of Sal working alongside Pat every day.

Sammy was still receiving training in England at the time of Sal's death. He would remain there until news came over the radio of the invasion of Omaha Beach, Normandy, on June 6, 1944, known forever after as D-Day. The Third Armored Division of which Sammy was a part didn't touch down on the sand of Omaha Beach until June 23rd. By July 7th, he was fighting in the Battle of Saint-Lô, which saw many causalities. On August 1st, on the day they were ordered to cross the See River, during the attack on the high ground east of Villedieu les Poeles, Sammy was seriously wounded by shrapnel in his head, neck and arm. Pete would once again receive a telegram to inform them that his son was wounded. Sammy would be awarded the Purple Heart a month later in the hospital in Belgium on September 4, 1944, but he returned to active duty when he recovered. "After we got the telegram about Sal," Pat said, "Mama used to scream in bed. It was hard. And then another telegram comes about Sammy."

Back home one day in Brooklyn during the spring of 1944, sixteen-year-old Pat was taking a walk with his friend, Frankie Slater, on Graham Avenue, when Frankie spotted a friend of his sitting on his stoop on Richardson Street, just off the corner from Graham Avenue. "Oh, that's a friend of mine over there, Pat," Frankie said. "I'll introduce you to him." Frankie introduced Pat to Johnny Morena, a fun-loving twenty-one-year-old neighborhood guy, and the two young men hit it off immediately. As they were talking, Pat's childhood friend from Herbert Street, Bobby Gentile, came by with a few other guys and the talking and laughing got louder and louder. All of the sudden, the screen on the window of the house opened and a middle-aged woman leaned out and yelled, "What are you guys doing on my stoop making all this noise?" Seventy-five years later, Pat said that he thought to himself, "Holy shit, he doesn't even live here! So, I started backing away and she starts to laugh and said, 'Come on back here! I'm only foolin!' And that's how I met Josie Morena, Johnny's mother. She scared the shit outta me!"

Like her son, Johnny, Josie Morena was a fun-loving, jolly woman whose constant ribbing would never lead a stranger to believe the sorrows that she carried in her heart. Her first husband, John Ferrando, died at the age of thirty-one in 1920 after they had only been married for nine years. Josie had been left a thirty-year-old widow with a seven-year-old son, Robert. "Josie's son from her first husband was a boy scout," Pat said, "and when he went diving from a pier in Brooklyn at the age of sixteen, he did not come back up to the surface. His bathing suit got caught on a nail and he drowned. The police officers dove in but were unable to find him. His uncle dived down and brought his body up," Pat said. "Josie lost her first husband and their son." She had remarried the year after her first husband's death, in December of 1921, to Dominick Morena. Nine months later, they welcomed the birth of their son, Johnny, on September 29, 1922. They had another son, Al, who was born the same year as Pat, on April 14, 1927.

Johnny's house, 170 Richardson Street, was next door to the Jewish bakery on Richardson Street, a few houses in from Graham Avenue. Sitting on the Morena's front stoop always was a delight from the aroma of freshly baked bread emanating from the windows next door. Josie used to send Johnny for some rolls and make mini pizza pies from them in the oven. "Josie used to say that she would make us pizzas if we would go and buy her Fox Head Beer," Pat said. "Nobody carried Fox Head Beer. I don't know why she had a taste for it. She would only drink a half a glass and that's it. And we went crazy to find a place that had it. We was all over. 'We don't carry that brand.' Where the hell she found it, I don't know." Regardless, Pat and Johnny always delivered and were rewarded with the mini pizzas.

"Josie got me drunk once on wine," Pat laughed over seventy years later. "We was playing cards in the house on Richardson Street. *Boss and Underboss*. She became the boss and the boss could tell you when you had to drink. 'Give him a drink!' She kept giving me the drink. I staggered going home. I get in the house and come up with all that wine I drank. It was coming out my nose."

Josie Morena was a favorite of the young people of her block, taking kids on the block on the boat trips with the 87th Precinct Police Athletic League. In addition to this, Josie sat on the Board of Elections and assisted immigrants in obtaining their American citizenship. Pat spent a lot of time sitting on the Morena's stoop thereafter, with Josie making mini pizzas and laughing with her son and his friends. Her husband, Dominick, had a concession in a club that he used to go to, but he was a gambler and nearly lost the house that they lived in, which was left to her by her first husband. The relationship between him and Johnny was difficult at best.

"Johnny always cursed his father," Pat said. "Dominick, when he hung around the house, used to hit up Josie for money. He had no money. When she used to see him hanging around, she used to whisper to Johnny, 'don't go out until your father leaves. When he borrows the money from you, he pays you back and pays you interest.' Sure enough, when Dominick saw we weren't moving, he asked Johnny to go in the bedroom and Johnny gave him the money and got back interest. That's why Johnny couldn't stand him. Johnny said, 'I had to pay my mother's mortgage one time because of my father.' He was a nice man, but he gambled it all. With Josie, I was like another son to her. She was always glad to see me."

When the boys weren't going far from home, they sometimes found themselves at the bar on the corner of Meeker and Graham Avenues. "I was sixteen years old and hanging out in the bar right on Graham Avenue across from where Johnny lived on Richardson Street," Pat said. "When Johnny and I didn't know what to do, we used to go to Flamm's bar. He was an old guy who had it. We used to sit there and have a few beers. We never got drunk. We didn't drink to get drunk. It was just a place to hang out that was not on the street."

Even seventy-five years later, Pat vividly remembered the adventures him and Johnny went on together. "He was a firehouse, that guy. He drove me crazy," Pat laughed. "We used to go to Ridgewood Grove and watch wrestling. It looked like London fog with all the smoke. Saturday was Golden Gloves. We used to go to the auto races in Freeport. We used to go to take tours around New York City looking at the buildings. A couple of times we went to Manhattan. The guy got to know us. He let us get on the bus for nothing. You know the buses that were open on the top? We used to pay to get on and go upstairs and watch the buildings. We'd ride around the city with the guy until he'd say, 'I'm going into the depot. You guys gotta get off.' We got that guy again and he let us go upstairs and ride. The bus was empty anyway. We even used to go see the ball come down with a bottle of whiskey in our pockets. We used to go all over. Sometimes we used to go and take the train to Manhattan and we used to go on the bus and we used to go to Union City, New Jersey, to see the burlesque show. They show more on T.V. today than they did in those movies. We used to get a kick out of the two comediennes, Stinky and Shorty, they were called.

"We had a lot of fun, Johnny and I. Fights? Forget about it. I used to break up all the fights, but I never got in any fights. I used to get hit a lot too breaking them up. If it weren't for me, Johnny would be in jail. Johnny and I was walking on Graham Avenue going to the subway going to New York. This kid was on the street going that way and says, 'Hey, Shorty!' Johnny was only 4'11". He punched this kid. I'm telling you, he was ready to slam his head into the cement when I put my arm around his stomach and pulled him off the kid. He scared me that one time with that kid on the bicycle. He'd be just getting outta jail now! I said to the kid, 'Get outta here! I don't know how long I can hold him!' The kid picked up his bicycle and he ran with it. I said to Johnny, 'What's the matter with you? Are you crazy?' He yelled back, 'I'll kill that son of a bitch!' 'Yeah,' I said, 'you'll be in jail.' Johnny was about twenty-two years old at the time."

Looking back on his youth gallivanting at night with Johnny Morena, Pat laughed as he said, "I was no lily when I was growing up. Not that I got in trouble. I always stayed outta trouble. I used to stay out late. I was young. Carmine used to get in trouble because of me. 'I want you to get your ass in here on time,' he'd say. 'Understand?' Mama would always think it was Carmine. My mother's bed was right near the door to go to our room, so you had to go by her and she was a light sleeper. So, I would never lie to her. She would say, 'Carmine?' 'It's me, Ma.' And the next day, she would get ahold of Carmine and say 'you come in two o'clock in the morning? What's the matter with you? Where were you?' Carmine would give me a dirty look, but he wouldn't squeal on me that it was me, but he would get on my back, 'get your ass in here on time.' The next day was the same shit. And the place was dark as anything. We knew our way around in the dark. The last one home locks the door. That was me. I used to stay out late."

Sammy was recovered by the end of 1944 as the Third Armored Division had crossed over the Belgium border and had set up camp in Verviers. The Spearhead of the West, as the Third Armored Division was called, had begun to prepare for the Christmas holidays when the German counter-attack had begun. The Battle of the Bulge would be the last major German offensive campaign of the Western

Front, from the Ardennes region of Belgium, northeast France, and Luxembourg. The intent of the German army was to stop the use of the port at Antwerp, Belgium, and split the Allied lines and allow the Germans to encircle and destroy the four Allied armies to force the Allies into a treaty that would favor the Axis' powers. In a battle that lasted from December 16, 1944, until January 25, 1945, The Battle of the Bulge was the largest and bloodiest single battle fought by the United States in World War II and the second deadliest battle in American history. On January 7, 1945, Hitler agreed to withdraw all forces from the Ardennes, which brought an end to all offensive operations.

While victory seemed so close, Sammy's unit, the Third Armored Division was not prepared for the attack on their general on March 30, 1945. Major General Maurice Rose's personal aide, Major Robert Bellinger, stated that while Rose habitually rode with the advance elements of the Third Armored Division, he had his driver turn around to check on reports of some men cut off behind them. Driving down a road that they thought was clear a few miles south of the city of Paderborn, Germany, their jeep encountered a column of German tanks. They fled across the field, only to find that they had been surrounded. Rose got out of the jeep, arms raised in surrender as he walked toward an armed tank soldier. The Nazi soldier shot Rose with a single shot to the head, killing him instantly. While the German soldier was in shock, Bellinger fled. Rose had been in full command of the Third Armored Division from Normandy on, as they swept across France following the breakthrough at Omaha Beach and St. Lo. Under his leadership, the Third Armored Division dashed through Belgium and was the first armor into Germany, first to get past the Siegfried line, helped to stem the Germans' Ardennes offensive and was first armor into the city of Cologne. Major General Rose was forty-five-years-old at the time of his murder. He was buried in the American Military Cemetery in Margraten, The Netherlands. According to the history of the Third Armored Division, *Spearhead of the West*, "The world mourned his passing. His troops scowled at the news and drove forward as he would have wished them to do." Sixty-years-later, in spite of age and illness, Sammy didn't hesitate in identifying a photograph of his long-ago lost general. The love and respect that he held in his heart for that man was evident in the intent way his eyes locked on Rose's face and his smile when he said, "General Rose!"

Back at home in Brooklyn, Lorenzina made the decision to prepare for the impending end of the war when the remains of her son could finally come home to her. She went to Calvary Cemetery on April 20, 1945, to purchase a 12-person family plot. While Sal was presently buried in India with a white cross marking his final resting place, she was adamant that he be returned home to his family, where he would be buried in a plot that would one day be the final resting place for all of them. In Section 4-B, Lorenzina selected a grave along the road only a few feet from the grave of the Spizio family plot where Tony was buried, and a few dozen yards from the grave of her parents, Salvatore and Angelina. This sorrowful mother was determined that no matter what had to be done, her son was coming home to her.

The month of April 1945 was a long succession of prominent deaths of the key players in World War II. President Franklin Delano Roosevelt, in the middle of his unprecedented fourth term in the presidency, suffered a fatal stroke at his "Little White House" in Warm Springs, Georgia, on April 12, 1945. As was his wish, his body did not lie in state and was buried in Hyde Park, New York, on April 15th. The Fascist Dictator of Italy, Benito Mussolini, was executed in Giulino, Italy, on April 28, 1945, and two days later, The Führer, Adolf Hitler, took his life in Berlin on April 30, 1945. German surrender was imminent and celebrations of V-E Day were celebrated throughout Greenpoint on May 8th. Celebrations commenced again on August 14th with the surrender of Japan, known as V-J Day. Japan's formal surrender on board the U.S.S. Missouri anchored in Tokyo Bay on September 2, 1945, brought about an official end to the war. Demobilization began two days later, and then on September 10th, Sammy would be on board the ship that would return him home three and a half years since having been drafted. He landed stateside on September 19th and spent the next nine days in New Jersey at Fort Dix, where he was separated from the army on September 28th.

PASQUALE

He had been over in Europe for two years and fifteen days and away from home for three years, seven months and five days.

Sammy returned home to his family in Greenpoint at the close of September and to the waiting arms of Josie, who had waited for him to come home. He would never discuss the horrors of war that he had witnessed as he drove in those armored cars, hid in basements, and was hit with shrapnel. No longer working in the family grocery store, now permanently closed, Sammy took a job alongside Pat working for Carmine. When Pat asked Sammy about his experience in Europe, he would simply say, "It was horrible," and walk away. Sal's best friend, Jimmy Glynn, also came home, with two tanks having been blown out from under him as he fought with Patton's Third Army. He too came to work at Brooklyn Box Toe, taking over the job that Millie had been filling at the rounding machine during the war. Millie and Jimmy were to be married that fall. While both Sammy and Jimmy came back home to pick up the pieces of the life they left behind, inside they could never be the idealistic boys from Brooklyn who had left home in 1942. And, so poignant for them when they got home, Sal was no longer with them, laying in a grave in a foreign land until the day came he could be brought home to rest.

The bells of Saint Francis de Paola rang on November 11, 1945, as Millie walked down the aisle on Pete's arm to marry Jimmy Glynn. Sammy stood best man and Margie was maid of honor as Father Passaniti pronounced them man and wife. The first of Pete and Lorenzina's children were now married. There were two apartments side by side on the second floor, which Pete had fixed up, so his daughter and her new husband could move in.

While Sammy and Josie now planned for their February wedding, the draft was still on in spite of the ending of the war, and Pat was drafted by the army. "Sammy came out and I went in," Pat said. "After my eighteenth birthday (September 5, 1945), I had to go down to the draft board. In fact, Sammy came down with me because there was something that he had to get, a discharge or what, but he came down with me and he did what he had to do and I did what I had to do. I didn't think they would take me, really. There were four fellas, husky guys, on the line. I was always skinny. He sees the first guy, 'You go on that line. Rejected.' He gets to the next guy, rejected. The stamp comes down again and again. Rejected. I'm thinking to myself 'Ooh! I'm getting out!' It comes to me and he looks over the thing and he says, 'Oh, you go on that line' and I'm thinking, 'No! No!' Well, when my turn came on the line, they asked what branch you want, army, marines, navy. I hear alotta guys sayin navy and they got hit with army. And I didn't want to go in the navy because I don't know how to swim and I heard they threw you in. Because I heard Johnny's brother, Al, he got drafted into the navy and he couldn't swim and they won't let you out of boot camp, but he could float. So as long as you could stay on the water for so many minutes, you're O.K. If you start to go under, they got a hook and they hook you out. It was fun and games. And I'm thinking, should I tell them that I want navy? I says, no, I'm gonna tell them army and he stamped it army. He says, 'you go home and you'll get a letter in the mail to tell you what to take with you and where you gotta go to and let you know when you're gonna leave.'"

Pete became hysterical and asked for Carmine to do anything to get his son out of it. He would never get over the fact that he had lost his son, Sal, and was not willing to stand by and take the risk of losing his youngest. Carmine explained to his parents that Pat had to go and there was nothing he could do about it. The letter came to 501 Humboldt Street to inform them that Pat was to report for service on Monday, December 17, 1945.

"When I joined, I had to go up to a building on Nassau Avenue," Pat said. "It was 165 Nassau Avenue. Five o'clock in the morning. They were crying in bed, my parents. They had lost a son and Sammy got wounded bad. When I got to the building on Nassau Avenue, the place was cold. There was snow on the ground. We had a snowstorm. They hadn't plowed the streets. There wasn't a soul to be had. There was a bunch of guys there. We're sitting there and we're sitting there. There was a lieutenant and a sergeant. Then they turn around and say to us 'I want you all to stand up as I call your name' and when they called my name, I stood up. They told us to raise our right hand and he mumbled stuff and swore us in. He said, 'your ass belongs to the government.' And I turned around and said, 'My ass is MY ass and nobody else's but me.' He turned around and said, 'Oh we got a wise guy amongst us?' 'No,' I said, 'I'm not a wise guy. I'm telling you facts. The government is borrowing this body. That's it!' Then he was mad at me. They didn't own me!

"We didn't leave the place on Nassau Avenue till eight o'clock in the morning. Then they put us on a bus and drove us to Jersey. When we got to Jersey, they put us on a tug boat and there was a camp there. I don't even know what kind of camp it was. It was on the water. We were surrounded by water and we were there until after New Year's. They didn't do nothing with us until after the holidays. Why didn't they just let us stay home for the holidays? All they did was give us a uniform. We had to get rid of our civilian clothes. They gave us a box and told us to address it and then they'd mail it home. They said 'say goodbye to your clothes because you ain't gonna see them again until after you get out of the service.' If you were on a leave or a furlough or anything, you were not allowed to take off that uniform. If you were caught out of uniform, you were considered a deserter.

"The second of January, they brought us back to land, put us on a cattle car train and took us to Arkansas. There was straw on the floor that we were laying on. We threw the blanket down on the straw and we laid down on there and you hear the train all night long.

"Little Rock, Arkansas was a small town. It had one bar, one movie, and a couple of stores and that was it. That's where I had my picture taken. I came across a sign that does weddings and stuff and when I went in, I asked the guy to make me the pictures. It was pretty expensive, although I was only getting $24 a month. I was a buck private then.

"We did nine weeks training in Little Rock. They didn't have barracks there. Where I trained, we had huts. It was four men in a hut and a stove in the middle. There were two men from the south, a Jewish fella, and myself. There were gas stoves and we weren't allowed to sleep with them on. We used to get up when they had reveille.

"There was a hill and then way back there was the target and it's pretty far back and it's got a red circle. It was on rollers. You roll the target up and you gotta be down in the hole. There were two flags. We used to call it Maggie's Drawers. So, when you missed the target, you put up the red flag. When you got it in the circle, you put up the white flag, if you hit the target. So, it was my turn to shoot the rifle. So, there was a puddle of water there and the drill sergeant says to me, 'Franzese, hit the deck!' So now I seen the water and I moved over and flopped down in front of the big hill and he yells, 'Hey! Hey! Get up!' So, I get up. 'Why did you go from here to there?' I says, 'There's a puddle of water there!' He says, 'When I tell you drop down, you drop down! You get over here and you drop down in that water' and he made me get all wet. All day long I was wet. And then I started to fire the rifle. I got a ribbon for sharp shooter.

Pat in uniform during basic training in Little Rock, Arkansas in 1946

"And then we had the machine gun. They're heavy. And who gets to carry the gun? Me! It's three men. One guy carries the legs. One guy carries the valise with the bullets in it. One guy carries the gun, which is heavy. Now, they time you. You gotta run up the hill with it. You gotta get on top of the hill. You gotta open the legs and you gotta put the gun on. You gotta put the string of bullets in. You gotta have it ready to shoot. They give you so many seconds to do it. And then you gotta take it apart and carry it down and then the next three guys do the same thing and they time you. I said, 'Son of a bitch! Why me all the time? Why couldn't I carry the legs or something?' It takes three men. We never fired it though. They didn't let us fire it. Then we had the hand grenades. They had these rooms and you were supposed to get it in the window. They used to explode when you pull the pin and throw it. Then you hear 'BOOM!' It was interesting. When you were doing it, you hated it, but when it was all over, it was a good experience.

"The one Jewish fella in my hut didn't want to do anything in the army. He wanted out of the army. They did anything and everything to that guy and he wouldn't do nothing. He wouldn't do what they told him to and they wanted us to straighten him out. The other two guys from the south beat the shit out of him, but I didn't have the heart. They wanted us to straighten him out, but we couldn't do nothing with him. And we got penalized for it.

"So, we had orientation on the field. When they were giving speeches, we were sitting on the ground and we took our rifles and we had to stack them standing up. They linked to one another and stood straight up. You gotta know how to hook them so that they don't fall over. So, we put our rifles there and we go past and we go and sit down and we listen to the speeches. I wasn't too far from our stack of rifles. The four of us. Before the orientation began, we're sitting there and we're sitting there, and all the sudden, I see the drill sergeant go over to our rack of rifles and he kicked them and let them fall into the dirt. He was punishing us because of the Jewish guy. We were picking up our rifles after the orientation and he says to us, 'Look at how you'se are keeping your rifles! These are the things that are gonna save your lives. Look, they're all dirty. Don't you clean em?' I felt like saying 'I just seen you kick the damn things down, you bastard,' but you can't get fresh with them. He said, 'When you get back to the barracks, you'se clean those rifles. And when you'se go to bed tonight, you put that rifle in your bed and you cover it with your blanket and you sleep on the floor.' We waited for him to come at night with the flashlight. He comes around at night with a flashlight. He looks to see that we were on the floor. He left. The four of us are on the floor and the rifles are in the bed, so after he left, I waited for ten minutes and I put my rifle in the rack and stood it up. I said, 'he ain't gonna come back no more,' so I got up and put my rifle in the rack and climbed into bed. All the sudden, I see lights shining in my eyes. It was him. He said, 'what did I tell you? You get that rifle and you put it in your bed and you cover it and you will sleep on the floor tonight AND tomorrow night.' I thought to myself, 'you son of a bitch.' I wanted to put the bayonet on my rifle and stick it up his ass!"

On February 16, 1946, Pat had to walk around an empty lot in Little Rock and was lost in thought about Sammy getting married on that day and his not being able to be there. "I was supposed to be Sammy's best man," Pat said. "Instead, I was doing guard duty walking around an empty lot in Arkansas on that day."

Back home in Brooklyn, it was a blizzard two days after Valentine's Day on that Saturday, February 16, 1946, when Josie Vizzari arrived at the back of Saint Francis de Paola wearing snow boots under her wedding gown. While the streets of Greenpoint and Williamsburg filled with snow, the warmth inside of the small church banished the cold as after five years of waiting, Josie walked down the aisle on the arm of her father, Vincenzo Vizzari. She was grateful to God on that day, as she knew that while her and Millie got this opportunity, Sal's girlfriend, Nancy, would never walk down that aisle to him. Father Arcesse pronounced them man and wife, as Sammy's cousin, Dominick "Doc" Croce, and his fiancé, Catherine "Kay" Angelicola, stood as best man and maid of honor. Josie had left her job as a forelady at a powder puff factory in the tradition of brides of her era. She loved her job and her boss sorely missed her. After the wedding, Josie and Sammy took the second apartment next to Millie and Jimmy on the second floor of 501 Humboldt Street. In spite of the first two marriages of Pete and Lorenzina's children, everyone was still living under his protective roof. A week after the wedding, Sammy celebrated his twenty-seventh birthday. "Sammy did a nice job renovating that apartment," Pat said. "He put in a stall shower. In fact, when I used to come home, I used to go up there to take a shower. We didn't have a shower downstairs. We used to go to a public bath house to take a shower on a Saturday. You had to pay ten cents and they gave you two towels and a small piece of soap. And the rest of the week we used to sponge ourselves off in the kitchen. It wasn't nice."

PASQUALE

Pat's eighteen weeks of basic training in Little Rock was cut short after nine weeks when it was decided to send the boys over to Germany for police action. "They decided they wanted us to go over as police action, so the boys that fought the war could come home," Pat said. "I had another eight weeks to go and Truman stopped the draft. We were supposed to finish our training in Germany for the rest of the time." When the boys were getting ready to ship out, the Jewish solider in Pat's hut would be remaining behind. "He stayed behind and I thought to myself, 'I feel sorry for the new guys coming in now. They're gonna have the same problem that we had,'" Pat said.

President Truman made a decree that if any families had already lost a son overseas that any current sons in the military would not have to be shipped overseas. After having been told that he would be going to Germany, Pat received this news and went to go see his commanding officer, "He says 'you gotta go,'" Pat said. "'Your papers are on the ship. When you get over there, you'll fill out the paper and they'll send you back home.' So, I filled out the papers and it was a couple of months before they shipped me back home." Pat's ship for Europe left on April 5, 1946.

"We went over in a cargo ship," Pat said. "You were in the hull where they put all the boxes and stuff. It was the bottom of the ship. Well, they hung the canvas things up for us to sleep in. There was two of them. One higher and one lower. They had them hanging from the ceiling. The rope was broken on it. I said, 'I need rope. It's broken.' 'We don't have no rope.' So, what I did was I took the shoelaces off my boot and I tied it up a bit, but it still wasn't right. And for eight days I was that way. There was a storm. Eight days it took us to get to Le Havre, France. That's where we pulled up with the boat. Then, when I got off the ship, I took my laces and put them back on my boots." Pat arrived in Le Havre, France on April 13th.

By the time Pat had arrived, the seaside port city of Le Havre was devastated by the Battle of Normandy when the city saw 5,000 people killed and 12,000 homes totally destroyed. As he looked back nearly three quarters of a century, Pat would remember the city as "this mud hole in France where we landed and they put us in these tents. They called it 'Tent City.' They didn't have barracks. They saved money by having tents rather than having barracks. They had these big, long tents with poles on both sides and there were soldiers on both sides of the tents. The place was a big lot we were in. The damned rats were bigger than cats over there! They weren't scared of anything, those damned things! And we used to throw our combat boots at them and then we were looking for our combat boots.

"The rain was terrible. It rained every day for the whole week that I was there and the place was muddy. Sleeping there was like sleeping in a mudhole. You went to the tent with your canteen and they put your food on the tray and the rain was coming through the tent and your food was soaking wet. It was disgusting. Some of the stuff I was able to eat. My food was floating around on my dish. I said, 'Holy Shit!' We carried the metal tray and canteen on a hook on our belts. And they had the Red Cross who had doughnuts, doughnuts, doughnuts. I couldn't look at doughnuts no more. They had the Red Cross there and I lived on their doughnuts. I used to go there and get two or three doughnuts and eat them. Well, I said, 'I gotta get out of this mud hole.' They were waiting to transfer us to someplace. I couldn't wait to get out of there."

One day, they made an announcement that they were looking for eight volunteers to be transferred. "They tell you 'Don't volunteer in the army,' but I wanted out of there. Nothing could be worse than this and I put my hand up. I was one of them that they picked to go and they took me and seven other fellas from France to Germany in a cattle car. There was straw. That's how I know it was a cattle car for cows. We rode a couple of days on the God damned train and we got into Germany and then they took us with a truck and planted us at the hospital over there.

"The hospital was in Erlanger, Germany. It was supposed to be ten or fifteen miles from Frankfurt. When I went to Germany, they made me a private first class. I had one stripe. I never put it on my uniform. There were seven guys they got to work in the hospital. I don't know what they did. I never even went in that part of the hospital. Most of the soldiers that were there took over the hospital. There were no civilians in that hospital. They were all soldiers and they used to have on these blue robes that they used to walk around in outside.

PASQUALE

Soldiers who had fought the war was there. Some had lost limbs. Most of it were soldiers with venereal diseases and I was one of the lucky guys out of the eight. I don't know what the other soldiers did, but I was lucky. They made me the security guard outside by the main gate. I worked four hours a day at the main street coming into the hospital. I had to check the people out and check the cards when they went in and out. I did that for four hours every day. And then we used to change shifts like the cops. One day you were 8-12, 12-4, all the way around the clock, so everybody got a share. I had to check in the women who came in to clean up the place. I carried a .45. I only worked four hours a day, seven days a week. I had to stand there by the gate. The women had buttons. They had to have the button on. If they didn't have the button on, they couldn't come into the hospital.

"I went to the village. I started walking and I seen a shop. I went into the shop and there were three or four women in there and hanging from the ceiling was prosciutto. They must have had ten or twelve hanging from there. Nobody speaks English and I'm telling the butcher. Finally, a woman opens her pocketbook. They must have had food stamps. 'You gotta have this.' 'But I got money.' I had plenty of money in my pocket. We used to trade. We'd give them a pack of cigarettes and they'd give us all kinds of money. They wouldn't give the prosciutto to me. He wouldn't cut it for me because I didn't have the stamp. He said he couldn't and I had to walk away. There was also an airfield there where they had the planes that were damaged and everything. It was like a junk shop, you know. The bombs and stuff they had."

While so much of Germany was in a depressed state in the aftermath of the war, the accommodations for the soldiers working at the hospital were very enjoyable. "You used to go into the mess hall in the morning and they would ask you what you wanted," Pat said. "The German people knew how to cook! They used to cook for us and we used to get good meals and because it was a hospital, when we had a waffle breakfast, it was like a restaurant. If you wanted pancakes, bacon, ham and eggs, whatever you wanted, they would make it. You tell them what you wanted and they cooked it for you and you go sit down and eat. It was like eating in a restaurant. And the girls used to clean our rooms and make our beds. If you were sleeping, you never heard them in the room. They mopped the floor, made the other beds, and before they go home, they came in and made your bed. We didn't have to make no beds.

"When we were on lunchtime, they would come down and relieve me for an hour, so I only put three hours in because I'm out to lunch. They sent another guy down to take over and then I would do the same. I'd go relieve him and stay there for the hour. And we used to hand the .45 from one guy to the other guy. The guy I used to relieve, I wanted to kill him. He always had a bullet in the chamber. I says to him, 'Why do you keep a bullet in the chamber?' He was afraid. I says, 'If I have to chase after somebody and I fall, I'll be shooting myself in the leg!' I knew he did that, so I would push the bottom and let the clip fall out and the bullet would go up and I used to catch it. I would put it back in the clip and I used to close it and lock the gun and put it back in the holster. I knew he did that, so that's what I used to do.

"And at night we used to get pot roast and all that kind of stuff. The food was delicious and the beer…you couldn't drink too much of their beer. They had strong beer. You drank three of those clay glasses they had and you started to feel it.

"One of the places they made into a nightclub and you used to go in there. They used to dance and they had a German band in there and all of the beer that was there. It was like a little night club. Guys used to pick up the women and they used to dance. With the women, they had a health card, so what the soldiers used to do, like I even did it, you pick up a girl and take her into the dispensary in the hospital. If the doctor examines her and says she's O.K., he gave her a button and she would have to wear that button and then she went into the club. If the girl didn't have a button, they wouldn't allow her in because they didn't know if she had a venereal disease or not. So, I had just met this one girl and I told her, 'You meet me here tomorrow morning and I'll get you a health button.' That night though I went over to the guards. They had guards on each side of the door where you go in and where you come out. They had guards there and she didn't have a button and they wouldn't let her in. So, I went over because I knew the guys and the guard said, 'Pat, you know I can't let you in.' I says, 'Alright, you aren't gonna let me in? When you come out of the street when I'm on, you better have a release paper that you are able to leave the hospital. Without that, you aren't gonna go past me. You carry a bat? I carry a .45. Now either you let me in…' The guard says, 'well, I'm not supposed to…but… oh, come on, Pat, don't be like that.' I says, 'Don't be like that? You're treating me like that! I'm getting her card tomorrow! And I'll show it to ya.' Then he says, 'Alright, but go sit in the corner.' And I said, 'I don't dance anyway.' So, he let me go in. He wasn't supposed to, but he didn't want to have to get a card with permission to leave the premises because if they didn't have that card, I wasn't supposed to let them go by, but I didn't bother stopping them." Unbeknownst to Pat, he wouldn't be back there the next night or ever see those soldiers ever again.

The next morning, June 1, 1946, Pat was sitting with the girl on a bench waiting for her name to be called for her examination for clearance when his name comes blaring over the loud speaker instead to report to the captain's office. "I says to the girl, 'I'll be right back,'" Pat said. "I told her, 'You go in that door when they call you.' She didn't speak English. I didn't speak German. We did sign language. So, I get to the captain's office and he says to me, 'I've got your records here. You never finished training. You got another eight weeks to go. Tomorrow, I want you to report to the drill sergeant and finish training.' So, I says, 'But I'm a security guard.' He says, 'I know what you do! You work four hours a day. You got plenty of time and make sure you go tomorrow!' So, I saluted him and left. I went back to where the girl was sitting, and no sooner did I get back there, not even fifteen minutes, and my name comes over the loud speaker again. 'Report to the lieutenant's office' I said, 'What the hell is this?' I go back to where I just came from and I went into the lieutenant's office. I saluted him and he says to me, 'Now what I want you to do is go back to your room and pack your stuff. Your records are in this manila envelope. Tomorrow, at five o'clock in the morning, be outside here. There's going to be a car that's going to pick you up. You're going home and you may as well take your papers with you.' I never finished training.

"A major picked me up in an open jeep. So, I never finished training. It was the major, a driver, and me. We drove from Germany to France. We had to get a boat. He drove us to Paris. When we got to Paris, I don't know where the major went. He disappeared and I met two soldiers who were cooks who told me they used to be sergeants, but they kept getting into trouble and they kept taking their stripes away and then they would get them back. So, they seen that I was a young kid, I was only eighteen, and they didn't want to see me get into any trouble, so they kinda took me under their wing. Now in Paris they had restaurants with tables outside and these goddamn tramp women come over and sit on your lap and wanna fool around with you and all and we kept chasing them. They seen I was a kid and they seen what these women were like and they made sure that I didn't get into any trouble. I was in Paris for a couple of hours until I got on the boat. Finally, I get onto the boat, and I never seen these guys get on the boat. I never seen these guys on the boat either. I don't know if they stayed in Paris or where the hell they went. I never seen them again. It took me eight days to get home on the boat back to the United States, but when we went over, we hit a storm. We weren't allowed to go up on deck for two days and that boat was jumping around the water. It was like a cork. The whole deck was soaking wet. When the weather finally cleared, we went up on deck. So, it took us ten days to get across. It took us two extra days when we went home because of the storm. We weren't allowed, and any time we went up on deck, you had to have your life preserver with you. We didn't used to put them on, but we used to sit on them. We would sit on the deck and on Sundays we used to have the three services: The Jewish service, the Lutherans, and the Catholics. They had a priest, a rabbi, and a minister. You had nothing to do, so you sat there and listened to them. And we sat there and watched the water. There was nothing to do." Pat left from Paris, France, on his father's fifty-ninth birthday on June 2, 1946, for a ten-day voyage across the Atlantic back home where they would land in New Jersey on June 12th. His European adventure had lasted for fifty days.

Upon his return to American soil, Pat believed that he would now be discharged and could return home to Brooklyn permanently.

Much to his surprise, he found himself stationed at Fort Dix in New Jersey. Instead of four hour shifts a day like he had doing guard duty in Germany, he now was putting in eight hour shifts as a clerk in the dispensary making 29 dollars a month. "I was sorry I came home," Pat said. "Had I known, I would have finished it all there in Germany. It was a regular job now. I'd never have come home." Pat mourned the thought of the breakfasts back in Germany, as he ate cookies and washed them down with a Coke for breakfast at Fort Dix.

"When I came back to Fort Dix, they put me in the dispensary with the doctors and I was the clerk," Pat said. "I used to get the cards and file them and I drove the lieutenant crazy. He was a guy from Upstate New York. The other guy was from Missouri and he was all right, but he went by the books, so I wouldn't fool with him. But with the other guy, I used to drive him crazy. They became captain then and the lieutenant from Upstate said, 'I want you guys to put the captain things on the uniforms.' I took the lieutenant ones off and put the captain ones on sideways. I didn't say anything. He went in the latrine and ran all around the dispensary after me. 'Get these things off!' I says, 'the lieutenant ones are no good to you now. Why don't you give them to me?' He said, 'what are you gonna do with them?' I says, 'I'm gonna put them on my collar!' He said, 'You know, you drive me crazy!' But he used to let me go home early on a Friday. In the afternoon there was nothing doing. I used to say, 'I'm gonna have the ambulance driver drive me over to the station.' He used to say, 'Who's running this place?' 'I am! I do more work than you. I gotta make the cards. I gotta file the cards.' He says, 'You're filing the cards in alphabetical order, right?' I said, 'What? No! I filed one, two, three, four...' 'Oh my God,' he says, 'No!' He opens the drawer and they're all in alphabetical order. 'I'm gonna shoot you!' he said."

In addition to making out reports and keeping books, Pat was administering inoculations and vaccinations at the dispensary. "When I went into the dispensary, they taught me how to give out shots. I had to work eight hours a day, and when new boys was coming in, we had to give out shots, we had to open up the dispensary at night and we were there till almost midnight giving out these shots to the boys coming in and I had to work. I was supposed to be corporal. That's what my job called for. I got in trouble for the easiest thing to give. We weren't supposed to give out the tetanus shots. You put the blue stuff on the arm and you take a needle and break the skin and then a week later you came back and if it scabs, it took. If it don't scab, it's gotta be done over again. The captain that was supposed to come do it wasn't there. I was there a half hour, so I said to the guy, 'line them up. I'm gonna give it to the guys.' 'You're gonna get in trouble.' I did, but I noticed on my discharge papers, they got it down. They had to have reported it. With one syringe, you can shoot ten guys. They sent a corporal. They didn't know what to do with him and sent him over to me. I'm a Private First Class and he's making money. He fainted on me! They says cause he was tired. He seen all these guys doing that and I had to do the work myself. I said, 'alright, you boil the needles and I'll give the shot.' He passed out on me. He said, 'I can't do this.' I don't know what the hell he did. I don't know why they sent him to me. Crazy!

"The only thing I gained by coming home was I had a Class A pass, so I could come and go like I wanted. I could come home almost every weekend, unless my name was on the board in the orderly room. Every Wednesday you go into the orderly room. If your name is on that board, you don't go nowhere. That means you got charge of quarters that weekend. It was a pain in the ass. We used to take turns. I couldn't come home that weekend. I was working. I had to spend forty-eight hours in the dispensary. I had to sleep in the main dispatch. We had one dispensary open twenty-four hours a day, seven days a week. The other dispensaries would be closed. So, anybody got hurt, they had to go there or we had a hospital on the premises, Tilden General Hospital.

"So, when I was working one time, this only happened one time, a guy turned over in a jeep. Now the doctor had a room and a regular bed. We got a cot to sleep on, so what I used to do was the back of the desk I used to put my cot and the phone right there. So, the phone rang about two o'clock in the morning, a guy turned over in a jeep at a certain spot, I called, and we had an ambulance outside and they sleep in the ambulance. So, I woke up and told the doctor that we got a call that the guy in the jeep turned over and then I told the girl there that the jeep was turned over. She was a war veteran. The doctor went underneath with his little briefcase and he told me that he gave the guy an adrenaline shot and he straightened the guy out a little bit, then he crawled out and he said to me and to the driver, the girl, you both take a foot and drag him out slowly. We dragged him out and put him on a stretcher. We put him in the ambulance and I sat in the front there and we took him over to Tilden General Hospital. We got him inside and me and the ambulance driver went out. He was in there for a while. Then I seen this doctor a couple of days later. I asked him about the boy and he says he was just bruised up a bit. They kept him overnight for observation. He was out."

When Pat checked the board for his assignment on Wednesdays and found he wasn't listed on the board for CQ duty, as they called it, he would drop a postcard in the mail to Johnny Morena with a message that he would be in Brooklyn that weekend. "I would come to Johnny's every Saturday morning," Pat said. "I would come home Friday night. I remember we got drunk upstairs in the room in Johnny's house. What happened was I got home from the army and we were supposed to go pick up the girls at three o'clock in the afternoon on Saturday. So, Saturday at like ten o'clock in the morning, I went and rang the bell. Josie was always glad to see me. 'Oh, Pat,' Josie said, 'come on in. Go upstairs. That bum is still in bed. Get him outta bed.' So, I went upstairs. Johnny was awake. He was just lying there. And he said, 'Hey Pat!' And I says, 'What are you doin in bed, you God-damned bum?' So, he says, 'Open the closet. There's a couple of glasses on the shelf and there's a gallon of anisette.' Now there was a few inches left in the bottle and we finished it. 'On the top shelf, I got a bottle of Canadian Club,' Johnny says. 'Get it down.' We started drinking the Canadian Club. We start making noise, singing. We were drunk. Josie came up the steps, 'What are you guys doing up here? You're making so much noise! Come on down!' So, she had a small lamp with a shade. I took it off the lamp and put it on my head. And I went by the stairs and I'm holding on the banister and kicking my feet. 'Come down here before you fall down,' she yelled up to me. 'What are ya's doin? You'se guys are drunk! I'll kill ya's.' She made a pot of coffee to sober us up. We're sitting there, sober now, and went to sit on the stoop. We got a lot of time to kill and now what are you going to do from now till three o'clock? I don't know. What shall we do? I'll tell you what! Let's go across the street to Flamm's bar. There was a candy store, then the street, then there was Flamm's bar. They were neighborhood bars. You didn't see women in those bars. Not in the neighborhood. And at that time, if you had two beers, the bartender would throw you a beer. So, we must have had four beers by time we went to pick up the girls. We had great times together, not getting home till two in the morning."

Another friend who sometimes palled out with Pat and Johnny was Frankie Fanaro. "Ralph used to drive our truck at Brooklyn Box Toe and Frankie was Ralph's son," Pat said. "I was Frankie's boss and then he quit. We palled around together. Him, Johnny and I. He was in the navy. So, he picks up these two girls and he said, 'I got a date for you.' He turns around and tells the girl that I was in the navy. I don't know nothing about the goddamned navy! And then the girl is asking me questions. So, I remember on TV I seen some of those pictures of those guys and they shoot the planes down. I said, 'oh, I was a gunner.' She said 'what's a gunner?' I says to her, 'you sit in this thing here and you shoot the planes down.' 'How fast does it go?' What the hell do I know? I says, 'it's not how fast it goes, it's the knots. It goes so many knots an hour. So, she goes, 'what's that like in a car?' 'It's like 120 miles an hour in a car, but you are on the water.' I says, 'son of a bitch! Why'd you tell her I was in the navy? Why didn't you tell her I was in the army?' But that didn't last. That was a one-shot deal, so I didn't care.

"Frankie was older than me," Pat said, "and in the navy before I was in the army, so he was out and I was still in, so Johnny turned around and told me that Frankie took that girl out to Manhattan and he didn't like her. He dropped her off in New York. I had words with Frankie about it and we almost came to blows. You don't do that to a girl. I went out with a few girls where I just didn't call them no more. When I came home, I threw their number out. I was Frankie's boss and knew his father and all, but it wasn't worth it. He's dead now. He was older than me.

"Johnny came to my house one day when I was home on a weekend pass," Pat remembered, "and he said, 'We got a date with two girls. They're cousins.'" Johnny was dating a Jewish girl named Nora Schaefer up on Bushwick Avenue, past Grand Street. Nora had a cousin named Gladys Goldberg, who Johnny wanted Pat to double date with him and Nora. "Johnny had Nora and I had Gladys," Pat said. "Gladys used to go to Nora's house for the weekend because I used to come home from the service so we could go out. I never met Gladys's parents. I don't even know where she lived. We used to walk far up Bushwick Avenue, Johnny and I. It was pretty far to Nora's house. Nora's mother was a nurse. She used to go to work at a certain time of the evening on a Saturday. She used to say, 'Nora, when you leave here, make sure you lock the door.' I used to say, 'Don't worry, Mrs. Schaefer. I'll make sure it's locked.' And she would say, 'Oh, thank you, Pat.' She talked to me more than she talked to Johnny and her daughter was Johnny's girlfriend. Maybe because I was in uniform? I don't know. Nora's mother liked me. She always talked to me. She never talked to Johnny. I think she was wishing that I took her daughter out instead of her niece. I was hooked up with Gladys, which was good, because Gladys was pretty tall and Nora was short like Johnny, more or less. She was a nice girl. I think Johnny liked Gladys more than he liked Nora, but Nora was more his size. We always went to Manhattan movies and that was always my biggest fight with Gladys. At the time I was getting $29 a month as a PFC in the army and she always wanted to go to New York and go to a restaurant in New York. I used to get in half price and I had to pay full price for her. I used to get on the train for nothing and I had to pay for her to get on the train. Now in Brooklyn, the movies houses had two features. In Manhattan, they only had one feature. You paid a dollar to see one picture. In Brooklyn, you used to pay fifty cents. I used to pay a quarter and fifty cents for her. In Manhattan, I was paying $1.50 to see one movie. 'Why do we gotta go to Manhattan and pay for the subway for?' I used to ask her. But they always wanted to go to Manhattan. That's what we would mainly do because it was only Friday night and Saturday night. Sunday night I didn't go with them because I used to go back to camp. So, it was only Friday night that I would come in and Saturday night that we would go out with them. So, it was usually a movie and then going to a restaurant. And in the restaurant, Gladys would order food, and if she didn't like it, she wouldn't eat it. I used to get pissed off because I was paying for it. I used to get pissed off with her all the time."

Pat never brought Gladys home to meet his family, as he didn't see the relationship as serious, and didn't want to hear his mother's questioning about the difference of religion. Was he surprised when he came home one day to find Johnny, Nora, and Gladys sitting at his mother's kitchen table and his mother giving him a glaring look across the room. Pat wanted to kill Johnny that day. Especially when he had to sit through his mother's interrogation about who were those Jewish girls.

Pat on a weekend leave with his sister, Margie, in 1946

PASQUALE

When Pat returned to camp on Sunday, he would go through the orderly room without signing back in, since he hadn't signed out. One week his negligence caught up to him. "I screwed myself up too because when you left the hospital, they had a book in the orderly room. Now if you left, you put your name in it and you go out. When you come back, you put your name in the book again that you're in. I never signed the book. I just used to go. I think that I was supposed to get the extra stripe because the next day one of the guys says, 'Hey, Pat, the captain was calling your name all day Saturday looking for you because he went to the orderly room and didn't see your name in the book. You better go see what the hell he wanted.' So, I went into his office. He says, 'I see you left the premises without signing in or out. You were due for another stripe. And, by the way, where is the one stripe that you got?' I says, 'It's in my locker.' He says, 'Well, if you don't want it, I'll take that one away from you.' I says to myself, 'ah, shit. It woulda meant an extra five dollars a month.' I didn't care about the stripe. I had one stripe which was five dollars more than private, so I never put the stripe on my uniform. How was I gonna sew it on? We didn't have thread and who knew how to sew it on? You have to take it to a tailor or somebody who knows, like some woman who could sew it on for you. Then you have to give her something for it."

One aspect of Pat's nearly six months at Fort Dix that he did not like was the demolition that took place. "You go there and there is this big mound of dirt and behind that dirt they're blowing up bombs and all the stuff they gotta get rid of behind that dirt," Pat said. "You keep hearing 'boom' and keep seeing all of the sky light up. We gotta be there with an ambulance in case somebody blows up. But I was lucky. We had to sit there for eight-hour tours doing nothing. I got that detail once. 'I hope I'm outta here before I have to do that again,' I said to myself. Imagine someone getting blown up and having to pick them up. They were getting rid of the stuff. What were they gonna do with it? So, I don't know if there is a big hole up there that they were in? I don't know because we never went to the other side. We parked the thing right in front of the big mound of dirt, the ambulance."

As December 1946 rolled around, President Truman demobilized the troops and Pat's year in the United States Army came to an end. "When I told the doctor in the clinic from Upstate that it was my last week with him, he was sad because I did good work," Pat said. "I says, 'I'm gonna leave you my phone number and my address.' 'What do I want your phone number and your address for?' I says, 'Why? When you go home outta here, you're gonna open up an office, right? You're gonna need a receptionist and I'll be your receptionist!' 'Oh God, no!' I drove him crazy. Sometimes, in the middle of the day, I would say, 'You want something from the PX? I'm going to the PX.' 'What do you mean you're going to the PX?' I made him crazy.

"President Truman wanted all the draftees out," Pat continued. "He just wanted regular army. The sergeant major came over to me. I never seen the guy in my life, so how does he know I work good? Bullshitter. 'Why don't you sign up and stay in? I like the way you work.' 'You never seen me work, you stupid bastard,' I thought to myself. They tried to get you to sign up. He didn't want the guys that were drafted. He was letting all the draftees out because he didn't need us. So, the sergeant major says they're changing the uniform. I had the Eisenhower jacket, the half-jacket. They went back to the buttoned jackets, longer jackets. And they were changing the color of it a little bit. It was something like the marines have. They're changing the color. They were getting new uniforms.

"When you get discharged, you go to the separation center. It's a special barracks and you stay there for three or four days because all the boys that are getting out have to get a physical to get discharged. In the corner, you threw all of the blankets, so I took my duffel bag and I grabbed two or three blankets and put them in my duffel bag and I left. My mother loved them. They were wool blankets." Pat was discharged from Fort Dix on Sunday, December 8, 1946. He was going home.

Before boarding the train in New Jersey on that Sunday morning for home, "I had trouble with an MP in the town," Pat said. "I was waiting for the train to come in. And even if you're a general, when you leave the building, you have to have your hat on. I had my hat in my shoulder pad. The MP comes over and said, 'Hey soldier, you gotta put your hat on.' I said, 'I'm not a solider.' 'You either put your hat on or I'll arrest you.' 'You can't arrest me—I'm a civilian! See this paper?' 'You are still wearing the uniform and you should wear it the way you're supposed to wear it.' 'You wanna arrest me? You go get a cop to arrest me!' We're arguing back and forth, the train pulls up, I got on the train and yelled to him, 'Why don't you get on the train? I'll show you New York!'" When the train pulled into New York City, while his uniform made him a soldier, in his heart, Pat had already put the army behind him.

When Pat got home to Brooklyn that afternoon, he headed over to Johnny's on Richardson Street. That night they had a date with Gladys and Nora. "When we went to pick up the girls, I said to Johnny, 'I'm breaking up with Gladys,'" Pat said. "Nora, says to me, 'Pat, take your jacket off. It's hot in here. We're gonna be here for a while.' So, I take off my jacket and she brought it in the bedroom. We didn't go nowhere that night. Gladys was there and I turned around and said, "Look, we're gonna part company because I'm not taking you out no more." So, I broke up with Gladys that night and then I said to Nora, 'Give me my jacket, I'm going home.' She hands me the jacket. I'm a little P.O'd and all at this point. I put my jacket on and I went home. Johnny quit his girlfriend too. 'What are you doin?' 'Eh, we'll find two other girls,' Johnny says to me." When Pat got home and took his jacket off, he noticed that Nora had taken all the buttons off of the jacket. "She stripped the jacket on me and I didn't know," Pat said. "I had a couple of ribbons over the pocket of my jacket. I had a sharp shooter ribbon and a good conduct ribbon and one that I had been overseas to Germany. I had three ribbons on there and they were gone and the U.S. button and the medic button on each side of the collar. Those two things were gone. I didn't know when she gave it to me because I was P.O.'d and I just put it on and when I took it off at home I said, 'Son of a bitch! She took everything off the God-damned jacket!' I never seen either one of them ever again."

Since he had no civilian clothes when he was discharged on Sunday, Pat was still wearing his army uniform on Monday morning when he walked over to Brooklyn Box Toe to say hello to the superintendent, Frank Keller, now that he was home again. "When I got out of the military," Pat said, "I didn't want to work there anymore. What happened was Frank said, 'Why don't you come back here? I could use you.' I said, 'No, I don't want to be a floor boy all my life.' Then the phone rang and Frank went to answer it, so I finished what he was doing and he's looking at me from the phone. Then he walked back over and said, 'Why don't you come back?' I said, 'I want to go upstairs, but you'se never put me upstairs.' He says, 'When there's an opening, I'll put you upstairs. Come back. I can use you.' And I figured that I had family there. I'd be with my family." Reluctantly, Pat decided to return. After leaving the shop, Pat went to go buy civilian clothes. His uniform shirt and pants would only be used in the future as work clothes at the shop. "If I wore the shirt, I didn't wear the pants and if I wore the pants, I didn't wear the shirt," Pat said. "Those clothes used to wear like iron. I wasn't too anxious to get out of the uniform. I went to the movie for half-price. I rode the train for nothing. I worked downstairs with Frank, and that's what I didn't want to do. Frank said, 'It's just gonna be for a little while until we get an opening upstairs. I was interested in the machines upstairs."

Now that Pat was home again, Lorenzina was impressed to hear that Pat knew how to give injections from working at the clinic at Fort Dix and was ready to volunteer him to take care of Pete's brother, Patsy. "Uncle Patsy was a sugar diabetic," Pat said, "and my mother said, 'Oh you could go give Zi Pasquale his shots.' I said, 'Ma, I gotta go to work.' Carmine, big shot, said, 'Go give him the shot. So, you're a few minutes late. What's the big deal? You go give him the shot.' And Uncle Patsy's skin was so tough that the needles were bending. The needles were so old and I didn't have much money and I kept telling Uncle Patsy to get new needles and he would say, 'No! No! No!' 'But I'm gonna break the needles and then we're gonna be in big trouble!' 'No worry,' he said. 'You're not gonna breaka the needle. Pusha! Pusha!' Yeah, pusha pusha and the needle breaks and we're in trouble. But I was lucky. His house was a two-family house, but the apartments were side by side. Downstairs was a garage and his tenant seen me going there every morning. It was a man. I don't know if he had a wife or not. I just seen the man and he seen me. 'If you show me how to give it, I'll give it,' he said. 'You don't have to come.' 'Really?' I asked. I stayed with him for a week because I had to go every day. I said, 'Look, here's the factory number in case you get in trouble, you can call me there. It'll take me five minutes to get here.' He said, 'I'll be all right.' He never called me or anything, so he was giving my uncle the shots. So, I got outta that."

When the family gathered at Uncle Patsy's on Christmas Eve of 1946, the three Franzese brothers were home and working together side by side at Brooklyn Box Toe, along with Millie's husband of one year, Jimmy Glynn. Millie had given birth to the first of Pete and Lorenzina's grandchildren that year with the birth of her son, James Anthony Glynn, on October 26, 1946.

Before being drafted, Pat had gotten his driver's permit, but due to the shortage of workers and the demand for work, Carmine had only one opportunity to teach Pat how to drive. Now that the war was over, Pat renewed his driver's permit and Carmine had the time now to instruct him on how to drive. "The first time I failed, and I did good," Pat said. "The guy was a big Irish guy. His face was red as a beet. I think he was half drunk. And I think I went out with the Hudson the first time. The second time I went out with the truck. Ralph Fanaro had the truck and the windshield was cracked and it's supposed to be in good shape and the seat on the passenger's side is busted. And they're all telling me to put a couple of bucks on the seat for the guy and the guy was mad. He says, 'take that money off. I'm gonna report you!' And he did report me. So, I drove any old way and I didn't give a shit because I knew he was gonna fail me, but he passed me. I get a letter in the mail from the license bureau. They said if you want your license, you gotta come down to the office for it. Livingston Street, Downtown Brooklyn. So, I went there, and I wore the ruptured duck pin on my suit jacket. It shows you were in the military. I had it and they said put that button on when you go down to the license bureau. The guy opened the drawer and he had my folder in there. He took it out and he gave me holy hell. He says, 'you're bribing? You know we could send you to jail? You're lucky because the guy passed you, but we wanted you to come down to let you know that you shouldn't be doing things like that, but you passed and you'll get your license in a couple of days.' And it was true."

The first car that Pat would drive was a green 1946 Hudson. "It was one of the first cars that came out of the showroom after the war," Pat said. Hudson Motor Company of Detroit, Michigan, began its post-war automobile production on August 30, 1945. During its time of production, the Commodore was the largest and most luxurious Hudson model. "It had no back seats and it had wooden bumpers," Pat said. "They hadn't had the bumpers on it yet because it was right after the war and they got the parts for it over time. They'd call my brother up and he'd bring the car in. They put the back seat in and then they put the bumpers on."

As 1947 began, Pat would arrive at Brooklyn Box Toe at six in the morning and work alongside men who could have been his father. "I worked down on the bottom floor with Frank Keller all the time," Pat said. "There was the skiving machine that they taught me how to use and I was running. Then I wanted to go up to stock fitting. They had the rounding machine, the apex machine, and I kept saying to Frank, 'I wanna go work upstairs with Artie' and he said, 'Nah, I need you down here, Pat. He don't need you up there. If he needs you up there, I'll send you up there. Just have a little patience.' I was doing all the shit jobs downstairs because I was the youngest in the whole place. Everyone was like Carmine's age and older, so they decided that I gotta go and buy the people's lunches. I had to go around with a pencil and paper. It was the same shit. Going out to buy lunch for people and stuff. You know how many times I quit my brother because of the lunch shit? Even my mother got involved and Carmine said to her, 'Ma, please stay out of it.' She said, 'He comes home to eat. Why must he go out and buy other people's lunches?'"

Three months after Pat started working at Brooklyn Box Toe again, an opportunity was about to come his way that he least expected. "Upstairs there was a guy named Artie Meyers," Pat said. "He was Frank Keller's friend. Frank used to play the guitar and Artie used to play a banjo. Artie Meyers had an ulcer and he was running the floor upstairs. So, when I was working downstairs, Artie came downstairs and he went to talk with Carmine and Frank and said, 'Look, I don't want to run the floor upstairs no more and I don't want to answer phones. I'm having trouble with my stomach. I just want a job.' So, my brother Carmine turned to Frank and said, 'Who do we know in the business that we can we hire to run the floor upstairs?' Right away, Frank Keller turns around to him and says, 'Your brother, Pat.' Carmine says, 'Pat? You think he could handle it?' Frank had confidence in me. Carmine had no faith in me. Frank says to him, 'He most certainly can.' Carmine says to him, 'Get him and let's talk to him. See if he wants to do it.' They called me down and asked me and I said 'Yeah, I'll try it.' I hadn't learned all the machines yet, so I went to talk with them and they both told me, 'You gotta keep one thing in mind. You gotta satisfy the customer,' and Frank said, 'Look, I'm friends with Artie and I'll tell you right now, Artie is not going to work under you. He's gonna quit. He'll stay for a couple of weeks, but he's gonna leave. Trust me on that. He'll leave. Now, he's not gonna teach you everything he knows. You're gonna have to steal from him and watch how he does things. You gotta watch how he sharpens the knife, how he changes the machines, and how he does this and that. You gotta steal that from him.' Frank sent me upstairs to Artie Meyers and he starts showing me and teaching me the machines. I took a liking to the rounding machine and I learned the apex machine. Artie was teaching me the machines, but he didn't teach me all of them. I would stand a little distance from Artie and watch him sharpen the knife. That's how I learned. Then when they came around and told him that I would be running the floor up there, I told Artie, 'the phone is ringing.' He said, 'you're the boss now, you answer it!' It's the first time I'm on the phone with a customer. I don't know what the hell I'm doing myself. It was hard learning everything. Sure enough, two weeks later, Artie went downstairs and told Frank and Carmine that he was quitting the factory and he did leave. You might as well say I was nineteen and a half and I was running the floor upstairs."

Once Pat got his driver's license in 1947, he would take off in the '46 Hudson and go to Coney Island. "I went a lot of times to Coney Island," Pat said. "I used to pick up girls in Coney Island. You know the cars that used to bump. Bing! Bang! I get in there and I see a girl by herself and I go and smash her all around the goddamned place, and when it's over and she got out before me, I'd say, 'I hope I didn't hurt you. You know I feel bad. Let me buy you a frankfurter or something.' 'No, get outta here.' 'Oh, come on! Make me feel better that I banged you all around. I hope I didn't hurt you. I'm sorry.' And sometimes they would let me buy them something and get to talk with them and set a date out of it and sometimes it didn't work. It didn't work all the time."

Before Pat had even settled back into civilian life, he was back having adventures with Johnny. The two of them used to go fishing together all the time, take some beer and their fishing poles and rent a boat for a day on the water fishing. "I used to go by the water because the salt water used to clear my head," Pat said. "We had good times, Johnny and I, especially fishing." Other times, they would head to the Ridgewood Grove Arena to the fights and the auto races in Freeport. Johnny wasn't fond of the movies like Pat was, but once in a while Pat could coax his chum into joining him.

"At that time, Johnny was working for a company that used to paint fire engines," Pat said. "Being that Johnny was small, he'd get underneath the truck and paint and the other guys there painted and he'd take the brush and paint the other guys shoes. Oh, he was a card! He was a lot of fun. One time, Johnny's place gave a barn dance in Manhattan. I started drinking and I got really drunk. So, what happened was, if you're doing something on the dance floor, say, if two guys are dancing together, you get thrown in jail and you don't get outta jail until a woman gets in the jail. Then you marry her and the two of you'se walk out, you and the girl walk out, and the other guy's gotta wait for another woman. Well, anyway, I get drunk and I go out on the dance floor and I'm jumping around there. Two guys come and grab me by the shoulder and threw me in there. Now there's a guy who wanted to be Johnny's friend for the longest time and Johnny hated the guy and he knew that I was good friends with Johnny. He had a bottle of whiskey and he was giving me drinks through the bars. They were fake bars. And he says, 'Eh, you're a friend of Johnny's. I tried to be Johnny's friend' and this, that, and the other thing. All of a sudden, a girl gets thrown in, so we get married, the girl and I. Then I'm on the dance floor with the girl and her real husband comes over and says, 'That's my wife.' I says, 'I just married her!' There was a big commotion. My friends all seen that and Johnny comes running over and he says to the guy, 'He's drunk and he don't know what he's doin. He's really a nice guy.' Well, anyway, we got by that, stewed as hell, and we have snow and ice outside, so

Pat with his 1946 Hudson

Johnny seen I was so sick. I had forgot my overcoat. He had my overcoat and had gone outside, and when we got outside, I went to the gutter curb and I threw up, and then I slid on the ice and I couldn't get up, and he's trying to get me up and he's got my coat. I'm in just a suit jacket. He gets me up and we both started walking. I said, 'Oh shit, where's my coat?' 'Your coat is right here, put it on,' Johnny said. I put it on. He's half holding me up. We got to 42nd Street and they got these stores and stuff, frankfurter places. They got the thing closed in because it's cold and it's all frosted. He decides he wants a frankfurter. So, he stands me up against the building and he goes to the window, and when the guy opens the window, the smell, I ran to the gutter curb and threw up again. I started to sober up a lot. Then, when we got to the subway, we're gonna get on the train. We're on the subway. I says to him, 'Hold my hand. I wanna see if the train is coming.' Then finally we got on the train and we came home. It was like two o'clock in the morning."

Other times, Pat would go with Johnny and his childhood friend, Bobby Gentile, up to Bear Mountain Park in Upstate New York. "There was a woman," Pat said. "I forget what her name was, and she used to have the Seven Dwarves. They were huts like all around. And we used to go to her all the time. One time, we went to the deli. We bought cold cuts and we bought beer and we went and sat on a park bench by the Hudson River. We pulled up our car to where the table was. We emptied the car and sat at the table. This man walks up to us and said, 'What are you guys doing here?' 'We're having lunch,' we said. 'You want a sandwich? You can have a sandwich with us.' 'No, no, I'm O.K.,' he said. 'But you know you're on private property.' 'There's no sign,' we said. 'It's my property,' the man said. 'Oh, sorry,' we said and started getting up. He says, 'No, you guys can stay here. Just make sure you don't leave a mess.' So, he sat down with us and we start becoming friendly and we asked about his motel. It was a nicer looking place. The man, Mike Monte, built it himself. He was an engineer. It was beautiful. I guess he had people working for him, but he was the one who designed it. So, we asked him what he charged, so we moved out of that lady and we started going to him and we started doing some jobs for him around the place. We became good friends."

Pat was settled back into civilian life working six days a week, with a half-day on Saturday, and hanging out with Johnny almost every night. Then, after four long years, the Franzeses were notified that Sal's body would be sent home to them from India. "My mother was on Carmine's back about getting Sal's body home to us, but the government takes their time too," Pat said. Under the direction of Franzese & Cucurillo Funeral Home, Sal's casket arrived with a military escort. Laying in state at Greenpoint Chapel, "one soldier stood at the head and one at the feet," Pat said. "They were holding rifles.

Carmine gave them a couple of bucks and chased them." Carmine wanted to relieve the soldiers because Sal was no longer one of theirs. He was back to being one of the Franzeses. Sal no longer belonged to the military; he had finally come home to his mother. After a solemn requiem mass at Saint Francis de Paola on the morning of Saturday, May 29, 1948, Sal's flag-draped casket was brought to Calvary Cemetery for burial in the grave that Lorenzina had purchased in 1945. On the hill that faced Sal's grave in Section 4-B, where a monument to the United States Civil War stands, seven soldiers were lined up to fire the 21-gun-salute. "Every time the bullets went off, Millie jumped," Pat said. With each shot, it seemed to tear apart her soul. "With Sal, they had the taps and Millie passed out," Margaret Dalto remembered. Following the salute and the folding of the flag that draped Sal's casket, the soldier presented the flag to Pete in honor of his son's service, as Lorenzina and his other living children looked on. For the Franzese family, World War II had finally come to end.

CHAPTER FIVE

Romance on Richardson Street

SUMMER 1948

The summer of 1948 began following the burial of Sal in the last days of May, and then by the death of the last ward boss of Greenpoint, Peter J. McGuinness, who died of a heart attack at the age of sixty, on June 10, 1948. Four days later, ten thousand Greenpointers lined the funeral route to bid farewell to the man who had coined Greenpoint as the "garden spot of the universe," as his funeral cortege went from Saint Anthony's RC Church on Manhattan Avenue to Saint John's Cemetery in Middle Village, Queens. By this time, all of the boys who had died in the war had been laid to rest on home soil or to forever remain interred overseas. The boys who came home, like Sammy and their brother-in-law, Jimmy Glynn, went to work, got married, and had children, but bore the scars on their souls from the atrocities of the war for the rest of their lives. Pat, who had not gone overseas until the fighting had ended, did not bear these scars, and once he came home to Brooklyn, had returned to the carefree life of working and going out with his friends just as before. After a day of work at Brooklyn Box Toe and the dinner plates had been cleared by his mother and sister, Pat would leave from the entrance on Herbert Street and walked up

Humboldt Street to Richardson Street, where he would sit on the stoop of 170 Richardson Street with his old chum, Johnny Morena, just as he had done before the war. The two would talk and laugh, razz one another, and "chippy chase," though rarely with neighborhood girls. Just across the way from Johnny's on the corner, Tota's store stood where Richardson and Herbert Streets came to a point, and the aroma of smoked mozzarella emanating from behind the store wafted down the block as Tota smoked the fresh mozzarella he just made by tying them to a stick and placing the stick across a garbage can he used for this purpose that had coal smoking in the bottom. The aroma of smoked mozzarella was mixed with the freshly baked bread from the bread store next door to Johnny's and would cause a passerby to suffer hunger pangs, even if dinner had already been over. Richardson and Graham, where Williamsburg ended and Greenpoint began, in 1948, was a closely-knit and unique neighborhood with the country ideals of Queens and the passion of the borough of Manhattan.

It was just about six in the evening on a weeknight on Johnny's stoop when Pat lost focus on the story that Johnny was telling. Johnny was always telling a story with a merry glint in his shining dark eyes and the mischievous grin of an imp. Pat also became blinded to the children playing stickball in the streets and the kids trading comic books and baseball cards. He would remember the street as being empty, which never happened on a warm evening on that street. With a moan of disbelief, Pat uttered, "Oh My God!" A young woman came walking around the corner onto Richardson Street from Graham Avenue and Pat became transfixed by her as if hit by a thunderbolt from which he would never recover. She had to be the most beautiful girl he had ever seen in his life. Where could she be from? In all of his years sitting on this stoop, Pat had never seen her before. Dressed in a black dress with a sequined bodice and black high heels, she looked like she could be coming home from a wedding. Her hair, the color of chestnuts, was down to her shoulders and bounced with each stride, as she crossed Richardson Street at an angle in front of Johnny's house. Pat broke from his reverie as the young woman glanced over to the stoop where he was sitting and called out, "Hello, Johnny!" and waved. "Hiya, Rose!" Johnny called back and Pat's eyes, mesmerized by her legs, followed her as she sauntered down Richardson Street, crossing Humboldt Street, and walking past Saint Catherine's Maternity Hospital, as the sound of her heels striking the sidewalk died away. Right before she reached North Henry Street, he watched her climb a stoop and enter a doorway. Snapping back to reality, Pat turned incredulously to look at Johnny. Who was this girl who Johnny knew and he had never seen pass here before?

Finally finding his voice again, Pat gave Johnny that incredulous look as he asked him, "You know her?"

"Yeah," Johnny answered nonchalantly, "she lives down the block. Why?"

Pat smiled, "I want to meet her!"

"You're wasting your time," Johnny tried to assure him. "She's engaged to be married to a guy who owns a candy store or something on Graham Avenue. She's already got her wedding gown."

Pat scoffed at the technicality. "What are you doing? Keeping her for yourself? I want to meet her anyway," Pat insisted.

"You're wasting your time. He's bigger than you. He'll kill you."

"That's a good way to die," Pat said, smiling ear to ear.

Seeing that his arguments were falling onto deaf ears, Johnny said to Pat, "Well then, come back tomorrow night around this time. She works in Manhattan and she passes here the same time every night and I'll call her over and you can meet her."

That night, as Pat walked home, he was determined to be there the following night when Rose walked past Johnny's house and figuring out how he was going to leave her a memorable first impression.

The following day, Pat walked into Carmine's office at Brooklyn Box Toe, where his brother sat in a leather desk chair in front of his massive desk piled with open mail and reams of papers stacked high. Carmine looked up, a Phillies cigar sticking out of his mouth, filling the room with thick plumes of smoke.

"Carmine," Pat said, "I was wondering if I could take the Hudson tonight."

"Yeah, what's going on?"

"Well, there's this girl I wanna take out tonight."

"Yeah, no problem. Have a good time."

Once again, when the dinner plates were cleared, Pat left home, but this time, he stopped at the garage behind the house to get into the 1946 Hudson. "It was a few years old," Pat said, "a shiny green."

Turning from Graham Avenue to Richardson Street, Pat made sure to pull up past Johnny's stoop to ensure that he had a clear view as Rose rounded the corner from Graham onto Richardson. While he sat with Johnny on the stoop, Pat didn't register anything that his friend was saying, his heart raced in anticipation. And then, like an angel, she appeared.

"Hello, Johnny," Rose called as she was just about to make her way diagonally across the street.

"Hiya Rose! Come over here! I want you to meet a friend of mine."

"Oh, Johnny, I'm tired and my feet hurt." Rose begged off the introduction.

"Aw, c'mon. It will only take a minute," Johnny reassured her.

Rose walked over to Johnny and Pat, who were now standing by the Hudson.

"Rose, this is Pat Franzese," Johnny introduced them. "He lives around the corner by the police station." Rose looked at Pat with her twinkling brown eyes and Pat noticed that when she smiled, she had two dimples on each side. She wore little makeup other than lipstick and a touch of rouge. She didn't need it.

"Well, it's nice to meet you, Pat," Rose said. "I'm Rose. Rose Porti. I live down the block."

"I can take you home cause I gotta go that way," Pat said and smiled.

"I only have one block to go."

"That's all right. I gotta go past there anyway. This is my car right here."

"O.K.," Rose said as her eyes appraised the highly glossed green finish of the Hudson. Pat opened the passenger door and Rose slid onto the seat. Running her hand over the dashboard as Pat slid behind the wheel, Rose said, "What a beautiful car, Pat! I love riding in cars. It's yours?"

PASQUALE

Thinking to himself of his brother, Carmine, Pat said, "Yeah, sure," but saw his opportunity.

"If you want to take a ride later," Pat said, "I'm going home to eat, so I could come back and we can go for a ride later to Coney Island or something." He smiled to himself, knowing that he had already eaten, but wanting to give Rose time to unwind and get ready to go out.

At the mention of Coney Island, Rose smiled. "I love Coney Island! Oh, this is my house next to those garage doors off the corner."

On the front stoop sat a middle-aged couple, the man bald and stern looking and the woman short and stout. "Oh, those are my parents. I'll see you later!" Rose got out of the car, closed the door, stepped back onto the sidewalk and waved as Pat pulled away.

Rose Porti, circa 1948

Pat returned with the Hudson and pulled in front of 207 Richardson Street around eight o'clock that night. Rose's parents, Tom and Victoria Porti, were still seated on the stoop. Rose emerged from the front door, said goodbye to her parents, and got in the car. Her parents looked very pleased as Rose closed the door on the

Hudson and they pulled away. That night, Pat and Rose walked the boardwalk on Coney Island and stopped at Nathan's for frankfurters with mustard and sauerkraut. Alternating between walking the boardwalk and riding the merry-go-round and bumper cars, Rose and Pat talked well into the night. Much to his chagrin, Rose told Pat that she was engaged and was wearing a diamond engagement ring. The wedding date had not yet been set and there was no wedding gown hanging in her closet. "Rose was having trouble with her fiancé," Pat said. "In other words, the timing was right."

While Pat gave Rose his shoulder to cry on, he couldn't help being hopeful that maybe her engagement would be coming to an eventual end. That is where he intended to step in. Rose spent most of her nights after working at the luncheonette, after spending all day in a clerical position at the Eagle Pencil Company in Manhattan. Yet, instead of spending this time working with her intended husband, she was often left to run the business alone, while her fiancé was out. They never spent any time together away from the store and their relationship was not progressing in any way at all. When the movie would let out next door at The Graham Theater, Rose couldn't help being filled with envy of the young girls on the arms of their fellas coming in for a malted before heading home. She would be selling candy, and serving sodas and malteds with longing in her heart and saying in her head, 'if only…"

On the nights that Rose pulled herself away from the soda jerk, she turned to the one person in the world who seemed to be listening to her. Carrying many burdens on her nearly twenty-year-old shoulders, where her secretary's salary kept her parents and five brothers and one sister afloat, she finally had someone to listen and let her cry when she could no longer carry her burdens. She had someone who cared enough to hear how disillusioned she was with the man she loved and rage at why he couldn't be who she needed him to be, in spite of her deep love for him. Without offering criticism and letting her vent her emotions, Pat would pull up to 207 Richardson Street in a shiny new car and take her away from all of the heartache for a few hours. On the other hand, Pat was ecstatic on the nights that Rose was available to go for a ride. For two months he endured the bitter tears and frustration that Rose had regarding the man who she said she loved and intended to marry. The 1946 Hudson would pull up in front of 207 Richardson Street, and Tom and Victoria Porti would smile in approval.

As Pat drove, Rose continued to unburden her problems and anguish, but as the weeks turned into months, he took all of this in and became frustrated himself. Pat could not help that he had fallen in love with the beautiful brunette with the twinkling brown eyes and sparkling smile that caused you to smile in return. But she belonged to someone else. While Rose continued to turn to him for solace and his car rides to help her to escape her unhappiness, she gave no indication that she returned those sentiments at all. The irony was that when she was with her fiancé, they only spent their time in the luncheonette. When she was with Pat, they were always on the road. "It was quite a few times back and forth between going for rides with me and going back to the store," Pat said.

After two months of sporadic nights of car rides and talks under the moon, Pat's resolve began to melt. He had fallen in love so deeply and completely, that he could not endure the talk of her loving another man any longer. He made the decision that he would have to tell her how he felt in return.

One summer night, Pat went to Richardson Street to pick Rose up. She was still moping about her fiancé, but Pat had had enough. Taking a deep breath, he pulled the car over near Cooper Park on Morgan Avenue and told Rose how he felt about her. How much he loved her and wanted a future with her. If she was so unhappy, he wanted Rose to leave her fiancé and have a happy future together with him. While Pat knew the risk in telling Rose what he felt, he made the decision if she did not feel the same way, he would walk away from his beautiful Rose tonight forever.

Rose listened to Pat's amorous feelings and intentions and looked back at him strangely. Her reply stung Pat worse than a slap across the face. After so many nights of drives and walks, so many talks through the night, she said that it was her fiancé that she loved and whom she would marry.

"I'm going to marry Lenny, Pat," Rose said. "I love Lenny. You're like my big brother."

Pat had no intention of filling the role as Rose's big brother. "She was just looking for a shoulder to cry on," Pat said in 2019. Devastated that Rose did not feel the same way about him and resentful that she saw him only as a shoulder to cry on, Pat told her with hurt pride, "I guess I'm just wasting my time. No, I am not going to be your big brother. You'll have to find yourself another big brother. I can't be your big brother. I care for you and you're turning me down! You know what's gonna happen to you? You're gonna end up with a couple of kids and be in the store and you're gonna have one kid in one arm and a kid hanging on your apron with the other hand and trying to make malteds and you're gonna be doing it alone just like you are now!"

"I'm going to change him!"

"Yeah, O.K. Rose, we've gone over this over and over. I've heard this already. You think you're gonna change him? Do you really love him?"

She answered automatically, "Yes, I love him." The words stung as his blood grew cold. "I know he loves me, Pat. It's just that there's always going to be something missing in our relationship."

"We just better cut it off." Pat couldn't understand what was really going on between Rose and Lenny, and to be truthful, he didn't care. He turned the car around and pulled in front of Rose's house on Richardson Street, clutching the steering wheel and staring straight ahead out of the windshield. She didn't love him. Why get out of the car? Why walk her up the steps? She walked down Graham Avenue alone every night in the dark. Rose had made her decision. She had chosen the guy who she cried and complained about all the time. Rose closed the car door and walked up her front stoop as Pat drove away.

"I used to walk her in the hallway because they lived in the back part of the house," Pat said. "It was front and back. They had the back apartment. When I used to take her out and brought her home at night, I used to walk her in the hallway. There was a little light, but it wasn't that bright, so this time she wasn't mine, so I didn't care. I just pulled up. She got out and went in the house and I went home. I put the car in the garage and I was upset."

As Rose mournfully climbed the stairs to her apartment, she wondered if she had made the right decision. The struggle waging inside of her was splitting her in two. She loved Lenny, but why in two years had nothing really progressed? Why did she always feel a nagging feeling that something was wrong? And did she really love Pat? Why had she chosen to spend so much time with him if she loved Lenny so much? How did Pat truly make her feel? Now, Pat was gone and she felt completely alone.

Eight, nine, ten days passed. The devastation of Rose's rejection so great, Pat refused to go anywhere near Richardson Street ever again. He refused to go to the movie theater on Graham Avenue for fear of running into her. Instead, he began going to the Meserole movie house on Manhattan and Meserole. He didn't want to see that beautiful brunette who refused to give him her heart. In avoiding Rose, Pat even stayed away from his best friend, Johnny, since he had no intention of going anywhere near Richardson Street. What Pat didn't consider was how hard it was to disappear in a little town such as Greenpoint-Williamsburg.

After a week and a half, Johnny ran into Rose as she was sitting out on the stoop with her parents.

Right away, Rose asked Johnny, "Have you seen Pat lately?"

"No, he hasn't been around. I don't know where he's been at. I guess they been pretty busy at the shop."

"Well, if you see him, tell him to stop by. I want to talk to him."

Johnny walked around to Herbert Street, where he found Pat sitting at home. Johnny sat down on the parlor chair with Pat.

"Hey, Johnny," Pat said. "How are you doin?"

"Hey, Bum, you don't come around no more!"

"Ah, Johnny, I don't want to run into Rose no more."

"Well, I just seen her."

"Oh, I guess she's married now, right?"

"No, she's sitting with her parents out on the stoop and she told me that if I seen you to tell you she wants to talk to you."

Pat couldn't conceal his hurt rage. "Like hell I'm gonna go see her! No one around to hear her problems? She's looking for a big brother! She cried on my shoulder enough! I'm still ringing out my undershirt from all her crying over her fiancé, so why don't you go be her big brother?"

"Ay, don't get mad at me! I'm just delivering you a message. Pat, why don't you go find out what she wants? I'm goin home!"

After the conversation was over and Johnny had left, Pat mulled the thought over in his mind. What could she want? What could he lose? "Maybe I'll go and see what it is all about," Pat said to himself. Pat went into the kitchen and found that his brother, Carmine, had not gone out yet for the evening. Between the three surviving Franzese brothers, they shared two cars, the 1946 Hudson and an old Ford.

"Yeah, I'm only gonna hang out on Broadway," Carmine said. "I'll take the Ford." Carmine was seeing a woman on Broadway in Williamsburg at the time. "He let me take the car," Pat said. "The Ford ran like a top. Second gear was broken on it. You shifted first and you give it the gun and then you pull it out in reverse. You had to park it off the corner so nobody parks behind you because you gotta put it in reverse, back it up really fast, and pull it out. Well, Rose never rode in that. I never took dates out in that. If I didn't have the Hudson, I'd take the bus to the movies or something." Pat walked around to the garage and picked up the Hudson and headed for Richardson Street.

"I seen Johnny was sitting on the stoop," Pat said. "I stopped. I said, 'I'm gonna go see what the hell she wants.' Johnny waved back and laughed."

With his mind racing with anticipation and guarded with a deep, wounded pride, Pat rolled down Richardson Street in the Hudson and parked in front of Rose's house. Just as Johnny had said, she was standing in front of the stoop talking with her mother and father. Her parents' eyes lit up at the sight of Pat and the car.

"Hey kid! How ya doin?" Rose's father, Tom, called out to Pat. "Where you been?"

"Hiya, Mr. Porti. Hiya, Mrs. Porti. I've just been busy at my brother's place."

Rose looked at Pat intently and asked, "Can we go for a ride, Pat?"

"Yeah, Rose, get in."

"Don't go too far," Rose said, as she slipped into the passenger seat.

As Pat drove near Greenpoint Hospital, Rose asked him to pull over by Cooper Park. She wanted to talk.

When Pat turned off the ignition, Rose began to speak. "Look," she said, trying to be as direct and honest as she could, "I can't promise you anything. I'm mixed up."

"What am I supposed to do?" Pat asked her.

She said, "I wanna be with you. Let's give it a try. Let's see what happens. I'm willing to give it a try if you'll have a little patience with me. I want to stay and go out with you for a while."

"Yeah, that's tonight, and tomorrow night, and maybe the next night. And then down the road you decide you want to go back to the store to him and I get kicked by the gutter curb again?"

"No, I don't think so…I doubt it…Just give me some time."

"Take all the time you want," Pat finished. "I'm not going nowhere."

"Well, I'm finished," Rose smiled. "You wanna go someplace?"

"I said, yeah, we'll take a ride to Coney Island," Pat remembered seventy-one years later. "I thought, let me hang in there and see what happens." Pat had fallen in love with Rose from the moment he first laid eyes on her, and finally, she was willing to give him a chance. How could he not agree to be patient and give them the chance that he had hoped against hope for since that first night?

Something had clearly happened between Rose and her fiancé one night in the store that had postponed her wedding indefinitely and she was now mulling over in her mind what decision would finally bring her happiness for the rest of her life. "After that, Rose was happier," Pat said. "It took a while. She loved the guy and it takes time. You don't get over things right away."

The summer was quickly drawing to a close. Lenny's mother, Regina, succumbed to cancer at the age of forty-seven. Although Rose had been supportive throughout his mother's final illness, they both knew that their time together was over. Neither of them could ignore the truth that they had now both found someone else, but

Rose knew that after having been together for two years, it was time to finally bring it to an end.

What Pat had no way of knowing when he began his pursuit of Rose Porti, those sparking eyes were those of a survivor and those shoulders were built to carry a weary load. While just turning twenty on August 7, 1948, Rose had endured more than he could have ever imagined already.

Rose circa 1948

CHAPTER SIX

The Portis and The Cilibrasis

1874-1948

Rose's grandfather, Pietro Porti, the son of Agostino Porti and Angelina Priola, was born in 1874 in Partinico, Palermo, Italy. A master candy maker, he married the eighteen-year-old Rosina Nania, the daughter of Gaetano Nania and Francesca Mancuso, on March 14, 1899, in her hometown of Lercara Friddi, Palermo, Sicily. Their first child, Rose's father, Agostino, known as Tom in America, was born in Lercara Friddi on March 5, 1900. A second son, Gaetano, followed in November of 1901, and died at the age of nine months on August 24, 1902, also in Lercara Friddi.

Pietro was sponsored by Barracini Candy Company to come to work in New York, so he left from the port in Palermo on the SS. Umbria on April 1, 1904, leaving behind his wife, Rosina, along with their two children, Agostino "Tom" and Angelina, who had been born on February 12th of that year. Rosina and her children would remain with her father, Gaetano, until the time came for them to join Pietro in the United States.

Their time came on December 5, 1907, when Rosina, along with her two children and Pietro's step-sister, Giulia Oliveto, set sail on the SS. Liguria from Palermo, arriving in New York Harbor on

Christmas Eve. Pietro had moved from 240 Elizabeth Street to 205 Forsyth Street (the current site of Sara D. Roosevelt Park), so it took time to notify him that his family had arrived at Ellis Island. The Portis spent Christmas Eve and Christmas Day in detention, having eaten breakfast, lunch, and dinner there for two days, waiting on Pietro's arrival. On December 26th, Pietro finally arrived and Giulia was released into his care at 10:15 a.m. and Rosina and the children at 10:30 a.m. They were the first detainees released on that morning. The Porti family were finally reunited on American soil, settling in Manhattan on East 11th Street.

Nine months after arriving in America, Rosina gave birth to her fourth child, a son, Gaetano, on September 29, 1908, named for her father and the infant son she had buried in Italy. Unfortunately, like his predecessor, he too died at the age of six months on March 28, 1909, from a gastrointestinal illness. He was laid to rest in Calvary Cemetery the following day. By April 15, 1910, they were living at 340 East 11th Street in Manhattan. At this time, Pietro worked for the railroad and not in the candy industry. The following year, they had a son, Pietro, on April 29, 1911, and a daughter, Francesca, named for Rosina's mother, the year after that, on December 2, 1912. In 1915, they were still living on East 11th Street and Pietro was once again working as a candy maker on Canal Street.

Sometime between the ages of ten and fourteen, Tom got into some kind of mischievous trouble, so his parents sent him back to Sicily to live with his seventy-year-old maternal grandfather, Gaetano Nania, on his olive ranch. One day, when they harvested the olives, Tom took the cart to Palermo to sell the olives. Instead of bringing the money back to his grandfather, he spent the money with his friends in Palermo. His furious grandfather sent Tom back to his parents in New York. "He wasn't bad, but mischievous," Tom's son, Pete, remembered in 2006. "He did crazy things. He was never locked up, just did crazy things."

Tom's grandfather, Gaetano Nania, put his fourteen-year-old grandson on the SS Canada in Palermo and he arrived at Ellis Island on his mother, Rosina's, thirty-fourth birthday, May 25, 1914. He was released into the care of his mother when she arrived to bring him home to 202 E. 11th Street.

Tom's parents, Pietro and Rosina (Nania) Porti

After finishing with school, Tom worked as a freight handler for the B&D Railroad, in Clarksburg, West Virginia, as he stated on his military registration card on September 11, 1918. He was working on a job in Cleveland, when he decided to join the US Navy from there on March 11, 1919. When the crew was ready to return home to New York, the boss didn't know where Tom had gone. On his return to New York, he had to tell Rosina that her son was gone and they didn't know where he had gone to. Six months later, Pietro receives a letter from Tom that he was on a tankard in Cuba and needed $100. There was talk that it had been because he had gotten a girl in trouble. His father scraped the money together and wired it to him.

It was dark when they pulled into the Brooklyn Navy Yard one night and Tom walked over the bridge into Manhattan. There was a knock at the door of the 561 East 11th Street apartment. The hallway was pitch black and Pietro couldn't imagine who could be knocking on the door at this time of night. After all, he would be back in the roasting department at the chocolate factory in the early morning. All he could make out was a dark figure in the hall when he opened the door. When the figure came into view, he was overcome at the sight of Tom in his Navy uniform. He had never thought that he would see his son, Tom, again. Pietro grabbed Tom, threw his arms around him and squeezed him tight. Tom wasn't able to stay long before being shipped out on the SS Wyoming. His sister, Angelina, and Cousin Anna, the daughter of Rosina's late sister whom Rosina had raised, saw him off at the Brooklyn Navy Yard.

Tom would never see his father again. Pietro died at home at 4 p.m. on November 6, 1922, at the age of forty-eight. The cause of death was chronic myocarditis with chronic intestinal nephritis. The funeral arrangements were under the direction of Filippo Rotella, Undertaker and Embalmer, at 446 East 13th Street, which arranged his wake at the family apartment. Pietro was laid in a wooden casket and two days after his death was taken to The Church of Mary, Help of Christians, where the American born children of Pietro and Rosina had been baptized on East 12th Street, for a solemn requiem mass in a horse-drawn funeral coach, followed by two carriages, and then laid to rest in Calvary. The entire funeral bill came to a grand total of $159.00. Tom was discharged on April 9, 1923. He came back to New York to find that his father had died six months before. Once he returned home, Tom found work as a chauffeur. On the application declaring his intent to become a United States citizen dated September 24, 1924, Tom is listed as a chauffeur, twenty-four years old, 5'6" 175 lbs., with dark brown hair and eyes, and a ruddy complexion. He was still living at 561 E. 11th Street

Tom's sister, Angelina, married Giocchino "Jack" Raia in Manhattan on July 26, 1924. A daughter, Maria, followed a year later on August 24, 1925, and another daughter, Rosina "Rose" on March 24, 1927. Jack had arrived in New York in 1921 from his native town of Bisaquino, Palermo, Italy. Sometime during the late 1920's, Tom and Jack started a trucking business. One day they got a job to move the contents of an apartment with their truck on 3rd Avenue, where the trolley tracks were by the elevated train. So, Tom backs up the truck into the sidewalk straight and he is blocking the trolley tracks. In the meantime, Jack is going into the house and moving out the people. Tom meets a friend of his and starts talking while Jack is going in and out of the house moving the contents. Meanwhile, a trolley car came. The trolley car cannot pass; it is blocked in. Tom is standing about fifteen feet away and the conductor rings the bell, 'bing…

bing' move the truck. Tom shook his head, "Eh, let him wait." He continued talking with his friend and Jack is still moving the house by himself. Another trolley car pulls up. Two are now backed up and both are ringing their bells. Tom kept talking. Before you knew it, there were five trolley cars backed up and all ringing their bells. Jack said, "Tom, move the truck!" "Eh, let em wait." Finally, the truck was loaded and they pulled away, trailed by the curses hurled at them from the disgruntled trolley conductors.

It was at a wedding in early 1927 that Tom met the nineteen-year-old Victoria Cilibrasi from Allen Street. The eldest child of Leonardo Cilibrasi and Maria Assunta Cerami, Victoria was born on March 30, 1908, in Manhattan. Her father, Leonardo, had been born on September 16, 1885, in Petralia Soprana, Palermo, Italy to Pietro Cilibrasi and Vittoria Macaluso. Leonardo departed from the port of Naples on the SS Citti di Napoli on November 22, 1904, arriving at Ellis Island on December 2nd. In addition to himself, Leonardo's sister, Angela, lived in New York as well. She was his senior by two years. Angela married to Leonardo Borromeo on September 13, 1913, and had four children, Sadie, Carlo, Victoria, and Peter, before eventually settling in New Jersey.

The twenty-one-year-old Leonardo Cilibrasi and the sixteen-year-old Maria Assunta Cerami, the daughter of Salvatore Cerami and his wife, Damiana Siefla, of Petralia Soprana, Italy, were married on July 17, 1907, according to their marriage license, or on July 21, 1907, according to the church register book at the Church of the Transfiguration on Mott Street by Rev. G. Giovannini. Their witnesses were Salvatore and Lilli Cancellieri. Maria, born on February 28, 1891, in Petralia Soprana, Italy, came to the United States shortly before her marriage in 1907. According to the church registry, both of Leonardo's parents were dead by this time and Maria's father, Salvatore, as well.

Following their marriage, Leonardo and Maria moved to 31 Allen Street and welcomed a succession of five children over a ten year period: Victoria on March 30, 1908, Pietro "Peter" on March 4, 1910, Damiana "Rita" on September 5, 1913, Salvatore on April 8, 1915, and Frank in 1918.

Victoria was baptized at the Church of the Transfiguration on September 21, 1908, by Rev. G. Giovannini, the same priest who had married her parents the year before. Oddly enough, she only had one person stand godparent, a woman named Maria Giovanna Marnelli. Victoria's brother, Peter, was baptized at the same church sixteen days after he was born on March 20, 1910. The names of his godparents are indecipherable in the register.

At the age of twenty-five, on September 26, 1910, Leonardo was described as working as a newspaper printer, standing at 5'7", 153 lbs., with a swarthy complexion, black hair, and brown eyes. It was noted that his right hand was mutilated. The family was living at 75 Allen Street in Manhattan at the time. Along with his wife and two children, they had two boarders living with them, Domenick Squadero, twenty-six, and Giovanni Messineo, twenty-five, both cigar makers who had arrived in America in 1905.

Tragedy struck the Cilibrasi family when Leonardo was stricken with lobar pneumonia and was rushed to Bellevue Hospital. He died at dawn the day after being admitted, pronounced dead at 5:30 a.m. on August 6, 1918, just six weeks shy of his thirty-third birthday. Two days later, Leonardo was laid to rest in Calvary Cemetery. He had been a naturalized American citizen for one year.

How Maria had wept when she was notified that her husband had died that morning at Bellevue. She felt desolate and alone with no man to protect her on this foreign soil. Her father, back in Italy, was already dead and she felt completely abandoned with no assistance, once the last shovel of dirt covered Leonardo's casket in Calvary Cemetery.

A year after the death of Leonardo, a new tenant freshly home from an overseas tour in France during World War I, came to live at 31 Allen Street. His name was Giuseppe "Joseph" Giarratana. Maria, a twenty-eight-year-old widow at the time who had been left with five children, soon after became involved with the thirty-two-year-old war veteran. When the census taker came to her apartment on January 10, 1920, Maria was still listed as a widow and had Victoria, Rita, Sammy, and Frank still living at home with her. Her ten-year-old son, Peter, had been institutionalized at the New York City Children's Hospital on Randall's Island for mental retardation. He was listed as being there in both the 1920 and 1925 census, but was transferred to the Rome State School For Mental Defectives by 1930 and remained there for the rest of his life. Once Peter was institutionalized, no one in his family ever saw him again. Peter died at the Rome State School at the age of thirty-five on June 26, 1945.

Born in Bompietro, Palermo, Italy, on October 27, 1886, Joseph Giarratana came to America in April of 1904 and served in the United States Army in Company E, 6th Infantry from his enlistment at Fort Slocum on July 27, 1917 until August 13, 1919. During his service, he served in the St. Mihiel and Meuse-Argonne engagements. He was slightly wounded on September 12, 1918, but was left with no disability. After his discharge from the United States Army, Joseph moved into an apartment at 31 Allen Street, where it is assumed he met Maria for the first time around August of 1919. She had been a widow for one year by this time. While Maria was listed as a widow in the January 10, 1920 census, Joseph claimed on his naturalization form to have married Maria in 1919, no specific date or place given. No evidence that a wedding ever took place was ever uncovered. Their granddaughter, Mary Lodato McCarthy, does not believe that they were ever legally married. While she was a "widow" in January, she was the mother of Joseph's son on December 7, 1920, with the birth of Leonard, known in the family as Sonny. It is unknown if the baby was named for her late husband.

As a stepfather, Joseph Giarratana was cruel and unloving and could only find love in his heart for the children he had had with Maria, not Leonardo's fatherless children. While Victoria was only eleven when Joseph came into their lives, he was not a father to her and never would be. Of the five children that Leonardo had left behind, only Victoria had those profound and lasting memories of him. How Victoria had loved him! She was the namesake of his beloved mother and his death devastated his eldest child so profoundly that the effects would stay with Victoria for the rest of her life. Maria knew this and how her union with Joseph Giarratana destroyed something in this child and how Victoria viewed her. But how could Maria make her child understand? Joseph came in and supported them and protected them when her and the five children didn't have a single male relative to defend them against the world. Maria had no family here in America and Leonardo had only one sister in New Jersey. Maria's father was dead and she had no brother in this country to watch over her. Entering a union with Joseph Giarratana had brought sorrow to her first child, who was already filled with rage and grief that her father had been taken from her. At the end of every day, Victoria would meet her father while playing in front of the Allen Street tenement and kissed his glistening, sweat stained swarthy face and carried his lunch pail up the long staircases to help her mother prepare the table for supper. Maria thought that one day Victoria would understand why her father's death had brought this stranger into their lives. The second husband. From the first day Victoria did not like him and was devastated that her mother had still been in deep mourning when Giarratana moved into their apartment and into Maria's bedroom. How strange that Maria was still wearing the black of deep mourning for Leonardo Cilibrasi when she was pregnant with Joseph Giarratana's child, and still decades later, when she died on January 10, 1961, at the age of sixty-nine.

When the ten-year-old eldest daughter, Victoria, returned to school that fall, she volunteered to help her teacher long after her classmates had gone home. When her teacher realized that her eager pupil was trying to stay later and later to avoid having to go home to an unhappy apartment where her father no longer returned, she forced Victoria to go home. It was at this time that Victoria showed the first signs of the highly fragile mental disorder which would plague her for the rest of her life.

Joseph's natural love for his first child, Leonard, who they called Sonny, gave him a love he never possessed for Maria's children. Sonny's birth was followed by Joseph on June 4, 1922. A month later, Maria's youngest of her children with Leonardo, Frank, died at the age of four-years-old on July 8, 1922, when he fell from the roof of their tenement house, 31 Allen Street, into the back yard. The cause of death was listed as a fractured skull and lacerated brain. He was buried the next day at Calvary Cemetery.

Maria went on to have two other children with Joseph: Cecelia on November 12, 1925 and Frances on February 7, 1928. By 1930, Joseph had walked out on Maria and never returned to her. Left with his four young children to care for by herself, Maria turned over Joseph and Cecilia into foster care until they reached adulthood. She kept the eldest and youngest Giarratana children home with her, Sonny and Frances. Joseph Giarratana died on November 9, 1946, at the age of sixty, and Maria would still mourn him as her husband, even though they had not lived together for somewhere between sixteen and eighteen years. He was laid to rest in Calvary Cemetery and joined there by Maria's son, Salvatore "Sammy," two years later, when he died from cancer on February 12, 1948, at the age of thirty-two. Maria too would be buried there in 1961.

It was a few years before all this that Victoria attended the wedding of a neighborhood friend when she first laid eyes on the World War I Navy Veteran from Sicily who would become her husband. She was nineteen and he was twenty-seven. "They knew each other about two or three months before they got married," their son Pete said.

Tom and Victoria were married in a civil ceremony at the Municipal Building in New York City on May 14, 1927. Tom's brother, Peter, and Rose Keiser stood as witnesses. With her left arm around the shoulder of her husband and her right clutching her handbag, neither Victoria nor Tom is smiling for the photographer. Tom is seated with his light-colored fedora on his lap and his right eyebrow arched. Victoria wore a simple, light-colored dress with a long strand of pearls and a long dark coat. It was topped off with a hat that came down to her eyebrows.

Tom and Victoria's marriage began while living in New York City. Tom had a widowed mother, a married sister with two children, and a single brother and sister. Victoria had a mother and her husband, a sister, a brother, an institutionalized brother, and four half siblings that were between twelve and twenty years younger than her. The old world of Sicily was quickly fading and the native tongue of the motherland would not be spoken in their apartment. By the end of 1927, Victoria would be carrying the first of her children in her womb. Uneducated in the ways of childbirth and fearful of having her stomach cut open, Victoria's mother, who was also pregnant at the time, simply told her daughter, "the way it went in is the way it comes out." Maria Giarratana would give birth six months before her daughter on February 7, 1928, to her ninth and last child, Frances.

PETER M. FRANZESE

Tom Porti and Victoria Cilibrasi on their wedding day, May 14, 1927

Rose Porti as a baby

PASQUALE

Rose Porti made her entrance into the world on August 7, 1928, at the Bellevue School for Midwives at 223 East 26th Street in Manhattan, the first official school for midwives in the United States. She was delivered by Jacques D. Soifer, the physician midwife. First opening their doors on August 1, 1911, the school had a small hospital with a house in the rear in which the pupil midwives lived. The school had accommodations for twelve patients in a second floor bright and airy ward, as well as a nursery, delivery room, lavatories and living room. The school shut its doors in 1936, due to lack of students. By then, it was more popular for a medical doctor to deliver children than a midwife. When Victoria was released to go home with her new baby, her and Tom were living at 429 E. 15th Street.

At the time when Rose was born, Tom was working for the United States Postal Service. He would remain there for three years during the late 1920's, but had difficulty because of an Irish foreman who gave him a hard time. This was in the times when there was animosity between the two immigrant groups. One day, Tom got so mad that while he was driving the mail truck, he parked it in front of the mail office in Manhattan and walked away from the truck, quitting on the spot.

Two months after Rose was born, Tom and Victoria were married on October 6, 1928, by Rev. P.C. Vassell in a second ceremony at Little Sisters of the Assumption at 246 E. 15th Street, down the block from their apartment. Their witnesses in this ceremony were Tom's sixteen-year-old sister, Frances, and Ellen Norton. One month later, the Rev. Joseph Schiano baptized their baby Maria Rosa Porti on November 4, 1928, at the Italian Church of Our Lady of Mount Carmel in Williamsburg, Brooklyn. Her godparents were Giuseppe DeFeo and Sarah LaMonaca. It is uncertain why Rose was baptized in Williamsburg, Brooklyn, when she was born in Manhattan. Also, it is interesting to note that her birth certificate lists her as "Rose Porti" and her baptismal certificate lists her as "Maria Rosa Porti."

According to the April 15, 1930 census, the Portis were living at 419 East 14th Street, a twelve-family tenement house, in Manhattan. Tom was driving the moving truck in his and Jack Raia's moving business and Victoria was the janitress of the tenement house, thus they lived rent free. Within a few months, they left Manhattan for good and moved to Avenue P and Kings Highway in Coney Island, where they were living when their second child, Peter, was born in Coney Island Hospital on October 22, 1930.

By 1932, the Portis lived on Metropolitan Avenue in Williamsburg, Brooklyn. Around this time, Tom had a portrait taken with his two children. Interestingly enough, Victoria does not appear in this photograph. Tom sits with a towheaded Pete on his left and a solemn looking Rose on his right. The photo shows Rose to be crossed eyed. She would soon be given corrective glasses that would correct this over her childhood. "Rose was my father's favorite," Pete said. "She was always a happy-go-lucky girl."

Around this time, the Portis had an oil burner in the front room, and because it was always hot, Victoria kept a tea kettle on top of it so she had hot water for a cup of tea throughout the day. It was a frigid day, and Rose was snuggled up close to the oil burner starving for warmth, when her two-year-old brother Pete climbed next to her to get close to the warmth of the oil burner and accidentally knocked over the tea kettle. The scalding water scorched Rose's legs and she was rushed to Greenpoint Hospital, where she was treated for 3rd degree burns. A constant regiment of salves and creams were applied, but the child was left with a scar on her leg nonetheless. She was three and half years old at the time. Toward the end of that year, Victoria had put Rose in a basin of water for a bath. It was a cold water flat in which the tenant had to create their own heat. While Victoria was bathing her, she had left the child in the basin for a while, and according to her younger child, Pete, Rose got a chill and came down with a fever. When the doctor came to examine Rose, he confirmed that she had contracted strep throat, which quickly manifested into rheumatic fever. The illness wreaked havoc on the small child and left her heart damaged with what is called a rheumatic heart. "The heart was damaged," Pete said. "She was a very active girl though, no slouch. She did her work, went to school, went out." Nonetheless, Rose's heart was damaged and compromised for the rest of her life.

With the ushering in of 1933, Victoria gave birth to her third child, Thomas, on January 16, 1933, and twenty months later to her fourth child, Theresa, on September 18, 1934. Both children were born at Greenpoint Hospital. The Portis went from living on Withers Street to Metropolitan Avenue and then to 298 North 8th Street. In the meantime, Rose began school at Public School 132 on the corner of Manhattan and Metropolitan Avenues, where she was enrolled in the "open-air" classes for the cardiac students, due to the effects of her rheumatic heart condition. At a certain point in the day, the students laid down near an open window and took naps. She was transported to school in a school bus from Varsity Transit Service.

Rose made her First Holy Communion at the Church of Our Lady of Mount Carmel, where she had been baptized, in May of 1936, as a solitary photograph survives of her in her white dress and veil, wearing glasses, and standing in a doorway. It was somewhere around this time that she was playing ball in the street with some neighborhood kids when the ball went over the gate, which had metal spikes on top. Rose tried to climb over the fence to get the ball when she slipped and got stabbed by one of the spikes. It ripped the inside of her thigh. The kids ran to get her father to come and pick her up off the fence. Tom ran with Rose to Greenpoint Hospital for her to get stitches. She was left with a scar on the inside of her thigh.

During the summer of 1936 when they were living on North 8th Street, Tom struggled to earn a dollar with a shoeshine box. Shoeshines cost between three and five cents a shine. During the depression, Tom came home with change after working all day. Victoria left a note for her oldest son, Pete, with a quarter to go downstairs to Marrone's grocery store. Pete brought the note with the quarter downstairs and gave it to the lady at the counter. The Marrones owned both the grocery store and the building they were living in. After reading the note, she gave the six-year-old Pete a bag of flour, a bag of cornmeal, some lard, and a small loaf of bread. And she returned it to him with change. Bread was seven cents a loaf and flour was a nickel. Potatoes were loose and he would get a few to make a pound. When Tom came home that night from a day on the street shining shoes, he took the flour and made cavatelli. They would shape the cavatelli with their fingers. With the cornmeal he made corn muffins. Sometimes he would take the dough and make doughnuts for everyone. Simmering in the Italian tomato sauce would be floating hard-boiled eggs, a Sicilian tradition. "That's how we ate," Pete said.

In return for a rent-free apartment, Victoria was the janitress in all the places that the Porti family lived. When they lived on Humboldt Street and Richardson Street, Rose cleaned all the hallways for her mother.

"Once in a while, my father [Tom] got slap-happy," Pete said in 2008. "He would slap my mother [Victoria] around a bit. She would do things sometimes she shouldn't do. He would give her money and say 'go easy on spending it' and she would buy ice cream and candy. She had a sweet tooth, but he would get mad. It was during the Depression."

**Tom Porti with his first four children in 1936
(clockwise) Rose, Tommy, Theresa, and Pete**

Victoria had her fifth child, named Leonard after her late father, on May 7, 1937, at Greenpoint Hospital. They were living at 21 Maspeth Avenue at the time. A year later, the Portis moved to 428

Humboldt Street from Maujer Street, on Pete's eighth birthday, October 22, 1938. Almost immediately, Rose became friends with the girl next door, Frances Milazzo. Frances was Rose's senior by two years, but the two girls quickly became inseparable. Frances's younger sisters, Annette and Gloria, also quickly befriended the Porti family, along with their parents, John and Mary. It was while they were living there that Augie was born on April 14, 1944.

During the summer on Humboldt Street, everyone came downstairs with their chairs to sit and talk at night. The whole block would talk into the night. Pitchers of beer would go around from the bar. They would talk until it was time for bed. The doors and windows would be left open to let the stifling heat escape. Tom would sit with Domenico A. Abramo in front of his funeral parlor at 405 Humboldt Street and tell the undertaker the old stories from Sicily for hours. Mr. Abramo was one of the sponsors for Saint Francis de Paola RC Church and he helped Tom get work building the grotto to Our Lady of Lourdes and Saint Bernadette Soubirous directly across from the church at the intersection of Conselyea Street and Old Woodpoint Road. The property had been donated by the owner, Vito Abate, to Saint Francis de Paola Church, along with his labor to build the grotto, which still stands over eighty years later.

It was at that church where Rose would receive her confirmation on May 20, 1939. According to Rose's sister, Theresa, Rose's confirmation sponsor had been Angelina Scalabia, the local florist. A month later, Rose finished Public School 132 and would attend PS 49, William J. Gaynor Junior High School in the fall. Although they attended the same school at the same time, Rose and Pat never met during their years going to school there. The main reason for this would have been because Rose was in the Cardiac Class and was transported back and forth to school by school bus. Because Rose's class was in the back of the building, her brother Pete never saw his sister at school, in spite of attending at the same time also. He remembered that Rose loved to write poems about nature and was always singing. Her outstanding voice drew the admiration of all the people in the tenement house where they lived. On a Saturday afternoon on Humboldt Street, the neighbors would ask her to sing louder as she mopped the hallways for her mother. In her free time, Rose adored going to the movies. Linda Darnell and Ann Southern were her favorite actresses. She thought that she bore a resemblance to Darnell. The leading men she found most romantic were Clark Gable and Tyrone Power. Her all-time favorite film was the Civil War saga, *Gone with the Wind*.

Rose graduated from the 8B Cardiac Class of Public School 49 on Monday, January 26, 1942. "When she graduated from Junior High School," Pete said, "Rose wrote in her autograph book, 'HaHaHa It makes me laugh to sign my own autograph.'" She went on to attend High School 196, Buschwick High School Annex.

Rose and her sister, Theresa, in 1942

Also, in 1942, Tom got a job in Union, New Jersey, making gray paint with the International Paint Company, which supplied paint for the US Naval ships. Tom stayed in New Jersey on the job site while Victoria stayed with the five children. One weekend, twelve-year-old Pete and nine-year-old Tommy took a train by themselves from Brooklyn to New Jersey to stay with their father. The two boys would go eat at the diner across from the boarding house. One weekend during the summer of 1942, Victoria brought all five children with her to Union, New Jersey to visit Tom and they went to see Alexander Korda's Technicolor spectacular of *The Jungle Book* starring Sabu as Mogli. "The whole family took the whole row up," Pete remembered nearly sixty-five years later. One night, two men carried Tom up the stairs of their Humboldt Street apartment. A 55-gallon-drum of paint had fallen and crushed his toe. He was unable to walk for a while and was let go from the job. Then Victoria suffered a nervous breakdown on Humboldt Street in 1943. She went to a rest home in Tuckahoe, New York to recuperate. One day Tom told the children that he had to go get their mother, so Rose took care of the children while he was gone.

"During the war, there were rationing books," Pete said. "We used to go to the bakery Clemente's. I used to take one of the stamps and go to the bakery and buy a seven-cent loaf of bread and get back eighteen cents. I would go and bring the bread upstairs and go to the movies with the eighteen cents. Movies were only twelve cents. We never starved. Once we had a small Christmas tree. One Christmas on Humboldt Street we each got a chocolate bar. We never got anything for Christmas. We were the poor kids on the block. We never expected anything and we never got anything because we knew it wasn't there. Other kids, their fathers had money."

The early part of 1944 had been a time of birth and death in the Porti family. Rose's grandmother, Rosina Nania Porti, died at 6:55 p.m. on February 20, 1944, in the 29 Skillman Avenue apartment where she had lived and rarely left for the past fifteen years. The diminutive grandmother, who stood only 5'3" and whose greying hair was carefully pulled back into a bun, was sixty-three years old and blind for years from the ravages of diabetes. Grandma Rosina had made some kind of vow that if she regained her sight, she would go out again. Although she was named for her paternal grandmother, Rose never spoke with her because they didn't speak the same language. Tom and Victoria never spoke Italian in front of their children, so none of the Porti grandchildren were able to communicate with their Porti grandmother, whereas their Raia cousins spoke

Italian and were able to communicate with her. She was laid out in her casket in the bedroom of the apartment. While Rose was sorry that her grandmother had died, she did not feel the deep grief felt by her cousin, Rose Raia, who had spent every day after school listening to her grandmother telling animated stories of the old country. Grandma Rosina was buried in Saint John's Cemetery on February 23, 1944. She could not be buried with her husband, who had been buried in an unmarked pauper's grave in Calvary Cemetery back in 1922, which had cost a total of ten dollars at the time. Two months after the death of Grandma Rosina, Victoria gave birth to her sixth child, Augustine, on April 14, 1944, at Greenpoint Hospital.

Once the 1943-1944 school year ended, so did Rose's formal education. While she aspired to become a nurse, the financial need of the family determined that it was necessary for Rose to leave school at the age of sixteen and go out to work full-time. Rose grew up learning to accept things as they were and make the best of them. She just felt lucky when things worked out in her favor, but never took that for granted. She was rarely bitter and even more rarely rebelled. She finished her formal education on the last Friday in June of 1944 and was out looking for work right away. Rose, like many Brooklyn girls who came from poor families, had to turn all her salary over to her mother. "There was a time my father wasn't working and my sister's money got us through," Pete said. "I was selling ice, newspapers, pretzels, and shining shoes." First, Rose had gotten a job as a cleaning lady and pretty soon after at Fruit of the Loom making underwear for the military on Metropolitan Avenue. One day, Pete was walking by the plant while Rose was having her lunch by the window and she called out to him and waved as he passed by.

But it wasn't only a life of work and drudgery. Rose was constantly taking the train out to Coney Island with her girlfriends for a day at the beach. Then, on weekends, the boys used to call on her to play ball in the street. On one afternoon, Rose hit the ball and sailed to first base when a neighborhood fella, Mike Ziccardi, caught the ball and said she was out. Rose insisted that she was safe, made a fist, and punched Ziccardi in the stomach. He landed into the garbage barrels! For the rest of his life, his lesson learned was to never make Rose mad!

PASQUALE

By Saint Patrick's Day in 1945, Rose was working at the Clarostat Manufacturing Co. at 296 North 6th Street. Inside the five story factory building, Clarostat workers dealt in radio parts manufacturing in Williamsburg from 1921 until 1950, but during World War II was involved in the war effort supplying equipment for war planes. According to the *Brooklyn Daily News Eagle*, Clarostat developed and perfected bombsights, as well as development of radar, rockets, and the atomic bomb. They were praised for helping U.S. pilots in the raids on Japanese installations in Guadacanal, receiving a telegram from Major General Echols, USA. He stated that "Army Air Force pilots, flying Airacobras you scored 38 out of 40 bomb hits in one raid. ... Army Air Forces are proud of every one of you whose skill and workmanship had a part in putting those planes into action." Clarostat also was awarded an Army-Navy E for increased production during the war.

In 1945, the Portis had to leave behind 428 Humboldt Street because someone had bought the building. With seven years and so many memories and friends made in their time there, they packed up their apartment to move to 207 Richardson Street, on the cusp of where Greenpoint ends and Williamsburg begins.

Rose in front of 207 Richardson Street with
her brother, Augie, in the carriage.

"In all the places we lived, Rose used to clean the halls on Humboldt Street and Richardson Street," Pete said. "My mother was the janitress. She took care of the building and didn't pay rent. I never knew my mother was pregnant with any of the kids. She was always a heavy woman and wore loose dresses." Although they usually got along, one day when Rose was mopping the floor around 1944 or 1945, she told Pete to do something and he became angry and picked up a knife and yelled at her to leave him alone. She got scared and her Uncle Sonny Giarratana, who was AWOL at the time, banged Pete in the ear for threatening his sister. "She got scared, the poor thing," Pete remembered. "I never would have hurt her. Uncle Sonny came and banged me in the ear! It still hurts," he joked in 2008.

It was November of 1945. The war was finally over and Rose was gazing out into the backyard, crisscrossed with the white clotheslines that had become frayed and weather-beaten to a gray color, the clothes flapping stiffly in the wind. Below was a small house in the backyard. She felt so incredibly tired. This time of year, it was impossible for her to ever really get warm, so she blamed the stretch into days and weeks without the nourishing sunshine and the long hours at the factory. There was an ache in her chest and behind her eyes and in her head. She felt a burning sensation throughout her body. But how could she afford to rest? Her parents and all those kids were counting on that sealed white envelope every Friday evening. Her cheeks flushed and she sat down at the kitchen table. The pain in her chest was suffocating her. She knew that she was sick. Then she began to be filled with dread. Had the rheumatic fever returned? Was it her heart that was ravaged by that childhood illness? She leaned over the table and cried with pain, spitting up little flecks of blood into the dishtowel. As soon as her parents came into the kitchen and found Rose in this state, they immediately sent for the doctor. By this time, Rose was back in the bed that she shared with her sister, Theresa. The doctor informed the anxious parents that she had contracted pleurisy and would have to go to Bellevue Hospital right away for X-rays and rest. She could not recover in the cold flat and surrounded by all the children.

PASQUALE

Following a stay in Bellevue Hospital, Rose was sent to convalesce at the Schermerhorn House in Milford, Connecticut. In the breathtaking home with a sweeping, columned porch, Rose rested and relaxed, made friends, and was relieved of the responsibility of taking care of the children and supporting the family. Pete helped to contribute and Victoria helped out in the Greenpoint Hospital kitchen to contribute. A photo dated January 1946, shows Rose with a group standing in front of the home.

By March of 1946, Rose was back home in Brooklyn, as photos taken with her new friend, Dorothy Columbia, show. Dorothy, known as Dottie, was born on May 26, 1928, in Brooklyn to Frank Columbia, a florist, and his wife, Loretta. They lived on Scholes Street. From 1946 on, Dot appears to have spent a great deal of time with Rose, as a handful of snapshots show them in Manhattan and Brooklyn through 1946. Dot was also wearing her Easter bonnet along with Rose and her family on Easter Sunday, April 21, 1946.

Rose stands with her father, Tom,
on Easter Sunday 1946 with her siblings (l.-r.)
Theresa, Lenny, Tommy, and their friend, Mary DeCurtis

It was also in 1946 that the song Rose loved most was released: Nat King Cole's *Christmas Song*. She adored his smooth tunes that evoked the image of chestnuts roasting on an open fire. She also loved Perry Como's *Prisoner of Love*, the latest rendition of Irving Berlin's *Always*, the song *Mama* in both English and Italian, which she sang to her mother, Victoria, as well as the song *Because*. At some point, she had made a recording in a booth on vinyl of her singing, although the record was broken and the song she sang forgotten.

Also in 1946, Rose's Uncle Sonny first introduced her to his friend, Lenny, home from the war and working in his parents' luncheonette on Graham Avenue, next to the theater. Watching his white-aproned hips as he shot soda water into a glass and generously stirred in thick spoonfuls of chocolate syrup, she was smitten when he turned around with his grin, his tousled wavy brown hair, bespectacled with round glasses. In spite of the fact that he was seven years her senior, Rose thought she saw in him the ending of her movie, her happily ever after. Lenny proposed to her in Cooper Park in October of 1946. Already a divorcee, the eighteen-year-old Rose may have not been prepared for a wedding in City Hall like her parents, versus the altar of Saint Francis de Paola.

The year 1946 drew to a close with the birth of the seventh and last Porti child. Victoria had Stepheno "Stevie" on December 1, 1946. She was thirty-eight and Tom was forty-six. There were eighteen years between their oldest and youngest. Tom and Victoria were just five months shy of their twentieth wedding anniversary.

By 1947, Rose was working in Manhattan as a clerk for the Eagle Pencil Company. Founded in New York in 1856 by Bavarian immigrant Daniel Berolzheimer, with a shop in Manhattan and a factory in Yonkers, the operation grew into a complex of buildings that made up the company on the south side of 14th Street east of Avenue C. A leader in the pencil industry for over a century, the company became Berol in 1969. At that time, Rose walked the length of Graham Avenue in high heels daily to take the train from the Metropolitan Avenue station into Manhattan, where she was always dressed impeccably in dresses, skirts with blazers, and hats. As in every job and classroom she ever entered, she quickly made friends. While there were a few good girlfriends that she made, her best friend quickly became the stenographer Katherine "Kay" Bagnuik, the American born daughter of Russian immigrants, who was from the Lower East Side. Born in New York City on January 10, 1928, the same year as Rose, Kay had an older sister, Sofie, also born in New York, and several brothers who had died of childhood illnesses back in Russia. Kay was keeping company with Andy Okpych until she met his brother, Walter, a pitcher for the New York Giants. Walter played under the name Walter Ockey and had the nickname of "Footie" and made his major league debut on May 3, 1944, in a home game against the Philadelphia Blue Jays at the Polo Grounds. He appeared in a second game on May 20th of the same year against the Saint Louis Cardinals at Sportsman's Park in Saint Louis, Missouri. He played for the farm team from 1944-1945. Walter's baseball career ended due to throwing his arm out, so he took the tests for the NYC Department of Sanitation and the New York Police Department. Kay didn't live too far from Eagle Pencil on 2nd Street between Avenues A and B. Her fiancé, Walter, lived on 11th Street. By the time that Rose met the couple in 1947, Walter was working for the Department of Sanitation.

During the summer of 1947, Rose stayed at the apartment of her Aunt Angelina Raia and her husband, Uncle Jack, to keep her cousin, Rose, company, while her aunt and uncle spent the summer at their bungalow in Selden, Long Island. Rose Raia was working in the city at the time and did not want to spend all that time commuting back and forth from the city to the island, so Rose stayed with her cousin. While Rose Raia was just a year and a half older than Rose, and the two first cousins having grown up in the same neighborhood, they rarely saw one another as children. While Rose Raia was constantly in the Skillman Avenue apartment of their Porti grandmother, Rose rarely if ever visited there. She was much more apt to visit her English-speaking grandmother, Maria Giarratana. Also, there was no love lost between Aunt Angelina and her mother, Victoria, whose shoulders Aunt Angelina placed all the blame for the problems in her brother's family. So, while the four Raia children were the Portis' only contemporary first cousins, only Rose and Pete seemed to really know them at all. Over that summer, Rose grew a very deep emotional attachment with her Cousin Rose and Aunt Angelina, who before then she only casually knew.

On weekends, Rose began joining her cousin Rose on train rides out to the Raia bungalow at 231 Dare Road in Selden, Long Island, and the solid bond they formed made Rose become an honorary member of Aunt Angelina's immediate family. The bungalow was built by Uncle Jack Raia, who was a carpenter. Far from the concrete jungle of the city, Rose enjoyed bicycle rides and days filled with laughter. Aunt Angelina taught Rose to cook in the Sicilian fashion, according to Pete. She became a second mother to Rose. The Raias always remember Rose for how happy-go-lucky she was and for always laughing.

When she wasn't at the Raias', Rose was on Coney Island, her favorite place to go besides Selden, and Rye Beach. Also, she helped he father purchase a plot of land in Smithtown, Long Island. There wasn't a house on the property, just an empty lot. The family took trips out there a few times and went camping. And then, of course, she had her on-again and off-again relationship with her fiancé, Lenny. And that was the state of Rose's life when Pat entered the scene on that evening in 1948.

Rose in Manhattan in 1946

CHAPTER SEVEN

A Coney Island Courtship

FALL 1948-FALL 1949

A few weeks had gone by since the night that Pat and Rose had sat in the Hudson on Morgan Avenue, just outside Cooper Park, when she pleaded with him to be patient with her. Since that night, they had practically seen each other every single night. Feeling relief that his patience had finally paid off, Pat was driving Rose home on a Thursday night when she said to him, "Pat, don't pick me up tomorrow night. One of the girls in the place is pregnant and they're giving her a baby shower, so I don't know what time I'll be home."

"Alright, Rose. Fine."

"So, maybe if you want to stop by like maybe eight or eight thirty to see if I'm home yet or not?"

"O.K."

After Pat had walked Rose up the stoop and into the hallway, he watched her climb to the second landing in the poorly lit hallway until her key opened the door that led into the kitchen as he always did. Then he went back into the Hudson and headed for Herbert Street.

As Rose walked into her room in the darkened apartment, she wondered if she had made the right decision. She struggled with it and her conscience was aching. She had lied to Pat and it was torturing her, but there was no way that she could tell him the truth just now. She knew what she had to do tomorrow night had to be done once and for all. She confided her plan in only one person. Her mother.

As Rose got off the subway at Metropolitan Avenue on Friday night, she did not head home but straight for Graham Avenue. She was going to the luncheonette to see Lenny. Twisting her engagement ring round and round her finger, Rose didn't know what exactly she would say to Lenny, as the marquis of the Graham Theater came into view. She was shocked at the shaking of her hands. She was never intimidated by anything in her whole life! It all had led up to this moment. She'd been so proud when he put this ring on her finger in Cooper Park in October 1946. She had dreams of their happy life together. The problem was, nothing had progressed since that day. Nothing between them had turned out the way that she had planned. His life was consumed with the luncheonette and she would be marrying not only him, but chaining herself to a life confined in its narrow walls and making malteds for couples in love who were experiencing everything in life that she felt that she was missing. She had tried to deny her feelings for Pat for the whole summer. She loved Lenny. There was no denying it. She loved his smile and his wavy brown hair. She had loved when they were alone, and at first, the sight of him with the white apron tied around his narrow waist made her heart leap in her chest. But first, there would be no church wedding. His divorce from his first wife had taken that away from her. How Rose longed to walk down the aisle of Saint Francis de Paola on her father's arm. And then, what life would she live in the luncheonette? She had pitied Lenny, who had told her how his real father disappeared when he was very small and his mother had just died from cancer. She had stood by him and weathered these storms together with him. But, she knew there was someone else for him, and truth be told, there was now someone else for her as well. Their love affair had run its course and it was time for Rose to return him his ring. Taking a deep breath, Rose lifted her head high, and walked through the door as she saw Lenny standing at the counter.

In the meantime, Pat pulled in front of 207 Richardson Street at eight o'clock, where Tom and Victoria Porti were sitting on the stoop. Victoria called out to him, "Rose isn't home yet, Pat!"

"Thank you, Mrs. Porti," Pat replied. "I'll try again in a little while."

Pat drove around for over a half hour, waiting for Rose's return. He hoped to see her before the night was over. He wondered how late a baby shower could go that started right after work in the office. Just before nine o'clock, Pat pulled in front of Rose's house again, and once again, Victoria told Pat that Rose still was not home.

"It's almost nine o'clock, Mrs. Porti," Pat said. "Tell Rose I'm not gonna come back no more tonight."

"I'll tell her when she gets home, Pat," Victoria called back.

Pat drove home and put the Hudson in the garage behind the house and then turned on the television set in the living room before bed. He had a half day of work ahead of him in the morning.

After getting out of work on Saturday afternoon, Pat came home and washed up before he drove over to Richardson Street to take Rose out for the day. As always, Tom and Victoria were sitting on the stoop and Rose was in the upstairs hallways washing the floor. While Victoria was the building janitress, which was the reason the family lived in the apartment rent free, it was Rose who did all of the cleaning by this point in both the building and the apartment during the early part of a Saturday.

"When Rose would clean the house on a Saturday, the windows would be open and she would sing," Pat said, "and the neighbors used to yell out, 'sing louder so we can hear you.' She sang like a canary." The only difference this time was when Pat got to the top of the stairs, Rose was on her hands and knees scrubbing the floor and she was not singing. "There was something fishy," Pat said. Rose was not her usually ebullient self and she seemed very high strung. She simply told him to come back and pick her up after four when she was done. Unlike the usual routine where he kept her company as she worked, he knew she wanted to be alone.

Pat returned at four and Rose still looked agitated as she slid into the Hudson. When Rose said to him, "Don't go too far. Go by the park. I want to talk to you," he felt a sinking sensation because this conversation sounded all too familiar. Pulling over by Cooper Park on Morgan Avenue, he felt defeated as he prepared for the news that she was going back to the store and into Lenny's arms.

Taking a deep breath, Rose began, "I don't want to start off our relationship lying to one another. I don't want to lie to you and I don't want you to lie to me." She looked deeply into Pat's eyes. Her could see that she was wracked with pain.

"What is it?"

"I went to the store last night. It wasn't a baby shower."

"What?" Pat couldn't contain his fury. "Why?"

"Will you shut up and listen to me!" Rose's fury matched his own. "I still had his engagement ring and I had to return it to him and he wouldn't let me outta the store. I returned it and he and I are finished. Now it is you and me."

"Why didn't you give it to me? I would have brought it back to him."

"Because I didn't want to see a murder on Graham Avenue! It was my place to bring the ring back to him. So, I did it this way. I don't want to start our relationship off with a lie, but if I had told you from the beginning what I was going to do, I know we would have had an argument. Now, it's done. I'm finished with him. Like I said, now it is you and me."

"What did he say?"

Rose paused for a moment. "Be careful, Pat. Lenny said he's gonna turn you over if he sees you on the street."

"Ah, he couldn't catch me with that piece of garbage he's got for a car! It's put together with rubber bands. I wouldn't worry about him."

Rose shook her head as the two men in her life made plans to show the other who she belonged to as her and Pat drove off into the night.

"After that, Rose was happier," Pat said. "It took a while. She loved the guy and it takes time. You don't get over things right away. In the end, I hadn't wasted my time. We were very happy."

A few months later, Pat and Rose were driving down Kingsland Avenue past Cooper Park, when lo and behold, pulled over with a flat tire and his car jacked up was Rose's ex-fiance, Lenny. On the sidewalk stood his new girlfriend, Lucy. Pat pulled up beside him and asked, "Do you need a hand?"

"No thanks, Pat," he replied. "I got it." And Pat and Rose drove away. Rose's eyes widened as she looked at Pat. "Are you crazy?" she asked him.

"Why?"

"You pull up next to him? He had a wrench in his hand!"

Pat shrugged, "Yeah, what's the big deal? Why would he care? Look, he's got a new girlfriend now!" Pat smiled as Rose shook her head and he drove on.

Once her engagement with Lenny was officially ended, Rose began introducing Pat to members of her family and her friends. They took the train to Delancey Street in Manhattan to meet Rose's grandmother, Maria Giarratana. They headed over to Metropolitan Avenue to meet Rose's favorite aunt, Angelina Raia, Uncle Jack, and Rose's cousins, Rose, Benny, and Little Patricia. One night, Pat and one of his friends took Rose and her Cousin Rose to the drive-in movie on Sunrise Highway in Valley Stream. In 2008, Rose Raia Suglia, reminisced with Pat about that night and how Pat, who was sitting in the front passenger seat next to his friend, put his hand over to the back seat to hold hands with Rose Porti, who was sitting next to Rose Raia. "I knew how much you liked my cousin, Rose, that night," she said to him as she laughed.

In addition to meeting Rose's grandmother, her favorite aunt, and her favorite cousin, Rose began taking Pat around to meet her friends. Dot Columbia and her boyfriend went out on double dates with Rose and Pat. And all of the time that Rose had been close with Kay Bagniuk at Eagle Pencil, Kay was always disappointed because she wanted to double date with Rose, but Rose's fiancé had never been available. When Rose confided in Kay that she had broken her engagement and was seeing someone new, Kay was ready to make plans to meet Rose's new boyfriend. Rose and Pat took the subway from Metropolitan Avenue into the city, where they met Kay and her fiancé, Walter Okpych, somewhere around Delancey Street. The two couples hit it off famously from the start. When Rose got to work on Monday morning, Kay told her under no uncertain terms, "Rose, don't let this guy go!"

"Kay was instrumental in convincing Rose to be with me," Pat said. "They were very nice. Kay was a blonde, a very beautiful girl. She could have been a model. And Walter was a handsome man. We had a lot of fun together."

Another couple that Rose took Pat out with to double date was her old chum she played baseball with, Mike Ziccardi. Mike played baseball in the street with Rose all the time, and in spite of their close friendship, he took Pat on the side to give him a warning.

"When I met Mike, he told me that I better never get Rose mad," Pat said, "because she'd punch your lights out. She used to go play ball in the street with the guys. The boys used to call her to play ball and this one fella who lived in the neighborhood, Mike Ziccardi, said 'So don't ever get her mad,' he said to me."

It was a Coney Island courtship for Pat and Rose, as so many nights he picked her up after work and they headed in the Hudson to the Belt Parkway for the boardwalk on Coney Island. "Rose used to love riding in the car, so I used to take her for a nice, long ride," Pat said. "We'd walk the boardwalk and buy a frankfurter, ice cream or something." Walking along the boardwalk and eating their Nathan's hot dog laden with mustard and sauerkraut, Pat and Rose would laugh as they ate and headed over to the rides. "At Coney Island we went on the bumper cars," Pat said. "I used to run into her with my car and we would bang into one another. She used to laugh a lot. Then we would go on the merry-go-round and the Ferris wheel, but we didn't go on the cyclone. We went on the boat ride and the cars on the track too. We used to go to Coney Island all the time, go on a couple of rides, buy a couple of frankfurters or something because she probably didn't eat much."

When Pat got off of work at 2 p.m. on a Saturday, he would go home, get cleaned up, and head over to the Portis' house. Rose's parents would be sitting on their folding chairs on the front stoop taking in the sun. He would greet them and climb the stairs to their second-floor apartment. There Rose would be on her hands and knees, scrubbing the worn linoleum floor.

"One time, Rose told her sister, Theresa, who was about fourteen at the time to take all of the shoes and put them on the top of the bed so she could mop," Pat said.

"I'm going roller skating," Theresa told Rose.

"I gotta mop in here! Pick up the shoes!"

Pat was standing in the doorway and said to Theresa, "You ain't goin nowhere. You either do what your sister told you or you ain't goin nowhere!"

Theresa burst into tears.

"Cry all you want," Pat said, "but if you wanna go roller skating, that's the faster you're gonna get outta here, so pick up the shoes."

Theresa quickly picked up the shoes and put them on the bed without a word, then darted from the room with her skates, the kitchen door slamming behind her. Rose just looked at Pat in amazement. She was so used to having to be sister and mother to the kids without any help from her parents and no one had ever stood up for her before. She was speechless.

"Theresa was only a kid, but I had to say something because no one was helping Rose," Pat said. "The carpet in their house upstairs was worn down to the wood in spots and Rose would be there mopping the floor." After Rose would finish her Saturday ritual of cleaning the entire apartment, Pat used to take her down to Sunnyside over on Johnson Avenue and Queens Boulevard to White Castle. They would eat in the Hudson, as the waitresses used to come to the car window on roller skates and hang the trays on the window. After they would eat, they would go over to Coney Island.

As months past, Pat became a permanent fixture on Richardson Street and a part of the lives of Rose's parents and her five brothers and sister. "Tommy was closest to Rose," Pat said, "but she took care of her brothers, like Stevie. Stevie wasn't even two years old in a carriage drinking coffee in a baby bottle when I met him."

One night in particular, Pat had picked Rose up at the Metropolitan Avenue station in the Hudson when she was paralyzed with shock as they neared her house and found an ambulance out front. "Rose didn't even give me a chance to stop the car," Pat said. "She jumped out of the car because the ambulance was there. She ran over to the ambulance, then I parked the car and got out and went over to the ambulance."

"We're going to the hospital," Rose said. "We're going to Greenpoint Hospital. Little Stevie drank CN! I'm going in the ambulance with him."

"All right," Pat said. "I'll follow the ambulance with the car."

Rose sat in the back of the ambulance, cradling her baby brother, not much more than a year and a half. Rose's father, Tom, had put CN, a liquid disinfectant, in a Coke bottle after the CN bottle broke while looking for another container to put it in and Stevie had drank it.

"Rose stayed there with Stevie," Pat said. "She stayed with her brother. She didn't want to leave him alone. We didn't go out that night because she wanted to stay with Stevie." Stevie was treated and released that night, but Rose was given instructions that she was to give Stevie plenty of milk for the damage the toxic chemical had done to his delicate infant stomach. Pat drove them home from Greenpoint Hospital, and once they were inside the apartment, he walked to the little store on the corner of Richardson and Graham, Tota's, to buy two quarts of milk for Stevie and brought them back to the Porti apartment. Rose nursed her baby brother back to health.

As 1948 began to draw to a close, Rose's brother Pete left for the service in November and joined the US Army. He was the first of the children to leave home. It would be a year before they would see him again. As the holidays drew near, advertisements for the Radio City Christmas Spectacular were on billboards all around Manhattan on Rose's way to work. With a sigh, Rose told Pat how she longed to see the Rockettes. "She always talked about the Rockettes because she was dying to see them," Pat said. Knowing that she had not ever been through the doors of the magnificent Art Deco theater, which first opened its doors in 1932, whereas Pat had been to the show many times, he decided that he was going to do something about granting Rose's wish.

Just in time for Pat and Rose's first Christmas together in 1948, a blizzard had swept through New York City and Pat had an idea that the time was right as he watched the Department of Sanitation work diligently to dislodge the streets from the crippling snow. The day that followed was going to be pretty warm and bright when he asked Rose, "Can you take off tomorrow from work?"

"Why?" Rose looked at him with a quizzical look on her face.

"I have a surprise for you."

"What's the surprise? What's the surprise?" She was as excited as a kid on Christmas Eve.

"If I tell you, it's not a surprise no more. If you can take off, I'll pick you up about ten o'clock and we are gonna go into Manhattan. So, if you take off, I'll tell my brother I'm not coming in tomorrow."

"Yeah, I'll call in sick. Where we goin? What are we gonna do?" Her eyes were bright with the excitement of anticipation.

"You'll see when we get there."

The next morning, Pat met Rose on Richardson Street and they navigated the tunnels of snow along the sidewalks and headed for the Metropolitan Avenue Station on Graham Avenue and headed for the city. They got off at Rockefeller Plaza, where the Christmas tree had snow in its branches overlooking the ice-skating rink full of skaters sailing along the ice. The mounds of snow along the sidewalk were so high that it was impossible to see what was happening on the other side of the street. Then, out from behind the mounds of snow, Rose saw the flashing red neon sign on the side of the building, Radio City Music Hall. They got to the end of the line on West 51st Street and 6th Avenue, waiting for the box office to open for the eleven o'clock performance of the Christmas Show. Rose marveled at the opulence of the Art Deco style, plush crimson velvet curtains, and the enormous crystal chandeliers, as they climbed the staircase to make way to their seats.

The curtain was made to look like a gigantic Christmas present, and when it opened, the stage revealed the renowned Rockettes, now in their seventeenth year of the show. Wearing black top hats topped with a white plume, a striped sash, and matching bowties, the thirty-six young ladies sporting the world class legs filled the stage. Wearing strapless, short skirted white dresses with a dice pattern and full-length gloves, the Rockettes kicked their legs to new heights, as the clatter of their black, high-heeled tap shoes made a music all their own. Rose was filled with glee mixed with astonishment and awe as the girls put on a show unlike anything she had ever seen in her whole life.

After the Christ child had been born on stage and the last of the camels had departed, Rose was nearly breathless with excitement over the spectacle she had just witnessed. "It's the most magnificent thing I've been to in all my life," Rose gushed as they left the theater and walked through the tunneled sidewalks of New York City. "She really enjoyed it so much," Pat said. "Rose never stopped talking about the Rockettes."

The church bells from the bell tower of Saint Cecilia's reverberated through the neighborhood to ring in the new year of 1949. While Rose lived around the corner from Saint Cecilia's, she never went to church on Sunday. She admired that Pat went to mass every Sunday morning at Saint Francis de Paola, even though she didn't.

"I want to start going to church with you," Rose said to Pat.

"But you live around the corner from Saint Cecilia's!"

"I don't go to church because I don't like to go alone."

"That's no excuse," Pat teased her. Regardless, he began leaving for mass earlier on Sundays to go meet her on Richardson Street and walk together to Saint Francis on Conselyea.

It was a week into the new year on Saturday night, January 8, 1949, when Pat asked Rose to marry him. "I asked Rose to marry me while we were driving in the car," Pat said. "I was always with her in the car. She loved the car. We used to ride all over the place." Pat had told his sister, Margie, that he wanted to get an engagement ring for Rose, so Margie spoke with their neighbor, Johnny Dalto, Marion Bonomo's husband. Johnny was friends with the owners of a jewelry store, DiNatale Brothers, in Downtown Brooklyn. "I let Rose pick out her engagement ring and her wedding ring."

The following day, Rose and Pat went to McCarren Park to take pictures. A little more than half a dozen shots show her in a black short sleeve dress with a corsage pinned to her left side, a black fur hat, and black open toe pumps. With her double dimpled smile, she proudly showed off her diamond ring to the camera, as well as her gams, sitting on a park bench. "We got engaged," Pat said, "we went to the park and took some pictures, we went out to eat, and we went to the movies."

PASQUALE

Rose on the day after her engagement to Pat, January 9, 1949

Both the Porti and Franzese families were thrilled to hear of Pat and Rose's engagement. When Rose returned to work on Monday morning, she gushed as she told her girlfriends that Pat had proposed and showed them the new ring on her finger. Unlike during her last engagement, she was already talking about planning for her wedding. Pat's Uncle Patsy Franzese and Rose's Aunt Angelina Raia were especially overjoyed over the engagement, as Angelina was fond of Pat and Patsy was fond of Rose right from the start.

Pat and Rose were not fazed by the long, bitter winter because they were in love and had a happiness that each of them had never had before. On the weekends they would head to the movie theaters in Greenpoint, sometimes both days. Other times on a Saturday night they headed to the Ridgewood Grove to see the Golden Gloves Saturday night fights. Wherever Pat wanted to go, Rose went eagerly as a child, as there was so much she had not done in her twenty years that Pat had taken for granted. Unlike the old days, he did not see Johnny Morena and Bobby Gentile like he had before. He always wanted to be with Rose.

When the warm weather returned, Pat and Rose would start driving out to Sunrise Highway to the drive-in movie theater on a Saturday night. "One night," Pat said, "we went to White Castle before we went to the drive-in movie over in Valley Stream. I used to go down by the 59th Street Bridge in Queens. Saint John's Long Island City Hospital was over there. That same street on the corner was a White Castle and at that time they used to bring the tray over to your car. You put your window half up. We used to go there a lot, Rose and I. They brought over the tray with the hamburgers and the ketchup. Rose wanted ketchup on her hamburger and they gave her the bottle and none would come out. I said, 'Give me the God-damn thing!' I hit the bottom and hit the bottom and splat…ketchup all over the windshield, all over Rose and all over me. I messed up her whole dress! Holy Shit! I went in the trunk and got some rags. She got napkins. We wiped everything down and cleaned it all up. Good thing we were going to the drive in and didn't have to get out of the car!"

On Sundays in the summer, Pat enjoyed driving out to Freeport, Long Island to the auto races. He began bringing Rose with him and one afternoon he sat marveling at the sleek cars and the incredible speed they traveled and confessed to her that he really wanted to become a race car driver. Rose's brown eyes that were always glistening with passion and mirth became stormy as she pulled off her engagement ring and handed it back to him.

"What's the matter with you?" Pat yelled at Rose in shock.

"Do you think I'm gonna sit in the bleachers and watch you get smashed against the wall?"

"C'mon, where did you ever see that? You see that in the movies maybe, but that never happens."

"You're not going to be a race car driver if you wanna marry me."

"Alright, here, put your ring back on! Forget I ever said it."

Other rides on a weekend took them to parts of Long Island even further out than Freeport. One weekend, Rose's father, Tom, decided that he wanted the whole family to go out to the plot of land that he owned in Smithtown and spend the weekend in tents.

"I didn't get a car all the time on a Sunday," Pat said, "so Rose's father went out and bought an old, beat-up truck. It didn't even have a front seat. He made a front seat out of boards. We piled all the kids in the back of the truck because, although it had a top, the sides only had wire screening. He used to get in the back with the kids because of the wire screening on the sides and he made a bench on both sides for them to sit. He asked me to drive. It was monotonous, but her father wanted to go out there. We slept in pup tents. Your feet stuck out the other end. I did that the one time. I was in the tent with Rose. We weren't married, but we both were in the tent. I don't remember how many of the kids were there at the time. The next morning, I said to Rose, 'never again! Don't ask me to sleep over! I am not going to sleep on the ground. I did that in the army. I ain't gonna do that here.' We sat around the lot and looked around. There was nothing to do.

"Another time Rose asked me to take her family to Smithtown to her father's property. Oh my God! What a disaster! We went there in the Hudson. We were nine people in the car. I think Stevie and Augie sat on two boxes where the back doors were and then there were three people sitting in the front seat and three people sitting in the back seat. So maybe we were eight people.

"On the way home, we were getting off the Grand Central near Queens Boulevard and the traffic was stop and go, stop and go. All of the sudden, the hose on my brakes broke, and when I stepped on the brake, I hit the guy in front of me and the whole front of my car got smashed. The other guy didn't get that much damage. He pushed the car in front of him and the cops were there. When the traffic moved, the cop said to me "You want me to get a tow truck?" "No," I said, and I came home on the emergency brake all the way home from Queens Boulevard and that's how I came home. I let everybody out. Nobody got hurt, thank God, and I put the car in the garage on Herbert Street.

"The next morning, I told my brother, Carmine, that I had an accident. He wasn't worried about the car. He was just worried if anybody got hurt. 'The hell with it,' he said, 'I'll take the car and I'll have it fixed,' and that's what he did. He took the car to the body shop and he fixed the car. They had to put all new chrome in the front because it was all chrome in the front. No one got hurt, so that was the end of it.

"We went out to Smithtown a couple of times. There was a sergeant that came from the 87th precinct on Humboldt Street, a Sicilian guy, and he bought the lot next to it and built a house there."

For the Fourth of July weekend of 1949, Aunt Angelina invited Rose and Pat to spend the weekend with the Raia family out at their summer home in Selden. Rose and Pat spent the holiday weekend with Aunt Angelina, Uncle Jack, and three of their four children: twenty-two-year-old Rose, twelve-year-old Benny, and five-year-old Patricia. Rose loved spending weekends at the Raia bungalow in Selden, where she and her cousin Rose would jump on bicycles and ride around the neighborhood, or take rides with Cousin Rose and her boyfriend, Vito Suglia.

"Don't go walking around during the night because I'm a light sleeper," Aunt Angelina said to Pat. "I knew what she was getting at," Pat said, "but she was such a nice lady. She always liked me. We went there a few times after that and spent the weekend with her aunt. Aunt Angelina's house was a nice house. It was a summer home, but it was a well-kept, nice house. We used to go there on weekends and on Sundays we would go to church.

"One time we went to Montauk at the end of the island with Aunt Angelina's daughter, Rose, and her boyfriend, Vito. We went in his old Model T Ford. The four of us sat on the sand out there and talked and had sandwiches. I don't remember anyone else out there. Then, coming home, Vito got sick and asked me to drive. Well, the girls didn't drive, and Vito was very particular about his car. I think he didn't want the car to go over 30 miles an hour. He sat in the back with his head on Rose Raia's shoulder and my Rose sat up front with me. Every time the needle on the speedometer went over 30, my Rose would nudge me and shake her head. I was used to driving fast. I didn't think we were ever gonna get back to Selden."

Other weekends when Pat wanted to take Rose away from the city, he took her to Upstate New York to his friend Mike Monte's motels.

"We used to go Upstate to Fort Montgomery," Pat said. "It was one or two miles past Bear Mountain Park on 9W and we used to go down to Bear Mountain. They have the Seven Lake Drive at Bear Mountain Park through the wooded area and it was beautiful down there. They had little private beaches and they were beautiful. They had rowboats at Bear Mountain Park and we would go at night on

Rose and Pat at Aunt Angelia's bungalow in Selden, New York in 1949

Rose's cousin, Rose Raia, with her boyfriend, Vito Suglia

a rowboat on the lake. One time (in June 1949), Walter and Kay had come up there with us as we went out on a boat with them. I used to do the rowing. I took Rose fishing there a few times too. We mostly went to the movies, Coney Island, and Fort Montgomery."

In the meantime, the wedding date had been set for September 18, 1949. Pat had asked his brother, Sammy, to be his best man. Rose asked her girlfriend, Dot Columbia, to be her maid of honor. Dot had lost her mother when she was a child and on February 16, 1949, her father, Frank, had died suddenly from a heart attack at the age of fifty-two. Dot and her brothers went to go live with relatives on Hayward Street in Williamsburg. Although Dot was thrilled to be Rose's maid-of-honor, she didn't have the money to buy a gown. Pat's sister, Margie, had been her sister, Millie's maid of honor four years before and said she would be happy to have the dress cleaned and loan it to Dot for the wedding.

In spite of being in the practice of going to mass for only a year now, Rose fell in love with the practice of being a weekly communicant at Saint Francis and it led her to make a final decision for the wedding ceremony.

"Rose decided that she wanted to have a high mass wedding and I had stopped going to confession," Pat said. "I said to her, 'You have to receive and I am not going to confession because I don't want to hear the priest's mouth. No, no, no.' She didn't like that answer. Then, her friend, Kay, turns around and tells her, 'Tell Pat there's a big church there on Lexington Avenue and they have monks there and they're very nice.' So, she talked me into going there."

On Kay Bagniuk's recommendation, Pat and Rose went to their prenuptial confession on a Saturday afternoon to the Church of Saint Vincent Ferrer on the corner of Lexington Avenue and East 66th Street in Manhattan, where the Dominican Friars would be in the confessionals. Dipping their fingers into the water font, they both made the sign of the cross as they genuflected before the altar and each entered one of the confessionals. Rose came out first and was on her knees in the pew saying her penance when Pat came out and knelt beside her and did his penance of five Our Fathers and five Hail Mary's.

PASQUALE

When Pat's prayers lasted longer than Rose's had, she turned to him and whispered, "Ain't you done yet? What did you do? It's taking you so long!"

"Don't ask me questions because I'm going to lie to you and I'll have to go into the confessional box again. And you're making me forget how many I said!" Rose bowed her head and rested them on her folded hands in prayer, but the jerking of her shoulders gave away that Pat's answer had her giggling. As the wedding date approached, finding an apartment was not turning out to be as easy as Pat and Rose had bargained for. Originally, Pete had bought a house meant for the newlyweds at 243 Frost Street, a few houses in from Kingsland Avenue, since the top floors of the Humboldt Street house hadn't been in use for so many years. There was also a great deal of talk that the house was going to be torn down by the city to make way for the Brooklyn-Queens Expressway. Pete thought he had solved the issue with the purchase on Frost Street, only to find out that he was unable to get the current tenants to move under the OPA. The only way that he could force the tenants to move was if he needed the rooms for his own use.

When the plans for Rose and Pat to move into the Frost Street house fell through, Lorenzina had heard that there was going to be a vacancy in her sister, Philomena Croce's house. "My mother found out about it," Pat said. "So she went to her sister, Philomena, so she said to talk to her daughter, Pips. We called my cousin, Millie, 'Pips.' I was supposed to get the apartment from Pips. She lived on the bottom floor of my Aunt Philomena's house and she was gonna move upstairs. Pips told my mother that if we wanted the apartment that we had to buy some of her furniture. My mother said to her niece, 'They're newlyweds! They don't want to buy used furniture. They want to start off new.' Pips told my mother that if we didn't buy the furniture that we couldn't have the apartment. So, my mother told her to keep the apartment."

A little while after that, Lorenzina's oldest sister, Lucy Maiello, was supposed to take a small apartment at 101 Jackson Street, but found out her estranged husband, Frank Maiello, lived on the same block. When Lorenzina found out that her sister no longer wanted the rooms, she said, "If you aren't gonna take it, I'll take it for my son."

"We took the apartment just temporarily because we had no place to go," Pat said. "It was hard to get an apartment. That was how we wound up on Jackson Street."

On August 7, 1949, Rose had her twenty-first birthday. On her birthday, Pat gave her a box from DeNatale Brothers that contained a golden cross on a chain. When Rose turned it over, he had it inscribed with her new initials. R.F. "Rose was crazy about that thing when I bought it for her," Pat said. She would wear it around her neck on her wedding day. Two weeks later, they went to Downtown Brooklyn to get their marriage license on August 23rd. Two weeks later, Pat had his twenty-second birthday on September 5th. The day that they had been waiting for was quickly approaching.

CHAPTER EIGHT

Jackson Street

SEPTEMBER 1949-SEPTEMBER 1950

Rose quit her job a week before the wedding. The girls gave her a little bridal shower during the lunch hour of the last day. She was beaming in snapshots wearing a black dress sitting at the break table. There was a white tissue paper bell with streamers coming down hanging above the table. Paper cups were filled with champagne to celebrate Rose on her marriage and to bid her farewell as she left their midst forever. The girls had chipped in and gotten her a radio and a vase of flowers. All of the girls there saw her as their best friend, but the one friend who she loved above the rest at Eagle Pencil, Kay Bagniuk, would remain her friend after she said her final farewell.

Sunday, September 18, 1949, Victoria was standing on the top step of the porch of 207 Richardson Street nervously looking up and down the block. Theresa had come out to the front porch as well and Victoria shook her head as she said, "She's gonna get a black eye! Tell her to stop playing ball and start getting ready! All she needs is getting a black eye on her wedding day! What's Pat gonna say?"

Rose was playing ball on Richardson Street on the morning of her wedding, running the bases, screaming, and laughing in the hours before she put on her gown. A few blocks away, at 101 Jackson Street, Pat had shined his shoes that morning and checked that his tuxedo looked perfect on the hanger, as he and Sammy left to go paint the ceiling of the new apartment.

As the hours went by, Pat kept looking at his watch and said to his brother, "Sam, we gotta go! It's getting late!"

"Nah, we've got time," Sammy replied.

When Pat and Sammy had returned home from painting, Pat went into his room to unwrap his tuxedo and bent down to get his freshly polished shoes out from under the bed. Much to his chagrin, they were not where he left them that morning.

"Ma! Where's my shoes?" Pat called out to his mother.

"Look on your brother's feet," she shook her head as she pointed to Carmine. Pat's shoes and suits were never safe when Carmine was home, as he felt that his taking of them was his prerogative as the oldest. When Carmine's cover was blown, he would pull out his wallet and offer money for Pat to buy new ones. Pat's wedding day was no exception. Pat shook his head with disgust as he dressed for the ceremony and he and Sammy headed for Saint Francis de Paola.

In the meantime, Dot Columbia had arrived at Rose's house in her gown that she had borrowed from Margie, the flowers had been delivered, and Fontana had arrived with his camera equipment. Rose put on her satin wedding gown with lace sleeves and bodice, covered with an illusion neckline. She sat in front of the mirror at the old, battered dressing table. The old dressing table had moved with them from place to place, bearing scars from each move and each new child running through the flat of each apartment where they had lived over the past twenty-two years. Opening her mirrored jewelry box, Rose removed the gold necklace with cross pendant that Pat had bought her for her birthday and fastened it around her neck. She sat looking at her reflection and couldn't help smiling as she applied her perfume from the crystal figurine of the little girl which sat atop her dressing table and then applied her crimson lipstick. Opening a drawer, she removed her compact with its pinwheel design and applied her face powder and smiled as Fontana, standing there in a light-colored suit and clutching his large, black camera in his left hand, looked through the lens and took his shot. Dot brought over Rose's silk tulle veil and they both smiled widely at one another as she helped Rose place it on her head.

PASQUALE

The photographer's camera too clearly showed the cheap, battered chest of drawers with the white paint worn away between the two bedroom windows, the faded paint on the walls with a framed print of the Sacred Hearts of Jesus and Mary, and the floral linoleum with black patches where its colored skin had worn through and the exposed wood had turned to black. Standing by the tall windows with their blinds drawn shut and framed by floral printed drapes, Rose pinned Victoria's corsage to her black, short-sleeved dress with fingerless gloves. Tom's smile could not have been broader as his eyes crinkled in delight as Rose pinned his boutonniere to his tuxedo jacket. Rose then stood between her parents in front of the window before Fontana's camera. Then the rest of the children joined them, except for Pete, who was serving in the army in Colorado. Rose's fifty-eight year old grandmother, Maria Giarratana, was also there for the wedding, dressed in a black dress with a floral print.

The Portis on Rose's wedding day (l.-r.) Tommy, Victoria, Rose, Lenny in front of Rose, Tom, Stevie (l.) and Augie (r.) in front of Tom, Theresa, and Rose's Grandma Maria Giarratana, September 18, 1949

Tom beamed with pride as he escorted his eldest child down the stairs and onto the front stoop with her maid of honor as a score of people stood outside on Richardson Street to get a glimpse of the bride. He sat in the back seat of the Cadillac with his daughter, while Dot sat in the seat in front of them as the car took off for Saint Francis de Paola. Victoria, with the help of Theresa, rounded up the rest of the children to head over to the church, including five-year-old Augie, and Stevie, two and a half months shy of his third birthday.

There was a crowd waiting for the bride outside of Saint Francis de Paola on the corner of Conselyea Street and Woodpoint Road when Rose's Cadillac pulled in front of the church and she exited the vehicle with Tom and Dot. Many of the women wore kerchiefs on their heads to conceal the curlers in their hair to make ready for the reception that evening. Inside, Pat, looking anxious and somber, stood with Sammy at his side on the altar.

Entering the wooden doors of Saint Francis, Rose clutched her bouquet as she smiled nervously and scanned the pews to identify who was there as Tom escorted her down the aisle. The guests were barred from entering the main aisle by rope that ran along the pews the length of the church. When she got to the front pew, Tom pulled back Rose's veil and kissed his oldest daughter's lips as he handed her over to a dour looking Pat as Victoria sat on the aisle seat of the first row with Lenny sitting beside her. Pat and Rose, and along with Dot Columbia and Sammy, walked beyond the communion railing and onto the altar.

The thirty-year-old Father Francis P. Mistretta, who said the hour and a half long high mass, had come to Saint Francis de Paola two years before, after having been ordained on April 3, 1945. Mistretta had grown up in the Bushwick section of Brooklyn and attended Eastern District High School and Saint John's University in Brooklyn, before entering the Seminary of the Immaculate Conception in Douglaston, New York. Saint Francis de Paola was Mistretta's second assignment since his ordination.

Pat and Rose knelt at the altar, which was lit by six tall candle sticks, and were blessed with holy water by Father Mistretta. As was Rose's wish, they both received holy communion on their tongues on the altar as well. When it came time for Pat to place Rose's wedding ring on her finger, there is a photo in their wedding album of Pat placing the ring on Rose's finger as Father Mistretta bends over their hands during the blessing and he is clearly laughing, as are Sammy and Dottie. Rose's face is concealed by Pat, but something transpired at that moment that made them laugh. Seventy years later, it will remain a mystery.

As the mass and nuptials came to an end, Pat looked nervous as he turned around on the altar clutching Rose's hand as they faced the full church as man and wife. He didn't finally start to smile until he walked down the aisle to leave the church with Rose's arm through his. After being greeted by all of the relatives and friends who had filled the church, Pat and Rose got into the Cadillac, where they took photos looking out the back window, as was customary at that time. Before they headed to their reception, they stopped at Fontana's Studio at 413 Graham Avenue at the corner of Withers Street to take their formal portraits.

A tall, cream-colored album contains four portraits taken during this session. The first is a full-length portrait of Rose and Pat. The photograph has become iconic in the family because it is the most well-known portrait of Rose. It was also cropped to create the thank-you cards. Another was taken with the couple and their maid of honor and best man. The other two are of Rose alone. The first captures her gown in a full length. The last is a close-up of her face and veil. It is almost like her "Mona Lisa" image in that anyone who views it cannot help looking into her eyes and feeling your soul has been moved as you try to figure out what is going through her mind at that very moment. Her twinkling eyes are full of inexplicable joy. Her ruby lips stretched into a smile that brightens up her whole face. The texture of the lace of her gown can almost be felt. Fontana was proud of his portrait of Rose and for well over a year after the wedding, her portrait was showcased in his front window on Graham Avenue.

Following the formal photographs, Pat and Rose headed to their reception at the Ridgewood Terrace Chinese & American Restaurant at 54-50 Myrtle Avenue in Ridgewood, on the same block as the RKO Madison Theater. "I had it upstairs in the Chinese restaurant and there was a choice of three meals, steak, chicken chow-mein, and another type of chicken. I had a live band too."

As scores of relatives and friends turned out to celebrate the marriage of Rose and Pat, Rose left the table where she was sitting with Pat and as the band played, she got onto the platform, and approached the microphone. As Rose's sister, Theresa, remembered in 1991, Rose looked at Pat and sang Irving Berlin's *Always*. "Rose had a beautiful voice," Pat said. "If her parents had money, she could have been a professional singer. She sang through half the affair. I got mad because all she wanted to do was sing and downstairs there was an RKO. She was up there singing with the band and I'm sitting there at the table by myself. Finally, when the band took a break, she came back to the table. I said to her, 'Look, if you're gonna entertain our guests, I'm gonna go down to the movies. When the wedding is over, come down and get me.' She said, 'You better not!' So, I says to her, 'Well, stay with me. You married me—stay with me. Don't worry about entertaining your guests!'"

Rose & Pat, September 18, 1949

PASQUALE

Rose & Pat with their best man, Sammy, and
maid-of-honor, Dorothy Columbia

Fontana was so taken with his portrait of Rose that
it graced his storefront window on Graham Avenue
for over a year and a half after the wedding.

Rose approached the microphone in the midst of the band for a final song and said, "I'm only married a short time, but my husband's ready to divorce me. He says he didn't get married to sit at a table by himself." The entire reception room erupted in gales of laughter.

Rose singing with the band at her wedding

Pat and Rose danced on the dance floor in front of the bandstand. His right hand clasping hers and his left was at her waist, as she gathered up her train with her other hand. Later on, they cut the three-tiered cake together, where there were boxes of Phillies cigars on the tables.

Rose and Pat took portraits with each of their families and Rose took a special, separate photo with Aunt Angelina and her father. After the last guests had said their goodnight, as Monday was a work day, Pat and Rose headed over to their new apartment on Jackson Street for their bridal night. The one-room, bath and kitchenette apartment at 101 Jackson Street had a small bedroom crammed with their brand-new bedroom set from Roma Furniture and a new wrought iron kitchen table and chairs. The appliances would arrive after they got back.

The Franzese Family at Pat & Rose's wedding, September 18, 1949 (l.-r.) Carmine, Josie (with Jimmy Glynn standing in front of her), Sammy, Rose, Pat, Lorenzina, Jimmy Glynn Sr., Millie, Pete, & Margie

Rose with Tom and her Aunt Angelina Raia

The next morning, Pat and Rose headed to Penn Station clutching their suitcases for their honeymoon destination of Niagara Falls. "I bought tickets for the express train out of Penn Station," Pat said. "We took a train to Niagara Falls. We were sitting in the train station when they announced the express, but we didn't hear it. We were waiting in the wrong waiting room. The train came and went. We went to the guy at the booth and asked him what happened to our train.

The train conductor looked out at them from the booth and said, "That train left twenty minutes ago! Didn't you hear it?"

"No," Rose and Pat told him. "We were sitting inside."

"Anyway, the local is pulling up. You might as well get on the local because the local and the next express is gonna get there the same time."

"We ended up having to take the local and making stops all the way up from New York City to Niagara Falls. We went for a week. Everything was right there. We went in a horse and wagon in Canada. There was a guide who showed us the houses in Canada. While we were on our honeymoon, Sammy ended up wallpapering our bedroom."

After a week in Niagara Falls, Rose and Pat came home and then headed for Fort Montgomery in Upstate New York to Mike Monte's motel. They spent another week away, where Rose rode horses and both she and Pat fished, went out on a rowboat, and took rides on the Seven Lakes Drive. By the beginning of October, they were back in Brooklyn and living on Jackson Street, where Pat went to work, and for a change, Rose stayed home.

"Rose wanted to go to work," Pat said. "I said 'no,' so instead I bought her the platform rocker because we didn't have no living room. It gave her some place to sit comfortably. Rose used to crochet a lot when she was home. She used to cook. She kept the house clean, which was only two rooms. The width of the bed was almost the width of the bedroom. There were two doors in the bedroom, one to the right where the refrigerator was and one to the left where the stove was. But they were just openings, no doors. There were two windows in the bedroom. There was only one bathroom. We didn't have a shower there. We had to take sponge baths. It was a big sink, one of the old-fashioned wide sinks—or I used to go down to the bath house. I used to go down there to take a shower sometimes. You used to buy the towels and the soap.

"I got the appliances from Capiello on Grand Street because Carmine was friends with him. In fact, Carmine was on the radio advertising for him. We had an ice box until the refrigerator came. At the time, you had to wait, so I had an ice box there. I had to wait I don't know how many weeks to get the refrigerator. Sometimes I would forget to empty the pan underneath and it would go all over the floor. The refrigerator came from Capiello and it was porcelain in and out. Then Ralph brought the refrigerator when it finally came in. On the bottom it had a potato drawer. He had taken it out and put it down. Meanwhile, Rose's mother came in. She dropped a teacup on the drawer and chipped it. Luckily, Capiello had another one of the same refrigerators in the warehouse, so Ralph went and changed it without telling Sam Capiello that he did that. Ralph came to the shop to tell me what happened.

101 Jackson Street, Rose and Pat's apartment when they got married, as it looked in 2019

"It wasn't a nice apartment at all. It was just temporary. We were two people in love and we were happy. I was on cloud nine. It didn't matter to me. The apartment was very hot in the summer and was freezing cold in the winter. The windows in the basement were broken and there were no windows down there. I was sick, I had gotten the flu, so I went across the street and asked the guy for a couple of boxes at the grocery store. I broke them up and closed off the draft because it was coming up into the apartment."

Rose's family came by often to visit the apartment. Her mother came by almost every day while Pat was at work. "When I came home from work, Rose was alone most of the time. Once in a while my mother-in-law was there. I would usually find Rose by the stove cooking the meal. It wasn't done, but almost done. Before I would get home, she would go across the street to the little grocery store to buy the newspaper every day. I would read it at night and she would read it in the day."

The second oldest brother, Tommy, was closest to Rose and he worked for the Italian grocery store, Graziano's on Graham Avenue. "Tommy used to bring the cold cuts home to us," Pat said. "I used to buy a pound of ham. Tommy was my favorite. He was always around me. We gave Tommy the key to the apartment so he could come in and help himself to everything he wanted."

By the time Pat would get to open the ham, he would find less than a half a pound left in the white paper.

"Hey, Tommy," Pat would tease his fifteen-year-old brother-in-law, "was the scale broken? There isn't even half a pound here!" Tommy would break into laughter. "I didn't really care. I knew what he was doing. The kid was hungry."

Practically every night after dinner, Tommy would come to the apartment and as Rose cleared the dinner plates, Pat would take out *Monopoly* and he and Tommy would play for the rest of the night, as Rose would sit in the platform rocker and crochet. "We would play all night until Rose would kick him out saying, 'Pat's gotta go to work in the morning,' and then he would come back the next night and we would play all over again," Pat laughed.

Unlike Tommy, with his smiling eyes and winning personality, Rose's third brother, the twelve-year-old Lenny was already a troubled child before having even reached his teenage years. At this age, Lenny was stealing and even from his own family. Tom had already been approached by police officers about his son and both he and Victoria were at their wits' end about what to do with him. Even an old-fashioned beating did not quell their son's behavior and that worried Tom a great deal. One day, Lenny decided to go visit Rose on Jackson Street while Pat was at work. "There was a little grocery store across the street from us on Jackson Street and Rose used to go there to buy stuff if Tommy wasn't bringing us groceries that day," Pat said. "Rose said to Lenny, 'Pat will be coming home and he'll want to eat,' so she gave Lenny money and asked him to go across the street to buy cold cuts and Italian bread." When a good deal of time passed and Lenny did not return, Rose began to get a sinking feeling that she had made a mistake. Lenny was not Tommy. Closing her apartment door, she walked across the street to the grocery store. Her suspicions were confirmed. There was no sign of Lenny. What was she going to tell Pat?

Pat came home from work after two o'clock on a Saturday afternoon to find Rose in a frantic state. "She didn't know how the heck to tell me," Pat said. "When she finally told me, I got so mad and took off out the door. I drove over to the Graham Theater and checked in there. I asked them to let me go in to look for somebody without paying. Then I went to the Grand Street Theater and checked there. I told them when I came out that I couldn't find him. I was ready to kill him. That time he got away with twenty bucks. When I got back home, I said to Rose, 'I don't want him in this house anymore!' and I meant it. I wanted to kill him."

As Thanksgiving Day approached, Rose and Pat were married just over two months, and in spite of living in an apartment that consisted of a kitchen and a bedroom, she decided that she wanted to invite her entire family for the holiday, except for one stipulation.

"Pat don't want Lenny in the house," Rose told her father.

"Well, if my son ain't welcome in your house, then I won't come to your house!"

While they were eating dinner that night, Rose told Pat about her conversation with her father. He saw the hurt and dejection in her eyes. She was so looking forward to having her family in her first home for a holiday, regardless of how small it was.

"Rose looked over at me," Pat said, "And I said, 'It's your family. I don't want to start trouble,' so I allowed him to come." Thanksgiving Day, November 24, 1949, Tom and Victoria came for Thanksgiving with Tommy, Theresa, Augie, Little Stevie, and Lenny too. "I kept my eye on Lenny the entire time they were there until they left. I had no use for Lenny after what he did to his own sister."

After thirteen months in the Army, Rose's brother, Pete, came home on his first furlough just in time for the holidays. As they sat in the kitchen talking about all that had happened over the past year, Pete sat in the platform rocker and Rose at the kitchen table when, as he was motioning with his hands in the middle of a story, he dropped his cigarette on the cushion and burned a hole in it.

"Let's turn it over before Pat gets home," Rose laughed. Eventually, she told Pat that it happened, but he just shrugged and said, "Whatcha gonna do?"

"When I came home for Christmas in 1949," Rose's brother, Pete said in 2008, "Pat and Rose were living on Jackson Street. I went to her house for Christmas and asked her to make me a lasagna. That day Tommy and I went to visit all his friends and they got me drunk. I fell asleep. I ate it later. Even Pat said, 'Let him sleep.' I hadn't been home in a year. I fell asleep on the floor in their bathroom. I got drunk. I never drank like that," Pete laughed.

Christmas Eve 1949 was on a Saturday night and Rose had made plans with her friend, Kay, for them to go out with their new husbands for the evening. Kay and Walter Okpych had gotten married four weeks after Rose and Pat on October 16, 1949, at Saint George's Ukrainian Catholic Church on East 7th Street in Manhattan. Rose and Pat had gone to their reception, where she was beaming in a black dress with diaphanous short sleeves and a white lace bodice. One photograph survives of her and Pat, dressed in a light-colored suit, sitting at a long table filled with plates, pitchers of beer and bottles of wine. While Pat loved getting together with Kay and Walter, he couldn't believe that Rose had made plans for Christmas Eve. That one night was so sacred to his family for his entire life and there was no way he could miss it, married or not.

"Rose! I gotta go to my Uncle Patsy's on Christmas Eve! Why'd you make arrangements for that night?"

Rose's family had no special traditions on Christmas Eve and it had never occurred to her that it should be different than any other night. Growing up in poverty, Rose never had a Christmas tree and she never received presents of any kind. While the Franzeses were not ones to worry about presents, they were big on the solemnity and the ceremony of the holiest night of the year. While Pat said they must go to Uncle Patsy's on Kingsland Avenue, he told her that she was welcome to invite Kay and Walter to join them if they wanted to. When Rose asked Kay, she said they would love to come. On Christmas Eve night, Rose and Pat met Kay and Walter at the Metropolitan Avenue train station and they walked to Kingsland Avenue for the festivities. When they walked into the apartment, there in the corner was the massive, hand-made Precipio of the manger and the surrounding town standing on mountains of papier-mâché. In addition, there were tables crammed with platters of food and bottles of wine to drink. The Franzese and Spizio relatives sat in chairs all along the walls while they talked and sang Christmas hymns in Italian. "Walter and Kay had never seen nothing like it," Pat said. "They really enjoyed it."

As family tradition had always dictated, the youngest boy would be the holder of the Christ child at midnight. The tradition had begun with Jimmy Spizio and had gone down through Carmine, Sammy, Sal, and then Pat. It was now Margaret Spizio Pisano's eight-year-old twin sons, Joseph and Anthony, who were supposed to carry the infant Jesus to the relatives, but this year the twins weren't there because they were home sick. "So, Uncle Patsy pointed his finger to me," Pat said. "He put the towel on my head and the baby Jesus in my hands. When I came to Kay and Walter, they were going to laugh and I whispered, 'Don't laugh. This is a very religious thing for my uncle. He gets very mad. He's very particular about that.' So, they didn't laugh. But I had the towel over my head and covering my hands and being that I was tall, my hand was almost to my mouth with the infant Jesus in my hands. I had to bring the baby to every person for them to kiss the feet. Then Uncle Patsy would take the baby and kiss the feet and put it in the crib. When it was all over and Jesus was put back in the manger, I walked over to Kay and Walter and I said to them, 'We can leave now.' They said, 'We have to leave?' I said, 'No, you don't have to leave. You want to stay?' They said, 'Yeah! We've never seen anything like this here.' There was plenty of drink and plenty of food, but I figured that everyone was singing in Italian that they might have been bored. But my siblings spoke English and my cousins were there. We didn't have to go nowhere. At the end of the night, we walked Kay and Walter to the train station and then for Christmas Day we ate by my mother."

When Pat and Rose got married, there were two Franzese grandchildren on the way. Millie and Jim Glynn had their second child, a son named Peter John Glynn, after both of his grandfathers, on October 29, 1949. On December 26, 1949, Sammy's wife Josie went into premature labor with her first child. She gave birth to a daughter born undeveloped named Laura after Lorenzina. Only Sammy and Lorenzina saw the baby, who Lorenzina baptized. The baby died the following day. It was with sadness that Pat and Rose stayed home that New Year's Eve thinking about Sammy and Josie mourning the loss of their first child.

It was a new year and a new decade, but it was a day that started out like every winter morning as Pat crept out of bed in the cold, winter darkness to go into the bathroom to get ready for his workday at Brooklyn Box Toe, where he was always at work by 6 a.m. Rose would wake up later on to an empty apartment and make the bed, when she would go into the kitchen and put the tea kettle on the stove.

Rose had a cup of tea before she washed and dried the breakfast dishes. She considered mopping the kitchen linoleum, but it was clean from mopping the day before. There was nothing more to do in the kitchenette. She swept and dusted, and later she would take her laundry to the laundromat on Graham Avenue—the shirt, shorts, pants, socks and handkerchief that Pat had used the day before, and a slip, brassiere, panties, handkerchief, and stockings of her own. It was nine in the morning and her work was done. How could she fill the rest of her day? She planned her marketing, but her brother Tommy, who worked at Graziano's, would deliver it for her. Her mother might drop by and share a cup of tea together while little Stevie played on the floor. It was all temporary. They would have their own house someday. Once his father got the tenants out on Frost Street, that cute little home would be theirs. And their children would be running up and down the stairs. She wouldn't have time to think about what to do. If only Pat would let her go back to work in the meantime…but he got so angry when she suggested it. "What am I gonna do all day in two rooms like this here?" His reply was always the same, "I don't care what you do." So, she would go and read the newspaper sitting in the platform rocker with her mug of tea or she would sit and crochet for hours. While Sammy had the attitude that it looked like a husband couldn't support a wife if she worked, Pat's was entirely different. Josie had made more money than Sammy as the forelady at the powder puff factory, but in Pat's case, he didn't want her working to support her mother and father's household and not his. His philosophy was that her parents were only in their forties and could support their own kids. She sighed. She missed the office. She missed laughing with the girls. At least she saw Kay often enough. Her and Walter came around quite a bit. When the day came and Rose had her own house, she imagined herself with an apron on and with pies cooling on the window sill, and babies crying in their crib. Just like in the movies. But that would be when they had their own house. All of this was just temporary.

This morning in particular, Rose decided to head over to Doctor Franzese's office. She hadn't been feeling well for a few days now and was concerned that she was coming down with the flu that Pat had just gotten over. What she wasn't prepared for was Doctor Franzese's diagnosis. She came out of his office walking home stupefied.

"It was three months into the marriage and I came home from work that night and I used to sit facing the stove," Pat said. "I was reading the paper and I hear sniffling. I looked up and I thought Rose was sick or something. She was frying something. I forget what she was making."

Pat asked her, "What's the matter with you?"

"I went to see Doctor Franzese."

"What, are you sick?" At that, Rose began to sob.

"I'm pregnant!"

"So, why are you crying?"

"I thought you'd be mad because we're only married a short time. What are people gonna think?"

"Let them count on their hands! I don't give a shit. I think I got a license in the drawer there that says that we're married. I don't care what people say."

"You're not mad?"

"Are you kidding? No, I'm happy."

"If you're happy, I'm happy," Rose smiled as she dried her eyes.

"Then stop crying and cook," Pat teased. "Let's eat."

That night, as Pat washed up at the sink, Rose put her arms around his narrow waist and held him tightly, laying her cheek against his back. She began thinking about her baby. If she had a boy, he would be named Peter after Pat's father and if she had a girl, she would be named Laura after Pat's mother. But, if she were to have a second son, she would name him Tommy like her father. "Rose was concerned about getting pregnant so soon after we were married, but I was so happy she would stop bothering me about her going back to work. She was so happy about the baby."

As the weeks went by, Rose's checkups all went well and she felt great. During the week, Tommy would join them at night and play *Monopoly*, but on the weekend, after mass on Sunday and dinner, they would head to the movies.

On one Sunday, Rose made the bed, fluffed up the pillows, and laid Pat's suit out on the bed. "At the time," Pat said, "you used to get dressed up for church, put on a suit, tie, and shoes. The women would all wear dresses. Rose would wear a dress and she would wear a hat to church. This one Sunday she made a roast beef and she had my suit on the bed. Rose used to put all my clothes out on the bed for me to get dressed. 'Pat, get dressed,' she said, 'we're going to the ten o'clock mass. You don't want to go to the eleven because that's the high mass and you get out after twelve o'clock.' I was sitting there reading the paper when she says, 'Put your suit on!' I said, 'Rose, we're not going to church today. I'm tired. I work six days a week. I don't want to go. If you want to go, you go by yourself.' She says, 'Pat, you go inside, get dressed, and we're going to church. If we don't go to church, I'm going to make your day so miserable today that you are going to wish you went to church. You can eat that roast beef by yourself and I'm going out!' "So, I sat there and thought, this is going to be a problem, so let me just put on my suit and go to church. So, I went inside, put on my suit, and we went to church. When we came out after an hour, she said, 'Now don't you feel better?' I said, 'No, not really. I'm still tired.' I thought after mass we would just go home, but she said after we were done eating that we were going to the movies. 'The movies?' I asked? 'We-are-going-to-the-movies!' she said adamantly. Since we had no TV, we went to the movies. We would stop by my mother's for fifteen minutes and then go to the movies."

As winter gave way to spring, Rose's appointments with Doctor Franzese continued to show that both she and her baby were doing fantastic. On Easter Sunday, April 9, 1950, Rose and Pat went to the 10 a.m. Easter Sunday mass at Saint Francis de Paola, before coming home and meeting up with Kay and Walter. Both Rose and Kay had corsages pinned to their suits and each wore their Easter bonnet. They took pictures that morning at McCarren Park before heading to Manhattan for a cruise around New York Harbor. While Rose was four months pregnant at that time, her friend, Kay, had found out in recent weeks that she was expecting a child that year as well. The two girls must have commiserated, laughed, and dreamed about their babies to come together and of all the things they would do together as new mothers.

Rose & Pat (right) with their friends, Walter & Kay (Bagniuk) Okpych

PASQUALE

Rose & Pat on Easter Sunday 1950

Throughout Rose's pregnancy, the only mishap she had was one afternoon following a trip to the local grocery store. "I had gone with Rose that one time to Graziano's to buy groceries," Pat said, "and I opened the trunk and I had taken the bags out and Rose slipped on the sidewalk and falls. I dropped the groceries all over the floor on Jackson Street, right alongside of the car in front of the apartment. The sidewalks then weren't all that great. She lost her balance and she fell. She scraped her two knees and all she was worried about were her nylons, but they were ripped." "I could give two shits about your nylons," Pat said to Rose.

She said, "You dropped the groceries all over the floor!"

"I don't give a damn about the groceries either!"

Pat picked Rose up off of the pavement and helped her into their apartment. "I got peroxide and gauze and dabbed her knees and put Mercurochrome, a general antiseptic, on them. She took the stockings off and she worried about her stockings," Pat said. "I went outside and picked up all the groceries."

Pete went on furlough before being shipped overseas in May of 1950. The whole family was proud as Pete went around the neighborhood in uniform. It was the stark opposite of Lenny, whose mischief had gotten him landed in Lincoln Hall juvenile detention center. "Rose was pregnant and we went Upstate to see Lenny at Lincoln Hall in Lincolndale, New York," Pete remembered. "Pat drove us with that big green Hudson. We all fit in there." Tom and Victoria assembled all of their seven children together in front of the Hudson while Pat snapped the picture for them with Tommy's camera. To hide her pregnancy, Rose stood in the back with her father. It would be the only photo ever taken of Tom and Victoria and all seven of their children together.

With Rose out of the house on Richardson Street and Pete in the army, Tom and Victoria began putting the responsibilities Rose had on Theresa's shoulders. Theresa, at fifteen going on sixteen, wanted to be out with her friends and not burdened with the care of her younger siblings. One night, Tom and Victoria had gone out to the movies after putting the two youngest to bed. Theresa was left home to watch them. "The kids were supposed to be in bed sleeping," Pat said, "and Theresa was supposed to be watching them. She went next door by the neighbor. They woke up and saw nobody was home and they walked all the way by themselves from Richardson Street to my house on Jackson Street. Rose and I were in bed and we hear a knock at the door. So, Rose was getting up.

Tom & Victoria Porti with all seven of their children standing in front of Pat's Hudson in May 1950. It would be the only photo ever taken of the entire family together.

I said, 'Where are you going? Let me answer the door. We don't know who the hell it is.' I opened the door and the two kids are standing there. They says to me that there was nobody home and they was scared, so Rose says, 'I'll get up and get dressed and take them back home, see what happened.' I said, 'No, you stay here. I'll walk them home.' She was pregnant after all. I walked them home and gave Theresa hell. I said, 'You were supposed to be watching them!' She said, 'I was only next door.' Rose was worried about her sister and said she wanted to give her more responsibility. That's when she turned around and decided that instead of asking her maid of honor to be godmother, she asked Theresa to be the baby's godmother. She wanted to start giving her sister responsibility. I turned around and asked Sammy to be the godfather."

On the weekends that they didn't stay in Brooklyn, Pat and Rose would go to Aunt Angelina's bungalow in Selden and spend time with the Raia family. Many times they drove over the George Washington Bridge to 9W and headed to Mike Monte's in Fort Montgomery. Johnny Morena would join them up there too, as well as his neighbor who he was now seeing, Marie "Micky" Culmone, who lived across the street on Richardson Street. Johnny's brother, Al, and even his parents, Josie and Dominick, joined them occasionally as well. One particular weekend in the summer of 1950 they were all there together, as the snapshots show. Rose is wearing a striped dress and her pregnancy is evident, as she is beaming, as is Pat. Other photos show them kissing and his arms around her, as well as others show Rose laughing at a table with Johnny as he probably told one of his mischievous yarns. They took their rides through the Seven Lake Drive and visited the little beaches when they weren't out picnicking with their friends. They were never more in love as they awaited the arrival of their first child.

Rose & Pat (center) with Johnny Morena and Micky Culmone hugging to their left, as Al Morena stands behind them and their mother, Josie Morena, stands to their right.

PASQUALE

That summer, Lorenzina's family suffered a terrible tragedy when her fifty-year-old brother, Lorenzo, drowned while clamming with his son-in-law in Lindenhurst, Long Island on July 13, 1950. The Nunziata sisters were screaming in the streets at the tragic loss of their youngest sibling and only brother. Pat and Rose attended the wake and his funeral, but something about this tragedy haunted Rose. Up until this point, Rose slept by the window so Pat could easily slip out of bed in the morning for work without disturbing her. One night following Uncle Larry's death, it was a rainy night and the rain was beating against the window. "There was a flash of lightning and Rose started to scream," Pat said. "I woke up and said, 'What's the matter?' She said, 'I seen your Uncle Larry's face in the window and the rain was falling down his face.' After that she wouldn't sleep by the window. I had to sleep by the window then, so I would have to climb around her to go to work. Other than the tragedy of Uncle Larry's loss, it was a time full of excitement and anticipation, as Pat moved the dresser into the kitchen when he assembled the crib that was now wedged next to their bed. One day, when Cousin Rose Raia came by to visit with Rose, she found her pregnant cousin with an apron around her waist and taking a fresh apple pie from the oven. Rose then proceeded to open the window to let the pie cool to surprise Pat with when he came home from work. After placing it on the window sill, much to Rose's shock, the pie fell out the window! "That never happens in the movies," Rose said as she was overtaken with fits of laughter. Rose Franzese and Rose Raia laughed the entire afternoon over the pie that fell out the window. Cousin Rose said years later, "Rose laughed if it was happy or sad. She was jolly no matter what."

After his trip home in May, Pete had been stationed in Camp Carson in Colorado and then was sent to Hawaii before being shipped out to South Korea. Unbeknownst to his family, after thirty-two days in South Korea, he was seriously wounded on September 2, 1950, and hospitalized in Tokyo, Japan. When Rose went to bed on Labor Day night, September 4, 1950, she had no idea what had befallen her brother, or that her entire life was about to change.

CHAPTER NINE

In Sickness and in Health

SEPTEMBER 1950 – DECEMBER 1950

It was in the wee hours of Labor Day night when Rose woke up and said to Pat, "I think I'm ready."

"I called Doctor Franzese and he said to take her to the hospital," Pat said. "I walked over to Herbert Street to get the car and then I picked her up. I brought her to Saint John's Long Island City Hospital, and at the time, they didn't let the father stay at the hospital. They took Rose's clothes, handed them to me, and told me to go home. So, I went home and I got in bed, but I couldn't sleep. In the morning, I went to work. When I got to work, I told Sammy, 'I took Rose to the hospital to have the baby and I don't know what's going on.' Sammy said he was going to find out." Sammy went into Carmine's office and dialed the hospital. Coming out of the office smiling ear to ear, he told Pat that Rose had given birth to a baby boy and that Pat could go to the hospital to see his wife and new baby. It was Pat's twenty-third birthday.

"I got in the car and shot over to Saint John's Hospital in Long Island City and the woman took me to where the baby was," Pat said. "They showed me the baby. He was a big baby and had a lot of hair. Then she took me to Rose."

"You have a baby boy and it's the best birthday present a wife could give a husband," Rose declared to Pat as she beamed so proudly.

"Yeah, I know. I seen the baby."

"You went and seen the baby before you came and seen me?" Rose delighted in teasing Pat.

"We were going by the place and the nurse went and got the baby so I could see him."

As dawn's early light hit Saint John's Long Island City Hospital on September 5, 1950, at 5:50 a.m., Doctor Franzese delivered Rose and Pat's child, a son, named Peter Franzese, after Pat's father. More poignant than that, father and son would forever share the same birthday.

"I used to go visit Rose at night," Pat said. "She had to feed Peter. They used to bring Peter to her so she could feed him. She was fine. She even walked all right after she had the baby."

When Pat returned that night, Rose grinned as she said to him, "Guess who came in to see me?"

"Who?"

"Lenny," she laughed.

Pat filled with fury immediately as he asked, "How did he know you was here? What's he gonna be a thorn in my side the rest of my life?"

"No, he came here to pick up his wife. His wife gave birth to a baby boy a few days ago. He seen me in the bed and he came over to talk to me and he wants us to go visit him."

"Oh yeah, I'm gonna be his buddy now."

Rose laughed as she said, "I don't know why I tell you anything. By the way, where are we going to put the baby?"

"In the bedroom with us," Pat said. "I took one of the bedroom pieces and I put it in the kitchen and I put the crib next to the bed."

After five days in the hospital, Rose and Baby Peter were released on Sunday, September 10, 1950. "Doctor Franzese said Rose was great," Pat said. That night, all was good with the world as they slept in the narrow bedroom with Baby Peter nestled in the crib wedged next to their bed. The following morning was Monday and Pat got up like usual to go to work. Rose's mother, Victoria, Pat's mother,

Lorenzina, and Rose's sister, Theresa, would be spending the day in the apartment to help Rose on her first full day at home. Lorenzina made a pot of escarole soup for them that night.

When Pat took over in the shop for Artie Meyers a few years before, Artie had given up his position as foreman because he had developed stomach ulcers. When Pat went up there as a nineteen-year-old fresh out of the army, he was healthy and carefree. Unbeknownst to him, the pressure and aggravation that the position brought with it was now having ill effects on him.

"I had a lot of aggravation from the factory," Pat said bitterly in 2019. "It was hard work, aggravating. I was the youngest one there at the time and I used to have to go out and buy lunch for all the people. One guy wanted cigarettes, so you had to go to the candy store. Another guy wanted Alka-Seltzer, so I had to go to the drug store. Sometimes I was short of money. I was getting sick over it and I didn't want to do it anymore. And I was going home to my mother's house to get my own lunch. And they just didn't want to hear it. I was running the floors upstairs and I still had to go out to get the lunches. Frank Keller would say that a certain customer called while you were out. They want you to call them back. Not only did I have to go out, get the lunches and give them to the people, I had to call the customers, and you know how many times I threw my lunch in the garbage because I was too aggravated to eat? And this is what brought it on. All the jobs I had there were junk jobs. It was my brother's place, he owned the place, and I was doing all the crap."

It was on that day after bringing Rose home from the hospital that Pat suddenly felt the urge to vomit and quickly grabbed a pail. When he looked inside the pail, it was full of blood. Shocked at the sight, Pat called over his cousin and godfather, Jimmy Spizio, who was working at the shop at the time. Right away Jimmy said to him, "I'll take you to Doctor Ciuffo, my brother-in-law."

Pat quickly replied, "No, take me home. I probably have a cold in my stomach."

Jimmy drove Pat home to Jackson Street, where he found his mother, mother-in-law, and sister-in-law, Theresa, with Rose and the baby. "I got in bed and I laid down for a few hours," Pat said. "I felt better and I got up to eat. I tried to eat, took a couple of bites, and I started throwing up blood again. I told Theresa, she was only a kid at the time, go to Doctor Ciuffo's office and tell him to come to the house. He came to the house and said, 'You've got to go to the hospital.' He seen that I was losing blood. He called an ambulance, they put me on a stretcher, and Rose seen them carry me out. They took me to Greenpoint Hospital."

Pat laid in bed in a room lined with beds along the wall. They gave him penicillin and blood transfusions. "They didn't even know if I was gonna make it," Pat said. "I got three blood transfusions at Greenpoint Hospital." When his friend, Walter Okpych, learned of Pat's dilemma, he rushed to the hospital to donate blood for Pat. Confined to bed and with his arm taped to a board with the IV's connected to him and the pole next to the bed, Pat lay there sick and discouraged. His weight sunk to an all-time-low of 127 pounds on a frame of five feet ten inches. "I was skin and bones," Pat said. While his parents and his mother-in-law came to visit him during his three-week hospital stay, he just couldn't understand why Rose had never come to see him.

"What's wrong with my wife?" Pat was hurt and angry as he spoke with Rose's mother when Victoria had gone to the hospital to see him. "She don't come see me."

"Oh, you know, Pat," Victoria said to him. "People come to see the baby."

"What's more important?" Pat continued to be hurt. "Is it more important that people come to see the baby or that she comes to see me?"

The shock of seeing Pat carried out of the house and spewing blood wracked Rose to the core and broke something in her that could never be healed. Pat claims it was from the shock. The Franzeses claimed that she went out in the rain when that happened and caught a cold. She told her sister, Theresa, that she was determined to have Peter baptized immediately, so in case that Pat died, he would know that his baby had been christened.

On the eve of Rose and Pat's first wedding anniversary, Sunday, September 17, 1950, Rose's sister, Theresa, and Sammy, brought

PASQUALE

Peter to Saint Francis de Paola to stand godparents to their nephew that afternoon as Father DiMarco poured the waters of baptism over his head. Too small for any cares, the child was unaware that both his parents were seriously ill only twelve days after his birth.

Rose's hysteria caused her health to begin to decline as soon as Pat became hospitalized. "Her heart gave way all of a sudden," Pat said. "All of the excitement stirred up her heart. She worked herself up. She thought I was gonna die." Sammy came over to Jackson Street and disassembled Peter's crib and took him and Rose to stay on Humboldt Street with the family.

In the meantime, the Franzeses kept the newspapers hidden because the news of Rose's brother, Pete, being seriously wounded on September 2nd in South Korea, was being reported daily. "My mother wrote me a letter," Pete said in 2008. "The letter was addressed to Hawaii and went to Korea. From Korea we went to Japan and that's where I was in the hospital. Peter was born on September 5th. I got the letter around the 15th or something like that and I was in the ward. My leg was up and I was in bed and read the letter and I read that my sister had given birth and the baby's name was Peter. I was thinking they named the baby after me, but it was after Pat's father, which I didn't mind. I told all the people, even the [Japanese] girls that worked there. I yelled that 'I'm an uncle!'"

One morning, someone in the family forgot to make the morning newspaper disappear before Rose got her hands on it and the shock at seeing her brother's name brought on a fresh wave of hysteria. Pete had been sent home from Japan on October 8, 1950, to Bethesda, Maryland, for the next eight months, except for a brief furlough home in December.

"My mother and Tommy took a Grayhound bus to Bethesda to see me in the hospital in October of 1950," Pete said. "My friends drove down. I gave my mother twenty dollars to go home. She had the money to get the gas to get home.

"When I was wounded, Rosie was sick. She had gotten sick. My mother said when she explained to her what had happened to me, my sister said 'Poor Petie.' She always worried about me."

After three weeks in the hospital for his bleeding ulcers, Pat was released, still looking pale, weak, and emaciated. Sammy came to Greenpoint Hospital to bring him home. Once they pulled away, Sammy told him gently, "You aren't going home. You're going to Mama's. Your wife and your baby are over by Mama's. Your wife took sick and we've been taking care of her and bringing her to the doctor."

"When I came home after three weeks," Pat said, "they told me I wasn't going home to my apartment, I was going to my mother's. Rose was next to bedridden when I got there. When they came to get me at the hospital, I thought I was going home to Jackson Street."

When Pat entered his parents' apartment, Rose was sitting on the couch and changing Peter's diaper. She looked over at him and said, "Don't ever do this to me again!" Pat said back sarcastically, "Do what? I wanted to get sick, right? What happened here?"

"I don't know," Rose said, "I got very sick. I was worried about you. I thought you were going to die."

Rose had been sharing Margie's bed with her, while Pat slept in his old bed next to Carmine's. Rose became weaker and weaker as the days went by. They brought a cot into the living room for Rose, who became too weak to stand.

"My mother was helping," Pat said, "My sister Margie, when she came home from work, was helping. When I came home from the hospital, Peter was still downstairs with Rose. He was with my mother and his mother downstairs for a while. My mother, my sister, and I were pitching in to take care of him. Rose was there, but she couldn't do much. My mother-in-law used to come. My father got angry because she was telling Rose sad stories and getting Rose upset and he wanted to throw her out. Rose's Aunt Frances, her mother's sister, came a few times too and my father wanted to throw her out too because she was filling Rose's head with a lot of crap. She was going to take her to Florida. They were gonna do this, they were gonna do that. My father got very aggravated. He was very protective of Rose."

As the weeks went by, they took Rose again and again to Doctor Franzese, yet she continued to get worse. Rose confided in Margie how she longed for Pat to buy her a phonograph. Music had always been her passion. Margie assured Rose that when she got better that Pat would buy her the phonograph she wanted.

"Doctor Franzese said it would be best if I took her home," Pat said. "So I took her home to Jackson Street. He thought that she would be more comfortable at home. For some reason he didn't want to put her in the hospital." After one night, Pat and Rose were back on Humboldt Street. By the time that Peter was two months old, Rose could barely take care of him and it was a comfort to Rose that Josie's willing hands and able arms were always there to comfort her baby, nine months after Josie had bore and lost her own first child.

Rose's brother, Pete, came home on leave from the hospital in Bethesda, Maryland, at the beginning of December 1950. "Pete came home with a cane," Pat said. "He was hurt pretty badly. I didn't know he got hurt that bad until I saw him."

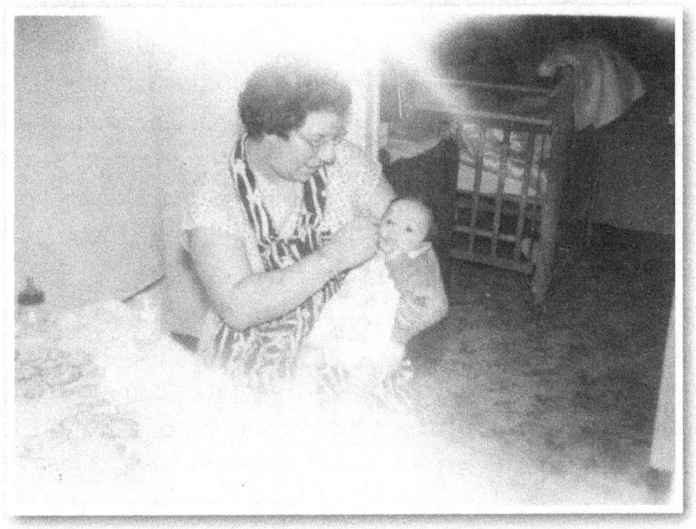

Josie taking care of Baby Peter in 1950

"Rosie was in the house on Herbert Street," Pete remembered in 2006. "When I went to the house to go see her, she looked pale. I went to see her with my cane and she was on a bed in the parlor. She had a cover over her. She wanted to see the baby. He was with his aunt. His aunt was holding him. Rosie said, 'I want Josie to take care of my baby.' She pointed to her when she said it. Rosie couldn't hold him, she didn't feel good, but she wanted to see the baby. She was worrying about me and I didn't know how sick she was. She kept saying, 'Poor Petie!' I said to her, 'don't worry about me. I'm worried about you! You're in bed!' She felt chest pains, like something was pressing on her. I had no idea she was building up with water, fluid. She was hurting and she was tired. You could see it in her face."

The pressure in Rose's chest became unendurable for her and she began yelling and screaming, keeping the family up all through the night. Josie and Sammy took Peter upstairs into their apartment. Lorenzina said to Pat, "I can't do it! I can't take it! We can't do this anymore."

Pat went to Doctor Franzese and begged him to put Rose in the hospital. Doctor Franzese was reluctant to hospitalize Rose, claiming she didn't need it, but Pat insisted, saying, "I don't know what's going on. She can't get out of bed and she's getting worse and worse."

Doctor Franzese put Rose in Queens General Hospital. "Queens General was like a house," Pat said. "It was a small hospital. Rose was in Queens General for quite a while. Josie's brother-in-law, Joe Manarano, was in there at the same time for ulcers or something and she was worrying about him. He was under Doctor Franzese's care too. They gave her medication by mouth. She wasn't hooked up to anything. They didn't have the facilities to care for Rose there. Carmine took a lot of time to take me to see Rose. Every night I was there. She didn't look too great. In fact, one time we had a hurricane. There were no cars on the street and we were going to the little hospital where Franzese put her near Queens Boulevard. Signs were down, wires were down, and Carmine was driving me there.

"When Rose was in that little hospital, Doctor Franzese had a heart specialist look at her from Sunnyside. He was supposed to be a cracker jack and Rose was filling up with water. So, they put a needle in her chest to draw the water out and she had a hole in her chest. When I went to see her, she said to me, 'Don't ever let them do that to me anymore!' I didn't know what they were doing. 'Do what?' She opened her top and showed me the hole there. So, I talked to Doctor Franzese about it. So, he says, 'We have to do that to get the water out. She's drowning.'

"Doctor Franzese sent me to see the heart specialist in Sunnyside and I sat down and the doctor, more or less, told me that Rose was dying. Her heart was surrounded by fluid. That was why they had to put the needle in her chest. They were trying to get rid of some of the fluid, but they weren't very successful. I don't know how I drove the car home. I was by myself. I got home, went upstairs by my sister, Millie, and I was crying. Millie said, 'Maybe you misunderstood him, Pat.' She was trying to calm me down. I said, 'No, Mil, I didn't misunderstand him.' Millie called Margie at work to ask her to speak with her boss' son-in-law for advice.

"My sister, Margie, worked for Mr. Cornbloom," Pat said, "And his son-in-law, Doctor Sax, was an internist on Fifth Avenue. Margie was one of his patients. So, she went to the doctor and talked to him about Rose. When Margie came home that night, she said she had spoken to Doctor Sax and he said that he didn't belong to that hospital, but if we wanted him to go look at her, we had to get permission from Rose's doctor and then he would go take a look at her.

"I went to Doctor Franzese and he said, 'Look, there is nothing we can do for her.' He said that the doctor was wasting his time and he didn't even know why he wanted to do it, but he did give his permission for Doctor Sax to go examine her. Doctor Sax goes and examines her. He told my sister that Queens General was entirely too small for Rose, for what she's got. She belonged in Montefiore Hospital in the Bronx and he could transfer her to Montefiore."

While Doctor Sax promised to transfer Rose to Montefiore, he told Pat that he couldn't promise him anything. Queens General didn't have the machinery or the facilities to help Rose, but he said, "I'll do what I can for her." It was the night of Wednesday, December 20, 1950, when Rose was transferred by ambulance from Queens General to Montefiore Hospital. Pat rode in the ambulance with Rose, while Carmine followed the ambulance with the Hudson. The technicians were amazed at their jolly patient who was so excited to see the Christmas lights go by and then teased when they picked her up by asking them, 'did I gain weight or did I lose weight?' "They were getting a kick out of her," Pat said. Pat and Carmine got Rose settled in for the night at Montefiore before they went home.

"The following night, Carmine and I went," Pat said, "and Rose said to me, 'Boy, what a big hospital this is! They got a tunnel underneath the street that goes from one side to the other side. They've done some tests and Doctor Sax says tomorrow they are gonna give me the works.' She wasn't hooked up to anything. She was jolly, she was fine. You wouldn't think there was anything wrong with her."

On that frigid Thursday night, when Pat laid down his head on the pillow of his childhood bed, it was with an easier spirit than he had had in weeks. His heart was so full of hope that Doctor Sax was going to be the one who was going to make the difference and save Rose's life. Although Doctor Sax was quick to say that he could not make any promises, Rose was beaming like her old self already that night. Pat hadn't seen that joy in her for weeks. "Tomorrow, Doctor Sax said they are gonna give me the works!" He left Rose that night so incredibly happy.

It was in the wee hours of Friday, December 22, 1950, when Pat was woken from his slumber by a firm kiss on his cheek. Startled, when he opened his eyes and felt around in the dark of his windowless room, there was no one there. A few minutes later, the silence of the apartment was broken by a loud knock at the Herbert Street door, which made both Pat and Carmine sit up in a jolt.

"I'll get it," Carmine said to Pat as he stumbled out of bed to open the door and see who it could be at this hour. When he opened the door, a young man in a Western Union uniform stood there holding a telegram for Pasquale Franzese. Carmine signed for it and tore it open. He was not ready to read the news. Pat's beautiful Rose was dead.

Rose Porti Franzese died at 12:50 a.m. on Friday, December 22, 1950. She was twenty-two years, four months, and fifteen days. "Rose knew it was her heart," Pat said. "She had it her whole life, so she knew. I don't think she knew she was going to die. And that night, just before we got word that Rose passed away, I could swear that someone had come. I could swear that I felt somebody had come and given me a kiss me on the cheek. And she was gone." Rose and Pat had only been married for 454 days. Peter, at three months and seventeen days, had already lost his mother.

PASQUALE

The entire household was awakened and gathered downstairs in Pete and Lorenzina's apartment. Lorenzina screamed, the tears poured down Pete's face, Margie, Millie, and Josie were hysterical. Carmine and Sammy could not hold back their tears either. But Pat just sat there in a stupor completely despondent. He did not cry. He refused to believe it could be possible. He was completely numb.

In the morning, Carmine dressed in his long, black woolen coat and fedora and drove alone over to Richardson Street. Climbing the stairs to the Porti's second floor apartment, the kitchen was bustling with life as it was the last day of school for the children before Christmas recess. The Porti children were excited to all soon be home for Christmas recess and a long, luxurious break from school. Tom and Victoria were sitting at the kitchen table drinking coffee when Carmine appeared in the doorway. He never had to say a word. He stood there grim faced with his head bowed. Tom's face dropped into his hands on the table as he wept bitterly. Victoria let out an animalistic wail of sheer pain and suffering that woke Pete from his slumber and shook the other kids to the core. "It was early in the morning," Pete Porti remembered, "and my mother's screaming woke me up. We were all home." Tommy, the closest of the brothers to Rose, took off from the apartment and was not seen for the rest of the day. Theresa was shaking.

Pete thought about the last time that he had seen Rose in Queens General. "Pat took me to visit her on a Friday or Saturday," Pete remembered. "She didn't look good to me. She was in pain and she said she was hungry. I said, 'Rose, you want something to eat?' She said, 'yeah, I'd like to have a sandwich.' I went to the store and got her a ham sandwich, I think it was. When I left her in the hospital, I gave her a kiss. I had never kissed her before. That was the last time I saw her alive."

Carmine took Pat to see the funeral director, Peter Cucurullo, of Franzese & Cucurullo at 18 Havemeyer Street. Peter's brother-in-law, Anthony Franzese, was a first cousin of their father, Pete. Franzese & Cucurullo had handled all of the family funerals since the deaths of Pete's mother and both of Lorenzina's parents over twenty years before. Peter Cucurullo wrote down all of the statistics for Rose's death certificate, as Pat sat there silently staring in a catatonic state. When Peter asked for a photograph of Rose for the prayer card, Pat pulled out his wallet, which opened to their wedding picture. Slipping the photo across the desk to Cucurullo, Peter made a light x over Rose in pencil. A bronze casket was selected and it was decided on that the wake would take place at Greenpoint Chapel on Kingsland Avenue starting the next day.

Victoria came to the Herbert Street door to see Pat in the hours after the death of her eldest child. A burning desire had given her the strength to seek out her son-in-law on the saddest day of her life. "After Rose passed away," Pat said, "my mother-in-law came to me at my mother's house and said, 'Pat, I need you to do me a favor.' So, I said, 'Mom, what do you want?' I was sick at the time. I was still bleeding. She said, 'Would you dress my daughter in her wedding gown?' I said, 'I don't know, Ma, I'll find out.' I didn't know what to do or if it was proper. I went to my two sisters and they said, 'You dress her any way you want to dress her. If you want her dressed in her wedding gown, we can have it dry cleaned in 24 hours.' They had the dress cleaned, and to make my mother-in-law happy, Rose was dressed in her wedding gown."

Flanked by his brothers, Pat walked into Greenpoint Chapel the next day, December 23, 1950, where Rose laid in state in her wedding gown. "She didn't have the veil on her head," Pat said, "just the dress. The train was out. Rose still looked beautiful." As Pat looked down at Rose in the casket, he balked at the fact that those didn't look like the lips he had kissed so often. That wasn't how she combed her hair. "I just didn't like how they combed her hair," Pat said. "They made it tight to her head. That I didn't like too much, but it looked like her. She was beautiful. When she smiled, she had two dimples on each side." Pat was waiting to see her smile with two dimples on each side that would never come again. "I wasn't in my right mind," Pat said. "I couldn't cope with it." In spite of everything, she was still beautiful, even in death, he thought to himself.

"Rosie was laid out at Greenpoint Chapel," Pete Porti remembered. "She was laid out in her wedding gown. She was still a bride, really. They were only married fifteen months. It looked just like

Rosie. She didn't change at all. There were a lot of people in there. A lot of friends were there."

"Oh, Rose's mother was screaming," Pat remembered. "Rose's sister, Theresa, couldn't even go up to the casket, and my mother-in-law kept insisting that Theresa go up. Theresa stayed in the back of the chapel. She just couldn't go up. I told my mother-in-law to leave Theresa alone. She was only a kid."

All of the Franzese's relatives, all of the Porti's relatives, and practically the whole neighborhood and the scores of friends Rose had made turned out to pay their respects to Rose over the Christmas holidays. All of the Christmas trees and Christmas lights had come down and a crepe on the front door had taken the place of the wreath. For the first Christmas of Rose's only child, there was no celebration, as his mother laid in her casket and his grandfather, Pete, watched over him in his crib. Pete was unable to attend the wake and funeral of his daughter-in-law. He had watched over and guarded her when she was under his roof. He delighted in her singing and her giggling when they ate together at night. Most devastating of all, he had lost his first wife, Carmela, at the same age and during the same week, back in 1908. He was not strong enough to face this same loss to come to his household once again.

On Christmas Eve, Pat sat in the front row silent and transfixed on his dead wife laying in her wedding gown. This couldn't really be happening, he kept saying to himself. "Pat was very remorseful sitting there looking at her," Pete Porti said. "His two brothers and Cucurullo had to keep pulling him back."

Monday morning was Christmas morning, which would be the third day of Rose's wake. Pat woke up that morning and put his suit on in a stupor and walked almost in a trace to Saint Francis de Paola for mass alone. It was snowing as he walked from Herbert Street to Conselyea Street, but he felt neither the cold of the wind or the snowflakes as they covered his blonde hair and coat. Although he had put on his suit and gone to mass, he sat in the pew stupefied. After the mass had ended, instead of going back home to Herbert Street, Pat walked to Kingsland Avenue to be with Rose. Walking into Greenpoint Chapel by himself, Pat stood there and saw Rose laying in her casket in a distance.

> Pregate per l'anima benedetta di
>
> **Rose Franzese**
> di 22 anni
> Morta il 22 Dicembre 1950
>
> Ohl Dio che hai lasciato a noi le vestigia della tua passione nella S. Sindone in cui il Corpo Tuo Sacrosanto fu deposto dalla Croce involto da Giuseppe, con cedi propizion che per la tua morte e sepoltura siamo condotti alla Gloria della Resurrezione. O Dio che vivi e regni nei secoli dei Secoli.
>
> "Blessed are they that mourn for they shall be comforted."
> St. Matt. V. S.
>
> **Rose Franzese**
> Age 22 yrs.
> Died December 22nd, 1950
>
> Gentlest Heart of Jesus, ever present in the Blessed Sacrament, ever consumed with burning love for the poor captive souls in purgatory have mercy on the soul of Thy departed servant.
> Be not severe in Thy judgement but let some drops of Thy precious Blood fall upon the devouring flames, and do Thou O merciful Saviour send Thy angels to conduct her to a place of refreshment, light and peace. Amen.
> Eternal rest grant unto her, O Lord! and let perpetual light shine upon her. Sacred Heart of Jesus have mercy on her. Immaculate Heart of Mary, pray for her. St. Joseph friend of the Sacred Heart pray for her.
>
> FRANZESE & CUCURULLO
> *Funeral Directors*
> 18 Havemeyer St.   B'klyn, N. Y.
> Phone EVergreen 8-8081

Rose's prayer card given out to mourners who attended her wake

She looked like an ice queen laying there all dressed in white. She would be eternally a young and beautiful bride. In his mind, Pat told himself as he walked up to Rose's casket and looked at her in eternal repose, "No. This can't be true. This cannot be happening. She wasn't dead. She couldn't be dead. She's only sleeping." Her beauty still enchanted him, but her lifeless body galled him. Where were those dimples and twinkling eyes? He refused to leave her in that casket.

"I was just dumbfounded," Pat said. "I was looking at Rose and I just started putting my arms underneath her to pick her up," Pat said. "I wanted to get her out of there. I was picking her up out of the casket when the funeral director caught me. He got me away from the casket and sat me down to talk to me. I was in a stupor. I wasn't in my right mind. I couldn't cope with it. I just wanted her out of there."

"Pat picked Rosie up out of the coffin," Rose's brother, Pete, said. "I think Peter Cucurullo was pulling him back. Pat was yelling 'come on, get up, you're just sleeping!' He took it real bad. He really loved her."

Pete remembered friends of Rose crying and screaming to the point of getting sick near the casket and trying to get them out into the hallway, which was packed with people, when it came time to say their final farewells.

Rose's funeral took place during a snowstorm on Tuesday morning, December 26, 1950. Rose's grandmother, Maria Giarratana, had come to Greenpoint Chapel for the wake to say goodbye to her oldest grandchild, but was unable to attend the funeral in the snow from Suffolk Street in Manhattan, where she lived. Carmine and Sammy stood on each side of Pat as he made the sign of the cross and kissed Rose's lips for the last time. She would always be his bride and wear her wedding gown and a plain wedding band on her finger for eternity.

The snow fell heavily and filled the streets as the funeral procession left from Greenpoint Chapel for Saint Francis de Paola Church. All of the key events in Pat's life had taken place there. He was baptized, made his first holy communion, said his first confession, and was confirmed there too. Rose had made her confirmation there as well and the two of them only fifteen months before had been joined in matrimony on that same altar. Only three months before, their son had been baptized at the same baptismal font as Pat. Now, Rose's casket was draped in the black pall, as Father Caliendo led the procession as Rose's casket made its way down the same aisle she had walked as a bride.

"At the end of the mass, Father Caliendo went around with the incense and then we went to the cemetery," Pat said. "We had snow. It was snowing when we brought her to the cemetery." The procession headed for the gates of the Greenpoint Avenue entrance of Calvary Cemetery. The funeral cortege made its right hand turn through the tall metal gates of the cemetery and around the alabaster statues of Jesus on the cross with his mother and Mary Magdalene at his feet. Down the winding road toward the dark gray Johnston mausoleum that looms on a hill overlooking the cemetery, looking like a replica of the United States Capitol Building or St. Peter's Basilica. The hearse made a right hand turn past the piles of snow that were growing by the hour as the heavy precipitation filled the streets around them. There, in section 4B, the snow was cleared before the large granite stone of the Sacred Heart of Jesus that was etched with the name FRANZESE at His feet. "The snow was up to the top of the tombstones," Pat said. "They had cleaned up around the grave, but it was very cold and snowing and there were piles of snow everywhere."

Father Caliendo stood by Rose's casket at the Franzese family plot and said the committal prayers as Rose's casket was blanketed in snow at 11 a.m. "We had the service at the gravesite," Pete Porti said. "In the car together were my mother, my father, me and someone else. Mom took it very hard." After Father Caliendo said his final prayers over Rose's open grave, the mourners stepped forward to drop their flower on Rose's snow-covered casket. Pat left her his rose and was led away from his beautiful Rose forever.

They laid Rose to rest that December morning five days before the year of 1950 came to an end. A snowstorm would bury the cemetery, covering the stone and her casket by the afternoon. Pat would feel the cold of that December day for the rest of his life. "Rose died on December 22nd," Pat said, "three days before Christmas, and the day after Christmas I had to bury her. There was a snowstorm. They didn't even bury her that day. They left her casket right on top of the ground. The reason I know it—on Johnny Morena's block—up the block from where Rose used to live, there was a guy that worked in the cemetery and he told my friend, Johnny. He said, 'We couldn't even bury her. The walls kept caving in. We had to leave her casket up on the top.' I didn't know this till my friend told me. I would have had a fit."

After Rose's funeral, the last five days of 1950 went by in a blur. Pat was sick physically, mentally, spiritually, and emotionally. All of his dreams and all of his joy were now buried with Rose in Calvary Cemetery. "I just wanted my family around me when it was all over," Pat said. "I was angry at the world. I didn't want to go to church no more, only if there was something going on in the family. I don't pray anymore. I don't do nothing no more. I am somewhat mad at God.

"Rose was a jolly person. She was a caring person. She took care of her family and everything. She was pretty. She was always laughing, joking, and singing. She sang like a canary. She really did. She used to play ball with the guys in the street. That's why I couldn't understand what happened to her because she was a tough cookie. She could be a tomboy and a lady at the same time. I used to wrestle with her. I can't see how she died! It baffles my mind! Rose didn't deserve what she got, dying so young at twenty-two years old!"

CHAPTER TEN

Life After Rose

1951-1962

The year 1951 was a year of transition for Pat in every possible way. He had buried the love of his life in the closing days of the previous year and he was still seriously ill and weak from the bleeding ulcers that had nearly claimed his life. After years of talk of the Brooklyn-Queens Expressway cutting its way through the neighborhood, Pete had been informed by the city that his house was right in the path of the exit ramp. After over a quarter of a century of calling 501 Humboldt Street home, the city was taking the property and the Franzese family had to move. Pete and Lorenzina would now be able to claim the house that they had originally purchased for Pat and Rose at 243 Frost Street and were able to finally get the tenants to leave. Immediately, Pete hired contractors to renovate the house for him and Lorenzina and their children still living at home, Carmine, Margie, and Pat.

In the meantime, Millie and Jim Glynn packed up their apartment and bought a two-family house at 17 Apollo Street. In the first half of the new year, they left Humboldt Street with their two children, Jimmy and Peter John. In March, Sammy and Josie also packed up their apartment and moved to the three-family house they had purchased in Greenpoint at 128 Calyer Street. This move had a much larger impact on the family because, when they left Humboldt Street, they were taking Peter with them. Lorenzina was vehemently against such an arrangement and felt that she should raise Peter, as she had raised her six children who had survived infancy. Rose had felt at ease knowing that Josie would be taking care of Peter, and everyone in the family felt that Lorenzina, at sixty-two, was too old to be raising a child from infancy. Lorenzina's true intentions were driven by the fact that she was adamant that Peter should not be separated from his father. While the battle carried on between Lorenzina and Sammy, Pat felt that his mother had already raised her children and that Peter would be in good hands with Josie. Three months after his mother's death, Peter left Humboldt Street in Josie's arms, as she and Sammy began a new life together in a home of their own.

During the first six months following Rose's death, Pat did maintain his connections with Rose's family. He brought Peter to see his Porti family over on Richardson Street. Three months after Rose's death, Tommy joined the United States Navy like his father had done. He did basic training in Bainbridge, Maryland, and was stationed in Norfolk, Virginia. Victoria visited Rose's grave constantly and ultimately suffered a mental breakdown over the loss of her daughter. She was placed in the care of Creedmore Psychiatric Center in Queens to recover and Pat would drive the family there to see his mother-in-law. "I found out my mother was mentally emotional when I got out of the army in 1952," Pete Porti said. "She was in Creedmore. Rosie's death affected my mother. Once in a while she would say foolish things and she was singing all the time, but there was no inkling that anything was wrong. She was an educated woman and had a beautiful handwriting. I didn't know anything was wrong, but she did have a nervous breakdown on Humboldt Street, maybe 1945, and they sent her to a rest home in Tuckahoe in Upstate New York. That one time she had a nervous breakdown. I had no inkling why. I just knew she had one. What that meant, I don't know. Now the next time I realized something was wrong with her was when I got discharged and I was home for a few days. Pat drove us to Creedmore in Queens and I found out she had another nervous breakdown. Now, she thought I was still in the Army. She asked me when I was going back. I told her I wasn't, I was discharged. She said

PASQUALE

'oh, that's nice,' very unemotional. We were sitting outside on the bench. How long she was there I don't remember."

Pat also went to Lorimer Street to see Rose's Aunt Angelina a few times. As she left Rose's funeral, she had said to Pat, "don't be a stranger and bring the boy to see me." It was during one of the few visits that he had made to see Aunt Angelina when her words brought him a great deal of comfort as he tried to come to terms with returning to life, a life without Rose. "After Rose passed away," Pat said, "I went to see Aunt Angelina a few times with my son, Peter, and she said, 'I have to say one thing. Thank you very much because you made my niece happy the last two years of her life. You made her very, very happy.' I never forgot that. She was a wonderful lady. I brought Peter twice to see Aunt Angelina."

A few months passed before Pat finally had the courage to clean out the apartment on Jackson Street, where he had been paying for months in spite of the fact that he had not been there since September. Going over to the apartment in the Brooklyn Box Toe truck with Ralph Funaro, they loaded the refrigerator, stove, and bedroom set, along with the platform rocking chair, and brought them to Frost Street to go in the new house. While his mother had tried to help Pat get someone from church to buy the bedroom set, he was so outraged by the low offer he had been given, he threatened to take his anger from losing Rose out on the furniture and take an ax to it in the yard. Lorenzina told Pat that he was crazy and agreed to take the furniture for her and Pete in the new house.

The Fontana photography studio on Graham Avenue still had Rose's wedding portrait featured in its storefront window. "Everyone that knew Rose would stop and tell him that she had passed away," Pat said. "After all of the passers by asking him to, he took Rose's picture out of the window."

By the summer of 1951, Pat was trying to return to a semblance of life, even if it was nothing like the life he had led only a year ago. In some ways, his life returned to a normal state of what it was before he had ever met Rose, except that he had his health then. In the evenings, he started going around to Richardson Street and sit on the stoop of Johnny Morena like he used to. One day, a new kid around eighteen years old was coming out of the last house on the corner of Richardson and Humboldt wearing a zoot suit with a long chain hanging all the way down from his pocket. At first glance, Pat was put off by the zoot suit and chain and was wary as the young man approached. "I thought he was a jerk because at that time he had those zoot suit pants that were tight at the ankles and loose everywhere else and they had that long chain," Pat said. "He came walking by Johnny's like a tough guy. I said to Johnny, 'where the hell did you find this guy?' Johnny said, 'He just moved into the corner house.'" Perhaps Pat's aversion to zoot suits stretched back to his junior high days when the zoot suit killers had murdered his math teacher, Mr. Goodman, in 1942. At any rate, the new kid had already become friends with Johnny and Johnny in turn introduced him to Pat. His name was Pasquale "Patty Boy" Sangimino. Patty Boy, five years younger than Pat, came to become an inseparable friend to him. Johnny was getting serious with Micky Culmone and they would be getting married within the year, and after their wedding, Johnny and Micky moved into an apartment on Powers Street. The only issue was that Patty Boy and Pat and Johnny's old friend, Bobby Gentile, just didn't get along.

At the start of the summer, Pat once again began driving up to Mike Monte's place in Fort Montgomery and Patty Boy began taking the ride with him. "Patty Boy and I used to eat in this restaurant all the time by Fort Montgomery," Pat remembered. "I would say, 'I want pie a la mode. If we rush, we will get there before he closes.' The owner was mopping the floor and he would say, 'if you don't want nothing cooked.' I would say, 'I just wanted pie a la mode.' The man would say, 'You're pain in the ass!' and laugh as he gave it to us. When we got there, Patty Boy and I used to go fishing together."

This summer, when Pat went to Fort Montgomery, Mike Monte was already making plans for how he was going to help Pat heal his broken heart. "Mike Monte was a matchmaker," Pat said. "He drove me crazy. He had a girlfriend that he was engaged to. Beautiful girl. He was a handsome guy. Her name was Jean and she came from the Bushwick section of Brooklyn. So, she didn't drive. She used to come up by bus and he used to go up to the bus station to pick her

PASQUALE

up. So, I had lost Rose and I started hanging out there the little that I could with the boys, so I was up there that weekend and he knew I was coming up that weekend and his fiancé, Jean, brings up her girlfriend, Ann. She was a short girl. Nice girl. Bobby Gentile didn't want to ride with me. Him and Patty didn't get along too good, so he was gonna use his own car. Patty was with me in my car. Bobby had a Lincoln Continental that he had bought. He used a truck load of gas for that thing. He didn't want to ride with me, so he used his car. We get up there and Mike says to me, 'Ann lives in your neighborhood. You're gonna take her home.' I says, 'No Mike, I'm not taking her home. I came with Patty. I'm goin home with Patty.' He says 'No.' I says, 'Bobby's by himself. Let her go with Bobby.' He says, 'No.' 'Mike, I'm not taking her home. Period!' So, we messed around for a couple of days. Now we're all together to go home and Mike says to Ann right in front of me, 'Ann, Pat's gonna take you home. He lives right in your neighborhood.' I said, 'Mike, you sonovabitch.'

Pat with his friend, Mike Monte, and Mike's girlfriend, Jean, on the left, and Ann, whom he briefly dated in 1951 in Fort Montgomery, New York

"I had to take her home," Pat said. "Mike says, 'Patty, you ride home with Bobby.' I said, 'Why can't he ride with me? The three of us.' No. No. Matchmaker. That's what he was doing. Rose died in the winter. This was the next summer. So, it was five, six months later. I wasn't in no mood for dating. Well, anyway, Ann lived on Bushwick Avenue, but past Grand Street. She lived in a big apartment house there right across the street from the library. I took her home. I made my U-turn and she got out and she went up into the entrance on the side street of that building. Nice to meet you. This, that, and the other shit. And I left. I thought I was done. Mike, that son of a bitch, he calls me up on a Friday night, 'Hey Pat, I told Ann you go see the Autoraces on a Sunday,' cause she used to go dancing with her girlfriends on a Saturday and she didn't date on a Saturday because she went dancing. I didn't give a shit what she did. He says, 'And I told her on Sunday afternoon to be downstairs and you're gonna take her to the autoraces.' I said, 'Mike, you son of a bitch!' I didn't have her phone number. She didn't have mine. I couldn't call her. I had to go. I couldn't leave her standing there. She was nice company, a nice girl.

"But then we went Upstate again and Ann was there again. And I see Bobby on the Big Stone with her with his arm around her shoulder. So, I figured-maybe him. No, it was me. I went out with her about five times. And I think she was starting to get interested in me because she said she doesn't date on a Saturday and her sister was getting married and she was gonna be the maid of honor and this particular Saturday they were going for fittings and she wasn't gonna go dancing, so if I wanted to go out. I says, 'What time do you think you'll be home from the fitting?' She said, 'Oh I should be home pretty early. Maybe about two o'clock. So, come about two o'clock. Then I'll be waiting.' So, I decide to go to Palisades Park because it is a ritzy Coney Island. It was nice. When you go over the bridge and make a left from the water, you could see the park and everything. So, we got out. I was hungry as hell. I have to eat a little bit, but often. What am I gonna eat there? I can't eat frankfurters. I can't eat what was there. Then I said, 'I know what I'll do. I'll get a tuna fish sandwich,' not remembering that they make it with mayonnaise. Mayonnaise is bad. I ate the sandwich anyway because I was hungry.

We went on rides and it was starting to get dark. And then there was this airplane ride. I don't know if we both sat in the one plane or we sat separately because it was going down and around. It wasn't going fast or anything. It was dark out then and I was planning on leaving anyway. So, we get off the plane and I start feeling sick as a dog and I said, 'Ann, we gotta leave. I don't feel good. That sandwich didn't sit too good with me.' So, she don't drive. She doesn't have a license. And you know what New York is like with the people and the cabs and all that and you gotta go around the park. I says, 'Holy Jesus, I feel lousy. Dear God, whatever you're gonna do to me, let me get her home safe.'

"When we got to her house, Ann said 'look, you got a pencil and paper? I wanna give you my phone number. When you get home, give me a call. I'll wait for your call because I'm worried about you. I wanna make sure you get home safe. All right?' I said, 'Look in the glove compartment.' So, she gave me her phone number and I had her phone number now. Well, I called her and told her I was gonna go to bed. She said, 'All right, keep in touch and let me know what happens.'

"I went to the bathroom during the night. I went all blood and I mean blood. It came out like a fountain and you get weak. I stood up. I cleaned up everything. I was holding onto the wall. I crawled into bed and I called my brother, Carmine. I was still living on Humboldt Street. So, I crawled into bed and I called, 'Carmine! Carmine!' 'What?' I says, 'I'm sick.' 'Whatsa matter?' 'I just went to the bathroom all blood.' He got all excited. He went inside and went to the phone and called Doctor Franzese. He had an answering service. You tell the operator. She decides if she should call the doctor or not. So, my brother explained everything to her. She said to Carmine, 'Give me your phone number. I'll have the doctor call you right away.' So, my brother sat by the phone, and sure enough, Doctor Franzese called. He says, 'Take him over to Saint John's Hospital and I'll call the hospital. They'll be waiting for him.' Soon as I got there, they put me in bed and they started giving me blood transfusions. That stops the bleeding and all. And they hooked me up to medication. At that time, they used to strap your arm to a board. Now they let you walk around and everything. Well, they took care of me. And then after about two or three days after that, Franzese used to come every morning. He came Sunday morning to see if everything was OK. How they took care of me and all and then he came Monday morning. He came Tuesday morning. I think it was Wednesday morning maybe he sat down on the chair and he says to me, 'I gotta talk to you. You need an operation. You talk it over with your family about what you wanna do and if you wanna be operated on. We can't do it right away because you're too weak. I have to build you up first, but if you don't have the operation, this is gonna continue to happen and it will happen again. And the next time you might not get to the hospital on time. So, when your family comes, talk it over with them.' Well, my father and my brother, Carmine, came and I told them and I asked them what I should do. Carmine said, 'Pat, we can't make that decision for you. You gotta make it for yourself.' Because they figure they tell me to go ahead and do it and I die, which I could've died, they didn't want to be responsible.

"Franzese kept me in the hospital for a week, and then he said, 'I want you to come once a week to the office. I'll keep an eye on you. And when I feel you're strong enough, I'll make the arrangements for them to operate on you.' I wasn't home too many weeks before I went to his office and he said that I was ready. 'I'm going to call the hospital to get a bed ready for you,' he said. 'Go home and when I get the bed, I'll call you and tell you when to go in.' I went in and they operated, but it took me almost two years to recuperate. I gave them a scare with that too. Doctor Franzese said they had me all opened up and everything and they were operating on me when my lung collapsed. So, they had to stop operating and get my lung going again. He says, 'you gave us a scare!' I says, 'I gave you a scare?' The guy that Franzese got to operate was a good guy and he told me that they took half my stomach out. He said it would stretch back again. It never stretched back again. He said, 'You're going to learn to eat a little bit and often.'

"We moved to Frost Street when I was recuperating. In the time that I recovered, I didn't bother too much with the women. I couldn't even take care of myself. Where was I gonna go? What was I gonna do? A lot of time went by with Ann and I just threw her phone number away. Mike Monte broke up with Jean and he married a girl named Mary. I heard he moved to Florida after that and I never heard about him again.

"I was able to go back to work after a couple of months, but I was never right. Franzese said, 'You can go back to work, but don't do any heavy work. And don't stay all day. Only a few hours a day.'

As 1951 was drawing to a close, Pat had survived a whole year without Rose. He was slowly recovering in his new home on Frost Street, and piece by piece, the crane pulled down the house full of memories at 501 Humboldt Street. The store with the living quarters and the garage on Herbert Street were reduced to rubble and carted away. Seventy years later, only the johnny pump that was on the sidewalk in front of the store and the now defunct police precinct across the street are the only remnants of what had stood there on Humboldt Street. As of this writing in 2022, only one neighbor remains, Margaret Dalto, the granddaughter of Pasquale Bonomo, still lives in the home on Herbert Street.

In the fall of 1951, Josie discovered that she was pregnant once again. Early on in her pregnancy, she began to suffer complications, so Doctor Franzese put her on complete bedrest for the six months remaining to her pregnancy. Now unable to take care of Peter while on bedrest, Peter, his crib, and all of his belongings, were packed up and he went once again to live with Pete and Lorenzina, now living on Frost Street. "What happened was Peter came back with us and between me and my sister, Margie, and my mother," Pat said, "we took care of him. My mother wasn't young."

On June 28, 1952, Josie gave birth to her daughter, Laura Ann. "When Josie had Laura and got back on her feet," Pat said, "my brother, Sammy, came and he started to take the crib apart."

My mother said, 'What are you doing?' Sammy said, 'We're taking Peter back.' My mother said, 'Well how do you know Josie wants him?' 'She sent me here to get the crib.' 'What if Pat gets married again?' 'Ma, if Pat gets married again, we'll worry about it at that time.'

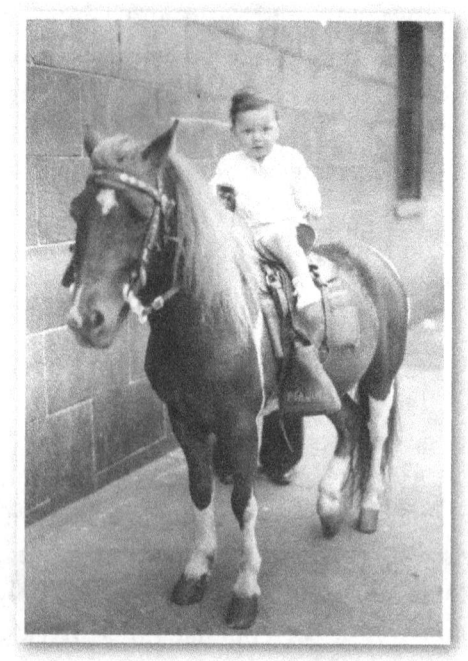

Baby Peter circa 1952

Pete the Grocer at the end of his life, circa 1950

PASQUALE

After Peter's return to Calyer Street, he became more Sammy and Josie's son than Pat's. While Pat paid for his clothing and any essentials that he needed, in addition to endorsing Rose's social security check to them for the use of Peter, he did not have an impact on the day-to-day life of Peter anymore.

Pete's last home, 243 Frost Street, where the family moved in 1951, as it looked in 2018.

By 1954, Pete and Lorenzina relished spending time with their five grandchildren. Millie had a third son, Robert Joseph Glynn, on February 1, 1953. Between Peter, Millie's three, and Laura, the cousins were inseparable and enjoyed playing together in their grandparents' backyard, shaded by Lorenzina's enormous fig tree.

The death of Pete's seventy-year-old elder brother, Uncle Patsy, on June 27, 1952, was a profound loss to the family. As the family gathered in Uncle Patsy's apartment on Kingsland Avenue for the wake, it would be a somber last family gathering of the people who had sat in joyful anticipation for decades to listen for the toll of the midnight church bells of Saint Cecilia's every Christmas Eve.

No more Precipio or ceremony of carrying the statue of the baby Jesus for each relative to kiss his feet. As Pat remained behind in Uncle Patsy's house to wait for the undertaker's men to remove their equipment needed for the wake when everyone left for his burial at Calvary, he thought about the papier-mâché mountains painted gray and the figures of the village, especially the figure of the butcher. Pete and their sister, Virginia Spizio, mourned the older brother who had paved the way for them in the new country. It had been the three of them always. The house would remain an iconic spot for the family for the next seventy years, until it was torn down to make way for condominiums in 2022.

By the summer of 1954, Pete's health had taken a rapid decline and he spent much of the summer in his bed on Frost Street. It was the morning of Wednesday, August 4, 1954, when Pat and Carmine were home to take Pete to Doctor Della Iacono's office. "Doctor Della Iacono smoked like a fiend," Pat said. "His desk had a tray full of smokes. His hands were brown from the smoking. Anyway, we got my father out of bed. He was wearing that long underwear and he says, 'I gotta go to the bathroom.' He went to the bathroom, and when I looked, it was all black. It must have been his liver. So, when we got him outside into the kitchen, he says, 'I want to sit down on the chair for a minute.' We sat him on the chair, standing next to him so he didn't fall. My mother came by and she stood next to him and he put his arms around her waist and laid his head against her and he stayed that way for a while. Then Carmine says, 'Papa, we gotta get you ready.' He let go of my mother and my mother walked away. It was the first time I seen my father put his arms around my mother like that and the last time. I never seen my father touch my mother in my whole life. He must have known he was going. We got him to the bed and sat him down on the end of it. We got his two legs into his pants legs and as we pulled his pants up, he gave out. He passed away. When my father passed away, me and Carmine were putting his pants on. We put him back on the bed. We got him onto the bed. Carmine called the ambulance and the guy came and he pronounced him dead."

PASQUALE

While Pat and Carmine were planning to take Pete to the doctor that morning, when an attempt was made to contact Doctor Della Iacono, it was discovered that he was out on Long Island at his summer home. Pete's body could not be moved from the house until they had the doctor's signature. Sammy got in the car and drove out to Long Island to track down the doctor to get him to sign the death certificate. In the meantime, Pat took his brother-in-law, Jimmy Glynn, and drove to Manhattan to Margie's job to inform her that their father had died. "Now in New York, you can't park, so I let Jimmy go up and call my sister and bring my sister down. When she got in the car, she screamed all the way home. And when my father died, he died with his mouth open, so when she saw my father, Margie went in the drawer and got a dish towel and she put it under his chin and tied it so his mouth would be closed. My father was there from morning until nighttime on the bed. When Sammy got back with the signed paper, the undertaker from Franzese & Cucurullo came at nine o'clock at night to take him. My mother wanted to wake my father in the house, but Carmine talked to her and told her that if she would have the wake at Greenpoint Chapel on Kingsland Avenue, she could have my father laid out an extra day." Pete's wake took place at Greenpoint Chapel on August 6th, August 7th, and August 8th, under the direction of Peter Cucurullo.

In a driving rainstorm that forced the family to remain in their cars as the Rite of Committal was performed at the family plot in Calvary Cemetery following his funeral mass at Saint Francis de Paola Church, Pete the grocer was laid to rest next to his beloved son, Salvatore, on Monday, August 9, 1954. He was sixty-seven-years-old. In a few short years, the grocery store was reduced to rubble and now the grocer was laid to rest. He was survived by his wife, five children, five grandchildren, and his sister, Virginia Franzese Spizio. Virginia survived Pete by three and half years when she passed away on February 8, 1958, at the age of sixty-eight. Buried only a few feet from her brother, the last of Michela Iovino Franzese's children were now gone.

PETER M. FRANZESE

> Pregate per l'anima benedetta di
>
> **Pietro Franzese**
> di anni 67
> Morto il 4 Agosto 1954
>
> Oh! Dio che hai lasciato a noi le vestigia della tua passione nella S. Sindone in cui il Corpo Tue Sacrosanto fu deposto dalla Croce involto da Giuseppe, con cedi propizion che per la tua morte e sepoltura siamo condotti alla Gloria della Resurrezione. O Dio che vivi e reani nei secoli dei Secoli.
>
> "Blessed are they that mourn for they shall be comforted."
>
> **Pietro Franzese**
> Age 67 yrs.
> Died August 4th, 1954
>
> Gentlest Heart of Jesus, ever present in the Blessed Sacrament, ever consumed with burning love for the poor captive souls in purgatory have mercy on the soul of Thy departed servant. Be not severe in Thy judgement but let some drops of Thy precious Blood fall upon the devouring flames, and do Thou O merciful Saviour send Thy angels to conduct him to a place of refreshment light and peace. Amen. Eternal rest grant unto him, O Lord! and let perpetual light shine upon him. Sacred Heart of Jesus have mercy on him. Immaculate Heart of Mary, pray for him. St. Joseph, friend of the Sacred Heart pray for him.
>
> FRANZESE & CUCURULLO
> *Funeral Directors*
> 18 Havemeyer St.   B'klyn, N. Y.
> Phone EVergreen 8-8081

Pete's prayer card given out to mourners who attended his wake

Lorenzina with Pete's sister, Virginia, following Pete's passing in 1954

PASQUALE

* * *

"Patty Boy met a girl on Boerum Street in Williamsburg in 1954 named Liz and she was Johnny's wife's cousin," Pat said. "They called her mother Tiger Lil. She sang in a bar. So, one day, I had gone fishing and Patty used to walk down the block, bring his car down to my house, and talk for a half hour and would leave to go pick up Liz. He had started dating that girl." One day, Patty Boy asked Pat to come along because Liz was bringing along another girl from her block. When Pat got in the car, a young girl with flaming red hair was sitting in the back seat. Immediately, Pat grew uneasy. 'What are you trying to get me arrested? You know I have son! How am I gonna support him from jail?' Patty Boy began to laugh. 'She's no kid. She's a secretary.' The girl from Boerum Street was the nineteen-year-old Grace MacFall. The second of six children born to William Henry MacFall and Margaret Michel, Grace was a 1953 graduate from Grover Cleveland High School and was indeed working as a secretary. Shortly afterward, Pat and Grace began dating.

One Sunday afternoon, Pat was to take Lorenzina and her sister, Rose Annunziato, to Saint Anthony's Church in Oceanside, Long Island, to pray at the shrine. Knowing that Grace was not Italian or Catholic, she was German and Scotch-Irish and Lutheran, he did not think that she would want to go, but Grace surprised him when she said that she would love to come. Pat sweated as his mother and aunt silently scrutinized the young girl sitting beside him in the car. The next morning, while Pat sat at the kitchen table drinking his coffee, Lorenzina came up to her son and said, 'Patsy! Who's that little girl?' Pat almost spewed the coffee across the room as he sputtered a reply to his mother that she wasn't a little girl and she was a secretary.

Grace was a member of the Lutheran Church of Saint John the Evangelist on Maujer Street in Williamsburg, where she was a member of the choir. Grace's pastor, Rev. Klopf, would stand at the door to say goodnight to all the choir members as they left and he would speak with Pat who was there to pick up Grace. Pat and Pastor Klopf developed a strong and warm rapport, as Pat and Grace navigated their relationship coming from different backgrounds. Pat's parents were foreign and Grace's parents were American. Grace was seven and a half years younger than Pat and Pat had been married and widowed and had a young son. Then the religious issue came up as the Franzeses were devout Catholics, although Pat had stopped attending mass after Rose's funeral, and Grace was deeply devout in her Lutheran faith. One night in 1955 while Pat drove down Grand Street Extension with Grace to go to a movie at the RKO that Grace wanted to see, she asked Pat, "When are we getting engaged?"

"I froze," Pat said. "I couldn't believe my ears."

"Pat," Grace asked, "what's the matter?"

"What did you say?"

"I said, when are we getting engaged? I hope you have intentions of marrying me and not wasting my time."

"I got into a stupor," Pat said in 2019. "Give me a chance," Pat said to Grace. "Let me ask you! Let me talk to my sister to talk to Johnny Dalto to get us an appointment with the DeNatale Brothers." Johnny Dalto was old friends with the DeNatale Brothers jewelers, where he had also gotten Rose's rings.

"When Josie found out that I had gotten engaged," Pat said, "Josie told Sammy, 'I want to talk to your brother.' Sammy came and told me. When I went to see Josie, she said, 'You're getting married again, Pat?' I said, 'Yeah.' She said, 'What's going to be with Peter?' I said, 'I don't know. Grace said, 'If you want me to, I'll raise Peter. I'll gladly raise him.' Grace was only twenty years old. I thought she was kinda young. Josie said, 'Well, Peter is five years old and I've had him since he was three months old. If you take him away from me, you'll break my heart.' So, what do you do to a person who helps you when you are down on your back? Smack them in the face? So, I said, "Look, Josie, if you want to raise him, I'll leave him with you." She was happy with that."

Lorenzina was devastated that Pat and Grace would not be marrying in the Catholic church and that Peter would not be living with them. Grace's parents had reservations about Pat because of his age, nationality, religion, and his having been married and having a son. Pastor Klopf became the defender of their love and spoke on Pat and

Grace's behalf that their marriage was God's will and blessed by Him and that no one had the power to keep them apart.

Pastor Klopf married Pat and Grace on Saturday, January 14, 1956, at the Lutheran Church of Saint John the Evangelist. Following a reception at the Brass Rail in Downtown Brooklyn, they went to Honeymoon Haven in the Poconos. When they returned from their honeymoon, Pat and Grace purchased the house next door to Sammy and Josie on Calyer Street, where Peter was living, which they had to wait to move into while it was renovated. They remained in that house for four and a half years, when they decided to sell the house, as having difficult tenants was not for them. The house was sold in 1960 when Pat and Grace left Greenpoint for the house they purchased at 97-11 129th Street in the Richmond Hill section of Queens, New York.

Pat Franzese and Grace MacFall on their wedding day, January 14, 1956

The Franzese's attending Pat & Grace's wedding, January 14, 1956 (l-r) Josie, Sammy, Grace, Pat, Lorenzina standing in front of Pat, Margie, Carmine, Millie, and Jimmy Glynn, Sr. The children sitting (l.-r.) Laura Franzese, Pat's son, Peter Franzese, Jimmy Glynn, Jr., Peter John Glynn, and Robert Glynn

Lorenzina with her five surviving children at Pat's wedding in 1956

PASQUALE

Pat & Grace, Easter Sunday 1960

Lorenzina with her grandchildren, Peter & Laura, standing by her fig tree on Frost Street circa 1957.

Pat with his six-year-old son, Peter, Christmas 1956

Lorenzina would survive Pete by eight years. She would live to see Pat remarry five years after Rose's death to Grace MacFall and Carmine marry for the first time at nearly forty-five-years-old to Hope Ysaguirre on June 28, 1957. She would also welcome four additional grandchildren, Sammy and Josie's daughters, Grace Ann, on May 19, 1956, and Jennie, on August 2, 1958, and Carmine and Hope's two daughters, Hope, on June 28, 1958, and Victoria, on September 3, 1959. Seven months after the tragic death of Millie's forty-one-year-old husband, Jimmy Glynn, on April 26, 1962, in which he left behind Millie and their three sons, ranging in age from fifteen to nine, Lorenzina would endure three operations at Saint Catherine's Hospital for internal bleeding. Pat believed it was due to diverticulitis. On the morning of Wednesday, November 21, 1962, Pat received a call that his mother was seriously ill and for him to get to Saint Catherine's Hospital right away. When Carmine had gotten to the hospital, his mother had held up three fingers for the three operations she had endured. She then made a hand signal that she could not endure anymore and then began to wave goodbye to her son. When Pat got to the hospital in Williamsburg, Brooklyn, from Richmond Hill, he found all of his brothers and sisters in the hallway. They were allowing one person in the room at a time. "So, I go in and see my mother," Pat said. "I am talking with my mother and she said, 'Hace Fria. I'm cold.' I said, 'Alright, Ma, I'll go out and get a nurse to get you a blanket.' I found a nurse and the nurse came and followed me into the room with the blanket and she looked at me and said, 'I think your mother passed away.' So, she took the blanket and covered my mother because she was cold and went to get the doctor. So, I went in the hallway and told them all that Mama had just passed away." Doctor Anton Smith pronounced the death of the Franzese matriarch at 9:15 a.m. on November 21, 1962. Lorenzina was seventy-three-years of age. That day, Pat sat in his mother's living room and cried for his mother, who had been his strength, his support, his disciplinarian, and the greatest source of comfort in life through all the tribulations he had endured. The following day was Thanksgiving, so the three-day wake took place at Greenpoint Chapel beginning the following day under the direction of B. Anastasio Funeral Home on Lorimer Street. Following a funeral mass at Saint Francis de Paola Church on Monday, November 26, 1962, Lorenzina was laid to rest with Pete and the rest of the family in the family plot in Calvary Cemetery. After fifty-two years, the saga of the grocer and his wife was now over. Their legacy would be carried on by their children and grandchildren.

Lorenzina with Carmine and his wife, Hope, on their wedding day in 1957

CHAPTER ELEVEN

In Search of Rose

1990-2007

Rose laid in her grave in Calvary Cemetery for forty years without barely a mention. By 1990, Pat had been married to his second wife, Grace, for thirty-four years, and they had had two children together, Michele on July 23, 1967, and Paul, on April 27, 1969. They had lived in Richmond Hill for twenty-two years before leaving Queens for Island Park, Long Island in 1982, during which their two children were born, with Grace's parents, William and Margaret MacFall, living upstairs in both of those homes.

Peter lived with Sammy and Josie until he married AnnMarie Boniface when he was twenty-two on May 5, 1973, and it was Josie and Sammy who were his mother and father and their three daughters who were his sisters. It was Josie who had nursed him through sickness, put him through Catholic school at Saint Anthony's School in Greenpoint, from which he graduated in 1964, then onto Eastern District High School, which he graduated in 1968, Kingsborough Community College, which he graduated in 1970, and then John Jay College of Criminal Justice, which he graduated in 1972. He had been a Boy Scout with his best friend on Calyer Street, Gregory Wielunski, and a Lionel train enthusiast, a Brooklyn cowboy walking around with his cap guns on his hips and an avid fan of Davey Crockett, Dick Tracy, and James Bond, along with his favorite cousin, Peter John Glynn. Beginning in the late 1960's, he began working

Pat & Grace with Peter & AnnMarie on their wedding day, May 5, 1973

with his cousin, Jimmy Glynn, on a variety show in the basement of the Frost Street house called The New York Variety Show on Channel BCF, which stood for Brooklyn, Calyer, and Frost. Peter John had been an early member of the show, but the draft had called him up for Vietnam and it was there that he lost his life on May 21, 1969, at the age of nineteen. Once again, the grave in Calvary had opened to claim another young soldier of the Franzese family.

It was in Jimmy's basement that Peter met a girl from around the corner, AnnMarie Boniface from Kingsland Avenue, on August 15, 1970. On November 15, 1970, AnnMarie became his girlfriend and they were engaged on the steps of Saint Cecilia's School on December 13, 1971. They were married at Saint Cecilia's Church on May 5, 1973, with Jimmy Glynn as Peter's best man and AnnMarie's sister, Susan Boniface, as maid of honor. For two years, Peter and AnnMarie lived at 90 Monitor Street in Greenpoint, while both were working for Greenpoint Hospital, before buying the house directly behind Pat and Grace in Richmond Hill in 1975.

PASQUALE

It was while living in Richmond Hill, at 97-12 130th Street, with their beagle-terrier, Mikey, that I was born, Peter Michael Franzese, their first child, Pat's first grandchild, at 9:13 a.m. on Monday, June 5, 1978, at Booth Memorial Medical Center in Flushing, Queens, New York. Born seven and a half weeks premature and weighing only four pounds, six ounces, I spent my first eighteen days of life in an incubator in the hospital. Only one day after I came home from the hospital, my only living great-grandparent, Victoria Cilibrasi Porti, Rose's mother, died from a stroke at Whitestone General Hospital on June 24, 1978. She was seventy-years-old. Throughout my father's life, his Grandma Porti came to visit him at the home of Sammy and Josie every week. She always brought him candy, was always warm and kind, and enjoyed Josie's company throughout the day. In his early childhood, Victoria would bring her two young sons, Peter's uncles Augie and Stevie, and they would play during the visit.

Victoria Porti's tragedy did not end with Rose's death. Her troubled son, Lenny, already a juvenile delinquent way before Rose died, continued to be in and out of institutions throughout his youth. By the time that he reached his twenties, his criminal activities became even more shocking. It was 2:30 in the morning on December 7, 1958, when off-duty plainclothes patrolman Thomas O'Brien had stopped at O'Sullivan's Tavern on 47th Avenue in Long Island City for a nightcap when Lenny Porti came into the bar and yelled, "This is a stickup" while clutching a .45 automatic. O'Brien, with his service revolver in hand, knocked Lenny down when Lenny's accomplice, James White, came in with a sawed-off shotgun under his arm. O'Brien fired once after he announced that he was a police officer and White refused to drop the rifle. Lenny then got to his feet and attempted to take aim at O'Brien. O'Brien shot Lenny twice and Lenny stumbled into the kitchen of the bar, where he collapsed to the floor and died within minutes. Lenny was twenty-one years of age. Much to the horror of the entire family, the story was on the front page of all the newspapers with a photo of Lenny sprawled on the floor dead in the bar's kitchen. Tom Porti went to his old friend, Domenico A. Abramo of Abramo Funeral Home on Humboldt Street, who handled the arrangements. Saint Francis de Paola Church refused to let the Portis have a funeral mass there because of Lenny's criminal activities and it is unknown where Lenny's final resting place is.

Two years after Lenny's death, Victoria's mother, Maria Assunta Cerami Cilibrasi Giarratana, died at Kings County Hospital on January 10, 1961. She was sixty-nine-years-old. Her services also took place at Abramo Funeral Home and she was buried with her estranged second husband, Joseph Giarratana, in Calvary Cemetery. Ironically, although Peter was ten years old at the time of his great-grandmother's passing, he had never met her and had no idea that he had had a living great-grandparent. Even more shocking was when he was sixteen and he had taken the ride with Sammy to drive his Grandma Porti home to Ten Eyck Walk in Williamsburg and his grandmother asked if he could come up to her apartment to meet his grandfather. Peter was in shock. He never knew that he had a living grandfather. So that evening, he followed his grandmother into her apartment and met his Grandpa Tom Porti. His grandfather shook his hand, said a few words, and then Peter left. A year later, his grandmother told him that his grandfather was very ill in Greenpoint Hospital, so he took his cousin, Peter John, with him to visit the old man. While he found his grandfather somewhat friendlier on this visit, he didn't know what to say to a man he didn't know, the father of a mother he had no recollection of. Tom Porti died from throat cancer at Greenpoint Hospital on Sunday, September 3, 1967. He was sixty-seven-years-old and had been married to Victoria for forty years. The funeral services also were under the direction of Abramo Funeral Home. Peter attended his grandfather's wake and saw his aunt and uncles for the first time since infancy and early childhood. Tom Porti's funeral mass took place on Thursday, September 7, 1967, at 10 a.m. at St. Francis de Paola, followed by burial with full military honors at Long Island National Cemetery in Pinelawn, New York.

Two years after Tom Porti's death, Peter was invited to his first event in the Porti family when the youngest of Rose's brothers, Stevie, married Diana Griem on August 17, 1969. Rose's brother, Tommy, picked Peter up on Calyer Street and drove him with his family out to Kings Park, Long Island for the event. At the wedding, Peter sat with Rose's aunts and uncles, Cecelia Giarratana Lodato, Sonny and Frances (Milazzo) Giarratana, and Angelina and Jack Raia. This was the first time that Aunt Angelina had seen Peter since 1951 and she sat next to him that afternoon and told him stories about his mother. This very well may have been the first time that anyone had ever done so. Rose was not a topic that was discussed in Peter's life, but at the end of the wedding, he thanked Aunt Angelina for taking such good care of his mother. He never had another opportunity, as Aunt Angelina died from a heart attack at her home in Selden, Long Island, on November 30, 1974. She was seventy-years-old at the time.

The only member of Victoria Porti's family that she introduced to Peter was her sister, Rita Cilibrasi Feinberg. Rita worked at John's Bargain Store on Manhattan Avenue near where Peter lived. One Saturday, Victoria told Peter to take a walk with her so he could meet her sister. As soon as Peter met his great-aunt Rita, the two instantly bonded and she told him to stop at her house. From that day on, Peter would visit Aunt Rita, her husband, Uncle Danny, and Victoria's other brother, Sonny Giarratana, who lived downstairs from Aunt Rita at their home on Leonard Street. He continued to visit her over the years, and when he met AnnMarie, he started to take her along for his visits to his aunt.

When Peter and AnnMarie were married, Victoria attended their wedding, along with Aunt Rita, and Victoria's children, Tommy and his wife, Vicky, and their daughter, Darlene, his godmother, Theresa, and his uncle, Augie. Peter stayed in close contact with his grandmother and Aunt Rita until they both passed. Aunt Rita passed suddenly in November of 1977 at the age of sixty-four and Victoria passed away seven months later. After his Grandma Porti's wake, Peter lost all contact with the Porti family.

Peter & AnnMarie with Rose's mother, Victoria Porti, in 1973

Pat holding his first grandchild, Peter Michael, in 1978

PASQUALE

Growing up in Richmond Hill during the 1980's, my mother's parents, Nettie and Bob Boniface, were a constant presence in my life. Grandpa Sammy and Grandma Josie were also a constant presence. Grandpa Pat and Grandma Grace lived behind us until I was four years old, when they moved to Island Park, so after that we did not see as much of one another. I can remember being as young as seven years old and being intrigued by Rose Porti Franzese. The information about her was so minimal and whenever you saw a photo of her, she was in her wedding gown. I felt uncomfortable to ask any of the elders about her because I was embarrassed to ask Grandma Josie because I thought in my child's mind at the time that she would think I didn't love her. I definitely did not feel comfortable to ask Grandpa Pat out of respect for Grandma Grace. My father didn't really know anything about her and I had never met a single one of her relatives. A few years before I was born, Grandma Grace gave my father Rose's wedding album and some of her photographs. I used to look at them over and over again. Besides the Franzeses, I didn't know anyone else in these black and white photographs. On the rare occasions that Rose did get mentioned, it was always in a somber tone and always revolved around the events of her last illness and death in December of 1950. She died three days before Christmas at the age of twenty-two and was buried in her wedding gown. We had an 8x10 wedding portrait of Grandpa Pat and Grandma Rose in our dining room. My father carried a wallet-sized copy of it in his wallet, and I was told that in spite of being married to Grandma Grace for many years, Grandpa Pat still carried his wedding picture to Rose in his wallet. It was also the photograph that was used for her prayer cards at her wake. I wanted one for my wallet to be like my dad, but of course, he only had the one he had gotten somehow. It was sometime in 1986 and my mom's Aunt Rosie Carrano was sitting on her front stoop when a man gave her an envelope and told her, "Give this to Peter." She didn't know who it was from and gave it to my mother. Inside was the wedding picture of Grandma Rose and Grandpa Pat that I wanted. My father gave it to me and I now had it in my wallet.

My father and I also visited Rose's grave pretty often. We would go see her and the rest of the Franzeses in the family plot in Calvary. I felt connected to the grandmother that I never knew from that time. I was also proud to visit the grave of the great-grandfather whose named both my father and I carried. I remember Easter Sunday in 1986 and we were at my Nana Nettie and Grandpa Bob's house on Kingsland Avenue. When dinner ended, my father and I left for an hour to go visit Grandma Rose for Easter. Just the two of us going to visit her was a profound memory for me. At that point, we were Rose's only two living descendants and we remembered her for the holidays, even if she really wasn't talked about. Also, while she may not have been discussed, her portrait did hang on the wall in our house.

Pat & Grace with their grandson, Peter Michael, in 1986

It wasn't until Grandpa Pat's adored older sister, Aunt Margie Franzese, died from Parkinson's Disease that I ever heard Rose mentioned in the family. After a few years of being bedridden from the disease that ravaged my aunt, who I adored and who had been so loving and kind throughout my childhood and my father's, Aunt Margie died in the same bedroom where her father, Pete, had passed away thirty-four years before, on the night of Thursday, June 16, 1988, at the age of seventy-three. Her wake took place at B. Anastasio & Sons Funeral Home on Lorimer Street in Williamsburg on June 18th and

June 19th and my father said to me with his cousins, Mary Spizio Baldanza and Frances Ciuffo Spizio, that if I had any questions about my Grandma Rose that I could ask them. I was ten years old at the time, and of course, my mind went blank. Later on, that Saturday evening, three women came into the wake and my father introduced them to me as "the Bonomos." They were the close neighbors that the Franzeses had had on Herbert Street in the days of the store. Marie Bonomo and Marion Bonomo Dalto and Marion's daughter, Margaret. The Bonomo sisters were so exuberant when they met me, and for the first time in my life, they referred to me as, "Patsy and Rose's grandson." I had never been referred to anything in reference to Rose before. I sat with them and they were telling me how incredibly beautiful she was, how she loved to laugh and was always smiling, how nobody sang as beautiful as her, and how much fun she was to be around. They told me how in love my grandfather had been with her and how tragic it has been for everyone when she died. I sat there mesmerized and excited that finally someone was telling me about my grandmother and also recognized that I was her grandson.

Over the next couple of years, whenever I attended the 5 p.m. mass on a Saturday night at Saint Cecilia's with my Nana Nettie, I would see the Bonomo sisters and they would always say, "There's Patsy and Rose's grandson!" I used to get excited to run into them just to hear them say that. They always had a few loving and heart-felt things to say about my grandparents. Those moments were very special to me.

Four months after Aunt Margie died, my mother had her second child. My brother, Robert James Franzese, was born at 5:29 p.m. on Thursday, October 20, 1988, in Long Island Jewish Medical Center in New Hyde Park, New York. Rose and Pat now had their second grandchild. On the same day that my brother was born, Cousin Mary Spizio Baldanza died at the age of sixty-five. It was a major blow to my family because she was so loving and fun and full of family stories that she loved to share. Some of her stories planted the seeds that would grow into my passion for learning about the family history of the Franzese family. Six months after the birth of Robert, just like Grandpa Pat and Grandma Grace, we too moved from Richmond Hill to Long Island, settling in Deer Park on April 29, 1989.

On October 22, 1989, my adored Nana Nettie Boniface died from complications after coronary bypass surgery she had had two days before. She was seventy-five years old. My Grandpa Bob had died at the age of sixty just two years before on August 1, 1987, and it was then that I began to wonder even more about my Grandma Rose.

Pat & Grace with their children, Michele & Paul, in the late 1980's

It was at the wake of William MacFall, Grandma Grace's father, who died on November 3, 1990, at the age of ninety-three, seven years after the death of his wife, Margaret, that the true search for Rose began. I was sitting in the chapel at Flinch & Bruns Funeral Home in Lynbrook when my Aunt Millie Glynn sat next to me and said that she was cleaning out furniture that hadn't been touched in years now that Aunt Margie had died. Aunt Millie and her son, Jimmy, now lived in the Frost Street house alone following Aunt Margie's death, and before that, Aunt Millie's son, Robert, had drowned while on vacation in Rio de Janiero, on February 21, 1980. He was twenty-seven years old at the time. While Aunt Millie was going through these old drawers, she found a stack of Rose's wedding portraits still in the folders and unopened since 1949, as well as a large wedding portrait, a wedding album, and an envelope of all of Rose's personal papers. She wanted to know if I wanted them. I was so excited, if I could have gone to her house in Brooklyn at that very moment, I would have. Of course, I told her that I would love to have my grandmother's photos and papers. She promised that she would give them to Grandma Josie and Grandpa Sammy to bring to me when they came to visit.

A few weeks later, Grandma Josie and Grandpa Sammy came with a bag full of photos and papers that had actually belonged to my grandmother. Finally, I didn't have to feel ashamed to ask questions. The most profound part of that day was opening a cardboard folder and seeing the closeup portrait of my grandmother's face that Fontana had had in his window all of those years ago. She was strikingly beautiful and it was at that moment that I felt like I met my grandmother and totally developed that intense love for her. She wasn't a myth anymore. She was my grandmother.

I was in seventh grade at the time and my English teacher, Lynn Simmons, gave us a project to complete on our family roots. It was then that I began to research my family history in February of 1991 and have not stopped since. It was during February break in 1991 that I went to Frost Street and spent the day with my Aunt Millie Glynn, who lived in the last home of my great-grandparents, Pete and Lorenzina Franzese. She took out old family papers and photographs and shared stories that she knew about the family. I sat there with a notebook and tried to copy down as many as I could. In the spring, I returned to Brooklyn and had my parents go with me to Our Lady of Mount Carmel and Saint Francis de Paola to get some records from the old register books the rectories housed. I went by myself to Saint Cecilia's, who took my address and said that they would mail me the records, which they did.

It was during a visit in April 1991 to my mom's brother, Uncle Anthony Lanzetta, who lived in my Nana Nettie and Grandpa Bob's house on Kingsland Avenue, that my mother's uncle, Charlie Abramo, had stopped by to visit. Uncle Charlie's father had been one of the neighborhood funeral directors and owner of Abramo Funeral Home at 405 Humboldt Street. My mother knew that Uncle Charlie had known the Porti family and that all of the Portis' funerals had taken place through Abramo. She asked Uncle Charlie what he knew about them, and while he didn't know how to currently contact them, he said that his brother, Sal, the current owner of Abramo Funeral Home, would be able to help me.

A few days later, I called Sal, and he was so happy to help me. He pulled his folders on my Great-Grandpa Tom Porti and Great-Grandma Victoria Porti. He told me when they were born, when they died, the names of their parents, and where they were buried—Long Island National Cemetery in Pinelawn, New York. It was only a few miles from my home! Within a few days, my father took me to the cemetery, where I paid my respects to my great-grandparents for the first time.

When Victoria Porti died in 1978, she left behind five surviving children, who we assumed were still living. I took out the white pages and saw a listing for an "S. Porti" in Nesconset, New York. I wondered if it was my grandmother's youngest brother, Stevie Porti. I knew that my father had reservations about my going ahead and contacting people after so many years, but I was obsessed at this point with the idea of contacting my grandmother's family and finding out about her. I had looked through the few snapshots and her wedding album countless times at this point. I had even put up her portrait in my bedroom. I was Rose's grandson and I needed to know about her.

It was April 26, 1991, and after the dinner plates had been cleared, I took the white pages in the kitchen and dialed the number for S. Porti. A young man answered and I asked if he was the son of Thomas and Victoria Porti. He said that was his father and asked me to hold on. When Steve Porti came to the phone, I once again asked him if he was the son of Thomas and Victoria Porti. When he said that he was, I told him that I was the grandson of his sister, Rose, who had passed away in 1950. He was completely stunned and right away said that I was Peter's son. He wanted to talk with my father. I put my father on the phone and they talked a while, and when I took the phone back from my father, Uncle Stevie said that I should call my Aunt Theresa, Grandma Rose's only sister. He said that she knew everything there was to know about the family.

That night, I called Aunt Theresa. She lived on Stanhope Street in the Bushwick section of Brooklyn. She had a husky smoker's voice and spoke with a dramatic flair that burst forth with vitality and excitement. When I told her that I was Rose's grandson, she immediately worried that something had happened to my Grandpa Pat. When I explained to her that I was calling because I wanted to know all about my Grandma Rose, she was immediately overcome with emotion. "To know her is to love her," was the first thing she uttered about her long dead sister. While I cannot recall everything that she told me that night about my grandmother on the phone, we did speak for hours, and she was insistent that she had to meet me. The one thing I remember asking Aunt Theresa that night was who was Rose Raia, the woman in my grandmother's photographs. She explained that Rose was their first cousin and that her mother and Grandpa Porti had been brother and sister. My grandmother had been very close to Rose Raia and her mother. I then asked Aunt Theresa if it was possible to put me in touch with Cousin Rose.

The following day, I spoke on the phone with my Uncle Pete Porti and my Uncle Tommy Porti. Uncle Pete gave me the phone number of Rose Raia's sister, Patricia. I called and spoke with her son, who said he would give his aunt the message. Later on that day, Rose Raia Suglia called. She was stunned and deeply moved that after over forty years that Rose's grandson was calling her.

I was ecstatic! I had spoken with all of these key people in my grandmother's story in a matter of hours! A few days later, I received a card from Aunt Theresa that said:

> Dear Peter,
>
> You sounded so interested in your grandmother's life, so I went through my pictures and sent some to you. I thought you'd like a picture of all seven of us. It was really wonderful to talk to you. Please call me anytime for information or just to talk. I'm always here. Love, Aunt Theresa

Inside of the card was photos of my grandmother that I had never seen. She had sent me my grandmother's baby pictures and photos of all of them. I finally felt that I belonged to my grandmother.

After calling back and forth with Aunt Theresa to talk, she invited us to visit her in Brooklyn and on Saturday, May 11, 1991, we went. My mother said to my father to get Aunt Theresa flowers because the following day was Mother's Day and she was his godmother. We parked on Stanhope Street and climbed the stairway to Aunt Theresa's second floor apartment. What I will never forget is the look of complete love and awe in her face as my father walked into her apartment holding flowers and she outstretched her arms and said, "You're back in my life!"

Over the next fourteen hours, the longest we have ever visited with anyone in our lives without sleeping over, we sat around Aunt Theresa's dining room table with her husband, Uncle Lou, and her children, Rosalie and Jackie for a day of animated storytelling and constant laughter. Uncle Lou filled the table with all of the different Chinese food that he bought and it truly felt like a holiday. Aunt Theresa kept us captivated as she told us story after story about Rose and growing up in the Porti house while she showed us Grandma Porti's photo albums. Perhaps the most touching thing that Aunt Theresa gave me that day was my grandmother's eight grade class pin from Public School 49. She said that she had always hoped that one day she could give it to us. The most shocking news that she shared with us that day was that Rose had been engaged to be married when she met Grandpa Pat. Even more interesting were the details she shared that made Grandma Rose a real-life person, such as the fact that she only drank tea and not coffee, her favorite song was Nat King Cole's *The Christmas Song* and what an incredible singer she had been, and that Grandma Rose and I had in common that we both loved to write and were both fans of Clark Gable and *Gone with the Wind*! When I heard that Grandma Rose thought she looked like the late actress Linda Darnell, I planned to go to the Deer Park Public Library that week to see who she was and what she looked like. The woman in the black and white pictures was coming alive and more

PASQUALE

had happened in her life than that she got married, had my father, and died at Christmastime. She had lived, regardless of how short.

I went home in the early hours of Mother's Day having met my grandmother's sister and invigorated with the feeling that I was starting to finally know her. On Memorial Day, May 27, 1991, Aunt Theresa, Uncle Lou, Rosalie, and Jackie came over our house for a barbecue. Grandma Josie, Grandpa Sammy, and Aunt Jennie came over too. For the first time in my father's life, he took a picture with both of his godparents. The connection was easy and Aunt Theresa fit so completely into my life, like a lost puzzle piece. It was then that I aspired to write a book about Grandma Rose, like I was going to write one about Nana Nettie.

In mid-June, Uncle Paul, the son of Grandpa Pat and Grandma Grace, was getting married to his high school sweetheart, Vicki Reilly. Aunt Theresa volunteered to come over for the days before the wedding and help my mother with sewing and hemming our clothes for the wedding. It was then that I got to really know Aunt Theresa, as she made homemade pizzas and we went for a walk in the middle of the night because I had a bad migraine headache. She was also there to take care of Robert when two kids snuck up behind me in school and smashed my head into a stone pillar, breaking my nose.

Peter with his godparents, Pat's brother, Sammy, who had raised him, and Rose's sister, Theresa, Memorial Day 1991

Pat with his siblings at the wedding of his
niece, Hope, to Jack Jordan in 1991

Pat with his grandson, Robert, in 1992

PASQUALE

The most profound moment that we shared over the few days she stayed with us was to talk about a taboo subject: Grandpa Pat in relation to Grandma Rose. I told her that Grandpa Pat probably didn't remember Grandma Rose very much. I had never heard him mention her. Aunt Theresa gave me one of her looks, "Peter, how can he talk about her if Grace is there? I may not have seen Pat in years and years, but I do know that I know him better than you do!" She then told me to get a pad and write down what she was saying. She then asked me if Grandma Grace was at work at the time. When I told her yes, she made me get the phone. "You are going to call your grandfather right now and ask him these questions. But don't tell him that I am here. I don't want to open up a can of worms."

With much hesitation, I picked up the phone as I sat on the couch next to Aunt Theresa and called Grandpa Pat. While I cannot remember all of the details thirty years later, I do remember that whatever I asked Grandpa Pat that day, he answered exactly how Aunt Theresa said he would. That day, Aunt Theresa told me that one day, when the time was right, that I would have the conversation with my grandfather about Rose.

Years would pass and I would only discuss Grandma Rose with Aunt Theresa, but even that waned because we were making memories of our own. In August of 1993, we received the shocking news that Grandma Grace was diagnosed with colon cancer. I remember telling Aunt Theresa and she was shaken because they were the same age of fifty-eight and she had gone to high school with Grandma Grace. Over the next six months, Grandma Grace went through intense cancer treatments and lost her hair and a great deal of weight. When I saw her the day after Christmas 1993, she was still a beautiful woman, but it was still heartbreaking to see the beating she had taken from her illness. After our visit, I started calling her every Sunday night and we would have fantastic talks. We had never had that before, but we bonded at the end. During a crippling snowstorm forty-three years later, Grandpa Pat lost his second wife when Grandma Grace succumbed to the colon cancer after it had metastasized to her brain on February 11, 1994. I cried as I shoveled the driveway that night, cried because we were finally becoming close and she was gone, crying because of what we had not had before. My grandmother was dead before I was born, but I didn't really have my grandfather or my step-grandmother either. I called Aunt Theresa that night to tell her the news and she was very somber. I think her thoughts were with my Grandpa Pat. She had been there for the first snowstorm and she knew far more than I would for many, many years.

Grandma Grace's wake took place over three days on February 13th, 14th, and 15th, at Flinch & Bruns Funeral Home in Lynbrook, New York. I was sitting in the corner of the back of the chapel on the afternoon of Sunday, February 13th when Aunt Theresa walked into the chapel escorted by a bunch of men. I couldn't imagine who she had brought with her. My mother was standing in the doorway with tears in her eyes as she watched them all walk to the front of the chapel to Grandpa Pat. "Those are your uncles," my mother cried, "they all came!"

"Pat," Aunt Theresa yelled out as she stood in front of my grandfather, who was devastated and a totally broken man standing there. Behind Aunt Theresa stood the Porti brothers, Uncle Pete, Uncle

Pat & Grace in 1991

Tommy and his wife, Aunt Vicky, Uncle Augie, and Uncle Stevie. After they spoke with my grandfather for a few minutes, I went with them and my parents into the smoking room to talk with and meet them. I just couldn't believe they were here. My grandmother's whole family. I remember that they were moved at the sight of seeing Uncle Carmine after so many years. It would be years before I would learn his role in their family story.

To the sounds of a bagpiper's playing of *Amazing Grace* amid snow mounds that concealed the tombstones, Grandma Grace's story came to an end as she was laid to rest in Greenfield Cemetery in Uniondale, New York on February 16, 1994, which was also Grandpa Sammy and Grandma Josie's forty-eighth wedding anniversary. At the age of sixty-six, Grandpa Pat had buried his second wife after thirty-eight years of marriage.

A few months later, I turned sixteen on June 5, 1994, and Grandpa Pat came over to celebrate with me. I had started calling him because it broke my heart the thought of him now all alone. Aunt Theresa had told me what my grandmother's death had done to him and I worried now. I wasn't afraid to call him now that I had a reason. I called and asked him to come over to celebrate my birthday with me and he sounded so happy when I asked him. It was then that my father asked him if he would be willing to teach me how to drive. One of Grandpa Pat's talents now well-known inside of the family is that he was a fantastic driving teacher. My mother always told him that he should have done it professionally. He had taught Grandma Grace, my father, Aunt Michele and Uncle Paul. I didn't take my permit test though until January of 1995.

I didn't want to have a junior license and then a senior license. I wanted a full license when I passed at seventeen. I also think that I was afraid of the permit test because the book seemed so intimidating. My high school buddy, Keith Byrne, sat with me and studied until the day came he insisted that I had it in the bag. I took the test and passed on the first try. Then I called Grandpa Pat to tell him that I had passed. He told me that he would start coming on Saturday to give me lessons.

One thing I can tell you about Pat Franzese is that if he tells you he is coming to an appointment to teach you how to drive, he will be there. On the other hand, Grandpa was absolutely thrilled that when he arrived at my house that I was sitting by the door waiting for him, unlike my father who he always found in bed when he was supposed to be taking him for driving lessons all those years ago.

I can still hear his directions and admonitions over twenty-five years later: "Don't get too close to the gutter curb." Or, "Go past the Johnny pump." Luckily, I had grown up for the first eleven years in the city. When my brother was learning from Grandpa a decade later, he was lost in the Brooklynese.

It was during these all-day driving lessons that the stories Aunt Theresa told me that he would tell me one day began to come to light. One week he would tell me about Grandma Rose and the other week he would tell me about Grandma Grace. Because he was still very much in mourning, the stories didn't go much past their final illnesses. He wasn't really talking about the marriages or the courtships. On the day that I had met Aunt Theresa in person, she told me that my grandfather had taken Rose out of the casket, which I found hard to believe. You could have knocked me over with a feather when he told me the same thing. Over those five months, I developed something with my grandfather for the first time, a relationship. We had our own private jokes and stories we shared. I was finally starting to know him as a person and not just a relative you kissed hello and goodbye at parties and around the holidays. On the day after my seventeenth birthday, Grandpa Pat took my mother and I to my road test. It was a sweltering day on June 6, 1995, but I got into my 1982 Chevy Impala that had belonged to my Grandpa Bob and was the car Grandpa Pat trained me on, and we took off. Right turns, left turns, parallel parking, and changing lanes. I did it all, and at the end, kept up my grandfather's flawless teaching record of his students passing on the first time.

During the summer of 1995, I was driving my 1982 Chevy Impala with my new-found freedom. For the first time in our lives, Grandpa started to come over our house for regular visits, and not just because it was a holiday or for a family party. That summer, my mother came up with the idea of giving him a reunion with the Porti family and organized a barbecue at our house at the end of August with all of the Portis in attendance. For the first time in decades, Grandpa sat with his former in-laws and reminisced and laughed about the days gone by. The stories stretched past the funeral and they talked about all of the good times that they had shared together too. Grandpa talked with Uncle Tommy about the days on Jackson Street playing *Monopoly* and laughing with Aunt Theresa about the time he yelled at her for not putting her shoes away when she wanted to go roller-skating. Our yard was filled with laughter and old ties were renewed. I took some pictures that day of them all together and it seemed that these times would be countless in the future.

Pat with Rose's sister, Theresa, and brother, Tommy, in 1995

Right after Thanksgiving 1995, Uncle Stevie Porti called my dad that Aunt Theresa was in Wyckoff Heights Hospital in Brooklyn and that she had cancer. My dad and I went to Brooklyn to her bedside and she cried at the sight of us. She told us that it was bad and she wasn't going to make it, but my father wouldn't let her talk like that. I couldn't believe this could be happening. After all of those years and she had become such a huge part of my life, and now she was dying?

From the moment of that first call back in April 1991, Aunt Theresa not only welcomed us with open and loving arms, but enfolded us back into the Porti family where we had always belonged. She called me to talk very often and never forgot a birthday. You could always count on her card in your mailbox and a phone call, no matter where she was. Aunt Theresa was an angel of mercy whose bags were always packed to go and stay with someone who needed help. A few months after Grandma Grace died, Aunt Theresa invited us all to our first Porti family party, the 25th anniversary of Uncle Stevie and Aunt Diana Porti. What an exciting event to be among my whole Porti family for the first time. The line from *Amazing Grace*, "I once was lost but now am found," felt so true of the day. I took pictures with all of my aunts and uncles and just relished that I was now a part of Rose's family. Aunt Theresa would give me the tightest hugs and dearest kisses and she hugged me constantly that day, so proud that I was a part of them. She did everything she could to make me a part of the family and fill the role that her sister should have been able to be in my life. A few months after that, we were in Brooklyn to celebrate Aunt Theresa's sixtieth birthday, which was on September 18, 1994. Finally, we were able to show her the love that she had given as generously as a queen to the entire family. More than her parents had ever done, Aunt Theresa was the glue that held the family together. She had filled the role that my grandmother would have held and I know my grandmother had to be enormously proud of her little sister.

The new year of 1996 came and I was coming to the end of my senior year of high school. Aunt Theresa was back and forth to the hospital, but on her better days, I was still able to speak to her on the phone. While that indomitable spirit gave her the strength, I clung to every word she said and cherished every second on the phone with her. In spite of her sickness and suffering, the love just poured through the phone and she never lost her childlike enthusiasm.

As the end of her life drew near, Uncle Stevie called to tell me that Aunt Theresa said that my grandmother, Rose, was with her and that she was braiding her hair. Uncle Pete and Uncle Stevie wanted me to come to be at her bedside with them, so they picked me up, and along with Uncle Pete's daughter, Lillian, we went to Brooklyn to be with her. My poor aunt laid there so sick and it broke my heart to see the injustice and indignity of this angel of mercy suffering so much. As I stood in that Brooklyn hospital, I couldn't help looking in the corners and wondering if my grandmother was standing beside me. At the end, it was my grandmother looking over the little sister she loved so much once again.

Aunt Theresa went to spend the rest of her days in the beautiful facility of Calvary Hospice in the Bronx. As we braced ourselves for the loss of Aunt Theresa, a call that was unexpected shook us to the core. It was the morning of July 8, 1996, and Grandpa Sammy had made breakfast for Grandma Josie and sat at the table waiting for her to wake up. When their daughter, Aunt Grace, came down to their apartment, Grandpa told her that Grandma was sleeping late that morning. When they went into the bedroom, they found that Grandma Josie had died in her sleep. She was seventy-seven years old. My father raced from work to his mother's house. He stood at her bedside and said goodbye to the only mother that he ever knew. Later on that day, in the living room sat Grandpa Pat, Uncle Carmine, and Aunt Millie. The children of Pete and Lorenzina stuck by one another through every trial and tribulation that the family faced, even now in their old age. My father was devastated by the loss of his mother, the only mother he had ever known, the loving hands that had raised him and the mother he loved to banter with. How I cried for my grandmother. Only a month before, she had signed herself out of New York Hospital so she could see me graduate from high school. I will never forget her being there and our last visit a week or two later when she sat in her reclining chair and I sat on the hassock next to her, holding her hand, and talking with her.

Grandma Josie's funeral took place on July 12, 1996, and I had eulogized her at Evergreen Funeral Home the night before. As we waited for the limousine on Calyer Street to take us to the funeral home, Grandpa Sammy became impatient because he wanted to be with Grandma Josie, his wife of fifty years, the girl who had waited for him throughout the war. He left and walked to the funeral home, and walking beside him were his two brothers, Grandpa Pat and

Uncle Carmine. That image is burned in my memory of the Franzese brothers, shoulder to shoulder, side by side, through all things. Between the three of them, they had buried four wives together.

Grandma Josie's casket was carried into her parish of Saint Anthony's Church in Greenpoint, where she had been a daily communicant before her health failed and a Catholic Daughter. Her mass was presided by the boy who had grown up across the street and was the best friend of my father, Father Gregory Wielunski. Throughout her illness, Father Greg's mother, Marie, my grandmother's dearest friend and neighbor, had brought her communion and spent so much time with her friend of forty-five years. From Saint Anthony's we went to Calvary Cemetery, but not before one last drive down Calyer Street with Grandma, where her grandson, Christopher, waved goodbye to Grandma Josie from her iconic stoop, while Aunt Laura's mother-in-law, Lucy Flugger, had the children rounded up on the sidewalk to say goodbye to Grandma.

Peter Michael with Josie, four weeks before her passing in 1996

I stood at the grave only a few yards from where the Franzeses, including my grandmother, Rose, were buried and looked at Grandma Josie's casket while Father Greg said the final prayers and then my grandmother's next-door-neighbor, Kevin Smith, lowered her casket into the grave. My grandmother was surrounded by love, from her family and her neighbors who had become family. She was now part of history and reunited with all of the Franzeses who had gone before again. I always pictured that when she got to heaven, Grandma Rose threw her arms around her with tears and thanked her for being such an incredible mother to her only son and exceptional grandmother to her two grandchildren. My father's two mothers were reunited. I looked back at the grave once more and Aunt Millie Glynn put her arms around me and hugged me as we walked back to the limousine together. I just remember staring at her grave from the limousine as we pulled away, knowing that I no longer had a living grandmother.

July of 1996 left us bereft at the loss of Grandma Josie, but then the inevitable loss that we dreaded came when Aunt Theresa passed away on July 30, 1996, at the age of sixty-one. My grandmother welcomed home the woman she had entrusted with her only child and her little sister who she had made his godmother. When Aunt Theresa died, I felt like I had lost my grandmother again.

These losses were difficult for Grandpa Pat as well. They conjured up the memories of the young girl Theresa Porti, who he always remembered as a kid and the decision that changed the course of his life, his son going to live with his brother instead of himself. Grandpa lived more in the past than the present that month and I remember driving with him, my mother, my Uncle Stevie's son, Karl, and his girlfriend, Abby, to Richmond Hill for Aunt Theresa's services. My one amusing memory of that ride was that it was a sweltering day and Grandpa Pat driving with the windows down and the air conditioner on at full blast. Abby, Karl and I were laughing in the backseat as my mother said, "Dad, you have the air conditioner on with the windows down," and he said, "I always drive like this. I like the cool and I like the feeling of the wind in my hair."

At the wake, Grandpa Pat was treated with so much respect by the nieces and nephews of Rose for whom he had been the mythological figure in the wedding picture now standing in front of them, looking so much like he had forty-six years before that it was mind boggling. It was like he stepped out of the long ago photograph. Grandpa Sammy, so fresh from the loss of Grandma Josie, came to be with us as we honored the life of Aunt Theresa. How lost the four Porti brothers were without the sister who held them all together. After a funeral mass at Holy Child of Jesus Church in Richmond Hill, where she was carried by the men in her family who she loved, Aunt Theresa was cremated. She left behind a legacy of love and had given me a treasure that I could never repay, the gift of my grandmother. As was her wish, her daughter, Rosalie, gave me the hand mirror of Rose and Pat's wedding picture that Aunt Theresa wished for me to have when she passed away. I will treasure it forever.

A few weeks after Aunt Theresa's funeral, I was in a car crash on Deer Park Avenue with my high school friend, Maria, on August 24, 1996, when I was rear-ended by an Isuzu Trooper in a three-car crash, totaling my 1982 Chevy Imapla. It was an emotional loss because it had been the car of one grandpa and the car my other grandpa taught me to drive with, but I was lucky to be O.K. A week later, I was an incoming freshman at Hofstra University in Hempstead, where Aunt Theresa told me to be careful because Hempstead could be sketchy. I began my studies in broadcast journalism with aspirations of being a television reporter.

I went from a person who had not known the Porti family to becoming one of them permanently, even after Aunt Theresa's passing. When Uncle Stevie's son, Karl Porti, married Abby Hutchinson on Grandpa Pat and Grandma Rose's 50th Wedding Anniversary, September 18, 1999, they asked me to do the reading at the wedding mass. Then two and a half years later, they asked me to be the godfather of their only child, Emily Carol Porti, when she was born on February 6, 2002.

Grandpa Pat was alone in the house in Island Park when Uncle Paul and his wife, Vicki, bought a house in Baldwin. They convinced him not to stay alone, as they had a separate apartment for him in their house, so he sold his house and moved into their house. At almost seventy-one, he welcomed his third grandchild, Grace Victoria

Carmine (l.) and Sammy (r.) stand behind Pat and Millie in 1996

Franzese, on August 1, 1998. I teased him at the time that he became a grandfather every ten years. Grandpa Pat now filled a role that he had never done before, in spite of having had three children and now his third grandchild. For the first time, he was a babysitter. Between 1998 and 2006, Grandpa Pat became the grandfather of four additional grandchildren, bringing the number to six with Grace in 1998, Aunt Michele's daughter, Samantha, in 1999, and Uncle Paul's two sons, David in 2001, and Joseph in 2006. While Uncle Paul and Vicki both worked as teachers, Grandpa Pat in his seventies and eighties was preparing breakfasts every morning for their children and walking them to Meadow Elementary School, where he became a beloved fixture along the route to the other parents and children, along with the crossing guard, and school staff. In the hours between dropping them off and picking them up, he puttered around the neighborhood doing errands and being ever attentive to Grandma Grace's grave in Greenfield Cemetery, in addition to visiting the graves of the MacFalls and Vicki's beloved Nanny, who passed away in 2001.

It was difficult for Grandpa Pat seeing his siblings age, as they were all significantly older than he was. He continued to drive to Brooklyn to see Uncle Carmine, who was slowing down as he approached ninety, Grandpa Sammy, now in his eighties and suffering from Lewy Body Dementia, and Aunt Millie, also in her eighties, and becoming physically infirm. When the four of them would sit on the couch of the family homestead on Frost Street, they were never as happy as when they were together. Pete and Lorenzina had instilled in them that deep love and loyalty for one another and it would be that love that kept them forever connected for the rest of their days. Uncle Carmine became too ill to live alone and he moved to Indiana to be with his daughter, Hope, and her family. It was difficult for Uncle Carmine, in spite of the incredible care and home Hope gave him with her family because his heart was always in Brooklyn. When Uncle Carmine suffered a stroke when he was ninety, Grandpa Pat was devastated and Uncle Paul offered to drive him to Indiana, which they did. In spite of all the trials and tribulations between them, Grandpa Pat had to be at his brother's side. They stayed a few days until Grandpa went home with the peace of mind that his brother would be O.K.

Pat and his siblings in the living room of the Frost Street homestead for a last time in 2003. (l.-r.) Pat, Millie, Carmine and Sammy. Carmine died on November 15, 2004 at the age of 92 and Sammy eight months later on August 2, 2005 at the age of 86. Millie died at the age of 90 on June 11, 2007.

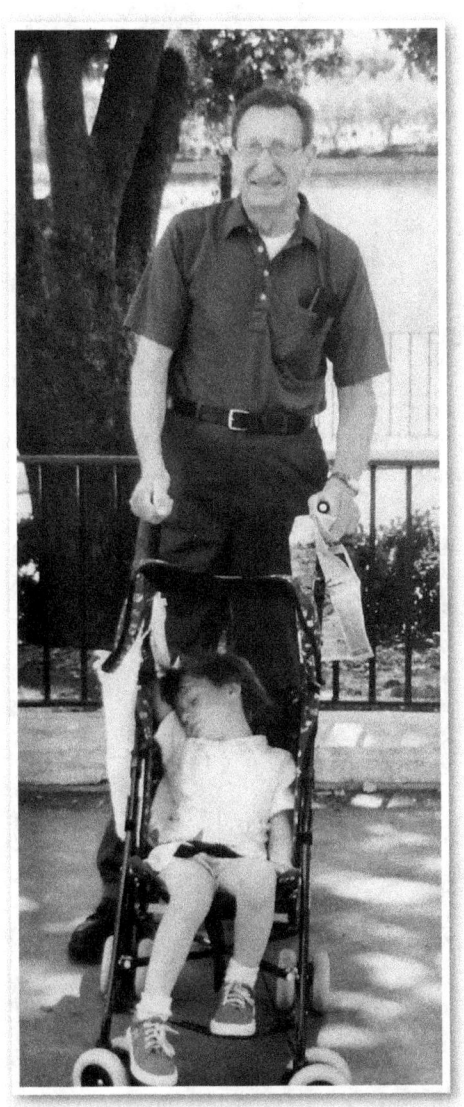

As Pat entered his seventies, he relished caring for Paul's children, as he is seen here pushing his granddaughter, Grace in a stroller

Pat became a major figure in the lives of his daughter-in-law, Vicki's family, especially after Paul and Vicki married in 1991

Pat walking his granddaughter Grace to elementary school

Another aspect of the new decade that was difficult for Grandpa Pat was the facing of the loss of his siblings, his in-laws, and his friends. Uncle Carmine had come home to New York and spent his remaining days with his daughter, Vicky, and her family in Kings Park, Long Island. It was there that he passed away on November 15, 2004, at the age of ninety-two. The death of Uncle Carmine saw the death of the patriarch, the oldest son who picked up the mantle when his father died in 1954. He had looked over each and every member of the Franzese family until his dying day. He was laid to rest on November 18, 2004, with his wife, Hope, who had died in 1982. On the hill in Calvary Cemetery, Grandpa Sammy and Aunt Millie, both so frail, stood and watched as we all said goodbye to Uncle Carmine. When everyone left the gravesite, Grandpa Pat stood with his hands in his pocket at the grave, refusing to leave until the casket had been lowered. He would not leave his brother alone. This scene would be replayed only eight and a half months later when Grandpa Sammy died at the age of eighty-six on August 2, 2005, his daughter, Aunt Jennie's birthday, a victim of a seven-year-battle with Lewy Body Dementia. How ironic that he died sixty years, almost to the day, of when he had been hit with shrapnel in the head in Germany. My father was devastated over the loss of Grandpa Sammy. Although Grandpa Pat had been his father, Grandpa Sammy had been his dad, and the two of them relished each other's company. Even when Grandpa Sammy was robbed of the ability to hold a conversation, my father spoke with him on the phone every Sunday and he would be smiling as my father talked with Grandpa Sammy as if he were well. I will also never forget the scene of my father walking him up and down the block, after Aunt Laura had confided in my father about the Lewy Body Dementia and how it was a seven-year death sentence. My father was taught love and selfless devotion at the table of Sammy and Josie Franzese. Neither of them would ever know the inside of a nursing home because of the example they set for my father and their three daughters, Laura, Grace, and Jennie. Their daughters had taken care of them around the clock.

On a sweltering day, August 5, 2005, two "little girls," as Grandpa Sammy would have called them, two members of the US Army honor guard, gave Grandpa Sammy the military honors that he more than earned sixty years before as we all stood around the grave and Father Greg performed the rite of Christian burial. Grandpa Sammy and Grandma Josie were gone. It was the end of an era for the Franzese family.

With the quick succession of the deaths of Uncle Carmine and Grandpa Sammy, as well as the passing of Grandma Rose's brother, Augie Porti, on April 15, 2004, at the age of sixty, the reality that with each year the opportunity to hear the story of Rose was diminishing. I called Grandpa Pat and told him that I wanted to come over to record his memories of her once and for all. With a notebook and tape recorder, my parents and my brother went to visit with Uncle Paul and Vicki, while I went to be alone with my grandfather in his apartment. He put two short glasses out for the both of us on the kitchen table and then went into his closet to take out the large gallon jug of Carlo Rossi burgundy, his trademark wine. Setting the jug on the table after the glasses were poured, he settled into the chair to begin. It was February 22, 2006. This time, the story was not going to begin at the funeral. It was going to begin at the beginning.

Pat pouring his signature Carlo Rossi Burgundy wine

Taking a sip of wine, Grandpa Pat set the glass down and began, "She was coming home from work and I was sitting with my friend Johnny on the stoop and she says to my friend, 'Hello, Johnny' and I said to him, 'You know her?'" He continued that afternoon to tell about the girl who walked down Richardson Street who was engaged to be married to someone else and his determination to be with her. Coney Island and trips in the 1946 Hudson to White Castle, the on-again-off again and tears parked alongside Cooper Park. Finally, these were the stories of her life and not her death. He talked for hours, as he refilled our wine glasses, as the pungent wine mellowed the mood and he reflected and remembered far better than I had ever imagined. I thought about Aunt Theresa, who had died ten years before, who knew him far better than I did. It was all still locked in his mind. It was if the story of Rose had been in a safe-deposit box that was finally ready to be opened. I left there that day invigorated that the story of Rose would finally be told.

I interviewed my Grandma Rose's brother, Uncle Pete Porti, a month later at his home in Coram, New York. He told me the stories of the history of the Porti family and the stories my grandfather would have no way of knowing. As the closest in age to my grandmother, they had pretty much had had the same childhood. I had called Aunt Millie Glynn, who was now very infirm and a few months shy of her ninetieth birthday, and was supposed to go to Frost Street to interview her about her recollections of Rose, but the whole world of my family was sent into a tailspin that none of us could have imagined in April 2006.

It was April 12, 2006, and after a late evening celebrating my tenth anniversary of my high school graduation with my friend, Joe Viruet, I was only sleeping a few hours when my father woke me up frantically that my mother was seriously ill. She was lethargic and could hardly breath. We rushed her to Long Island Jewish Medical Center because that is where her doctor, Harry Jacob, MD, was affiliated with. By time we got her to the emergency room, she was unable to get out of the car. After she had been evaluated, we were informed that she was going into septic shock and she had to be placed in a medically induced coma. We were in complete shock. How could this be happening? Before she was placed under, my mother told me to pray the Chaplet of Divine Mercy for her. The Chaplet of Divine Mercy, said on ordinary rosary beads, is a prayer that was revealed by Jesus to a Polish nun, Sister (now Saint) Faustina Kowalska, in 1931. That night, Aunt Susan Boniface, my mother's sister, flew in from North Carolina to be with us at this difficult time.

The following morning, Dr. Multz, the senior doctor handling my mother's case, told my father that my mother had a ten-percent chance of survival and that he had to administer a medication that would either save her or kill her. With a ten-percent chance, literally next to none, we braced ourselves for the worst as we headed for the hospital.

Kneeling at my mother's bedside, as she lay in a coma on the respirator, I cried as I clutched my rosary beads and said the Chaplet of Divine Mercy as my mother had instructed me to. As I knelt on the hospital floor, a Catholic nun came into the room, and taking out her rosary, she knelt beside me and joined the prayer. After I had completed the chaplet, I turned to the nun and thanked her so much for joining me in prayer. When I asked her for her name, she told me that her name was Sister Faustina. I started to cry and told her my mother's request was to pray to Saint Faustina and she hugged me and started to cry too. Perhaps there was still hope in spite of the news from the medical point of view.

I called Grandpa Pat from the hospital and told him everything that had happened. He immediately jumped in his car and came directly to Long Island Jewish Medical Center. Grandpa sat vigil with us for that whole day and I realized that with Grandpa Sammy gone, my dad needed his dad now more than ever. Grandpa sat next to my father in the waiting room and he said to him, "God took your mother. He's not going to take your wife." My grandfather, angry with God for almost fifty-six years for the death of Rose, was confident that He was not taking my mother.

As the days wore on, it became apparent that the cause of my mother's illness was diverticulitis and that it had caused a hole in her intestines and the fecal matter had entered her blood stream, causing the sepsis. On Good Friday, April 14th, the doctor said that if my mother was still alive on Easter Sunday that there was a good chance that she would survive. Grandpa sat with us day after day as we sat vigil and hoped for the best. On Easter Sunday, I called the hospital for a status update on my mother and the nurse told me that she was stable. She was alive! When I walked into the eight o'clock mass at my parish of Ss. Cyril & Methodius Church in Deer Park, the tears rolled down my cheeks as the song, "Jesus Christ Is Risen Today" echoed through the church. There was hope.

My mother finally came out of the coma and went into rehab, only to develop a blood clot in her lung and end up back in the hospital. She was back and forth between Long Island Jewish and Parker Jewish Institute for Health Care and Rehabilitation, which was next door to the hospital. Having left the house on April 12th, she finally was released to come home, albeit very weak, on June 2, 2006. My brother, Robert, graduated from Saint John the Baptist Diocesan High School in West Islip, New York, on the next day. While my mother was unable to attend, she was there when he returned home from the ceremony.

My mother had a very long road ahead of her and my father's new full-time job, having retired a year before from the NYC Department of Sanitation, became my mother's care. Life as we knew it would be forever changed, but my mother was alive and that was all that mattered. Only a few months later, my mother's bachelor brother, Uncle Anthony Lanzetta, became terminally ill with bone cancer, which had been a manifestation of the prostate cancer which he had had surgery for in 2000. It was right back to the intensive care unit of Long Island Jewish Medical Center for him, but in this case, the cancer severed the nerves to his lungs and he ended up on a ventilator permanently. By the end of 2006, he was placed in Gurwin Jewish Nursing & Rehabilitation Center in Commack, New York. There was no hope of him coming off of the ventilator. In the meantime, Aunt Millie Glynn also had become seriously ill and hospitalized with infection. She spent her ninetieth birthday, November 7, 2006, in the hospital and amputation of her leg was inevitable. The year 2006 had tried and tested us. Once my mother became ill, the thought of writing this book had gone on the backburner and would remain there for a long time.

After nearly six months on the ventilator, Uncle Anthony made the decision to have the machine shut. He did not want to fight this losing battle anymore. After being transferred to Stony Brook University Hospital for what they called a terminal wean on April 18th, he was transferred to Hospice House in Northport, New York, a few hours before he died on April 20, 2007. He was sixty-eight years old. In the meantime, Aunt Millie Glynn was in Cabrini Medical Center in Manhattan, where her leg had been amputated by this time and she was unconscious. Grandpa Pat wanted to go see her and he and Uncle Paul invited me to join them. We went on the Long Island Railroad from the Baldwin Station to Penn Station and I was quite impressed by my almost eighty-year-old grandfather running up the stairs and running after trains. In spite of the fact that we were in Manhattan to say goodbye to his last sibling, it was a bonding experience between my grandfather, my uncle and I as we walked the streets of Manhattan together, stopping for a slice of pizza, and spending a very meaningful afternoon together.

Aunt Millie Glynn died on June 11, 2007, at the age of ninety. Just shy of eighty, my grandfather was now the sole survivor of the children of Pete and Lorenzina. Her funeral took place four days later and eerily reminiscent of the funerals from his youth, he walked behind her casket as it went down the aisle of Saint Francis de Paola, just like he had after Rose, his parents, Sal, and his grandparents. The Franzese family plot was opened and Aunt Millie's casket was placed on top of Uncle Sal's. Grandpa's eyes were transfixed on the hole of the open grave as he stared at the side of an exposed casket. "That's my mother," he said, deeply moved. I stood with my arm around him as I paid tribute in my heart to the family matriarch.

On September 5, 2007, Grandpa Pat turned eighty. Uncle Paul and Vicki had a birthday party for him at their house and we celebrated his long and eventful life. The book was still in the back of my mind and I planned in the coming months to return to his table and have his story be heard.

Pat with Peter Michael in 2007

CHAPTER TWELVE

Finding Grandpa Pat

2008-2012

It was January 16, 2008, and I decided to call my Uncle Tommy Porti to wish him a happy seventy-fifth birthday. To be honest, I had never been very close to Uncle Tommy, but I knew the history that he shared with his sister and Grandpa Pat, and I wanted to reach out to him on his special day. I never interviewed him about Grandma Rose because when I broached the topic, it was too painful for him to discuss. Her death had the biggest effect on him of the six siblings who survived her, and it was evidently a topic he clearly did not want to discuss. I respected that, but wanted to speak with him just because he was so special to her and Grandpa Pat. We talked about my grandmother's photos and I told him about the pictures I had of him with my grandmother and the others when they were small children. He was very eager to see them and I mailed them the next day. I wasn't prepared for the phone call two weeks later that he had suffered a heart attack and passed away on January 30, 2008. When I called Grandpa Pat that Uncle Tommy had died, he was truly shaken. "Oh my God! Tommy was my favorite," he said in shock. "We used to play *Monopoly* every night. I really wanted to see him again." That night, Grandpa Pat took out the *Monopoly* game that he used to play with Uncle Tommy all those years ago. "I found the chest that I had it in and sat there with it and fixed the money," Grandpa said. "I just couldn't believe he was gone."

On a rainy night a few days later, my father picked Grandpa Pat up at his house and we drove into Queens to attend the wake for Uncle Tommy. Of all the deaths in the Porti family, this one really had Grandpa Pat shook up. He stood the entire time with his hands in his pockets and telling his stories to a new audience of the younger generation of the Portis. He had buried Lenny, then Theresa, then Augie, and now Tommy. Only Pete and Stevie remained. "They were all kids," he said over and over, and yet one by one he had to say goodbye to them all. A few weeks after Uncle Tommy's funeral, it was more evident than ever that I had to get the story down. The key people in Rose's saga were disappearing before our eyes.

Almost two years to the day since our last interview, I finally sat down with Grandpa Pat to continue our interviews in his Baldwin Harbor apartment on February 19, 2008. Since it had been two years, we went back to the beginning. What impressed me most this time around was his attention to detail. "The first time I laid eyes on her," Grandpa said, "she had a black dress on and it had sequins in the front and she had high heels. She didn't have on a hat. Her hair was down to her shoulders. Her hair was chestnut colored. She had a beautiful voice." And thus, the woman in the black and white photographs became vibrantly alive with color.

When we are young, it is through our parents that we forge a relationship with our grandparents. When it came to the relationship of my father and Grandpa Pat, it was awkward for both of them from the day he left Humboldt Street in Grandma Josie's arms for a life with her and Grandpa Sammy on Calyer Street, instead of a life with him. Grandpa Pat spent the rest of his life trying to justify the decision. Sometimes I wasn't sure if he was doing it for my father's sake or for his own. As he revealed in his eighties, it was not easy for him to watch his son call Sammy his dad. But Grandpa Pat had made the decision not to fulfill that role, a role that Sammy filled for my father flawlessly for the nearly fifty-five years he was in my father's life. Needless to say, their story was a series of missed opportunities and regrets. They looked to the past for the answers instead of looking at the here and now and what time was left. In 2008, I was turning thirty years old and I was on my own. I owned my own house, thanks to the generosity of my Uncle Anthony who had passed away the year before, and was forging my own life. I didn't need to develop a relationship with my only living grandparent through my parents. I was an adult now and it was up to me. It was also up to Grandpa Pat if he indeed wanted that. Thus, I began another chapter in the saga of our lives. While I had spent the last eighteen years in search of Rose, I was about to discover the only grandparent I had, and the one of whom up to that point, I knew the least.

Thursday, August 7, 2008, marked what would have been Rose's eightieth birthday. A few months after each of the deaths of Uncle Carmine, Grandpa Sammy, and Aunt Millie, there had been a private memorial mass to commemorate them and bring the family together at the old family parish of Saint Francis de Paola in Brooklyn. After having attended Aunt Millie's in late 2007, I decided that my father, brother and I had never been given an opportunity to celebrate Rose's life in any way. We were her living legacy, yet never had experienced anything in connection with her. With the help of Aunt Millie's son, Jimmy Glynn, who was the sacristan at Saint Francis de Paola Church, I was going to plan a full day to celebrate and commemorate the life of Rose Porti Franzese. Jimmy helped tremendously with booking and planning the mass. Grandpa Pat joined us for the mass, along with my parents and my brother, Robert, as well as Grandma Rose's two surviving siblings, Uncle Pete and Uncle Stevie, with his wife, Aunt Diana. The portrait that had once graced Fontana's studio window on Graham Avenue stood on a table on the altar, along with a vase of red roses. Uncle Pete was so excited to be back inside Saint Francis and he searched for his bugle award that had once hung there, but to no avail. After mass was over, both of Rose's brothers marveled at being on Humboldt Street after so many years. Then, which was inevitably fitting for the day, we all ended up on Richardson Street where the Portis had grown up and Grandpa Pat had first seen Rose turn the corner and change his life. I was standing in front of 207 Richardson Street when Grandpa pulled up in his Buick with Uncle Pete in the passenger seat. I thought about the times in his stories when he pulled up and imagined Grandma Rose coming out the front door while her parents sat on that very stoop. So long ago, yet so vivid and fresh on that day with the key surviving members of the saga. After reminiscing on Richardson Street, we headed in a procession for Calvary Cemetery to all come together to visit Rose for her eightieth birthday. Whenever my grandfather would pull up to that grave, he would stand there silently with his hands in his pocket, slightly stooped, and the tragedy would be etched into his face. All those who he had loved and lost, except for Grace, were laid to rest on that small plot of land. In spite of that fact, it was the top etching on the right that still seared his soul nearly sixty years later, "Beloved Wife, Rose, 1928-1950." He would always say, "She was only twenty-two. I still can't wrap my mind around it. She was so pretty. She was a toughie. I just don't understand how she could have died like that." We all gathered around the grave and Grandpa Pat laid his rose on the headstone just above her name. For this time, we were all there together. Her husband, her only child and his wife, her two grandchildren, her two surviving brothers and her sister-in-law. We celebrated her and remembered her, and although only Grandpa Pat and Uncle Pete standing there had vivid memories of her, their stories would keep her alive for more years to come.

Rose's eightieth birthday mass at St. Francis de Paola Church in 2008 (l.-r.) AnnMarie, Diana Porti, Peter, Stevie Porti, Robert, Peter, the priest, Pat, Jimmy Glynn & Pete Porti

PASQUALE

During the summer of 2008, I began spending a lot of time with Grandpa Pat. He loved to help with chores around the house, even as an octogenarian. My father always bragged about his father because, in his eighties, he was still mixing cement. In spite of their awkward relationship, there were things about Grandpa Pat that I know my dad was proud of. It was far more complex than the age-old line, "he gave me away." Anyway, there was a window well on the side of my house and there was a thin tree growing out of it. Grandpa Pat told me that he would come over and we would take care of it together. We took a ride over to Sears and we bought a small saw, since it was a very small area we had to work with. When we got back to my house, we had gotten pizza and then spent the afternoon sawing away at this tree for hours. I was sawing and Grandpa was pulling and all of the sudden the branch broke and Grandpa fell and ripped his pants. We sat on the grass "laughing like hell," as he would say. We got to the root of the problem and fourteen years later, the tree has still never grown back.

That afternoon, Grandpa Pat told me that his old friend, Johnny Morena, who had introduced him to Grandma Rose, was living in a camper on his son Michael's property in Medford, somewhere off of "Grandmother's Path." He wanted to go see him and wanted to know if I would like to go with him. Since he had been the man who introduced Grandpa to Rose, he thought I might like to meet him. I thought that would be fantastic and agreed to go with him the next day.

The next day, Grandpa again drove out to North Babylon for another adventure. Well, after driving for almost twenty years to my parents' house in Deer Park, he would get off the Southern State at Exit 39N, even though I lived blocks off of 39S, and drive the three miles to my parents' house because he knew where it was. Then I would meet him in front of my parents' house, even though they weren't home, and he would follow me the three and a half miles back to my house. Until he stopped driving out east on the highway almost a decade later, that was our ritual, no matter how many times I tried to convince him when he got off of the highway he was almost at my house.

On this particular afternoon, we headed out east and I told Grandpa that there was a Granny Road, but I had never heard of Grandmother's Path. "That's what Johnny told me," he insisted. We drove up and down North Ocean Avenue and were at a total loss as to where Johnny lived. Grandpa said let's drive up and down and look for a house with a camper. We had no luck. We passed the turn off where Grandma Rose's brother, Uncle Pete Porti, lived and we decided to go and see him and ask his advice about where Johnny might live.

Always so jovial, Uncle Pete was ecstatic when he came to the door and found us there. He invited us in and we sat with him at the kitchen table to chat. Of course, he remembered Johnny from years ago. "The little guy," Uncle Pete exclaimed. "I was Short Cut, and he was littler than me! So, he's still alive!"

Shortly after I had interviewed Grandpa in the beginning of 2008, I had called Uncle Pete and asked him if I could interview him for my book about my grandmother. He was so happy to be a part of my project and invited me to come to his house for dinner when we talked about his childhood and memories of Rose. With his pot of tomato sauce simmering on the stove with hardboiled eggs floating at the top, a Sicilian-style "gravy," as sauce is referred to among the old school Brooklyn people, Uncle Pete had gladly opened up about the history of his grandparents, the early lives of his parents, and his memories of Rose from early childhood until her passing. I was so grateful for his perspective, especially because he was only two years younger than my grandmother and they had lived through it all together.

Grandpa showed Uncle Pete the address and the old postal worker that he was gave us flawless directions for how to get to Johnny's son's house. Before we left, Uncle Pete said that the three of us should make a date and take a ride out to Mattituck to visit Cousin Rose Raia Suglia. I had first gone to see Cousin Rose with my parents and Robert in September of 1995. She was so warm and kind and her house on Rose Lane, which was built by her late husband, Vito, was like an enchanted cottage in the woods near the water. As my father and grandfather both shared the common trait of loving to tease, my father told Grandpa Pat that when she moved out to Mattitick there was no one there, so they named the street after Cousin Rose. Well, my father never told Grandpa Pat that he was kidding, so every time he would hear Grandpa telling someone, "You know, they named the street after Rose Raia," we would step out of the room laughing hysterical.

Rose told me from the minute that she met me that she saw Grandma Rose in my twinkling eyes. We formed a bond that would last for decades. She loved to share stories with me of Rose and of the history of the Porti family, as she was very close with the grandmother that she and my grandmother were named for, Rosina Nania Porti. Rose, whose actual name was Rosina, first showed me photographs of Grandma Rose's Porti grandparents, Pietro and Rosina. I will never forget seeing the photograph of Pietro Porti with his arched eyebrow, which passed down to my father. We had visited Cousin Rose a few times over the years and had taken Uncle Pete with us one time. As he got out of the car when we went with him shortly after my college graduation in 2000, he yelled to Rose, "Rosie, this is God's country!" There was no one like the irrepressible Uncle Pete and no one like the good natured and always warm Cousin Rose. Now, in August of 2008, Grandpa Pat and I made plans with Uncle Pete for the three of us to go see Cousin Rose. Grandpa had not seen her in so many years, in spite of his fond memories of her and her mother. He still had snapshots of her and Aunt Angelina from back in the summer of 1949 in his album. We said goodbye to Uncle Pete and promised to call him with a date, after I called Cousin Rose to see when was good for her.

We set out for Johnny Morena's, and lo and behold, there was the camper on the side of his son's house. Wearing a baseball cap and a striped golf shirt and shorts, Johnny Morena emerged from the trailer with a mischievous grin and naughty merriment in his eyes. "Ey, bum, you finally got here," he yelled at Grandpa Pat. Grandpa Pat immediately laughed, and that afternoon, I saw my grandfather for the first time as the naughty kid who bummed around with Johnny Morena making mischief. He introduced me to Johnny and we all went inside to sit with him in the camper.

Johnny regaled me with tales of Grandpa that I had never heard. He laughed like a little imp telling me about their Jewish girlfriends, Gladys Goldberg and Nora Schaefer. "Your grandfather hit Gladys in the face with pie because she wouldn't eat it," Johnny laughed. My grandfather protested that that had never happened. Then the story turned to Rose and Johnny proclaimed to have been in love with her and that Grandpa had stolen her. "She was engaged to Lenny," Grandpa protested once again. "What was she going to do with you? You were only up to her bust!" Johnny knew just the right buttons to push to get Grandpa's goat and he played the role flawlessly. While Grandpa liked to joke with everyone, the easy banter and feigned indignation they enacted with one another was different than any other interaction I had ever seen him have with anyone else. It was also interesting to see him refer so much to Rose with someone, since in all fairness he spent the better part of forty years of his life with Grandma Grace. But Johnny's friendship was a time capsule of the 1940's and very early 1950's and that's where their history and their reminiscences remained. Once again, while I went looking for Rose, I was finding Pat as well. The two old friends parted warmly and Grandpa laughed all the way back to North Babylon as he told his side of the story about Gladys and the true story of Johnny's role in his meeting Grandma Rose.

In keeping with memory lane that we were going down to remember Rose in the month of her eightieth birthday, I did call Cousin Rose and asked if it would be alright if Grandpa Pat, Uncle Pete and I came to visit her. She was so excited at the news, doubly so because she couldn't even guess how many years it had been since she last saw Grandpa Pat. Uncle Pete was thrilled as well and Grandpa drove out to me and we picked Uncle Pete up along the way. I remember we were driving down Sound Avenue in Wading River and Grandpa Pat started critiquing my driving, saying he didn't teach me to drive like that. I feigned insult and pulled over and told him he could walk to Rose Raia's house. He told that story for the rest of his life. We laughed the whole way there, with Uncle Pete telling story after story about Aunt Angelina and her family.

Pete Porti, Rose Raia Suglia, and Pat in 2008

Pat joking around at home in 2008

Rose had cold cuts for us laid out on the table for when we got there and she was so excited to see Grandpa Pat after so many years. Uncle Pete was so excited that he just couldn't stop talking. We started laughing because Rose said to Uncle Pete, "I haven't seen Pat in forever! Give him a chance to talk." Grandpa said, "My God, could Pete talk." We laughed so much. Rose took out some photographs when Grandpa reminisced with her about Vito and driving out to Montauk in his Model T Ford. She told him of the time that she remembered going with him, Grandma Rose and Johnny to a Drive-in movie and his holding my grandmother's hand the whole time. "I knew how much you liked my cousin that night," she said as she smiled. There was a wistfulness too as they remembered those bygone days, when the love of each of their lives were alive and young and the four of them together had countless hours of fun and filling the air with their laughter in those Selden summers. As we left that afternoon, Rose whispered to Grandpa, "Come back yourself without Pete next time, so we can talk!" We left that afternoon and Grandpa said, "It was so good to see Rose again. She was always such a wonderful lady. You know, she was very pretty when she was young! I got the pictures in my album!"

Three months after our month of honoring Rose, I was invited to play a game of Texas Hold'em on a Saturday night at the Wading River home of my friends, Deanna Baisley and Stavros Lilimpakis. It was a rouse for me to meet the friend of Stavros's sister, Shauna, who Shauna had attended nursing school with at Helene Fuld School of Nursing in Harlem. I had heard about this friend a year before at Deanna's father Brian's fiftieth birthday party, but nothing had materialized. In the meantime, I went on a few failed dates in the interim, and then once again, in September of 2008, when it was the birthday of Brian's wife, Janice, they began to mention Shauna's friend again. It was nighttime and we were sitting in the Cracker Barrel rocking chairs on the Baisley's front porch drinking wine when Janice said that they had to figure out who they know that I had to meet. Deanna had brought up Shauna's friend. I told them that I had heard about this nurse friend from Shauna at Brian's birthday party the year before, so I told Deanna to just let me know when and I would be there. It was weeks later, and I thought it had been forgotten, but the night was set for Saturday, November 1, 2008. I went to Kohl's to buy a black button-down shirt and new pair of khakis. When you are a bachelor, it is just easier to buy new rather than iron. That night, I sat at Deanna and Stavros's kitchen table with my eyes affixed on the kitchen door. I didn't want to forget a single moment of this night, hailing back to Grandpa Pat's story of sitting on Johnny's stoop. It was somewhere around eight o'clock and Shauna's friend arrived. She was beautiful with large, expressive eyes and red hair, but she was reserved and did not really make eye contact with me or even speak to me. I tried a few times during the game to strike up a conversation, which fell miserably flat. The only thing that we had established was that her cousin, Alda Martino, was a high school friend of mine, but when I asked how she was doing, all she said was "fine." When I saw that the conversation was going absolutely nowhere, I totally lost interest in the game and gladly lost. Impressively, it came down to Shauna's friend and one other coworker of hers, who in the end won. When I went back into the kitchen, Shauna's friend had left without saying goodbye and Deanna apologized for my having come out all that way for nothing. Then, Shauna came back into the house saying that her friend said that I could have her phone number. At this point I was insulted and said, "What, does she think she's doing me a favor?" Shauna was insistent that her friend wanted me to have her phone number. I reluctantly saved it in my phone. The friend's name was Vanessa Elizabeth Paula Kelsch.

The next day, I texted Vanessa and said that it was nice to have met her. She texted me back pretty promptly the same, and after that I had no intention of ever speaking to her again. It was a few days later and I was in between teaching classes of English at Shoreham-Wading River High School, when I received a text from Vanessa that she hoped that I was having a great day. I was stunned. I never expected to hear from her again. Later on, she would tell me that she was on the train to the city with her sister, Vicki, and her sister convinced her to text me. Thus began Vanessa and I texting back and forth for the next two days when I finally got the courage to ask her if she would like to go on a date.

It was Friday, November 7, 2008, and Vanessa and I had been texting back and forth all day. I got off of work and we were talking that night leading up to our first official date. She was hiding in the medicine closet at work to speak with me privately as we got to know one another. She mentioned during the conversation that she had twin brothers named Matthew and Michael. This completely took me aback. Four years before, I had been the teacher of Deanna Baisley's twin brothers, Matthew and Michael Baisley. At the end of their junior year, Matthew was diagnosed with Ewing's Sarcoma, a pediatric cancer that attacks bone and muscle. Matthew fought an incredible seventeen-month battle with the entire community standing behind him and I taught him his senior year of English at home. I developed an incredible bond with the entire Baisley family through the experience that extended far beyond graduation and continues until this very day. While I was single at the time, Matthew always teased me that he was going to find me a good woman. He died at the age of eighteen on November 15, 2004, only a few hours after Uncle Carmine on the same day. Now here I was, a week before the fourth anniversary of his passing, going on a date with a girl that his sister had introduced me to. And she had twin brothers with the same names to boot! When I left for Bellport to pick her up that night, I felt really hopeful and I said a quiet prayer to Matt to pull for me with this one. This wasn't going to be anything like our disastrous first meeting six days before!

Vanessa came running out the front door of her home and got in my car and we pulled away. Even in the dark as she got in, I was drawn to her large, luminous eyes. She laughed as she admitted to me that she hadn't told her family that she was going on a date. So unlike six days before, conversation was easy and I immediately noticed how beautiful she was when she smiled and laughed.

For our first date, we headed to Port Jefferson Village. After we parked, the village officer on duty came over to me immediately and Vanessa thought that our date was short lived and I was being arrested. The officer was a friend of the Baisley family, Jeff Campo, who had driven me back and forth to Sloan Kettering in Manhattan when Matthew was getting his treatments. Walking around the village together, we settled on a restaurant not too far from the water and had dinner. I secretly felt dizzy with excitement because I really liked being with Vanessa and silently prayed that she was the one.

As we walked around the village and talked that night, it was a few days before the full moon, but it looked so large and luminous in the sky. I mentioned to Vanessa how it reminded me of the movie *Moonstruck* and she smiled and said how much she loved that movie. As one of the movies I enjoyed seeing most again and again, we found our first thing we had in common.

When I brought Vanessa back home that night, I could feel the excitement between us. Although it was far from my first date that I had ever had, it wasn't like any of the ones that I had before. The following week it was pouring rain and we ended up at the Olympic Diner in Deer Park. She was graduating from Helene Fuld School of Nursing that week, but was embarrassed to invite me because we just started going out and she still didn't tell her family about me yet. It was the third date that clinched everything. This time, Vanessa and I went to Babylon Village to a restaurant called the Carriage House. While it was very loud and we had to scream to talk to one another, it was that night that she asked me if I would like to come over to her house for Thanksgiving brunch. I immediately said "yes" and she said that she would come over to my house for dessert. Later on, she told me that it was that night that she knew that I was the one she was going to marry.

Thanksgiving Day fell on November 27, 2008, and that morning, Vanessa tells me that she still didn't tell her father about me yet. With butterflies in my stomach, I drove to their house in Bellport, not knowing what to expect. When the door opened, I found out that Vanessa had just told her dad that I was coming. The house was abustle with activity, as the stove had something on each burner and Vanessa was making gluten-free pancakes, the first time that I ever heard of such a thing. Her mom, Vicki, was on the phone and both of Vanessa's twin brothers, Matthew and Michael, and later on her sister Vicki, came by with her friend. We all sat around the table and, although I was nervous, I felt welcomed and I looked at their faces and around this house and briefly thought to myself, will these be my in-laws? Will they be the grandparents of my children? Obviously, I kept my thoughts to myself, but in truth, all felt good with the world and it all felt right.

Later that evening, Vanessa came to meet my family and got lost on my parents' street, so I had to stand on the stoop to wave to her. She was so nervous to meet my family, but she received a warm welcome and not the Marie Barone from *Everybody Loves Raymond* treatment that we always teased my mother about. She just treated me like Raymond and never treated Vanessa like Debra. My brother, Robert, and I are never having more fun that when we are imitating our mother.

So now, we met the families and the holiday season was upon us. This was my second Christmas living alone in my own house in North Babylon. The Christmas of 2007, I decorated alone. This year, Vanessa was there to put up the tree with me and decorate the house. As I watched her decorate the tree, I hoped that this would be forever and she would never have to leave to go home again. Every time I saw her, every text that I received, I was determined to never let her go. I remember with previous girls that I had dated, I always felt that I was making a list of things I would have to put up with, get used to, or tolerate. Sometimes those things filled more than a page. I was thirty-years-old, older than anyone of my parents, grandparents, or great-grandparents had been for their first marriage. On his death bed, my Uncle Anthony told me that when I moved into his house, he wanted me to be married and have children running through the rooms. He regretted as he died that he had never had that and was adamant to me that he didn't want his life for me.

The weeks flew by and it was Christmas week and time to meet The Franzeses. We took Vanessa to Brooklyn for Christmas Eve at Aunt Jennie's in Bay Ridge, and afterward, to midnight mass at Saint Matthew's Church in Dix Hills. She had to work on our first actual Christmas together. On one of her days off that week, we went to Baldwin so she could meet my legendary Grandpa Pat. As always, Grandpa was charming and kidding around and won over Vanessa's heart immediately.

We had an amazing Christmas week together, spending two days exploring New York City, going on the aircraft carrier the Intrepid with childhood friends of Vanessa's and then running into students of mine on the line for the Empire State Building. As the year that we met drew to a close, we both knew in our hearts that each of us was "the one."

Three months after that first date, it was Saturday, February 7, 2009, which happened to be Lorenzina's 120th birthday. I had decided during the holidays that Vanessa was the one who I wanted to marry. I knew that I had Vanessa's mother, Vicki's, blessing because she called me in January and asked me if I was planning to ask Vanessa to marry me. I told her that I was going to and she knew that I was the one Vanessa was going to marry. She suggested Valentine's Day, but I wanted Vanessa to have a date that was all her own.

My mother's sister, Aunt Susan Boniface, found out that I planned to ask Vanessa to marry me and said she was coming on a plane to New York and that she was going to be giving me the engagement ring that Grandpa Bob had given to Nana Nettie. Nana Nettie was the most incredible woman to ever touch my life and in 2004 I had published her life story entitled, *Nettie: Tales of a Brooklyn Nana*. Aunt Sue wanted to give me the ring for my marriage to be blessed by the love of Nana and Grandpa.

The scene was set and both my family and Vanessa's conspired with me. Vanessa's mother invited my family over for dessert on that Saturday night. I was bringing the cake. What Vanessa didn't know was what was on the cake. After everyone greeted one another and settled in, I said, "I forgot the cake in the car," and ran to the trunk. Smiling, I knew this was our moment and I was on. I walked into the house, opened the white cardboard lid, and called Vanessa over to inspect the cake. In chocolate icing and in pink script, she read, "Vanessa, will you marry me?" I got on my knee and produced the ring that had ties to my favorite love story and was ready to give it another chapter with the love story of my own. Vanessa cried and said "yes" and my father started opening the bottles of the Verdi champagne that he loves. How lucky we were to be surrounded by our parents, my brother, Vanessa's brother, Mike, and my Aunt Susan. We could have gone to the top of the Empire State building or a secluded beach, but at the heart of Vanessa and I will always be family and home. So, in the home where all of her life story had played out thus far, from when she was a toddler on, I proposed marriage there in her living room with both of our families to see. It was the beginning of another Franzese love story… from Pietro and Lorenzina, to Pat and Rose, to Peter and AnnMarie, to US.

We were engaged for seventeen months, but on July 17, 2009, we had our engagement party at Papa Joe's Restaurant in Deer Park. Surrounded by our family and some very close friends, and the DJ we had selected to play at our wedding, Brett Jacob, we celebrated our love on the same day that we were to be married the following year. I was so thrilled that Grandpa Pat was there to see me be engaged and I prayed that he would be there to see the milestones to come.

While the year between was filled with the endless wedding preparations, how quickly we found that the year 2010 rolled in and the months fly by from January to July. Our venue was settled on, the church was booked, the priest was coming, the flowers and photographers were ready, our wedding party was bedecked in Vanessa's choices, and the honeymoon awaited us.

Saturday, July 17, 2010, was such a gorgeous day. The sun was ablaze and there were no clouds in the azure sky. As I put on my tux, I realized how after a lifetime of thumbing through the wedding albums of my parents and grandparents, this was my time. I imagined Vanessa at her house and wondered what she was feeling and could not wait to see how she looked. My brother, Robert, was my best man, and one of my ushers was Michael Baisley, my once student, and then forever friend. We had a history and, in my heart, Matthew, the mastermind behind all of this when he was alive, had to be there with us getting ready too. My parents drove Robert and I to Saint Matthew's Church in Dix Hills, where we were to be married, and Msgr. Greg Wielunski, my father's lifelong best friend from Calyer Street, the priest who had baptized me as an infant, was giving me the enormous honor of saying the mass and bestowing on us the sacrament of matrimony. How blessed I was to see sitting in the pew his mother, my Grandma Josie's dearest friend, Marie, and his sister, Barbara. When Marie hugged and kissed me, she kissed me twice and said to me, that one was from Grandma.

How much I missed having Grandma Josie and Grandpa Sammy at my wedding, and here, her beautiful friend gave me the sign that Grandma Josie really was there.

As I stood on the altar with Robert at my side, I was exhilarated, emotional, and nervous as hell. In the video you can hear me emotional and giggling second by second. When I looked out at the pews, how daunting to see a person who represented every key moment of my life. My aunts and uncles were all there assembled, some cousins, my friend from kindergarten, Jaime Laura, and her mom, Debby, my college professor, Ellen Frisina, coworkers, students, and the entire Baisley family who had been instrumental in making my dreams come true.

I saw Grandpa Pat slip in the back door and felt so moved knowing that my grandfather had lived to be at my side to celebrate this day. Leaning heavily on Dad's arm, Mom walked down the aisle resplendent in a salmon-colored sequined gown and it brought tears to my eyes how amazing they looked and how close we had come to not having Mom walk down that aisle only four years before. God is good. I hope her story inspires people to not lose faith and believe in miracles.

The doors opened and under the clock I saw my bride on the arm of her dad, Ken Kelsch, clutching a bouquet of yellow and white roses. My nerves got the best of me, as I felt tears in my eyes, my heart race, and the nervous sensation that made me giggle. Her strapless white gown was magnificent and I remember those large eyes filled with excitement as she made her way down the aisle smiling the entire time. Her tiara and the lace veil made her look like a fairy princess. Everyone always has that lifelong dream. As a small child laying at night with a pile of hardcover Disney books, I decided that I wanted to marry Cinderella, and here was my Cinderella, and the beginning of our happily ever after.

In a mass where we both honored our love and those who were not alive to be there, among others, we mentioned Grandma Rose and Grandma Josie and Grandpa Sammy. All of their lives and all of their stories had inspired me and I asked them to be blessed as I hoped they would be blessing me from above. From the church, we headed to Argyle Park in Babylon Village for our portraits with our immediate family and our wedding party. Grandpa Pat was with us, and when we took our Franzese family portrait, Grandpa was standing right beside me. We took so many family shots before our portraits alone, but I truly treasured taking the photos of Grandpa Pat, Dad, and I. Three generations of Franzese men and I had them with me to celebrate my marriage. To pay homage to Rose, Vanessa and I took pictures looking out of the back window of the Rolls Royce that was taking us to our reception, just like Grandpa Pat and Grandma Rose had done.

From Argyle Park, we drove along the Sunrise Highway to our reception at Sunset Harbor in East Patchogue, New York. Along the way, Vanessa and I laughed as we drank champagne and cars honked at us in congratulations. The setting of our wedding was a secluded spot on the water, with a magnificent vista of the water and a dock where we took our portrait kissing as the sun set between us. Three generations of our families watched us dance and laugh and celebrate our love. We walked into the reception to the theme of *Star Wars* and

Pat with Peter's family on Peter & Vanessa's wedding day, July 17, 2010

PASQUALE

Pat with Peter on his wedding day

I held a lightsaber high, thanks to a gift from my former students, Bobby Reilly and Joe Tricarico. My parents sat with Grandpa Pat, Aunt Susan, Don, my godfather, Joe Rizza, and our family doctor, Harry Jacob, and his wife, Marion, as Dr. Jacob's son, Brett, was back in the DJ's booth as the master of ceremonies making all of the music we selected work and the night a magical night for the both of us. I danced with my mother to the *Godfather Waltz*, thanks to an inspiration that I had gotten from my Aunt Theresa's daughter, Cousin Rosalie Accardi Kinstel, when she danced at her wedding with her father, Uncle Lou, in 1997. I had always said after that when I got married that was my song with Mom.

Two days after the wedding, Vanessa and I went on our honeymoon to Secrets Maroma Beach, an all-inclusive couples' resort that was an absolute paradise on the outskirts of Cancun. The pools, the beaches, the tiki bar, and the outstanding restaurants, where our love affair with Hibachi began. We also loved exploring and going snorkeling in a cave and so many magical moments that are perfect when you first say "I do" and before real life once again begins. When we returned after a week in Mexico, we fulfilled another dream we both had, which was to explore Chicago. A distant cousin of mine, Pier Davide Luppino, was visiting from his home in Campobello di Mazzara, Trapani, Italy, and we had so much fun as he was our tour guide showing us the city.

It was August 2010, and we returned to our lives, but my house was now a home and it was no longer filled with loneliness, but love. How incredible to have my wife there always. My dream came true that Vanessa wouldn't have to leave ever again. I enjoyed having not a house but a home where I could invite my family for dinners and barbecues and anticipated the day when we became parents. Life was happening and life was exciting and busy, so although I still called and saw Grandpa Pat pretty often, I was living my own story for now before I returned to the computer to continue telling his story.

It was in the afternoon on Christmas Eve, December 24, 2011, when a phone call came regarding the blood test that Vanessa had taken that confirmed the hopes of our biggest dream. She was going to have a baby! Vanessa and I were crying and leaping for joy and could have never imagined a more spectacular Christmas gift in our lives. We went to the store and bought two baby bottles and wrapped them. First, we went to my parents' house and gave it to my mother as my father looked on. She was stunned to silence before the tears when she found out that they were going to be grandparents. We did the same thing that night when we had Christmas Eve dinner with Vanessa's parents, Ken and Vicki, and her sister, Vicki. A new generation and a new chapter of our lives was about to begin. I was so excited to call Grandpa Pat and tell him the incredible news. In the Franzese line, there had never been a Franzese male who had lived to see his great-grandchild. At eighty-four, he was excited and amazed.

Pat with Peter & Vanessa on Easter Sunday 2012

    Vanessa's parents, Ken and Vicki, hosted Easter Sunday dinner on Sunday, April 8, 2012, and invited my parents and brother, Robert, as well as Grandpa Pat. We were all filled with the excitement and anticipation that in a few short months that our child, grandchild, and great-grandchild would be here. Grandpa sat next to me at dinner, as he always did, and we laughed and talked all day and took pictures until he said, "Isn't that enough?" And we ended up making plans that the next day we would spend the day together again and go to Brooklyn.

    The following day, I drove to Baldwin to pick him up and we headed toward the city. The first stop would always be Calvary Cemetery. For decades he went to visit the Franzese grave weekly, but now that his siblings were all gone and his reason for driving to Brooklyn no longer existed, he only got to go to Calvary Cemetery when he went with me. His memory of all the different relatives and friends was flawless. First, we got off the highway at 48th Street and stopped to see my mother's parents' grave, Nana Nettie and Grandpa Bob, and her Aunt Rosie Carrano. Then we went to the other side to see, "the first wife and the baby." Grandpa was referring to his father's first wife, Carmela Nunziata Franzese, who died in 1908, as well as his infant sister who he never knew, who died in 1912. The first time that I remember him showing me this grave was on the 100th anniversary of Carmela's death, December 30, 2008. There was a monument over their grave that just said Franzese. We walked up and down the row until we spotted it. He was the grave whisperer. He always found them. We then continued on to Greenpoint Avenue and drove through the majestic main gate of the cemetery. As I was ready to drive down the hill, Grandpa told me to pull over. When his mother, Lorenzina, was alive, she always told him to pull over by this certain path because she used to go to visit the grave of her sister, Concetta Nunziata Caliendo. He decided that he wanted to find it. I followed him down this path, as he walked fast—a man on a mission. Looking intently at each stone, he stopped and yelled, "here's my aunt!" And there was the grave of Aunt Concetta and her family. He found it so effortlessly, even though he had not been in this spot since at least 1962. Back in the car we went, and down the hill, where the enormous Johnston monument loomed and the plot of land where Don Vito Corleone's funeral scene was shot in the 1972 film, *The Godfather*, was just a few yards away. Once again, Grandpa yelled to stop. This time, he had to go see the uncle he was named for, Uncle Patsy Franzese, who died in 1952. The fondness he had for the old man and the memories of Christmas Eve clearly flashed through his mind as he smiled and said, "My uncle was crazy about me. He was so proud that I was named after him." After a quick prayer, well, I said a prayer. I was never completely sure what Grandpa Pat was doing when he stood there staring at the stone with his hands in his pockets. Was he just forlornly remembering those buried there or saying a silent prayer? Only he knew and I wasn't going to ask. Once again, we were back in the car to drive the few feet to section 4B, where most of the rest of the family was buried. First, Grandpa Sammy and Grandma Josie's grave. When he would go to their grave, interestingly enough, he would only tell a story about Josie and his visits to Calyer Street, but never about Sammy. I always found interesting what he did not tell in addition to what he told. There was definitely something complicated there as he stood at the grave of the people who had raised his son for him. A few

PASQUALE

yards down was where his mood would turn somber, the big Franzese grave where his parents were buried, Sal, Margie, the Glynns, and Rose. The monument is divided in the middle by a large sculpture of the Sacred Heart and Grandpa Pat always stood to the right side, in front of Rose's name. I watched him each time from a few steps away. He would get this same somber look each time he went, and yet, he was upset when a very long time passed that he did not stand on this plot of land. "You know, we haven't taken a ride to the cemetery in quite a while," he would say to me. That's when I knew that I had to figure out my schedule and make it happen. From there, he would stop two graves down and see his Aunt Virginia Spizio and her family, then we walked a few rows back and then it was to his Grandma and Grandpa Nunziata, Salvatore and Angelina, who were also buried with his Uncle Larry Nunziato and his Aunt Rose Annunziato and some of their family. Then, it was a long trek to the way back of the section, which was dark from the line of trees there. There was one more grave to pay our respects at in Section 4B. A single, tall monument, dull and gray, bore the names of two Franzese women who he would never let be forgotten. One was his Grandma Franzese, Michela, and his Uncle Patsy's wife, Aunt Anna. He had no remembrance of the grandmother who had died when he was not much over the age of two-years-old, but he honored her memory every time he came here and had named his daughter, Michele, after he and Grandma Grace visited the grave when Grandma Grace was pregnant with her in 1967. It was then the long walk back to the car across a large, empty field, which I found out one time was a mass grave for the Spanish Influenza of 1918. On the way out of the cemetery, we turned the corner and stopped at the grave of the oldest brother, Uncle Carmine, and his wife, Aunt Hope. Grandpa Pat and Uncle Carmine, the oldest and the youngest, had a deeply loving and deeply tumultuous relationship for their entire lives. As we left through the Greenpoint Avenue gate of Calvary Cemetery and made the left onto Greenpoint Avenue, we were headed for spending a day where his story began.

When we got to Frost Street, we were lucky enough to get a parking spot across the street from 243 Frost Street, which was the last house where his parents had lived, where his two sisters also had lived, and where his nephew, Jimmy Glynn, currently resided. After parking the car, Grandpa Pat and I walked across the street, opening the latch of the short black fence, went up the stoop and rang the bell. Jimmy greeted us and we followed him down the hallway that opens up into the kitchen. We chatted for a few minutes and Grandpa looks at me and says, "Why don't we go take a walk and get some cold cuts or something? It's lunch time." We told Jimmy that we were just going to take a walk up Graham Avenue and be back in just a little bit. Now the one thing that has not changed in the century of my family living on Frost Street is that you cannot walk from the corner of Kingsland Avenue and up to Graham Avenue without constantly running into relatives or lifelong friends. Only a few yards into our journey, Grandpa Pat saw his first cousins, the Nunziatos in front of their house: Carmela and Johnny Nunziato and Josephine Nunziato Viola. They were so excited at the sight of Grandpa that they refused to hear about us going up to Graham Avenue to get lunch, we HAD to come in their house and visit with them. We followed Cousin Carmela up the long staircase to her second-floor apartment, and all of us sat around her kitchen table. She started opening her refrigerator and was warming up this and taking out that while she made sure that we each had a cup of coffee. As we sat there and chatted with his cousins, my grandfather smiled as he looked at me and said, "Imagine, I'm sitting in my grandmother's kitchen all these years later with my grandson." It was then that I learned that Carmela Nunziato's apartment had been the apartment where Salvatore and Angelina Nunziata had lived in the early years of the century. Cousin Johnny brought up old photographs from his apartment, where his mother, Aunt Mary Nunziato, had lived until her death in 1987. I have vague memories of Aunt Mary, who Grandpa's sister Aunt Margie referred to as, "Aunt Mary with the red hair." When I met her, I couldn't understand why, since they should have called her, "Aunt Mary with the white hair." I also wondered if there was an "Aunt Mary with the brown hair." I never did find another Aunt Mary in the Franzese/Nunziata family.

While we had told Jimmy that we would be right back, every time Grandpa started to say goodbye to his cousins, Carmela took something else out of her refrigerator. Coffee and cake became lunch…and then she decided we just had to stay for dinner. By the time Grandpa and I left that house, it was well past seven and it was starting to get dark outside. Grandpa started laughing and said, "We better get to Jimmy's before he goes to bed. You think he'll still let us in after we told him we'd be right back?" Jimmy let us back in and we had a short visit before we headed back to Long Island after the sun had gone down. Grandpa and I laughed all the way home about how our day went completely different than the one we had expected, but that is the magic that still existed when you returned to Greenpoint-Williamsburg. Grandpa had left that block over fifty years before, but like they say in the theme song of the TV sitcom, *Cheers*, everyone still knew his name, and, yes, they were all still glad that he came.

Shortly before my daughter's birth, we had the heartbreaking loss of Grandma Rose's brother, Uncle Pete Porti, on Father's Day, June 17, 2012, at the age of eighty-one. Uncle Pete had been battling cancer and the entire family had assembled at his home in Coram to sit vigil as we leaned on one another for support, reminisced about our family legend, and mourned the passing of time. He was a man who had a heart of gold and had worked hard to not only make a better life for his wife and children, but also for his siblings. It was because of Uncle Pete's support and help when anyone in his family was down on their luck that the family had survived. As I said my goodbye to him in his bedroom the day before his passing, I pictured that good-natured man with the enthusiasm of a kid and incredible warmth. I was so grateful for the conversations that we had about the family, as he was now becoming part of the legend. Grandpa Pat was so sad to yet say goodbye to another of the Porti brothers, as they had rekindled their relationship over the past few years. I can still hear the two of them "laughing like hell" in the car together. His passing conjured up many memories for Grandpa about Rose and it was while we were sitting alone that he began reminiscing about a couple that were very close friends of his and Grandma Rose's throughout their short marriage. I had seen photographs of them taken on Easter Sunday 1950, but didn't know any more about them other than the woman had been a coworker of Rose at the Eagle Pencil Company. "Their names were Walter and Kay," Grandpa said. "She was a beautiful blonde, and he was a big, husky, handsome guy. They were wonderful people. He came to the hospital to give me blood when I had my ulcers." I was intrigued by the intensity of his memories of them. I never realized before that they had meant so much to him. He had no idea what had happened to them after Rose died, other than that Walter had left the Department of Sanitation and became a New York City police officer. I asked him if he remembered their last name, and without the slightest hesitation, he said, "Okpych!"

I was then determined to find out if Walter and Kay were still alive and if I was able to find out what had happened to them. After an internet search, I located a woman named Kristine Okypch Marks, and everything I found seemed to point out that she might be a child of Walter and Kay. After I sent her a note, she promptly responded that she was Walter and Kay's daughter and she was eager to speak with me on the phone.

Walter Okpych passed away from a massive heart attack while out shopping with Kay on December 4, 1971, leaving behind two children, Kristine, and her brother, Walter. He was only fifty-one-years-old. Kay had passed away on April 4, 2004, at the age of seventy-six. Grandpa Pat was deeply moved that the young, vibrant couple whose memory he cherished and whose photographs that he had kept all of those years in his photo album were gone. Two years later, I finally got Grandpa Pat and Kris to connect when I was in his apartment showing him an envelope full of pictures she had sent of Walter and Kay on April 7, 2014. It was really awesome seeing Grandpa Pat light up as he talked on the phone with Kris and shared with her his cherished memories of her beloved parents, the friends who stayed so fresh in his memory. Two years later, Grandpa was very saddened when we learned from Kris that her brother, Walter Okpych, passed away at the age of sixty from a heart attack while on vacation in Florida on February 29, 2016. While he had hoped to find his friends alive on this journey, he couldn't believe that he was hearing about the death of their son.

CHAPTER THIRTEEN

Victoria's Pa Pat

2012-2019

The light of our lives came shining into our world at 4:36 a.m., on Thursday, August 30, 2012, with the arrival of Victoria Rose Franzese, coming in at 6 lbs. 11 oz. and 19 1/2" long. She was born at Saint Catherine of Siena Medical Center in Smithtown, New York. The four proud grandparents arrived by the afternoon to see the new princess who was born. The following night, I was moved when Grandpa Pat walked into the room and the excitement in his face at the sight of his first great-grandchild. As I sat next to him and

Pat with Peter and Victoria Rose on the day after her birth, August 31, 2012

Four generations of the Franzese's.
Peter, Peter Michael holding Victoria, and Pat
September 2, 2012

held Victoria in my arms, he caressed her head as his eyes filled with incredible love. Due to his gnarled hands from all of those years working the machines at Brooklyn Box Toe, he was afraid to hold a baby so small at that time, but relished being so close to her. When I told him that Victoria had been named Victoria Rose, he was thrilled that I had honored my late grandmother in my daughter's name. His beautiful Rose of long ago would live on in their great-granddaughter.

Three days after Victoria was born and nestled safely at home with us in North Babylon, the four generations of Franzeses came together for the first time. Sitting in the middle of my living room couch with Victoria nestled in my arms, my father sitting at my right and Grandpa Pat sitting at my left, we smiled for our first four-generation Franzese photo. Grandpa was celebrating his eighty-fifth birthday and my father was celebrating his sixty-second. The excitement that filled me that I had them both at each side of me and that we had accomplished something great. Next to my grandfather on the end table, was the portrait of Rose from their wedding that Fontana had had in his window all those years ago. Grandpa Pat looked at me and said, "Imagine, I'm here with our great-grandchild and she didn't even barely get to see her son." It moved him that he sat there with this little infant that was a great-grandchild that he had never in his wildest dreams imagined that he would live to see.

Only two months after Victoria's birth, Long Island was blasted with a storm like it had never endured before—Super Storm Sandy. In the days leading up to its landing on Long Island, I begged Grandpa Pat to pack up his stuff and stay with me, as where he lived in Baldwin Harbor was in the line of the devastation. At eighty-five-years-old, as loving and fun as my grandfather was is how equally stubborn he could be. He refused to come and stay with me and refused to leave the house. I just told him to pack up all of his pictures and stuff that meant a lot to him and get it all into the attic. Luckily, he listened at least to that, as his entire ground level apartment in his son's house, that of my Uncle Paul, was filled with three feet of water. Grandpa complained that he was sleeping in a sleeping bag on the floor like he was back in the army, but he refused to leave, in spite of the house not having any electricity or heat and feet of water below swirling around in the rooms that he called home.

In spite of the storm, Victoria's baptism took place on Saturday, November 10, 2012, in the chapel of Ss. Cyril & Methodius Church in Deer Park, New York. Msgr. Greg Weilunski, along with his mother, Marie, and sister, Barbara, had made the trip from Brooklyn. Marie nestled Victoria in her arms and kissed her like she had me on my wedding day and said it was from Grandma Josie.

Victoria's four grandparents were present, my brother, Robert, was her godfather and Vanessa's sister, Vicki, was her godmother, but due to the devastation and personal loss that Grandpa Pat and Uncle Paul's family had endured, Grandpa Pat was unable to attend Victoria's christening. The impact of Super Storm Sandy did not just leave him with the devastating loss of personal items, but a disruption for a while of his routine, his way of life, and the loss of some artifacts that were touchstones for him of his past. Although most people would not understand, he was very upset that in the flood he had lost the famous *Monopoly* game that he had played with Uncle Tommy in the Jackson Street apartment in Brooklyn all of those years ago. For him, it was like the loss of an old, lifelong friend. Luckily, all of the photographs that he treasured were saved.

Grandpa Pat came on Palm Sunday, March 24, 2013, to my parents' home in Deer Park to spend the day with us and connect with his great-granddaughter. It was the first time that I had seen Grandpa since the devastation and it was so good to be together again. It was very sad not to be able to see one another for the holidays for the first time ever, but Grandpa said not to come just yet. How awesome to see him come alive when he held Victoria in his arms and he bent down on the floor to her level to play with her. The delight in his smile as he held his nearly seven-month-old great-granddaughter melted my heart. He delighted at seeing her when she was a newborn, but I saw them develop a permanent bond that day.

As the years began to go by, the bond between Victoria and Grandpa grew stronger and stronger, and, truth be told, so did the bond between Grandpa and I. Grandpa never missed a single one of Victoria's birthdays, and the time he took to send the most meaningful and heartfelt birthday and Christmas cards with a twenty-dollar bill tucked in, always warmed my heart. The conversations on the phone stopped being only once in a while. The visits stopped being only a few times a year and became adventures that were very often ones that we would never forget. Instead of just sitting at his kitchen table and drinking Carlo Rossi, we got in the car and went places. He wasn't a feeble and sedentary grandfather. He was full of life and always down for an adventure. As Victoria grew and I had made the transition from being a high school English teacher to finishing my schooling to becoming a licensed funeral director, life began to settle down for me once again, and it was time to focus more on listening to the stories that only Grandpa Pat could share. As he approached his ninetieth birthday, the grim reality could no longer be put off. The time to record the stories was now. The grains of the hour glass were running out. But, the stories did not have to be told from his reclining chair. He was very eager to show me the places, walk in the footsteps of his younger self, pass the stoops he knew so well, especially the ones where he once sat and the sight of a certain woman had stopped his heart and changed the course of his life. Every time

Pat, Victoria and Peter Michael on August 30, 2016

Pat and Victoria play ball on August 30, 2016

that I visited with my grandfather, as I approached forty and he approached ninety, I continued to discovered something even more profound about him.

In this life we never know how long we will have the ones we love, so it was incredibly important to me that Victoria spend as much time with her grandparents as possible. Unlike my wife and

I, Victoria had four living grandparents when she was born, all of whom were very active in her life. In addition to that, she also had one living great-grandparent as well. I tried to bring them together as often as possible. I was off on New Year's Day 2016, so Vanessa and I invited our parents to come celebrate, as well as my brother, Robert, my cousin, Jennifer Flugger, and Grandpa Pat. Grandpa had driven out to my house, and after dinner and conversation and pictures, which included one that I was big on taking, Victoria with her parents, grandparents, and great-grandpa all together, the sun was starting to go down and Grandpa wanted to get home. As he drove home that night westbound on the Southern State Parkway, he said the headlights going east really bothered his eyes and he was very nervous getting home. It was then that I made the decision that in the future I would be picking up Grandpa Pat myself. He was eighty-eight years old and if I wanted him to spend the time at my house, I would go to get him.

It was shortly after New Year's 2016 that I went to learn how to embalm during my funeral directing residency, and the gentlemen at Taglia, Lysak, and Co. in Lynbrook, New York, were good enough to have their embalmers show me their craft and share with me their incredible expertise in embalming. One embalmer in particular, Joe Gallipani, took me under his wing and became my mentor and one of my closest friends practically overnight. It's always amazing how a person can be a stranger at the beginning of your day, and by time you go home, feel like they have been one of your best friends since you were born. That's just how it was for me with Joe on that January 12, 2016, when I first walked into the embalming room with him. After a day of learning so much from Joe, Grandpa Pat was only a few miles away and was waiting for me after my first day of "embalming school" to have dinner with him. He made chicken cutlets and vegetables and mashed potatoes all by himself. There were two short glasses on the table and the Carlo Rossi Burgundy jug was waiting to be poured. He was in the middle of cooking when I walked through the door. "Do you want a glass of wine?" Grandpa loved his wine, but he loved to share it as much as he enjoyed it. I wasn't planning on leaving any time soon, and at this stage of my life, I really enjoyed sitting at Grandpa's table with him drinking a glass of wine and just talking about everything between the past and the present. I just watched him work before we were ready to eat, and he wouldn't allow any help. You couldn't throw off his routine. What was even more impressive was how delicious everything was, and sipping the wine, we had really come to be in a comfortable groove with one another. Although I never lived with him, after a long day at work, it was nice to come home to Grandpa's home-cooked meal.

After dinner was completed and the dishes were done, because a dish or a spoon never rested in his sink for long, we went to sit in the living room. As Grandpa Pat sits in his reclining chair in the ground floor apartment in the home of his youngest child, the image of the girl he loved so long ago is present in every room. She had not been his first love, nor his last, yet the two years that they spent together played and replayed in his eighty-eight-year-old head over and over, like the old films on Turner Classic Movies. Like those films too, the print has not faded, the dialogue and her voice remain strong for him. For the rest of us, she only lives through his retelling of her stories accompanying the old black and white snapshots that she left behind. For Grandpa, Rose is as vibrant as when Dorothy steps out of the black and white world of Uncle Henry and Auntie Em's house into the vibrant world of colors awaiting her in Munchkinland. For me, she is a legend.

"Rose was the backbone of the Porti family. She was the oldest, the big sister. I loved her very much. I went through a lot of hell and high water to win her over. To have something like that for so short a time after you worked so hard to get it is hard to accept. She liked me, but she didn't love me at the time. I told her to give me time. Then she was going with me to Coney Island, she was going Upstate. I was taking her out. She would go to the movies. We would go to restaurants to eat. She worked in the pencil factory and she hung around the candy store all night long with her old fiancé, but they never did anything together. Sometimes he used to leave her in charge of the store. Things weren't working out between them. They seen that she was always sad. And she had my shoulder to cry on, and after a while, I told her 'You gotta do something here.' I had to tell her how I felt and see what I had to do. And when she turned me down, I figured, let me wash my hands of this."

That was far from the end of their story. You might ask, what can you say about this woman sixty-six years after she died? What did Grandpa Pat teach me? Plenty.

Every few months, I would take a ride to Baldwin in the late morning when Victoria was at school and spend a few hours with my grandfather talking and visiting in his apartment. I would sit on his couch and he would sit in his recliner as the stories of the past tumbled out. When we weren't talking about the past, he would inquire and listen intently about what was happening with Victoria or Vanessa or my job, or I would listen to his angsts and complaints that were the price of living a long time. "My doctor says that I'm gonna live a long time," he would say. "I already lived a long time!" Before I would leave to head back home for Victoria, Grandpa would always say, "Let's go take a ride for a frankfurter." Right near his house, parked on the side of the road, we would pull up right behind the hot dog truck. We would get three between us, him only eating one, the reason that his wife, Grandma Grace, referred to him as the "skinny guinea." Grandpa loved hot dogs from the truck. He may have not eaten many when he did, but he truly enjoyed them. I thought about how he always talked about getting hot dogs on Coney Island with Rose, and here we were, generations later, still doing the same thing. Life is good.

The beautiful Victoria Rose turned four years old on August 30, 2016. My daughter was resplendent in her white party dress with beading in the front and a white sash tied in a bow at her waist, as she emerged into our back yard to celebrate with her family. Besides her parents, she had all four of her grandparents, her great-grandpa, both of her godparents, great-aunts and great-uncles, her great-great aunt and uncle, Stevie and Diana Porti, and her cousin, Joni Pisano Roderka, the great-granddaughter of Grandpa Pat's Aunt Virginia Spizio. The scene that touched me the most that day was as I was busy running around with Vanessa, making sure that everything was going well with all of our guests, I saw Grandpa Pat and Victoria walk to the back of the yard and play catch. Here he was, six days shy of his eighty-ninth birthday, laughing and playing ball with his great-granddaughter. I stopped what I was doing and grabbed the camera. I never even laid eyes on any of my great-grandparents. This was a moment to treasure for the rest of our lives. Later on, my brother Robert took a picture of Victoria with Grandpa Pat and I. Victoria put her arms around the two of us and gave us the biggest smile as the three of us had our heads together. It will always be the picture of the three of us that I will cherish most. Then, my father came over and Robert took another photo of the four generations together. Every year we tried to take this photo all together at least once or twice. We have a treasury of photos of Victoria growing bigger alongside her Franzese lineage.

It was Christmastime 2016 and you try to figure out, what can you buy your eighty-nine-year-old grandfather for Christmas? He loved the home-made gifts he received from Victoria, but when it came to me and I showed up with a gallon of Carlo Rossi Burgundy for him, he would yell, "Don't buy me anything! Save your money. These are hard times for everybody." He says this in spite of sending my wife, my daughter, and I each a separate Christmas card with a twenty dollar bill tucked inside. For the over twenty years since Grandma Grace had died and he had been on his own, not one birthday or Christmas had gotten by him.

It was four days before Christmas 2016 and I had decided on the Christmas gift that my grandfather could not object to. All it would cost me was my time…time for making memories. I called him and offered to pick him up to spend a day just the two of us and return once again to where his story began. He never came as alive as when he was back walking those old sidewalks, running into relatives, smiling and telling his stories as we passed the homes of friends who were long gone, and in spite of the pain it caused, it was very meaningful for him because of the passion he felt when we drove through the gates of Calvary Cemetery to honor his family.

When I rang the doorbell on the house, Grandpa was all ready to go on our adventure ahead. He was dressed in a red plaid shirt and khakis with a black buttoned sweater. He put on his heavy black coat and he was ready to go. He got in the car and we headed for the Southern State Parkway and talked about his different memories of relatives long gone as we drove. As we turned onto Greenpoint Avenue, it is a difficult merge into the extreme right lane. A tractor trailer pulled out in front of us and Grandpa goes to me, "Don't fight with him. He's too big!" Then a smaller car was trying to merge with us and then he goes, "Knock him on his ass!" So much for him criticizing my driving! Finally, we make the left hand turn into Calvary Cemetery, and as I drive around the statue of the crucifixion to head down the hill, I said to Grandpa, "We went down this road in our lives more than a couple of times."

"Oh my God," Grandpa said. "I used to come here every other Sunday and I used to leave here and go see your father when he lived on Calyer Street."

As we turned past the Johnston Mausoleum, I said, "Aunt Millie would have been a hundred last month."

"A hundred? Really? She died when she was ninety."

"Yeah, in June she will be gone ten years."

"Ten years? Really? Wow. Slow down because Uncle Pat is over here someplace. Here. It's right here."

We got out of the car to pay our respects and he laughed that one time he came with Uncle Paul and Uncle Paul didn't like seeing "Pasquale Franzese" on a tombstone, so he walked away and went back to the car. Then we stopped at Grandpa Sammy and Grandma Josie. Then we pulled up to the big grave. The next day would be the sixty-sixth anniversary of Rose's death.

"Rose was eleven months younger than me," Grandpa said. "With Grace, I robbed the cradle," he said with a laugh. As he stood in front of the grave, he pointed out the position of where each of his nine family members were in the plot. It was something very important to him to know where each individual person was. Although this grave was very important to him, Calvary Cemetery would not ever be his final resting place. His family were all together, but Grandma Grace was by herself in Greenfield Cemetery, and he would never leave her by herself when he left this world.

"If I wouldn't have thrown up blood in front of Rose, she never would have died. It was all from the aggravation of Brooklyn Box

Toe. I should have never accepted the position. Imagine you have me running the floor upstairs and then expect me to buy all those separate lunches for all those people. I quit him a few times and even my mother got involved and Carmine told her to stay out of it." Grandpa would hold a deep resentment toward Brooklyn Box Toe and Uncle Carmine as his boss, not as his brother, for the rest of his life. "I lost my wife and nearly lost my own life because of that place," he finished.

Then Grandpa turned to look on the hill that faces the Franzese grave and said, "The soldiers were up there when Sal died. They shot off the rifles and I seen my sister Millie jump with each shot. Even with Sammy. When Uncle Pete Porti died and we went to the military cemetery, now they play taps from that recording."

"My mother never put all these flowers," Grandpa said as he looked down at the grave. "Nobody ever made it look beautiful like Jimmy makes it. What I do with my grave now is I put one or two flowers and I made a bouquet of artificial flowers and they stay forever." Grandpa was known for going to Michael's to buy artificial flowers and make his own arrangements to decorate Grandma Grace's grave, which he tended to lovingly almost every single week. "Now when this Christmas stuff is all over, I take the blanket off and I put something else."

A few feet away, we stop at the Spizio grave and he smiled as he said of his cousin, "Mary was so nice." We then walked to see his Nunziata grandparents, our feet making the crunching sounds as we stepped onto fallen leaves. "Aunt Rose was such a nice lady," he said at that grave. "She was my godmother." And then he looked at the only grandparent he remembered, Angelina Nunziata, and thought about how they had picked blackberries together in his early childhood. The wind was bitter cold in the cemetery and I suggested that we not walk to the back where Grandma Michela Franzese was buried and to head back to the warm car. We drove past Uncle Carmine and Aunt Hope's grave on the way out.

I helped Grandpa with his seatbelt and he looked at his hands and said, "My hands are shot." As we drove down Greenpoint Avenue and headed for Greenpoint, he started to reminisce about when Rose saw Johnny and she asked Johnny to tell him to stop by because Rose wanted to talk to Grandpa. "She was standing by the stoop with her mother and father that summer day." You could still hear the hurt from her initial rejection all of these years later as he says that he and Johnny bickered about if he was going to go to Richardson Street to see Rose. He retold once again all the events that took place as Rose's relationship with Lenny came to an end and their relationship began. The amazing thing about his stories was that not one word deviated in spite of the fact that he told me the story dozens of times before. That glint in his eyes and the passion of which he spoke about Rose after all of those years still fascinated me.

As we came down the ramp of the Brooklyn-Queens Expressway's Meeker Avenue-Morgan Avenue Exit, I asked Grandpa, "You wanna get a slice of pizza?" I know that one of the two things he liked when we went to Brooklyn was either to get a slice of Brooklyn pizza or a freshly cut cold cut sandwich from Graham Avenue. Jimmy the Hotdog Man's iconic hotdog stand, where my Uncle Anthony Lanzetta always stopped for a hotdog with onions and a Yoo-Hoo, was now just a faint memory on Meeker Avenue.

"Yeah, you know where to go?"

As I parked my car under the Brooklyn Queens Expressway by Graham Avenue, Grandpa had already gotten out and was crossing Meeker Avenue before I even got out of the car. I sat there and watched him for a minute to observe how being back here brought a spring to his step. "Today is sixty-six years since the last time he saw Grandma Rose alive," I thought to myself, "and today we are going on a walking tour of memories. I'm thirty-eight years old going on an adventure with my eighty-nine-year-old grandpa. What a gift today is going to be."

When I crossed Meeker Avenue and caught up to Grandpa, I found that, well, the pizza place I was excited to take him to was no longer there. Still, Graham Avenue not have a pizza place? I knew Graham Avenue was the mecca for some of the best places to have a good lunch in the neighborhood. I assured him we would find a place.

After we had crossed Meeker Avenue, Grandpa came to the corner and walked up Herbert Street and stood by the fire hydrant on Humboldt Street, or Johnny Pump, as he called them, where Grandpa Pete's store, Grandpa Pat's birthplace, had once stood. He then walked over and stood in front of the Bonomo's house and remembered those dear friends of his family for his entire lifetime. All of the Bonomo's were deceased since Marion Bonomo Dalto passed away in 2001, but Marion's daughter, Margaret, still lived there. We then headed toward Graham Avenue in search of pizza.

Graham Avenue comes to a point at Richardson Street, and Grandpa pointed to the building on the angle and said, "This was Tota's. That's where I got the milk for Uncle Stevie Porti when he got sick as a baby." He then pointed to another building across the street from Tota's and said, "This used to be Sam's candy store. He sold ice cream and candy and stuff."

"Which one was Johnny's house?" We were so close now and I had to see the scene of his stories.

"That one with the brown awning. And here this brick building next door to his house, this used to be a store that made rolls, and next door, right here, that's the stoop Johnny and I used to sit on. I don't think it is the same one, but that's where we used to sit."

"So now that we're here, how was it that you met my grandmother?" I needed to hear him explain it at the very scene of the story. He was eighty-nine years old. How good were the chances that this would ever happen for us again?

As he pointed from where we stood to the corner, he said, "She came around that corner from Graham Avenue. Just as she came to the front of Johnny's stoop, she looked toward us and called, 'Hello, Johnny,' and walked across Richardson Street at an angle and then continued down the street, crossing Humboldt Street, to where she lived all the way toward the end." His eyes trailed for a few moments down Richardson Street toward Rose's house and I couldn't help but wonder in my mind if he was watching her walk down in his mind's eye. Could I tell in detail about the love of my life, Vanessa, as he could nearly seventy years later about his first great love affair? The old man could put anyone who had a great love to shame.

As he turned once again toward Johnny's stoop, he stood there with his hands in his pockets and laughed. His pale blue eyes crinkled in merriment as his long nose grew redder from the cold as he laughed and said, "We had some good times on this stoop. We laughed like hell every night." Before we left the front of Johnny's house, I took a picture of Grandpa smiling in front of the famous stoop where the magical evening took place sixty-eight and a half years before. We then continued to walk up to where Rose's house was, which looked pretty different from how it looked in 1949, but the garage doors next door to Rose's house, 207 Richardson Street, were still there that were the iconic backdrop in so many of her pictures. As we stood in front of the stoop, he pointed to the front door at the top of the stoop and said, "That's where I used to stand with her in the vestibule and say goodnight and watch her go up the stairs."

I offered Grandpa for us to go to Frost Restaurant, but since his ulcers, he never could eat much, and just wanted a slice of pizza. Frost Restaurant wasn't offering pizza like they did in the old days, so we turned back and started going down Graham Avenue. Grandpa commented that Grandma Rose walked the length of Graham Avenue from Metropolitan Avenue to Richardson Street every day back and forth from the subway. Until I did it with him, I never realized how long it actually took. When I think about how compromised her heart was supposed to be since childhood, and then what an active life she had led, no wonder he was still in shock and baffled all of these years later that she was dead at twenty-two.

"Your Grandmother Rose and I never did things together here in the neighborhood. We always got in the car when I picked her up and headed to Coney Island mostly. It was pretty far way out on the Belt Parkway. She loved riding in the car and it was a nice, long ride. We didn't want to do things around here. And after rides and walking the boardwalk eating a frankfurter and an ice cream, we had a nice long ride back ahead of us. I spent a lot of time on Coney Island. That one time I took her to Radio City to see the Rockettes." He retold the story of fulfilling Rose's lifelong dream of seeing the Rockettes in real life. "She loved those Rockettes," he ended.

PASQUALE

As we walked up, Grandpa and I saw the deli where we were supposed to go to get cold cuts that time we were supposed to be visiting Jimmy Glynn and ended up at Cousin Carmela's house instead. I said, "There's the deli where we get the cold cuts." Grandpa laughed and said, "Yeah the one we never got to get the cold cuts at." Four years later, we still laughed about how different that visit to Greenpoint went. As we walked up Graham Avenue, we stopped someone to ask how far up the pizza place actually was. The lady told us that two more blocks we would be hitting two. Grandpa laughed as he said, "There's none and then you have two in the same place?"

After walking two and a half more blocks of Graham Avenue, we finally got to Carmine's Pizzeria, which was across the street from Tony's Pizza, and we gratefully sat down to piping hot slices of Brooklyn pizza right out of the oven and warmed up from our long walk in the cold. When I checked on how he was feeling, he would always shoot back, "I'm fine!" He was very adamant about not showing his age on our adventures, while when he was home, he talked endlessly about every ache and pain, how his back hurt, and how he couldn't do things he used to do and how long his simple tasks took him. When he wasn't mentioning his aches and pains, he talked endlessly about his medical coverage, or his "hospitalization" as he called it, which he was constantly complaining about and changing over the years. When I brought him back to Brooklyn, he never talked about that at all.

After our pizza was done and the white paper plates were shoved in the garbage, we walked back out onto Graham Avenue and headed back the way we came for Frost Street. This time we had every intention of visiting the family homestead to surprise Jimmy Glynn, but unfortunately Jimmy wasn't home this time. As we went back up toward Graham Avenue, we saw Grandpa's cousins like we had a few years before, Carmela Nunziato and Josephine Nunziato Viola. As we had the last time, we went up to Carmela's apartment for a visit to have coffee and reminisce, as well as Carmela telling Grandpa what a beautiful great-granddaughter he had, as I had sent Carmela photos of Victoria. At the mention of Victoria, Grandpa's face lit up and he was clearly proud. The visits were infrequent to Frost Street and four years had gone by so quickly. When we left that house that day, there was always that concern if it would be the last time. I quickly banished those thoughts from my mind, as I continued to enjoy walking in the footsteps of the young Pat Franzese with the old man he now was.

We had gone all of the places that we intended, and saw some familiar faces, as well as told the old stories and taken some pictures. As we crossed Meeker Avenue once more to get back in the car to go home, we passed Humboldt Street, where the site of his birth was a mound and the site of an exit ramp. History can be torn down, as we saw piece by piece of this beloved neighborhood disappear before our very eyes. We may not be able to preserve the buildings, but we must persevere in protecting the stories.

The year of 2016 ended and it was amazing to me that in the year 2017, Grandpa Pat Franzese would be reaching the milestone of age ninety. Shortly after the new year began, Grandpa's doctor said he found that the aorta of Grandpa's heart was leaking and he suggested Grandpa have his aorta replaced. When Grandpa heard about the supposed success rates with the operation, even at his age, he was very receptive and wanted to have the operation done. When I heard that Grandpa was going to be having the surgery, thinking about how risky an operation on someone over eighty-nine would be, I wanted to make sure that we spent time with him. It was Grandpa's decision and not up to me whether he went through with the surgery, but I wanted to make sure that Victoria and I got to spend time with him should the surgery not be successful. On my day off, January 25, 2017, I drove to Baldwin with Victoria to pick Grandpa up and bring him to my house for the day. There were no interviews on this day. This was a day for Grandpa and Victoria to bond and make memories. When we got back to my house, Grandpa sat on my living room couch and Victoria dragged her plastic yellow table in front of him, put one of her play houses on top of it and Grandpa and Victoria played for over an hour with the little figurines inside. Victoria wanted to make a video with her "Pa Pat" and also teach him the art of a selfie. My phone had a few of both after Victoria had her way and he really got a kick out of making them. How interesting to know his life had begun without a phone and photos were taken in studios, and now the same contraption you made calls on could photograph you as well. I just stood there and smiled how the hearts of the very young and very old connected. The two of them just giggled

Victoria teaches Pat how to take a selfie in 2017

Pat and Victoria playing together in 2017

together non-stop that afternoon, and when I asked, "What are you two doing in there?" they looked at each other with big grins and said simultaneously, "nothing!" Their laughter together was priceless. Later on, that afternoon, my parents came over to my house and Victoria cuddled with her grandpa, "Pa Pete," and wrapped her arms around and squeezed her great-grandpa, "Pa Pat," and kissed his cheek, and I said to myself, "If only I could keep them together in this moment forever."

Shortly after Grandpa spent the day at my house, he went into Saint Francis Hospital in the Village of Flower Hill of Nassau County, New York. I was apprehensive at the thought of him there only because both of my grandparents on my mother's side had died there from heart related issues. After conducting all of the testing, which Grandpa Pat had absolutely no patience for, the doctor decided not to replace his heart valve at all and sent him home. We would all be left with questions about what was the story with Grandpa's heart and valve after the doctor's sudden and abrupt change of heart. It would baffle us for the rest of Grandpa's life.

It was around this time that through Ancestry.com that the granddaughter of Grandpa's Aunt Rose Nunziata Annunziato, Joanna Pasquale, connected with me and we had made plans to have lunch at Ben's Deli in Carle Place, Long Island. After sharing our passion for family history, we made plans that when she returned to Long Island, she wanted me to bring along Grandpa Pat and she would bring along her aunt, Grandpa's first cousin, Teresa Annunziato Sciortino. Joanna's mother was Teresa's older sister, Angelina Annunziato Pasquale, who had died the year before. Joanna made plans for us to meet at Major's Steak House in East Meadow, New York, on March 21, 2017, and I picked up Grandpa Pat to take him. He was excited to be seeing his Cousin Teresa, as they had grown up close and he had not seen her at that point in many years. As always, he chatted and kibitzed, as he complained about how he didn't like going to restaurants because he couldn't eat much. Joanna and I laughed because you just come to accept that no matter what you did for the elderly, even though they were enjoying themselves, they were always complaining.

PASQUALE

After the scare we had experienced with Grandpa's heart in January, he was fine and still doing all of his routines and insisting that he didn't need any help from anyone. I picked him up to spend Easter Sunday with us on April 17th and he enjoyed spending the day with everyone. Then Grandpa called me one night after I had gotten home from work in May and he sounded very excited. When I asked him what his news was, he told me that he was having company for dinner on Saturday, his old friend, Johnny Morena, with Johnny's son, Michael, and his wife, Tina. The next thing was, would Vanessa, Victoria and I come. He had never asked me for something like that before, and since I was already off to take Victoria to the circus at Nassau Coliseum that morning, I told him that we would love to come.

On Saturday, May 13, 2017, after going to see the Ringling Brothers and Barnum and Bailey Circus, we ran in the pouring rain to our car and drove over to Grandpa's in Baldwin. When we arrived, Grandpa was so excited as he was finishing up cooking dinner for his guests, who had already arrived. I met Johnny's son, Michael, and his wife, Tina, for the first time, and although we did not know one another, we were both thrilled to meet because of the history that our family shared through Grandpa and Johnny. Grandpa had put a large bowl of ziti in the middle of the table, with meatballs and sausage, that he had made all by himself. Not bad for a man a few months shy of ninety. Everyone was very impressed by how delicious everything tasted and what he was able to pull together single handedly. Grandpa sat next to his old pal, who at nearly ninety-five had become much quieter and more subdued than when I had first met him nearly a decade before. With nearly seventy-five years of history between them, Grandpa still coaxed Johnny with memories of the things they had survived together, laughing about those girls they had dated in the forties, and showing off his and Rose's great-granddaughter to his oldest chum. As we sat there, I said to Michael, "If it wasn't for your father, my daughter and I wouldn't be here." I looked at this very old man and although I didn't have a personal profound history with him myself, it was him who introduced Grandpa to Rose, whose sole purpose was to bring my father into the world, so he could have my brother Robert and I, and I in turn could have

Victoria. I was very moved at the thought of this, and after the dishes and been cleared and we sat around the table and talked, we took pictures of the old chums and all of us with them. One that struck me much was Victoria taking a picture with Grandpa and Johnny, the little girl whose middle name was after the woman in the greatest story the two of them had ever shared.

Pat and Johnny Morena, friends for nearly seventy-five years, in 2017

Victoria Rose with Pat and Johnny Morena in 2017

PASQUALE

At the end of the evening, when we all got ready to say goodbye, we were all grateful to have spent the day with the two icons of our families whose legendary friendship had inspired us, as a new friendship formed that day now with Michael and I. We left feeling profoundly grateful having gotten to witness firsthand this inspiring friendship that had lasted longer than any other relationship of their lives.

During the summer of 2017, Grandpa had the opportunity to see much of the extended family that he had not seen hardly at all in recent years. The days of weekly visits to Frost Street were long gone, and running into cousins was extremely rare. In fact, he did not even get to see his nephews and nieces very much anymore either. Greenpoint had become close to a closed chapter, except for the trips we made to revisit and remember and honor the past.

On June 3, 2017, Grandpa was invited to accompany Joanna Pasquale and Teresa Sciortino to a luncheon at the Westchester Country Club by his first cousin, Teresa Caliendo Taormina, the only living child of his Aunt Concetta Nunziata Caliendo. I was sorry to miss the luncheon because I was working, but Joanna picked Grandpa up in Baldwin and brought him. On the trip in the car was Joanna, Teresa, and Joanna's sister, Terry Ann Mosso, who Grandpa had never met. It was almost immediate on the trip up to Westchester how Grandpa and his cousin, Terry Ann, made an acquaintance and in the matter of a few short hours, were laughing and teasing all the way there. Always dressed in his suit but tieless in the warm weather, Grandpa sat next to his cousin, Teresa Taormina, after having not seen her in probably over sixty years. Teresa sat at the head of the table and Grandpa sat to her right, as Terry Ann sat next to him. In addition to seeing Teresa Taormina, he met additional Caliendo cousins, Paulette Young, and her two sons, and Annie Brucato. They enjoyed an outdoor luncheon at the country club and Grandpa enjoyed a few glasses of his pungent red wine.

A month later, we had another day of celebrating with Grandpa's cousins when we attended a Nunziato family get together at Rhea Nunziato Passarella's home in Howard Beach, New York. Rhea is the daughter of the youngest of Uncle Larry and Aunt Mary Nunziato's children, Larry Nunziato. On this day, Grandpa accompanied Vanessa,

Victoria, and I to Rhea's home, and he was delighted to spend the day with his Nunziato cousins for a barbecue. Grandpa enjoyed taking pictures with his cousins, Larry, Mickey, and Carmela, who he spent most of the day talking with. Victoria played with Rhea's grandson and we enjoyed spending time with Rhea, her husband, John, and her whole family, her brother, Larry, and Mickey's son, Jeffrey, and his wife, Wendy. Victoria screamed in delight going down the slide into the pool and there was constant laughter echoing through the yard, as four generations of Salvatore and Angelina's descendants spent the day reconnecting or getting to know one another.

Pat (right) with his Nunziato cousins, Mickey, Larry, and Carmela, in 2017

"My grandfather will be ninety in September," I thought to myself as I drove him home after a day spent with most of his remaining living cousins. "This blessed milestone, although joyous, still carries with it waves of melancholy for him I can see. He is coming to the end of his run. There isn't another twenty years ahead. Perhaps ten, if he is lucky enough to reach a century. Although still alert and agile for a nonagenarian, I know that time is of the essence to tell his story. I must confess, although it is only the first quarter of a century that fascinates me, the story of the grocer's son, the last of the seven children, I must get all of the stories before time runs out." I glance over and although it is hard to conceive of his not being here, as he still looks the same that he has had his entire life, I also know that time is moving rapidly.

As the summer began coming to an end, Grandpa got to see Victoria turn five, as well as a few days later reach his milestone birthday. On August 31st, my dad and Uncle Paul and their families, including my family, all celebrated Grandpa's ninetieth birthday at Miller's Ale House in Deer Park, five days early. Then, on September 5, 2017, he officially turned ninety.

A month later, Grandpa's cousin, Teresa Taormina, invited us to join her for a luncheon at the Columbus Citizen's Foundation Headquarters located in Manhattan's Upper East Side. Cousins Joanna Pasquale and Terry Ann Mosso, were also invited and the four of us went into the city together. I sat upfront and talked with Joanna, while Grandpa and Terry Ann sat in the back and joked and kibitzed with one another the whole ride in. When we got to Manhattan, we walked down a stoop, where the restaurant was inside of the club. With so much warmth, Teresa Taormina was there to greet us and led us into the restaurant, where we sat with her at a corner table, as we spent an afternoon having the most delicious Italian fare, as Teresa shared with us stories about the Caliendo family, mainly about her mother, Concetta, and Grandpa told some stories about his mother, Lorenzina, Concetta's sister. After our lunch, Teresa took us on a tour of the Columbus Citizens Foundation, where we walked through a vista of rooms that were more and more breathtaking through each one. Like a tourist at the Museum of Art, my neck craned as I took in the exquisite art and décor and carvings in every corner of every room. As always, a fabulous afternoon drew to a close too quickly and we thanked Teresa for such an exquisite afternoon before heading back for Long Island.

At the end of the year, I was unable to take Grandpa on our Christmastime cemetery and Brooklyn visit after Victoria had gotten sick and then I quickly did as well, ending up with pneumonia. I was disappointed that we didn't get to spend that special time together as we had grown accustomed to.

After I had recovered from a severe bout with pneumonia in early 2018, I began interviewing Grandpa again both on the phone and in person. When a poster online was being sold of him as a three-year-old boy in his father's grocery store, along with his father, his brother, Sammy, and their friends, the Formatos, I was impressed how at ninety he was able to tell you the products on every shelf and what every can was, eighty-eight years later. I started to realize that the book I had to write was the story of the grocer's son. Without much effort, Grandpa was able to transport me to the living quarters behind his father's store, where he had been delivered by a midwife in his mother's bed, the stickball games, the neighbors, the schools, everything came flooding back in stories so detailed, once again, I was left awed.

Pat (center) and his grandson, Peter Michael, spending the day in Manhattan with his cousins, Teresa Taormina, Joanna Pasquale, and Terry Ann Mosso.

Easter became the holiday that Grandpa Pat spent with us, and he enjoyed watching Victoria hide eggs and make him walk around with a basket looking for them. As the months passed, every time that I took Victoria in the late morning to visit Grandpa in his apartment, I saw the bond growing between them. She would walk in and immediately put her arms around him and he would squeeze her in an embrace and immediately get up to go in the freezer and get her an ice pop. Another thing was he would go to her, "I got something for you." He would go into his closet and take out an old beer glass that he had with a bell attached to it. He would pour Victoria a glass of milk, and when she wanted more, she had to ring the bell. It became a ritual that whenever she went into Grandpa's apartment, the first thing she would ask him was for her glass. Grandpa and I would sit and talk while Victoria sat and either drank her milk or ate her ice pop and watched a cartoon until it was lunchtime. "You feel like having pizza pie?" he would ask Victoria. Since Grandpa knew that Victoria wasn't as big a fan of frankfurters like we were, he would suggest that we go take a ride and bring home a pizza. I would drive and he would direct where to turn and where to go and where to park. My favorite memory of this was watching Victoria and Grandpa holding hands and looking inside of a glass case in the pizzeria and him asking her what she wanted and what she liked. It was so sweet to watch them and how much he enjoyed being with her. After eating pizza back in his apartment, Victoria would be looking to go play with Uncle Paul's dogs and go exploring, and I would see how after a few hours poor Grandpa Pat lost her attention to her passion for puppies.

Once again, summer came to an end and on August 30th Victoria turned six, and on her first day of first grade, September 5th, Grandpa Pat turned ninety-one and my dad turned sixty-eight. Earlier that afternoon, my parents drove to pick up Grandpa Pat and bring him to spend the day with them at their house. The one thing Grandpa really enjoyed was going down the basement with my father to look at the Lionel trains that he had bought Dad over sixty years before. Later on, Victoria and I came over after Victoria got home from school and we all spent the day together celebrating our two Franzese birthday boys.

Pat sitting with his three children, Michele, Peter, and Paul

Pat and Peter celebrating their birthday together

Over the next few months, Grandpa and I talked for endless hours as I captured all of the stories of his youth. Cousin Joanna Pasquale came to New York and set up another cousin reunion, but this one would take place on the street where the story had begun, Frost Street. Working with Cousin Jean Petraglia Capobianco, the daughter of Grandpa's late cousin Loretta Nunziato Petraglia, a host of Nunziata descendants came together at Frost Restaurant on the corner of Frost Street and Humboldt Street, just a stone's throw from where Salvatore and Angelina's house stood at 224 Frost Street. Just as we had done when we went to Manhattan, Grandpa Pat and I joined Joanna and Terry Ann to drive from Long Island into Brooklyn together. It was Thursday, December 20, 2018, a day with a steel-gray sky and drizzling, with the windshield wipers going wildly back and forth to keep the view clear. A driver had driven all of us together into the city, and on the way in, Joanna had the car stop at Calvary Cemetery so Grandpa Pat could pay his respects to his family for Christmas, and his first wife, Rose, on the 68th anniversary of her passing. As we pulled up to her gravesite, Joanna and Terry Ann waited for Grandpa and I, as we exited the car and he stood as he always did in front of Rose's name. Forlornly, once again, he said as he did every time, "And she was only twenty-two." He let out a sigh as he lingered for a few more moments in silence as he stood there and stared at her name on the monument. Grandpa had been visiting this grave for seventy years, beginning with the day when Sal was buried there in 1948.

Pat visiting the Franzese family plot in Calvary Cemetery, where Rose, his parents, some of his siblings, and nephews are buried

The rain had begun to come down more steadily as we rolled down Frost Street and pulled in front of Frost Restaurant. A long table stretched along one of the walls of the restaurant and you couldn't help but wonder what Salvatore Nunziata, ninety years since he walked the length of Frost Street, would think of three generations of his descendants coming together to celebrate the family that he and Angelina had begun in Palma Campania one hundred and forty years before. Grandpa sat next to his new best friend, Cousin Terry Ann, and settled in with his glass of red wine. The glass door of the restaurant opened and Jean Petraglia Capobianco came in, as did her aunts, Carmela Nunziato and Josephine Viola. The door opened once again and the Caliendo cousins arrived, Paulette Young, Annie Brucato, and Rosemarie Murray, and her husband, Al. Grandpa enjoyed sitting with Rosemarie and Al, talking and laughing over wine. I sat between Cousin Carmela and Cousin Jean Capobianco, talking with Cousin Paulette across from me. The room was filled with the din of our laughter and the joy of the Christmas spirit. Throughout all of the fun we had, we celebrated the awesome fact that well over one hundred years since our ancestors first settled on this street, we were still a family, regardless of how far stretched the branches had gone. With a toast, we all held our glasses up high and toasted the memory of Salvatore and Angelina. Without them, all of this would not have been possible.

After the cappuccino and empty dessert dishes had been cleared, the Italian goodbyes took a good hour as always. First you kissed the cousin goodbye at the table while you put your coat on, then again as you were walking out together, and a last time coming out of the doorway and standing on the sidewalk. It's that longing that you hate to say goodbye, the gratitude for the moment, and the uncertainty of when you will see each other again. As Grandpa and I had been attending these get togethers so frequently, always talking about and visiting the old neighborhood often, I didn't realize when we stepped out into the pouring rain on Frost Street and entered the waiting car, how that very moment would be pivotal in my relationship with Grandpa. After ninety-one years, Grandpa Pat would never see Frost Street again.

PASQUALE

Victoria Rose with Pat in his kitchen

Pat with Peter's family (l.-r.) Vanessa, Victoria, Peter, Robert, AnnMarie (sitting), Peter Michael and Pat, November 2018

Pat with his sons, Peter and Paul, November 2018

Victoria Rose and Pat in November 2018

PASQUALE

Pat (center) having fun at a family wedding with his niece Jennie and her husband Henry (left) and his son, Paul, and daughter-in-law, Vicki (right) in 2019

Grandpa Pat was invited by Cousins Joanna and Terry Ann to spend Christmas Day at Terry Ann's home in Carle Place. Joanna had picked Grandpa up and he had spent the day talking and laughing with them at their table. Within a few days, the year of 2018 came to an end. The interviews continued at a rapid pace, as we spoke once a week and we were now tackling the years of World War II and their impact on his life and the Franzese family.

In the first few months of 2019, I would call Grandpa while Victoria was in school and spend a good three hours a week interviewing him about different topics of his life, as we navigated his time in the Army and his antics with the chum of his youth, Johnny Morena. I wasn't home very long from attending Sunday mass on April 28, 2019 with my daughter Victoria, when I went to turn the sound back on my phone and I noticed that I had a missed call at

11:40 a.m. from Michael Morena, Johnny's son. With a feeling of foreboding, and thoughts immediately to my grandfather, I paused for a moment before pressing his number to call him back. I knew what the news would be. Just as I had suspected, Johnny had just died in his Patchogue apartment in a senior citizen community. My grandfather's best friend of over seventy-five years was gone. Johnny was ninety-six-year-old.

Although I knew that Johnny had reached an advanced age and that he had been in ill health for a while, it sobered me to think that my grandfather's lifelong partner-in-crime, the man who had introduced my grandfather to his first love, was now part of history. After making the initial phone calls as the funeral director in charge, the momentous moment came when I had to call my grandfather. Besides having to tell him when his siblings had died, three over the course of two and a half years, this was one of those moments you dread more than most.

While I only met Johnny three times that I can distinctly remember, what an impact he had on the course of my family history, which ultimately resulted in the lives of my father, my brother and I, and my daughter. Taking a breath, I dialed my grandfather's number. After he answered and asked how everything was, I began.

"I got a call from Johnny's son." Words failed me for a moment as I couldn't think of what else to say.

"He died?"

"Yes, just now."

Grandpa let out a long sigh. "Shit." He too was now at a momentary loss for words. As quickly as his old chum's soul left, he regained his composure and the tidal wave of stories came tumbling in his mind once again. They were back on Richardson Street. Josie was in the window. Dominick was trying to get money to gamble. Al was reading a book in the parlor. Him and Johnny were heading over to Flamm's Bar across the way. Double dates with Gladys and Nora. And then that fateful night when Rose came walking at an angle and called "Hello, Johnny!" After seventy-five years, it was really over.

Five days later, I picked Grandpa up at his Baldwin apartment before noon. He was dressed in his suit and looking forlorn. "My best friend died," he began. "You know how many years we go back? I was sixteen when I started hanging out with Johnny!" As we drove from Baldwin to O.B. Davis Funeral Home in Miller Place, Long Island, he talked about meeting Johnny through Frankie Slater, finding out they had a common friend in Bobby Gentile, breaking up fights between Johnny and anyone who would make a reference to his small stature. Although my grandfather knew his old chum had been ill, the thought of the finality of this day really had thrown him.

Dressed in his navy-blue trucking uniform, Johnny lay in a hardwood poplar casket, his hands folded in repose holding a black rosary, the only hint of the Saint Cecilia's boy he had once been. Surrounded by family photos throughout the years, his wedding album to Micky close by, and their wedding picture propped up near him in the casket, they told the story of his life. Not far off to the right, a collage told further stories with Johnny's best friend, Pat, over seventy years ago and then the two of them as nonagenarians. Grandpa Pat knelt down slowly onto the kneeler in front of the casket and gazed into the face of his old friend. The black wavy hair was gone, but the mischievous grin had remained until the end. Johnny still knew the secrets to get under Pat's skin, whether it was about Rose or Gladys, the girls of their youth. Quiet and somber throughout the day, he sat on the side couch and spoke with others who had come. No one had known Johnny as long as he had, other than Johnny's sister-in-law, Judy Culmone Vail, who lived just across the street from Johnny as a girl all those years ago. Later that afternoon, we sat at a table at the home of Mike and his wife, Tina, thumbing through the old photos Johnny left behind. My grandfather was the only person who knew the grinning faces along Johnny in those old black and white photos. The enormity began to hit him that he was the last one standing of a long history that began in those long-ago streets in Greenpoint, Brooklyn.

At the end of the evening, Mike, Tina, my Uncle Paul, and I were standing in the front of the chapel when my grandfather approached Johnny's casket for the last time. He made the sign of the cross and clasped his gnarled hands together as he bowed his head. Then he looked up and stared intently into Johnny's face and then squeezed

Johnny's arm in goodbye. The tears rolled down his cheeks and he was quick to press a tissue to his eyes. Mike and Tina and Uncle Paul and I were very moved. There are so few people that I have ever really seen my grandfather cry for. Feeling the full weight of the role that made us closer than we have ever been before, my grandfather looked at me and said, "This is how the story ends." I look at my grandfather as *The Giver* like in Lois Lowry's dystopian novel and me as the "Receiver of Memory." He had entrusted me with all of these stories of growing up with his parents and siblings, with Johnny, and ultimately with Rose. And this is how the story of three quarters of a century with Johnny ends. I walked my grandfather to my uncle's truck and made sure he got in all right. I gave him a hug and he thanked me so much for making this possible for him to say goodbye to his best friend.

The following morning, with Mike and Tina, Mike's children, Nicole and Anthony, and Mike and Tina's friends, Paul and Tracey, we said goodbye to Johnny before his cremation at Long Island Cremation Company in West Babylon, New York, a stone's throw from where he had once been a truck driver. As the funeral director, I was in the passenger's seat while my driver, James Bizzaro, made the journey from Miller Place to West Babylon, on this key figure's final earthly journey. After a brief service at the intimate chapel of Long Island Cremation Company, we said our farewell to the legend who was Johnny and then proceeded to honor the memory of his late wife and son. The day ended at Pinelawn Memorial Park where we laid Johnny's flowers on the grave of his wife, Micky, and his late son, Johnny Boy. On that overcast, rainy day, we stood there on the lush green grass, trying to stay dry, but all thankful to Johnny for something unique and profound. As for me, I was grateful for that summer day in 1948 when he called Rose Porti over to meet his friend, Pat Franzese. Because of that small gesture, four people lived today, myself included. How do you adequately say thank you for that?

"You know, my last friend died," Grandpa began to tell everyone. "He's the last of my friends. I got no friends no more." He was devastated by this fact on so many levels. He made a comment to me in the weeks that followed that the only person he still knew from those long-ago days left was Rose Raia Suglia, Grandma Rose's cousin. He said that when I had time over the summer that perhaps we could take a ride to New Jersey to see her, as poor health had made it impossible for her to remain alone on Long Island in Mattituck and she now lived in a facility nearby to her daughter, Maria, in New Jersey. It was for this reason that I found it very upsetting to call him on May 31, 2019, to have to tell him that Cousin Rose had died at the age of ninety-two. Once again, he let out a sigh and then after a few moments he said. "She was a wonderful lady...she was really a great lady...she was so pretty when she was a young girl...we had such good times with her in Selden. I really thought that we were going to get to see her again."

As Grandpa lived in Baldwin and Rose's services were held near her former home in Mattituck, I felt very badly that I was unable to take him to her services to say goodbye. On the day of her funeral, my forty-first birthday, June 5, 2019, Grandma Rose's only surviving sibling, Uncle Stevie Porti, accompanied me to her services. He was reunited with his only Porti first cousins, Benny Raia and Patricia Raia Ochs, Aunt Angelina's only surviving children. After Rose's burial with her husband, Vito, and a few feet away from her parents, Aunt Angelina and Uncle Jack, we attended a luncheon where the first cousins were able to spend time together as they had not in many decades. Although it was impossible for him to be there, Grandpa's presence that day was keenly missed.

Over the summer of 2019, Grandpa and I talked every week. Sometimes it was interviews for the book. Other times, I would call him as I drove long distances to a hospital for work, and see how he was doing and just let him talk. On my days off every few weeks, I would take a ride to see him and would try to take my daughter, Victoria, if I could. He would delight in his conversations with her and the thrill he would get in us taking a short ride and his treating us to lunch. He was also somber after having lost two key people from his past in a month's time and feeling very alone where his contemporaries were concerned. He would begin, "There's so many people that I know that died! My God! Everybody's gone. But I carry on! I'm the only one left. The guys that we all palled out with are all gone."

Pat and Peter Michael in August 2019

Pat with his three children, Paul, Peter, and Michele, and great-granddaughter, Victoria Rose, in August 2019

The Four Generation Franzese photo Pat (age 92), Peter (age 69), Peter Michael (age 41), Victoria Rose (age 7)

Four generations celebrate Victoria Rose on her seventh birthday (l.-r.) Peter, Pat, Peter Michael, AnnMarie sitting in front, Vanessa, Vanessa's mother, Vicki Kelsch, with Victoria Rose standing in front of her, and Vanessa's father, Ken Kelsch

Victoria turned seven years old on August 30, 2019. Surrounding her to celebrate her birthday were her parents and her dog, Lady, her four grandparents, and her great-grandpa, "Pa Pat." I had everyone gather around her to have my brother, Robert, take a picture of Victoria with all of the living people that she had descended from. I had everyone take that picture as often as we could, as it was a treasure to have them all living and all there to celebrate her. Six days later, after I directed a funeral in the morning, I came home and changed and jumped in the car to pick up Grandpa Pat for the day. It was Thursday, September 5, 2019, Grandpa's ninety-second birthday. It was just around lunch time and Grandpa mentioned we should get a frankfurter or something soon, so I said to him, "Let's head out my way. If you want to have a frankfurter, I know just the place." We got off of the Southern State Parkway at Exit 33 Route 109. Heading south toward Babylon, my friend, Angelina Badalamente, had her hot dog truck on that road and I parked alongside of it on Route 109. The warmest and kindest woman that you ever wanted to meet, Angelina was ecstatic when we walked up to the truck, as she knew me very well from my job as a funeral director at Claude R. Boyd-Spencer Funeral Home in Babylon. When I introduced her to Grandpa Pat and mentioned that today was his ninety-second birthday, she gave him the most exuberant birthday wishes and brought a smile to his face. She refused to let him pay for his hot dog, and even though he tried to insist on paying, she said it was his birthday and to just have a happy birthday. As we drove down Route 109, he kept saying over and over what a kind lady Angelina was.

On the way to my house, we stopped at the funeral home, so I could show Grandpa where I worked. He met my coworker, Joan Alfiero, as we walked up the front stoop. She was so impressed that a man his age didn't even hold onto the railing. After he spoke for a while with Joan, I showed him the facility, and introduced him to everyone in the office. I introduced him to my fellow funeral director, Anthony Estremo, because both he and Grandpa had separately taken the Ancestry.com DNA test and found that they were distant relatives. Grandpa was excited to meet Anthony and Anthony really got a kick out of Grandpa, telling everyone what a nice old man he was. After spending a little time at my job, we said goodbye to everyone and then headed to my house.

As it got closer to three in the afternoon, Grandpa and I started heading to Marion G. Vedder Elementary School in North Babylon to pick up Victoria, where she had just begun in the second-grade class of Mrs. Jennifer Kreuscher. After years of walking his grandchildren to and from school, he was now getting an opportunity to do it for the day with his only great-grandchild. Victoria had no idea that "Pa Pat" was coming to pick her up with me, so when she came out the side door with the "walker" students, she ran down the steps to hug us and yelled "Pa Pat!" Grandpa talked with the other parents with me, who are also friends of Vanessa and mine, while Victoria ran across the lawn with her friends as they did every day during dismissal. After Victoria ran around for a while and Grandpa began to get tired, I rounded her up and the three of us headed back to my house, where Grandpa and I sat on the couch and talked while Victoria played.

Pat celebrating his 92nd birthday and Peter's 69th birthday. (l-r) Robert with Victoria standing in front of him, Peter, Peter Michael with AnnMarie sitting in front of him, and Pat

That evening, as it was also my father's sixty-ninth birthday as well, we made plans for my parents and Robert to meet Grandpa, Victoria and I, at Mangia's Pizza to have a family dinner for both birthday boys in that restaurant. We all sat around the table and Grandpa, as always, was happy with his glass of wine. As soon as dessert was served, Grandpa started to get antsy for me to bring him home. I had wanted to wait for Vanessa to get home from work, but as I saw him grow more and more anxious to leave, Robert said that he would stay at my house with Victoria while I drove Grandpa home. Safe at home and putting his slippers back on, Grandpa spent the rest of the night sitting with his feet up in his reclining chair, as I sat talking with Uncle Paul on the couch.

As the weeks were passing, Grandpa had been mentioning to me that one day he had taken a shower, and when he looked down, he thought that his foot was bleeding. When he sat down and looked, he realized that his foot had turned purple. He immediately went to go see his doctor, who gave him a salve for it, but it did not improve at all. He made a few visits to his doctor, but still he had no improvement. I spoke with Grandpa every week, and although he sounded perfectly fine, all of us were concerned that he was not having any improvement and we did not know what was wrong.

In the weeks following his birthday, Grandpa was having more issues with his leg, and by Friday, September 27th, his doctor was treating him for cellulitis and had put him on an antibiotic. Grandpa had been taking antibiotics all along for this issue, but it seemed to be getting continually worse. I was on the phone with Grandpa while I was at work on Sunday, September 29th and I suggested going to the hospital because he didn't want to end up losing his leg like his sister, Millie. Grandpa, always stubborn, refused to consider it. The next day, Monday, September 30th, I was alarmed, but not shocked, when I received a text that Grandpa was being admitted at Mercy Hospital and the doctors were saying he had acute kidney failure. In spite of the seriousness of this diagnosis, our entire family was baffled when he was being released a few days later, on October 3rd, and just told to follow up with his medical doctor and a nephrologist.

PASQUALE

While Grandpa did come home, he struggled to do the things in his routine that made him happy. They included cleaning his apartment, washing the floor, laundry, shopping, cooking, making his morning coffee, and making the bed. He prided himself on his independence, but he was almost panting doing any activities that weren't sitting in his recliner chair. On Monday, October 21st, Uncle Paul took Grandpa to the nephrologist who turned around and said Grandpa really needed to see a urologist. When they saw the urologist, he said that Grandpa was in heart failure. Grandpa had been declining daily, so Uncle Paul took him to South Nassau Community Hospital. Just by the fact that Grandpa didn't fight Uncle Paul about going to the hospital proved how ill he must have felt. Uncle Paul really wanted to bring him to Winthrop or Saint Francis, but Grandpa insisted on South Nassau. By this point, both of Grandpa's legs were purple and swollen with edema. He had also started to become incontinent and was exhausted before he even did anything. In spite of the fact that Grandpa was ninety-two, this was never the story and never an issue until now. In a matter of days, this vibrant and independent man began to lose all of his vigor and independence.

Uncle Paul sat with Grandpa in the emergency room all day and none of the news from there was promising. Grandpa's kidney function was only at twenty-five percent, his blood count was low, and he had heart failure. Then the nephrologist came in to say that it was not heart failure, but was kidney failure and that Grandpa might need dialysis because the X-ray of his lungs had come back clear. His kidney function had gotten worse since his hospitalization at Mercy.

That night, I picked up my father and the two of us headed to South Nassau Community Hospital. Grandpa was in a private room and Uncle Paul was there with him. Grandpa got the biggest smile when I walked in and said, "There's my buddy!" Over the past thirteen years, we had become buddies and copilots on many adventures. I talked with my uncle while my dad talked with his father. Uncle Paul and I noticed how in spite of the fact that my father and Grandpa had never lived together, they had experiences and people they knew that neither of us had any idea about. While for most of the visit, I was relieved to see them kibitzing with each other back and forth like always, when we got ready to leave after two hours, I was moved when my father told Grandpa that he had to get better because after sixty-nine years he didn't want to start celebrating his birthday alone.

Three days later, Grandpa was still in the hospital, but his heart and kidneys were still major issues, in addition to an infection in his leg. The following day, Friday, October 25th, was very concerning because Grandpa was hallucinating that he was floating up near the ceiling and that the nurses were floating by into the room. He was very frightened by the experience. He was also having constant issues with his bowels. The healthiest man in our family had everything changing on him like the collapse of a house of cards. He remained in the hospital for four more days before being released on October 29th.

After he came home, Grandpa was so incredibly tired and just walking to his chair made him so out of breath. Vicki's mom, Vicki, took Grandpa to the nephrologist the day after he came home from the hospital. In addition to all of the care Uncle Paul and Vicki were so diligently giving to Grandpa, Vicki's mom, Vicki, was devoted in helping Grandpa whenever Uncle Paul and Vicki were at work. He was irritable and completely exhausted and when I suggested that he go back to the hospital if he was so ill, he snapped at me that he would rather just die then. I became frantic and was on the edge of getting hysterical for the first time. And I felt completely powerless. I was at work, but even if I weren't, he didn't want to go anywhere. He had argued with Uncle Paul and Vicki through every step of this when they wanted to get him medical attention. His legs were swelling up again, in spite of the fact that he was happy to be home and sleeping in his own bed. This wasn't how he usually acted, so I was very upset. Over the following days though, he was getting rest and happy to be sleeping in his own bed, but his legs continued to fill with edema and his ability to walk was getting more difficult. The simple act of making a cup of coffee left Grandpa panting for breath. He was talking about wanting a new bed like my parents, a Craftmatic, so he could make the back of the bed go up since he was having trouble breathing in bed.

After only being home for a week, Uncle Paul and Vicki had to rush Grandpa to the hospital on Wednesday, November 6th, because he was doubling over in abdominal pain. After disappointment with Mercy and South Nassau, they took Grandpa to Winthrop University Hospital in Mineola. The doctors there once again said that Grandpa was suffering from kidney failure. The abdominal pains were the kidneys not working. After laying in the emergency room for twenty-four hours, they found his creatin levels had risen to 4.2. They administered morphine for pain. His leg was infected and he was put on antibiotics.

After work, my brother Robert and I went to see Grandpa at Winthrop on Tuesday, November 12th. We found him in great spirits and full of fun, retelling the stories of his adventures with Johnny and his love stories with Rose. My brother had never spent time with my grandfather like I did and was truly impressed by the captivating stories of this ninety-two-year-old man, as well as the connections of the stories of our father with Grandpa. I was glad that my brother had this opportunity to see our grandfather more like I did, beyond saying hello and goodbye at family parties. On the other hand, I never got tired of hearing him tell and retell all of his old stories. It was when he started to complain about the here and now that I tried to redirect him back to the good old days.

Grandpa was released from the hospital on Thursday, November 14th. He sat in his reclining chair and had the soundest sleep that he had in a while. When Uncle Paul checked on him a few hours later, Grandpa had a wash going on and had changed his bed sheets. No matter how much he had gone through, his determination kept pushing him on. Uncle Paul tried to tell him to take it easy, but Grandpa did not like being told that he couldn't do things.

Four days later, Uncle Paul took Grandpa to the cardiologist who said that he had a strong heart and looked healthy for his age. His incontinence continued to be a major problem that they couldn't seem to get a handle on. He had to see the cardiologist again and the nephrologist back to back four days later on that Friday, November 22nd. The cardiologist had taken blood from Grandpa and wanted to go over the results then.

Grandpa's daughter, Aunt Michele, and her husband, John, drove in from North Carolina on Sunday night, November 17th, and Tuesday, November 19th, the urologist said that Grandpa's prostate was a little swollen, but not bad. Aunt Michele and Uncle Paul brought Grandpa to the Winthrop Hospital urgent care walk in, based on the recommendation of the cardiologist, thinking that it would be OK, since they had all his records at the hospital. Grandpa had been completely exhausted after the urologist appointment, but he was clearly very ill, so they took Grandpa to the walk-in, but they said that he would have to go to the hospital. Crestfallen that they had not been helped, they ended up going back home that night. By the next day, Grandpa was looking somewhat improved, so it seemed like he was just still recovering. Aunt Michele and John returned to North Carolina that night, so she could return to work. I spoke with Grandpa the next day on Wednesday, November 20th, and he sounded so much better. I was so relieved.

When the nephrologist got the results from Grandpa's blood test, he told Vicki's mom, Vicki, that Grandpa had to go straight to the emergency room. Grandpa's kidneys were now functioning at only 4% and his creatin level was 6.59 when he was rushed back to the hospital on Friday, November 22nd, and was being treated in the critical care department of the emergency room. When I got the news, I jumped in the car and drove over to Winthrop to sit with Grandpa and Uncle Paul to see what was new. A doctor spoke to Uncle Paul and I once again about the possibility of dialysis. The nephrologist was suggesting that Grandpa had a blockage in his urinary tract that was causing his kidney failure and they might have to go in through the back to get rid of the blockage.

Grandpa seemed to grow more and more tired and spent more time asleep than awake most days. He said he was constantly nauseous and refused to eat anything. The nephrologist was now saying they would have a put a nephrostomy tube in his back to drain his kidneys. They were not able to conduct the test to check for a blockage because the contrast needed would cause him a lot of harm. This was another step to try to avoid Grandpa going on dialysis because of his weak heart.

Grandpa underwent the procedure for the nephrostomy tube in his right kidney on Monday, November 25th. He came through the procedure fine, but he continued to have no appetite. My father and

PASQUALE

I were supposed to go to see Grandpa the next day, but they were supposed to be able to do the second kidney and then cancelled at the last minute that night. We were disappointed that we didn't get to go see Grandpa that night, but kept praying and hoping for the best. They ended up doing the procedure the next day.

On Wednesday, November 27th, I had to direct an interment service at Calvary Cemetery and the mausoleum was right around the bend from the Franzese plot. After the service was over, I asked my driver, James Bizzaro, to pull up in front of the Franzese plot and take a picture of me standing behind the stone. Grandpa had always found a lot of peace visiting that grave for over seventy years and he always enjoyed seeing how it looked decorated by his nephew, Jimmy Glynn. As always, the grave was resplendent with fall colors and decorations and I texted the photo to Uncle Paul so Grandpa could see it. What Grandpa didn't see was me kneeling down on the grave in my suit over Rose's resting place and with tears in my eyes praying for her to help Grandpa in this desperate hour.

The following day, Thursday, November 28th, was Thanksgiving Day. Vanessa, Victoria, and I, went to Vanessa's parents' home in Bellport for the holiday, but before we all sat down to dinner together, we got to Facetime with Grandpa, Uncle Paul and Vicki. I was so happy to see Grandpa and Victoria talking on Facetime together, bridging the longing they both had to see one another. Trying to coax Grandpa to eat, they had even brought him a glass of his Carlo Rossi Burgundy wine, which he did not have the desire to drink. His failed appetite was very concerning and was stretching into day after day. He was getting more tired and cranky by the hour when anything was asked of him.

Uncle Paul texted me on Saturday, November 30th and said that it had been the worst that he had seen Grandpa so far. He was in excruciating pain, sleepy, cranky, and very weak. He continued to refuse to eat because he was nauseous in spite of taking anti-nausea medicine. A doctor told Uncle Paul that dialysis was inevitable. They replaced the nephrostomy tubes in his back because they did not seem to be working, so Grandpa was very exhausted and out of it after the procedure. I went there that night and found Grandpa asleep. After a while, I woke him up and found his memory to be completely jumbled. He would be confusing his wives and his in-laws, and I was only able to know the difference after years of having heard all of his stories multiple times. He was quieter than I ever saw him, but he watched the television pretty intently and I held the cup full of ice water so he could drink from the straw. When I Facetimed my father so he could see Grandpa, I could see the surprise in my father's face by seeing how weak and frail Grandpa had become in only a week's time. By December 3rd, the doctors said that the nephrostomy tubes were not working and that they would stent the kidneys, but they did not believe that would work either. Then they sent an end-of-life doctor to come to speak with Grandpa. When I saw that end-of-life care was now on the table for discussion, I went into an empty chapel at the funeral home where I work and just cried. The tears just poured down my face as I felt broken and lost. I didn't want to lose Grandpa. We had so much more to do together. We were writing this book together. For the first time in our lives, we were having the time of our lives together. I just couldn't stop the tears.

After Grandpa talked it over with Uncle Paul and his family, he decided that he would give dialysis a shot, instead of just accepting end-of-life care. Having known that my father-in-law, Ken Kelsch, lived an active life on dialysis gave Grandpa hope. The major problem that compounded everything else was that he still refused to eat and it was stretching now into weeks. Grandpa lived in this unrealistic world that he would eat when he got home and that everything would return back to normal.

The following night, Wednesday, December 4th, my father and I headed up to Winthrop to go see Grandpa when I got home from work. Uncle Paul was there as well when we got there and a young female doctor came in to talk with Grandpa about end-of-life care once again. She immediately turned us off as she tried to make it sound like we were speaking for Grandpa about his decision for the future. She was adamant about end-of-life care, but Grandpa clearly wanted to give dialysis a shot. My father spoke to his father and said, "Are you giving up, Dad? The doctors are giving up on you because you need to push yourself. Fight and push like I know you're capable of. I know that you have the strength to get better." He finished by saying to Grandpa that if he didn't start eating and forcing himself to get out of bed, that he was not going home. "You're never going to be cooking in your kitchen again if you don't get out of that bed now. Forget about by time you go home. The decision is yours, Dad. You have to do this stuff now."

The doctor made the comment to Grandpa that at ninety-two, he had had a good run. He looked at her and mustering his spunk shot back, "When you're twelve years old, it appears that way." After she left, we talked more at length and he said that he wanted to try dialysis because he really did not want to die. When he told the nephrologist and palliative care team that he wanted to go home, they took that as that he wanted to go home to die. The truth of it was that Grandpa was in complete denial about what was happening to him. He continued with this fantasy in his head that if he only went home, all of these problems he was facing now would go away. He would be back washing his floors, making his morning coffee, cooking his fabulous meals, and putting his feet up in his reclining chair with a glass of Carlo Rossi Burgundy. Uncle Paul and I went downstairs to his truck to talk things over and we left my dad alone with his father so they could talk too.

When we got back to the room, I was deeply moved at watching as Grandpa laid in the bed and my father sat in a chair near the foot of the bed and how they laughed and laughed together. I took a picture of them with a lump in my throat as I thought that I would probably never see this scene again. These are the two Franzese men I come from whose nature to tease and kid around I inherited. I had teased my grandfather a few months before that he had lived so long that now his son was his oldest living friend. That night I remember my father in a fit of laughter as Grandpa told him the story of going with Rose and the Portis to their property in Smithtown, Long Island in 1949 and finding when they got there it was only an empty lot. Although he was weak, Grandpa still had the mischievous glint in his eyes and he laughed easily that night. There was hope amid all the uncertainty if Grandpa would indeed see the new year.

The following day, the nephrostomy tubes were put inside to connect the ureters to the bladder and Vicki had to argue with the palliative doctor from the night before that Grandpa did not want to go home to die, but very much was fighting to live. Over and over he said that he wanted to get his car painted, he wanted to buy new clothes, and he wanted to get a Craftmatic bed like my father and mother. That was not a person who wanted to go home to die, she argued.

As the days went by, Grandpa grew more upset and depressed and irritable and still continued not to eat. Every time I visited him, I could see him always growing thinner and that he was fading before my eyes. Not too much kept his interest, other than watching Steve Harvey on *Family Feud* and admiring his suits and ties. Even at ninety-two, Grandpa still admired dressing well.

On Monday, December 9th, they took Grandpa to install the port in his chest at 8:30 p.m. after waiting without eating or drinking the whole day so he could have the procedure. It was over by 10 p.m. and he was slated to start dialysis the next day.

It was 2:40 p.m. on Tuesday, December 10th when Vicki texted me at work that my dad and I should go to the hospital that day because Grandpa was not doing well. Vicki's mom, Vicki, was at the hospital visiting Grandpa and found him not doing well at all. He had developed a huge hematoma at the site of where the port was installed. His blood pressure was very low and not rising, so they were unable to do dialysis as planned, because he was too weak. The doctors thought that there was a blockage in his stomach, so they were planning to do an endoscopy. Grandpa said that he suffered through the entire procedure putting in the port into his chest. The doctor was talking about doing a 24-hour dialysis, so it would not be as intense on his body as three days a week. They also needed to give him medication to try and bring his pressure back up. Grandpa told Vicki's mother that he just wanted to die. He didn't want to go through all of this anymore. I left work immediately, went to pick up my dad at 3 p.m., and we went to Winthrop Hospital. Uncle Paul and Vicki were there with my dad and we sat around his bed until well into the evening. He got to speak with my mother, Vanessa, Victoria, and my mother's sister, Susan, all on Facetime, as well as a phone call with Kristine Okpych Marks, the daughter of his old friends, Kay and Walter Okpych, from long ago. Everything just seemed to get worse by the day.

The following day, Wednesday, December 11th, a doctor told Vicki that they would try dialysis again, but if Grandpa was not able to tolerate it or it did not work, then he would have to just be kept comfortable on hospice. Aunt Michele was preparing to board a plane from North Carolina and had a temporary transfer to the bank where she worked to the branch near Uncle Paul's house. When her flight got postponed, her daughter, Samantha, drove her through the night to Long Island. Grandpa was so happy that Aunt Michele was coming, and always the cleaning fanatic, he was worried that his refrigerator needed to be cleaned out and that his apartment was going to be dirty. Aunt Michele cleaned it out and straightened up around his apartment so she could put his mind at ease when she saw him that morning.

After Aunt Michele settled in at Uncle Paul's house that morning, she and Uncle Paul went to the hospital to be with Grandpa and everyone was very concerned. Grandpa was not able to tolerate the dialysis treatment, so they had to stop treatment. The plan was to try dialysis one more time the next day. I didn't sleep that night full of angst, crying, and just lying there and staring at the ceiling thinking about Grandpa's mortality.

Friday, December 13th, the doctors were going to try to drain the fluid mounting in his body and get dialysis to work with one last attempt. They said that if dialysis failed this time, he only had between a matter of days or weeks to live. Grandpa still didn't focus on dying. The night before, he was still asking for Uncle Paul and Vicki to buy him the Craftmatic bed.

When I got to the hospital that afternoon, Grandpa was alone and he told me that the doctors wanted to meet with the family because they had attempted dialysis again and it didn't work that morning. He then told me that he had vomited blood during the night and that they hadn't given him fluids since. I felt the hairs on my arms stand up. All I could think about was the ulcers he suffered in 1950 and 1951 that had nearly claimed his life. He never mentioned throwing up blood other than those two instances in his life.

I knelt down next to Grandpa's bed and we held each other's hands and I asked him how he was feeling about everything. "I don't want to die," he said as he looked into my eyes. "Who wants to die? I want to stay here with youse. I want to see Victoria. I want to see my girl make her communion. No, I don't want to die." The tears were burning my eyes because, in spite of the fact that the two women who he had ever loved were in heaven waiting for him, he didn't want to leave his three kids, six grandkids, and one great-grandchild.

Uncle Carmine's daughter, Hope, had texted me that afternoon that she was in Detroit and waiting for a flight to JFK Airport and was taking the Long Island Railroad to the Mineola stop and coming to Winthrop to see Grandpa that afternoon. I told Grandpa that his niece was on her way and he was shocked and very happy to hear this, as he had not seen her in fifteen years. Uncle Paul, Aunt Michele, and Aunt Michele's daughter, Samantha, got to the hospital and I told them that Hope was on her way. Everyone's spirits lifted when they heard she was on her way.

The spirits of Grandpa's room lifted when Hope arrived at the door with her suitcases and Grandpa was so happy to see her. Once she settled in, Uncle Paul, Aunt Michele, Samantha, and I walked to a pizzeria to have dinner, while Hope and Vicki sat and talked with Grandpa. It felt good to relax and spend time with my aunt and uncle, since life makes these opportunities so rare. Grandpa enjoyed talking with his niece, complaining about working for her father, his oldest brother, Carmine, and reminiscing about both of his wives. He said wistfully that no one should have to bury their wife at twenty-two.

Grandpa was looking very tired by time we came back from dinner and I insisted on driving Hope to her sister's house on Long Island. After I kissed Grandpa goodnight and Hope said her goodbye to him, we went to the parking garage and were just about to pull away when we got a call that Grandpa had started to vomit blood. We turned the car around and parked once again and raced back up to his room.

My family members were all standing outside room 3110 completely shaken by Grandpa's violent vomiting fit of blood and his blood pressure plummeting. A rapid response team had been called and Hope went into his room, as she is a practicing medical doctor in Indiana. I was silently praying, but inside I felt hollow, empty. He was slipping away. This was the end. Only a few hours ago he had told me that he didn't want to die. He didn't want to leave us. And yet, he was slipping away. For hours, I stood vigil with Uncle Paul and Vicki, Aunt Michele, Grace, Samantha, and Hope, as we tried to see if they could stabilize Grandpa. I called my father to tell him what was happening. It was just so hard to accept that the end was drawing near and could be coming at any moment. All I could think was how I would miss the glint in his eyes when he talked about Rose. When his time came, it would be like losing her again. She lived on through his stories.

After a few more hours and they seemed to have stabilized Grandpa, Hope and I left and I drove her to her sister's home. Before I went to bed, I got a message that at 11:46 p.m. he had had another episode of vomiting blood and had been transferred to the intensive care unit. As I saw Friday become Saturday, I couldn't sleep because I just couldn't cope with the thought that this was truly the end.

On Saturday, December 14th, I worked all day at the funeral home, but after I got out after five, I drove to pick up Hope because she had volunteered to stay at my parents' house with my mother while I took my father to Winthrop so he could say goodbye to his father. Grandpa had been in and out of it all day, but was in a great deal of pain with his back from the kidneys and they were unable to complete an MRI. They were going to make one more attempt at dialysis, which did not work, and he was spitting up more blood during the process and said that he felt so sick. They paused the dialysis after only a half hour because his pressure dropped and he felt dizzy. The doctor confirmed that Grandpa had a bleeding ulcer. After nearly seventy years, his bleeding ulcers had returned. All of those stories of what happened to him in the first days of my father's life while he and Rose struggled to live made me sick as I thought that at ninety-two he was going through it all over again.

When Dad and I got to the hospital that night, Grandpa was on the third floor ICU in bed 3514. He wasn't conscious, but was very restless in the bed and looked like someone having nightmares. Among the jumble of things he was saying, I did hear him say my name, Peter Michael, a few times. It moved me to see his three children sitting together by his bed, as well as his oldest grandson, me, and oldest granddaughter, Grace. The room was kept dark and was serene, but none of us were ready to say goodbye to Grandpa.

On Sunday, December 15th, I was working late at the funeral home as I do on every Sunday. They had done an endoscopy on Grandpa in the day, after he had another episode of vomiting blood around 11 a.m., which had to be stopped, because his blood pressure dropped. They said that the bleeding was coming from a clot in the neck and they saw fluid around his lungs. Then the ENT was contacted, but he also couldn't tolerate another procedure. His liver was now having issues draining into the small intestine and there was another blockage somewhere. His white blood cells were elevated. By 6 p.m., Grandpa was shutting down. They were keeping him comfortable because too many systems of his were shutting down.

As the evening was wearing on, I was overwrought and agitated at the thought of my grandfather in his last hours and wanting to be with him. I reached out to my friend, Father Dave Atanasio, who is the current chaplain of my alma mater, Saint John the Baptist Diocesan High School in West Islip, for some spiritual guidance. He came right over to the funeral home to speak with me. I discussed with him my concerns because Grandpa had been a practicing Catholic in his youth, but after the tragic death of my grandmother in 1950, that he had not attended church of any kind since, although he did not change his faith. I was concerned about his soul. Father Dave talked with me privately for a long time and gave me definite peace. The most profound thing that he said to me that night was that when I closed the funeral home for the evening at 10 p.m., that he would join me in going to Winthrop to go to my grandfather's bedside and pray with our family and give him the sacrament of last rites of the Catholic Church.

When I got to the hospital about 10:40 p.m., Uncle Paul, Vicki, and Aunt Michele were at Grandpa's bedside. He was crying in agonizing pain from his back, but was unable to communicate with us and his eyes were unfocused. I held his hand and spoke with him and told him that I was there, but there was no personal response. I was losing him.

Father Dave arrived a few minutes after I did and offered words of comfort to each member of my family. He then offered to pray with all of us and to give Grandpa the anointing of the sick, the last rites of the Catholic church. While Grandpa was no longer religious, his family was. During those final days, he had been visited by Uncle Paul and Vicki's pastor from One Life Christian Church in Baldwin and now my friend, Father Dave. I felt so overcome as I saw Father Dave say those comforting words in prayer as he blessed Grandpa with the chrism, the consecrated oil used at baptism and at last rites. Having led the spiritual leaders of our lives to Grandpa's bed, we were getting him ready to face God once again, in spite of their falling out back in 1950. My pastor, Fr. Gius Garcia, at Ss. Cyril & Methodius Church had assured me that morning that Grandpa was going to give God a piece of his mind when he saw Him, but that God was going to take it because He can take everything, and after Grandpa finished, He was going to give him a great hug and welcome him home.

Father Dave remained with us for a while before saying goodnight to all of us and assuring to please let him know if we needed him. Grandpa was administered fentanyl to help his agonizing pain that he was experiencing and he began to settle down and go back to a more slumberous sleep. As it became apparent that we were in Grandpa's final hours, Uncle Paul and Vicki had made the decision not to go to work the next day, and Aunt Michele would not be reporting to the bank either. After how hard everyone had worked to save him, coax him to get better, pray for a miracle, we were coming to the moment of acceptance of God's will that Grandpa's body could not fight anymore. I stayed until after midnight and told everyone that I would see them after work the next day.

I did not sleep that night. How could I sleep when I knew that at any moment that Grandpa Pat's life was coming to an end? How could I not dwell on anything else? He had become such a huge part of my life and my best buddy. Although I knew he was ninety-two, he was our own Dick Clark and never changed and never aged. Over the past two and a half months, everything had just come crashing down around us. What made him so unique was that in spite of his loving to tell the stories of the past, he was very present and interested in what was happening in our family and in our world currently. His energizing spirit and his love for kibitzing, his infectious laughter over a glass of Carlo Rossi burgundy wine, and even his constant complaining about things that didn't really matter were all a part of him. But we loved him for all of his good and in spite of all of his faults. And it was the same with him. In spite of all of his complaints and gossip about us to others, we were the ones he wanted to be with. He wanted to be at Uncle Paul and Vicki's house, even when he complained about the noise from their hot tub keeping him up, even when it wasn't plugged in. He loved his grandchildren in spite of complaining when they did laundry in the night and the machine kept him up. He loved me in spite of the fact that when I borrowed his photos to make copies for this book that I didn't bring them back to him fast enough or that I was always digging up long lost relatives for him to reunite with. He complained when Aunt Michele called him at dinner time, but you knew he relished her phone calls because he would then call me to tell me everything happening in her life. He complained about us all, but loved us all. My father's joke about his father had always been that if he stopped complaining, take his pulse. Whenever Grandpa complained to my father, my father would start laughing hysterically, especially the time when Grandpa told him that the very old can't live with the very young. This is our family and these are Pat's descendants. We don't have it all, but we all have love for one another and we were all there.

My grandfather had lived multiple lives. He lived the life of the youngest son of the grocer on Humboldt Street. He had lived a short, but tempestuous and utterly happy life with his first love from which I came. He lived the life of a sick, young widower who had lost his way. He lived the life of a hardworking and devoted husband and father in Queens and Long Island. He then had to navigate a quarter of a century as a widower once again, but also that of a grandfather. That role was so unique, as he had grandchildren in their 40's, 30's, 20's, teens, and a young great-grandchild. He had outlived all of his siblings and all of his contemporaries, but still very much wanted to live. He talked about dying when he was disgusted or frustrated, but never lost interest in living. But here we were, for better or worse, at the end of his amazing life. He had chosen to share his past with me, something that my father never achieved with him. He also let me into his present, and I ended up making more memories with him than any of my other grandparents. Those memories were also not through my parents, as happens so much with grandparents. The memories were made of an elderly grandparent with his adult grandchild. I was blessed and I know that he felt the same way too.

After a restless night, I got up for work on Monday, December 16th, because I was directing a funeral from my home parish of Ss. Cyril & Methodius Church in Deer Park. Grandpa was resting comfortably after they had administered the fentanyl and Vicki's mom, Vicki, was sitting with him while everyone had gone home after a very long, stressful and draining night.

After the funeral mass, I was standing at the grave of the decedent that afternoon in Saint Charles Cemetery in Farmingdale, and began my closing comments following the deacon's prayer service. I was sharing a poem with the family called *The Fallen Limb*, and as I began with the opening line, "A limb has fallen from my family tree," all of the sudden I was hit with a burst of snow. All of the mourners commented about how it was only snowing on me. Something else happened to me that had never happened before while I directed a funeral. Tears started to roll down my cheeks and I couldn't stop them. After I had finished the funeral service and expressed my condolences to the family, I saw that my grandfather's cousin, Joanna Pasquale, who had just come to Long Island for a visit from Louisiana, asked if she would be able to visit Grandpa that afternoon. When I texted Vicki to ask her, she told me the words that I had been dreading all along. "He just passed." I felt my blood turn to ice. He had died just at the moment when I had been reciting that poem. Also, although they were not with me and in other parts of Long Island, my aunt and uncle had seen the snow too. Vicki's mom had gone to put money in her parking meter outside the hospital and he had passed in the few minutes she was out of the room. She was so upset because she wasn't there when he passed away, but knowing my grandfather, he had wanted it to go that way. Knowing all of his stories, I realized this was a Franzese tactic at the end. In Lorenzina's last minutes as everyone sat vigil at her deathbed in 1962, she had sent my grandfather from her deathbed to get her a blanket. When he returned a few minutes later, Lorenzina was gone. I also thought about the snow. He told and retold the story about how he had been sleeping when Rose died and was awakened by a kiss. The snow has been his goodbye to us as he left this world and reunited with all those whom he loved in heaven…the last link in the chain that was the family of the grocer, Pete Franzese, and his wife, Lorenzina…was now in heaven.

When I received the news, I just couldn't stop crying as my hearse driver, Phil Maniaci, drove me back to the funeral home, and I called my father to tell him that his father was gone. My coworker, Jade Martin, closed the doors on the hospitality room inside the funeral home to give me privacy as I sobbed because the story had truly come to an end. After I calmed down enough to drive, I went to pick up my father, and we headed to Winthrop.

Uncle Paul, Vicki, Aunt Michele, and Grace, as well as Uncle Paul and Vicki's pastor, Scott Solimine, were all there at Grandpa's bedside. I stood there and saw my grandfather laying there lifeless in the bed. He was gone. I hugged him and cried. Everyone had tried everything in the world to save him, but it was his time. We would never have enough time. I cried for him, I cried for Rose whom I never knew, I cried for the end of the family of Pete and Lorenzina, I cried for the grandpa who had been my copilot on so many adventures, I cried for the loss of a generation, and for my last grandparent. I cried for my father, who had lost his mother at three months old and now stood at his father's deathbed at sixty-nine-years-old. I cried for my Uncle Paul and Vicki and their children for how much they had devoted their life to saving Grandpa and all they had done for him for his last few decades not to be alone. I cried for Aunt Michele whose heart was breaking for having had to be so far away and juggling life in North Carolina and all that was happening here. I cried for Victoria who would never sit and giggle with her great-grandpa, "Pa Pat," again. My father cried for Grandpa Pat for the first time in his life because he said that it was the first time in his life that he could say that his mother and father were together and that they were standing together and looking down on him.

Pastor Scott led us in prayer as a family and offered us the use of his church, One Life Christian Church in Baldwin, which was around the corner from Uncle Paul and Vicki's house, to have Grandpa's wake service. He was so kind, so compassionate, and so accommodating to all of the members of our family.

After everyone had said goodbye to Grandpa, Dad insisted on staying behind with me before the funeral home came to release him from the hospital. I was deeply moved after the room had grown so quiet and my father sat next to Grandpa's bed. This journey had begun with Grandpa and my dad alone when Rose died in 1950 and the two of them now once again were alone together at the end. Unlike the rest of us, they never spent time alone together during life. After my father went to live with Grandpa Sammy and Grandma Josie and Grandpa Pat had started a family with Grandma Grace, they had never really been alone with one another. It was time for them to say goodbye, and it was time for them to do it alone.

"Goodbye, Dad," my father said to his father as he left. "Say hello to Ma for me."

The funeral business is my business, so we are both hardest on ourselves for perfection because this is what we do for strangers on a daily basis, and because this is our final act of love that we can tangibly do for our loved one before their physical presence leaves the Earth. I could not have gotten through that day without my buddy, Joe Gallipani, because I know that he would treat my grandfather like family, as he has always watched out for and guided me from the days I was a resident funeral director. When I was getting my grandfather ready for his casket, I cried harder than I had ever cried in my adult life as I held him in my arms. I wasn't ready for how hard my heart would break when this time came. The lump in my throat was so hard as I saw him wear the suit that I had taken him to buy on a long day excursion because he couldn't find a suit that he liked. When I saw him in his casket, I was so glad to see that he was him again, all dressed up in his suit and freshly shaven, and looking like the dapper old gentleman who everyone loved.

Thursday, December 19, 2019, Grandpa laid in his Batesville Mediterranean Copper casket with champagne velvet interior and dressed in his suit and wearing the tie he wore to all of the family weddings, including mine. In the four corners were sculptures of Michelangelo's Pieta and the sides bore images of DaVinci's The Last Supper. Grandpa's casket sat in front of the altar of the One Life Christian Church, while soft music played and on the wall above the casket played the video of the photographs of his life from cradle to casket of the ageless man who had lived ninety-two years while the world changed instead of him. It was just for that reason why it was so difficult to accept that he was truly gone.

The room was festooned with flowers from all of the people who loved him, along with photo boards and two easels holding 11X14 portraits of him on his two wedding days. On the floor in front of his casket sat three of his iconic objects, his small, two cup percolator coffee pot, his half-empty gallon jug of Carlo Rossi Burgundy wine, and his short, stemless cut-glass wine glass. Grandpa's three children were there, along with their spouses, five of his six grandchildren, and one great grandchild. From Brooklyn came his nephew, Jimmy Glynn, along with his niece, Laura Franzese Flugger, her husband, Larry, and his grand-niece, Jennifer, and his niece, Jennie Franzese Ramos, and her husband, Henry. From his mother's family, his Aunt Lucy Maiello's grandson, Vincent Maiello, as well as his Aunt Rose Annunziato's granddaughters, Joanna Pasquale and Terry Ann Mosso, and Aunt Philomena Croce's grandson-in-law, Tommy Carlo. Members of Rose's and Grace's families, old family friends, and friends of his children and grandchildren, all filed through. Johnny Morena's son, Michael, came in the evening as we mourned the two great friends who had both gone to their eternal reward in 2019. Pastor Scott offered some prayers for Grandpa as well as a reflection, and both Uncle Paul's wife, Vicki, who had lived with Grandpa for most of her and Uncle Paul's twenty-eight years of marriage, shared key words and stories about the Dad who had raised her husband and the Papu who had helped her and Uncle Paul raise their three children. I eulogized him as the Grocer's son and the Grandpa who had joined me on so many fun adventures in my adult life.

PASQUALE

Friday, December 20, 2019, I woke up anxious as I thought about the enormity of all that would take place that day. On this date sixty-nine years before, Grandpa Pat had ridden in an ambulance with Rose from Astoria, Queens to the Bronx, where she would enter the hospital, Montefiore, and where she would die two days later. On this day one year before, he had been at Calvary Cemetery and Frost Street, in what would have unknowingly been his physical farewell to the past. On this date only two days before Rose's anniversary, we were now saying goodbye to him. When it came time for us to say goodbye, and I had all of the friends and extended relatives say their farewells, I called for all of his grandchildren to come together around his casket. With only one unable to be there, he had been Grandpa Pat, Papu, and Pa Pat. We all loved him, but he had been such a different icon in each of our lives for so many different reasons. Uncle Paul and Vicki's son, David, wanted Grandpa to be buried with his wine glass and his coffee pot, so I placed both in his casket. The wine glass would be in his hands for eternity. After that difficult moment when his three children said goodbye to Grandpa, my hearse driver, James Bizzaro, assisted me as I closed and locked Grandpa's casket and we draped his casket with the American flag and solemnly led the casket outside into the frigid air to the open door of the waiting hearse. The pain was palpable as I was the last person to see his face and to have to close the lid. After everyone had gotten into their cars, we began the procession to Greenfield Cemetery in Uniondale, New York.

In those last days of his life, all Grandpa had discussed over and over was his wish to go home. On the way to the cemetery, I stopped the hearse in front of his house and walked up to the front door and left a single rose, while I heard the dogs inside barking their goodbye to him on the other side of the door. His car that he had had for twenty years that he wanted to have painted so badly sat there parked on the curb. It just seemed so surreal that he really was no longer among us.

Pat with his grandson, David

Pat's grandson, Joseph

At Greenfield Cemetery, the frigid wind was stinging my face as the cemetery workers took Grandpa's flag-draped casket and placed it on top of his grave. Grandma Grace's name filled one heart and the other now awaited his name. I stood beside his casket as all of the mourners stood there and the two soldiers performed taps and folded the flag, presenting it to my father as the oldest child. I then performed the committal prayers of the Rites of Christian Burial for the first time for a member of my immediate family. And then it was time to say goodbye. All of the mourners left their flower, leaving him a bouquet on top of his casket, and walked back to their cars. When I first became a funeral director, Grandpa made me promise that I would never leave the grave until the casket had been lowered into the grave. For almost seventy years it had haunted him that Rose's casket had been left sitting on top of the grave that was still not buried the next day. He never left the cemetery until every person in his family was buried. And now, I would be staying behind for him. After nearly everyone had left, my daughter, Victoria, was adamant that she was not going to leave me. She held my hand as we both stood there and watched as Grandpa's casket was lowered into the concrete vault below. Before they lowered the lid onto the vault, Victoria pulled a rose out of the floral arrangement and tossed it onto the top of his casket. She wanted to give him a rose from Victoria Rose. Once the lid had been lowered and sealed, we looked at the symbol of the soldier above his name and dates. In spite of having only spent a year of his life in the US Army, he would forever be a veteran who had served his country. My shoulders shook as the tears poured down my face. Pasquale Franzese's story was over. As my daughter and I walked away from that grave, I looked back over my shoulder once more and said goodbye to Grandpa. Like he had said to me back in April, "this is how the story ends." Two days later, on Sunday, December 22, 2019, I woke up that morning and immediately thought about the fact that it was the sixty-ninth anniversary of Rose's death. I felt peace that this was the first time that Grandpa wouldn't be sad on this day any more.

Five days after Grandpa's funeral was our first Christmas Day without Grandpa. As I sat at the head of my dining room table, with Vanessa, Victoria, my mother and father, my brother, Robert, and Vanessa's parents, Ken and Vicki, I had filled one of Grandpa's stemless cut-glass wine glasses with his Carlo Rossi Burgundy wine and we toasted his wonderful life. Although it was Easter that he usually spent at that table with us in the years since I had been married, his loss was keenly felt and his presence was deeply missed.

Pat & Grace's grave in Greenfield Cemetery

My daughter and I each have a glass that we cherish to make us remember Grandpa Pat. I will forever cherish his wine glass and Victoria will always cherish the glass with the bell he used to give her milk to drink in. I will forever miss sitting at that kitchen table as he deftly filled out glasses in spite of his gnarled hands always giving him difficulty, as we sipped that pungent, dark liquid, and the stories that made us a family were shared again and again.

CHAPTER FOURTEEN

Life Without Grandpa Pat

DECEMBER 2019-JUNE 2021

The day after Christmas 2019, Vanessa and I took Victoria to Manhattan to see the Radio City Christmas Show and the Christmas Tree at Rockefeller Center. As I watched my daughter's neck crane in wonder at the opulent Art Deco theater, I marveled at the thought of her great-grandmother Rose doing the same thing seventy years before and thinking how pleased Grandpa Pat would be knowing that I had brought his great-granddaughter to see the Rockettes. A few days later, I came down with a harsh case of the flu, and when the ball touched down in Times Square at midnight on January 1, 2020, I was sleeping for the first time that I could remember since I was a child. How I had been looking forward to celebrating the New Year with Grandpa and the fact that he would be living through the '20's for a second time. This was not to be.

All of us who were part of Grandpa's immediate family were hurting in our own unique way as we welcomed this new year. How odd it felt not to be calling him every week whenever I had to drive great distances for work, whether it be to Stony Brook or Manhasset or Roslyn. It felt absolutely bizarre that I couldn't call him on January 14th, his sixty-fourth wedding anniversary to Grandma Grace, or on February 11th to let him know that I was thinking of him and had not forgotten that it was the twenty-sixth anniversary of Grandma Grace's passing. I always called him on those dates that were vital to his story where either of his wives were concerned. In spite of his advanced age, he never forgot the significance of the key dates of his story and we honored their memories through his retelling of their stories.

My daughter, Victoria, would be making her First Holy Communion on Saturday, May 2nd, and I was brokenhearted at the thought of Grandpa not being there to see her on her big day. I thought about that keenly as she made the Sacrament of Reconciliation on Saturday, March 7th, when I had no idea that there would be no communion ceremony taking place on May 2^{nd,} and that after that weekend was over, it would be a very long time before Victoria and I would set foot in Ss. Cyril & Methodius Church together again. A week before, an illness had its first confirmed case in New York City called the coronavirus, or Covid-19, a new virus that had begun in China and was spreading like wildfire. There were now thirty-three confirmed cases in New York. New York State Governor Andrew Cuomo declared a state of emergency, and after visiting my parents that evening after Victoria's ceremony, we did not know when it would be safe for us to visit my parents inside their home again.

On Thursday, March 12, 2020, I went to Greenfield Cemetery in Uniondale to visit Grandpa Pat and Grandma Grace's grave. The blank heart on their monument had been etched with "Pasquale 1927-2019." I really just couldn't believe that he was really down there. He had always been my cemetery-visiting buddy. Now I would be doing it alone. I felt so alone and empty as I stood there staring at the pink stone and on this day just could not find peace and consolation that he was in heaven and with all of his loved ones who had gone before. I wanted him here. I wanted to go on so many more adventures with him. Victoria wanted to spend so much more time with him. Uncle Paul and Vicki and their kids wanted to have him there with them. Aunt Michele wanted to share with him all of her stories as she drove home from work at night in North Carolina. We were lost without him.

The following day, Friday, March 13th really was Friday the 13th in every way. When Victoria walked out of the second-grade class of her teacher, Mrs. Jennifer Kreuscher, the school door would be shut

Peter Michael and Victoria on March 7, 2020

and my beautiful little girl would never again set foot in her school as a second grader. With 21,000 confirmed cases in New York State by March 16th, the New York City Saint Patrick's Day Parade was cancelled for the first time in history, and churches would only be open for funeral masses...and then...not open at all.

Saturday, March 28, 2020, I came into contact with my first decedent who had died from the coronavirus. In spite of being decked out in personal protective equipment, I was very concerned. Then, masks called N-95 masks would become as much a part of my attire for work as a suit and tie. As March gave way to April, the floodgates of cases of coronavirus deaths seemed to break open. In spite of the fact that we were not having visitations at the funeral home, our workdays were extending from eight hour shifts to fourteen to sixteen-hour shifts.

There was no palm on Palm Sunday and there was no mass. Good Friday I was home, but spent the day in prayer reflecting on the Lord's passion and death and in tears about what was to come as I began my work week on Holy Saturday. I thought a lot about Grandpa and about how frantic I would have been about his health because he was so stubborn and would he understand how vital it would be for him to stay home, had he still been with us. As I fell asleep that night with my rosary in my hands and tears in my eyes, I kept praying for God to send me a guardian angel, like Saint Michael the Archangel, to get me through the trial that I would be facing. God, I missed Grandpa!

When I got to work the next day, Saturday, April 11, 2020, I was shocked to see that a man and woman who I did not know were working alongside my coworkers. I was soon to find out that they were funeral directors from other states who had volunteered to assist us for the next two weeks through the pandemic. Later that afternoon, I got to work with one of the funeral directors, Eric Daniels, a funeral director and location manager who lived in Melbourne, Florida. When Eric and I had gotten into the van to go to a home where someone had passed, he immediately disarmed me with his supportive kindness and his ability to see that, in spite of my smiling, how my eyes revealed how much pain that I was actually in. The truth was that in the week before he had arrived, I had felt overwhelmed and defeated and could not figure out how my fellow coworkers and I were going to get through Covid hell. After only one day of working together, I went home that night thanking God that He had heard my prayers and had sent me the guardian angel I had asked for in Eric. Grandpa would have been frantically worrying about me, and I can't help but wonder if he had his hand in sending me a friend when I needed one most. Constantly on the road because of the spike in Covid deaths over the next two weeks, I was able to keep focused, in spite of the relentless workload, because of the person who was in the passenger's seat. Eric Daniels helped me through all of the situations that I encountered while bringing a decedent into my care. There were many situations that were far from easy. In spite of this, I never lost faith and I never lost hope because Eric stayed the eternal optimist and always knew what to say to make me not lose hope, because I had lost all of my optimism weeks before. Not only did he have the right words to say, they made an impact and helped me to become stronger and focus on the silver lining while we were making our way through a time of darkness. Eric was a superhero in my eyes and I told him that he was Superman without the cape. Truth be told, I really thought that when I had prayed to God for a guardian angel to help me, he had sent Michael the Archangel in the human form of Eric Daniels. While we drove together for hours on end traversing Long Island, Eric and I never stopped laughing together, and each of us were constantly bubbling with stories of our lives to share with one another. Overnight, we went from strangers to friends to brothers.

When Eric went home on Friday, April 24th, I was truly sad to see this heroic man leave, but he did leave me with the tools to get through that he had learned as a paratrooper in the US Army before he had ever been a funeral director. What neither of us could have realized was that the Covid battle we had just fought together was not the worst one that we would actually be fighting together.

The sun had not yet risen on Saturday, April 25, 2020, when I woke up before 3 a.m. in a stupor and felt like my body was on fire, my skin hurt, and I felt extremely woozy. I had slept on the couch that night to keep with social distancing from Vanessa, since she was working in the hospital, and if one of us did get sick, we wouldn't bring the other one down with us. Vanessa had started feeling ill and had stayed in her room the day before, but we did not have any idea yet that she could have the virus. She had been working such brutal shifts at the hospital that we wanted to believe that she was just run down. I took my temperature and my fears confirmed that I had a temperature of 100.8. At 4 a.m., I got on my phone and scheduled to get tested for the virus at the AFC Center in West Islip. I felt so incredibly ill, and so did Vanessa, and we did not know what in the world we were going to do if we had indeed caught the virus. I texted my boss that I had a fever and was going to the doctor.

Peter Michael and Eric Daniels during the
Covid-19 pandemic, April 2020

    Vanessa tested positive first and I felt my insides sinking. I needed to muster all of my strength to get dressed, put on my mask, and get in the car to drive to the testing site. When I sat on the table, and exposed my nose, I felt dizzy as the swab probed up my nose, feeling it twist up my nostril to my brain, and came popping out again. Then it was time to get the results. And the survey said, "Positive." Vanessa and I had both tested positive for the Coronavirus before 2 p.m. Victoria was already exposed to us, so there was nowhere for her to go. We each had compromised parents who we had not seen in weeks. Vanessa felt like she was holding her own, but I definitely felt like I was sinking. She told me to walk around and not to lay around so much so that the lungs continue to expand and I didn't get pneumonia.

The next morning, Sunday, April 26th, Vanessa told me that I should go take a shower to wash away all of the Covid germs. I was holding onto the walls to avoid falling down in the shower, when I started to scream. As the water poured down my body, I howled in agony, "Vanessa, there's acid going down my body! There's acid going down my body." When Vanessa rushed into the bathroom, she discovered that my body was covered in a red rash and the contact with the hot water made it feel like I was getting an acid burn. I took Benadryl to try and calm down my skin enough to put my fresh pair of sweatpants and undershirt on. Vanessa was dealing with a headache and cough that would take her breath away. Hour to hour, I would range from not feeling so bad, to so horrific that I had never been that sick in my life. The illness pretty much baffled me. I was relieved that Vanessa didn't have these violent swings. All of this was happening while Victoria and our dog, Lady, had to witness this war going on within our bodies.

My parents and Robert were on edge as they got reports of my declining health every few hours. I laid on the couch lifeless and I was beginning to have an issue catching my breath. A throbbing headache worse than my migraines drummed through my head, giving me vertigo and uncontrollable vomiting. I couldn't keep food, fluids, medication, or anything down without a violent bout with vomiting or diarrhea. My entire body felt like it was having a Charlie Horse from my neck to my arms, my legs and down to my ankles. For reasons I couldn't understand, I was uncontrollably crying all the time, and although I was taking the recommended Tylenol, my fever refused to come down, and each day I felt sicker and sicker by the hour.

By mid-week, I woke and knew all the signs and went to the doctor. When my oxygen level, which was supposed to be 100, was 85, I was not shocked when the doctor told me that I had developed

Covid Pneumonia in both lungs. What did I feel in spite of not being in shock? Doom. I started to doubt that I was going to survive this illness. I saw myself as being taken away to Good Samaritan Hospital and being placed on a vent. I saw myself going back to work in a body bag. There was absolutely no relief, no good days, no improvement. Tylenol did absolutely nothing. I had to lay prone (face down) for sixteen hours a day and using a C-Pap machine in place of a ventilator because Vanessa said that is how they treated the patients at the hospital with Covid. Vanessa would boil water and I would put a towel over my head and breathe in the steam. I took every vitamin from A-Z all day long. Later on, Vanessa said that since I showed no improvement, she was getting ready to accept defeat and have me hospitalized. I began telling her all of my funeral arrangements that I wanted. I looked at Victoria and cried because I was not going to live to see her make her First Holy Communion. I was so devastated that Grandpa Pat was not going to be here for it, and now I wouldn't be either. I wouldn't see my only child grow up. I thought this was the end. I prayed to Grandpa Pat for the first time. I couldn't call him and talk about things, but I could ask him for help. I knew that if there was anything he could possibly do, he would be there for me. I knew that if he had any say in the matter, Grandpa would not let God take me now.

    A legion of people were contacting me that they were praying for me and my family. The prayers had to have worked because modern medicine had not been able to help me. When it seemed like nothing would get better and the end of my life was coming, my fever of 102.8 finally broke after over fifteen days. My hair eschewed and more than a week's worth of facial growth, I looked in the mirror and was just taken aback by my reflection. After living on sips of Gatorade and no solid food, I slowly returned to the living. I was over twenty pounds lighter on the scale. Slowly, most of the symptoms little by little subsided, except the excruciating lung pain, loss of breath, tiredness, and intermittent cramping of my body. I retested and found I was still Covid positive. I went on a second antibiotic and prednisone for the lungs. A week later, as I felt no improvement, I returned to the doctor and the X-ray showed that, instead of bilateral pneumonia, I now had it in my lower lobes. Interestingly enough, both times they never heard anything bad on the stethoscope. It was only revealed through X-rays. Another week in bed, another antibiotic.

In the meantime, many of my coworkers had tested positive, but most were either asymptomatic or suffered from only mild symptoms. Although he was now home in Florida, Eric too had been stricken with Covid-19 right after returning home, and most of our symptoms mirrored one another, except that I was diagnosed with pneumonia and he became sick with a urinary tract infection and kidney stones. We were both laying on our couches feeling defeated and hopeless and we Facetimed daily to promise that we were going to keep fighting and get through this together. He was home with his wife, who was taking care of him, and I was home with Vanessa, Victoria, and Lady. Had it not been for the intense care that I received from Vanessa, who was like a lioness in the ferocity of which she fought to save my life, the constant support of the medical advice from our friend, Christine LaPersonerie, who is a nurse practitioner, and talking with Eric every single day, while we kept one another from losing faith and hope on a daily basis, I might not be here anymore for my wife and daughter. My brother Robert was constantly leaving stuff for me on my front stoop whenever he went to a store, which helped so incredibly much. My parents were always there, feeling powerless, and it broke my heart that my illness had to cause them such anxiety. Right before I returned to work, it made me so happy when they pulled in front of my house one day and I talked with them a bit from a distance. We still had to speak through the phone because my voice and lung power wasn't strong enough for them to hear me.

Once I recovered from my second bout with pneumonia, I returned to work once again extremely fatigued and weak on May 25, 2020. It took enormous effort to muster enough strength to get through the day, in spite of constantly losing my breath, but I must admit that it was also with the fear of getting sick once again.

Regardless though, I had survived a nightmare, but took away from it some gifts and lessons tucked in. Vanessa taught me how as a couple and as a family we can overcome mountains and beat the odds stacked against us, coming out stronger than before. From Victoria, I learned never to stop smiling although your heart is breaking. Because of her, I had to smile when I wanted to cry and laugh even though my lungs hurt. But I wasn't just going through the motions—she can always make me smile and make me laugh. Because of her, I felt a sympathy for my parents that I never really would have understood as they were panicked over the thought of never seeing me again and burying me. That is every parent's greatest fear, and I have seen it so many times in my line of work, that I know how easily we could have been there. From Eric, who came to me like a guardian angel out of nowhere when I needed one most, I learned how to keep looking for good in every day, even when suffering, and even during a pandemic when the world is telling you that nothing good could come out of 2020. This was not the time to lose faith. It was from this experience especially that I started to take the time out of my day to look up at the sky and never stop having complete faith in my beliefs.

Eleven days after returning to work, I celebrated my forty-second birthday on June 5th. While it was not a milestone birthday, I never felt so blessed and grateful to be alive on that day before. I missed hearing from Grandpa Pat that I wasn't young no more either, or all the years of his sending such heartfelt grandson cards with a twenty tucked in. That little gesture made you feel like you were still a kid, but it was the cards I cherished most. I always felt that they told you how he felt, since he wasn't one to overly share his loving sentiments for others like my father and I have always done. Nine days later, it was six months already since he had passed away! It was inconceivable to think that I had not spoken with or seen him in half of a year. Aunt Michele and her family had moved from North Carolina to Florida and I know it was sad for her not to share her new adventure with Grandpa. Uncle Paul was keeping busy and doing incredible projects on his cabin in

Upstate New York. We were all looking for ways to fill this void that we all keenly felt.

On July 17, 2020, Vanessa and I celebrated our tenth wedding anniversary. How different the world was from a decade before or even the year before. We renewed our marriage vows and went to the park where we had taken our wedding portraits. We found the tree where the wedding photographer had taken the pictures of us and I took a photo of Vanessa and Victoria under it. Just like us, the tree had weathered a lot of storms in ten years, but was still standing. Four days later, July 21, 2020, I was blessed to celebrate the day that I thought I was not going to live to see. Victoria made her First Holy Communion at our parish, Ss. Cyril & Methodius Church. Wearing a resplendent white gown with Vanessa's bridal veil and tiara, Victoria walked down the aisle wearing a mask as she received. Grandpa's presence was deeply missed on that day and Victoria mentioned him quite a few times. She was blessed that she did have her four grandparents there with us to celebrate, as well as her godfather, my brother, Robert.

Peter & AnnMarie on their 47th wedding anniversary, May 5, 2020

Victoria on her First Holy Communion Day, July 21, 2020 (l.-r.) Robert, Peter Michael, Vanessa with Victoria standing in front of her, AnnMarie, and Peter

A month later, Victoria celebrated her first birthday without "Pa Pat" when she turned eight years old on Sunday, August 30, 2020. Unlike all of her previous birthdays, our backyard was not abound with relatives and friends or little children. Under the overhang in our backyard, Victoria sat around a table of just her parents, her four grandparents, and her two godparents, as our dog, Lady, and her godmother's dog, Riley, ran around the yard. Grandpa was deeply missed and it felt so strange not to take our four-generation birthday picture with him on that day. As we sat together eating pizza and drinking pink lemonade with a mermaid decorated yard as Victoria wanted, we had to not focus on what we had lost in the past year, but what we still had. Vanessa's dad had spent most of the summer of 2020 hospitalized and my mother suffered from chronic ill health, and look at what Vanessa and I had survived only a few months before, so we had to focus on the blessing that for her Communion Day in July and for her eighth birthday on that day, she still had her parents and grandparents with her to celebrate. Grandpa's passing made it very evident to us in 2020 that nothing is guaranteed and

PASQUALE

you never really know how long you have with the ones you love. On that day a year before, it seemed that we had a long road ahead left with Grandpa. In reality, we had only three and a half months left.

Saturday, September 5, 2020, I was elated at the thought that at 5:50 a.m., my father officially turned seventy. While I was elated at the fact of my father's milestone, the emptiness of another milestone was still there. This was Grandpa Pat's ninety-third birthday as well, and our first without him. How odd it was for me not to be calling him or going to Baldwin to pick him up so the birthday boys could celebrate their day together. As I worked that morning, a somberness overtook me, as much as I tried to fight it. After work that afternoon, I got off of the Southern State and paid him a quick visit at Greenfield Cemetery before the gates closed to see him on his birthday. Staring at his name now engraved into the left of the two hearts, I couldn't help once again feeling disbelief that he could really be there. How I missed him and I always would. What a heavy heart I had while driving away from the gravesite.

Later on that evening, I went with Vanessa, Victoria, and Lady to my parents' house to celebrate my dad. Not wanting to lose the tradition, in spite of Grandpa Pat's death, Victoria and I took a picture with my dad of the now three living generations of Franzeses. The tradition must not be lost and we must not forget that we must carry on, as Grandpa used to say. Watching my dad blow out his candles with my daughter made me smile. Grandpa had spent three fourths of his life celebrating his birthday with my dad. Now we would celebrate the rest of my dad's with him, but learn how to do it without Grandpa.

Two weeks later, on Friday, September 18, 2020, I woke up to a gray and rainy day as I remembered that today was Grandpa Pat and Grandma Rose's seventy-first wedding anniversary. How sad to think that this was technically the first anniversary that they had ever spent together. Their first one was when he was hospitalized with bleeding ulcers, and by their second anniversary, she was in her grave for nearly nine months. I was thinking about a year ago, the last time that he came to my house, when he asked me to see his wedding album. The cream-colored album with the gold lettering of "Our

Wedding/Rose and Pat/September 18, 1949," was now tinged with the yellowing and brittleness of antiquity. I laid it on a table in front of him, as he sat on my couch, and I sat next to him. He paused as he looked at the cover at their names in faded gold. I can only imagine the memories that must have conjured in his mind that were left unsaid. His gnarled hands gingerly opened the cover and he peered at each imagine in silence. "She was such a beautiful girl," he said as he looked at Rose smiling back at him from those crisp black and white photographs. "I still can't wrap my mind around what happened to her." As we came to the end of the book, he smiled and said, "She sang like a canary… she sang with the band throughout the whole affair." The cream-colored book was closed, and little did we know, it was his farewell on Earth to that chapter of his past and looking through that album he had thumbed through so many times for the last time.

At 12:15 p.m. on that afternoon, I attended a memorial mass for Grandpa Pat and Grandma Rose with Vanessa and my parents at Ss. Cyril & Methodius Church. It was moving as the four of us sat in the pew together and heard the names of "Pasquale and Rose Franzese" mentioned, and to think that these two marriages sitting in that pew carried on the legacy that Rose and Pat had begun seventy-one years ago that day. After mass was over, Mom, Dad, Vanessa and I went to the Olympic Diner in Deer Park to honor and celebrate the legacy of our family together.

On September 22, 2020, Grandpa Pat's Aunt Virginia Spizio's only living grandchild, Joe Pisano, passed away at the age of seventy-eight. Cousin Joe had been the last living person who had attended Uncle Patsy's Christmas Eve celebrations on Kingsland Avenue all of those years ago. In recent years, Grandpa and Joe had enjoyed reminiscing about those old times of which they were the last two surviving members. As we prepared for Joe's wake five days later, my father called me that my mother had become unresponsive in her reclining chair. As I was at work overseeing the wake for my cousin, I was filled with angst as my mother was taken by ambulance to Good Samaritan Hospital, where they found an infection had caused her to lose consciousness. After staying there a week on IV antibiotics, she was transferred to Affinity Nursing & Rehabilitation Center in Oakdale, New York, where she spent a few weeks building up her strength and walking again. Due to Covid restrictions, she was not allowed any visitors and had to speak with us solely through phone calls and Facetime. After spending a few weeks there in October, she was determined to be home in time for my brother, Robert's thirty-second birthday. Her determination paid off when she was home on October 19th, the day before his birthday. It was so heartwarming for me when I entered her house on October 23rd and she was back in her kitchen with a radiant smile and sitting in her wheelchair at the stove making Chicken Francese. It felt like we had totally turned the corner with her ill health and that life was going to be good again.

AnnMarie back in her kitchen cooking on October 23, 2020

Two weeks later, I was ready to venture off Long Island for the first time since the pandemic hit. I had thought that the pandemic would have been over by November, but I was wrong. Armed with my mask, my antibodies, and prayer, I knew that I could not take a trip to Florida as I had planned, but instead drove four hours to Boston to spend a few days with my best friend, Eric, who had gotten me through the pandemic in April. After Eric had gone home on April 24th and then the next day we were felled by the illness, we had continued to talk on the phone daily at 7 a.m. The stranger who had flown in to help had in hours become my favorite coworker, and by time he had gone home, had become my best friend in the world. After fighting, beating, and recovering from the harrowing illness that had almost claimed our lives together, we had become brothers. Eric became the big brother that God forgot to give me, but in the end, gifted me with this treasure at the age of forty-one. We met up on November 8th, the day after Eric's fifty-eighth birthday, and we laughed nonstop as he showed me the streets where he had grown up in Peabody, Massachusetts, introduced me to his brother, Tony, who we went out to dinner with, and on our last day went touring with at Harvard. Eric also introduced me to his sister, Maureen "Mo" Twiss and her husband, George, his son, Joey, and his daughter, Jessie, his grandson, Giuseppe, and his childhood best friend, who we all went out to dinner with. We visited Joey's brand-new barber shop, South Mane Barber Shop, in Concord, New Hampshire, which he had successfully opened during the pandemic. Joey got to give his father a haircut in his new shop while we were there. We toured Richardson's Dairy in Middleton, Massachusetts, which was owned by his cousin, David, which his Uncle Bill Daniels had run for many years. His Uncle Bill had died from Covid on April 17th when we were working together in New York. This kid from Long Island was awestruck at the process of watching ice cream made from the cows to being filled into containers and put into deep freeze. I never tasted ice cream that incredible in my entire life. Another day, we went to Jordan's Furniture Superstore, where Richardson's had another location. This was unlike any furniture store that you could imagine. The ice cream location is a 60x40 foot ice cream stand, topped with a gigantic banana split made out of jelly beans. This is surrounded by a replica of Boston's major landmarks sculpted out of jelly beans and the town is surrounded by jelly bean tables to sit at with your ice cream. While you sit and eat your ice cream, you are watching a Liquid Fireworks show. While we didn't do it, they also had an adventure ropes course to go through and an IMAX 3D movie theater. All of this in a furniture store! I definitely didn't have all of this when I went to Ethan Allen on Route 110 in Farmingdale back home! As only funeral directors would do, Eric and I also visited Saint Mary's Cemetery in Salem, Massachusetts, to visit the graves of his grandparents on both sides of his family, in addition to some of his ancestors. While I lost my main cemetery buddy, Grandpa Pat, in 2019, God had definitely sent me a new cemetery buddy in Eric in 2020.

As it always is when you are having fun, the hours flew by, and before I knew it, I was wistfully driving back to Long Island. After Covid, every good time was cherished all the more and the ending of those good times were just more keenly felt. As I drove home all of those hours, I missed Grandpa Pat so much. On long car rides, I always loved calling him because he loved to talk for an hour or two whenever you called him. While I was on the road driving, he would enjoy reminiscing about yesteryear and complain about today. I enjoyed the former, tried to be sympathetic to the latter, but was always grateful to have been in my forties and still had a grandparent with whom I could laugh with and have meaningful conversations. In the meantime, as I drove home from Boston, it was a torrential rainstorm and the roads were pitch black and the visibility was non-existent. Mom was on the phone with me instead and was awesome company for the ride home. She made me laugh because she was like a little kid always looking for presents whenever I went away. One of the days, Eric and I were speaking to her through the car speakers as I drove and she said she wanted a present. Eric said, "But AnnMarie, we are going to a furniture store." Her reply was, "Peter has his car. You could buy me a lamp. He could put a lamp in his trunk." We roared with laughter. She got a magnet from Harvard because, by the last day, I was sweating that I hadn't found anything yet. Disappointing AnnMarie Franzese was a cardinal sin, just like her birthday, April 23rd, was always treated as the high holy day of the calendar.

Thanksgiving Day fell on Thursday, November 26, 2020. Mom had had such trouble with her legs that she had only been able to come over for events in my backyard most times in recent months because she had not been able to climb the stairs of my stoop. Since having been released from rehab, she was confident that she could come over for the holiday. The last time that she had been inside my house was on Christmas Day 2019, when we toasted Grandpa Pat five days after his funeral. Vanessa had told my mother that she only had to bring dessert for the holiday, that she had everything covered. As we prepared that morning, we watched the Thanksgiving Day episode of *Everybody Loves Raymond*, which Vanessa calls our life story and "home movies." Later in the afternoon when Mom, Dad, and Robert arrived, yes Mom had brought dessert…but she also brought something else. She brought her own stuffing and gravy. We howled because here was our very own Marie Barone who always found a way to do it her way. We would always laugh because it would be a little competition as the focus was my plate and whose food was going to be on it, Mom's or Vanessa's. Victoria's eyes would be filled with glee and the three most important women of my life had their eyes on me. The pressure was on. In the end, I made them all happy. It was the first holiday that we got to spend together as a family in nearly a year and we were really just incredibly thankful on this Thanksgiving. In fact, it was the most thankful that I had ever felt on Thanksgiving ever. I spent so many holidays thinking about what and who were missing, either through distance or death. On this Thanksgiving, I was finally just grateful for who and what I still had. Inspired by my daughter making a thankful tree in honor of Thanksgiving for school, I made a Thanksgiving Day post on Facebook to share what I felt on this holiday, who and what I was grateful for, and what each person and event had done to enlighten my life.

On this Thanksgiving 2020, I took nothing for granted, I was more thankful than I have ever been, and I appreciated all of these incredible people who make me feel like George Bailey every day. It really is *A Wonderful Life* and God is so good because He gave me my beautiful girls, Vanessa, Victoria and Lady, my parents, my brother, Aunt Sue and Don, my in-laws, Ken and Vicki, and this year brought me my best friend, Eric. In the end, 2020 was the year to be grateful and not bitter. "Happy Thanksgiving and much love on this day for giving thanks!"

Thanksgiving Day 2020 at Peter & Vanessa's house

    As Thanksgiving came to an end and we got ready for the season of Advent, once again, everything that we planned was about to have the rug pulled out from under us. Following Thanksgiving, the Covid numbers were once again out of control. I had to start social distancing again from my parents who were so compromised. When I did visit them, I would always wear my mask and stay at a distance and not hug and kiss them like we always did.

    We had gone a whole year without Grandpa Pat's living presence in our lives. How I missed him when I stopped to think about him and the great times that we shared in those last years, but this year did not give me a lot of time to dwell on that fact. There was a survival fight for all of us who remained behind that had filled my time and also humbled me and made me grateful for whatever I could hold onto. On that cold and dank day of December 16th, I stood at Grandpa Pat and Grandma Grace's grave, the pink of his stone dull under the steel gray sky, as I marveled at the fact that he was truly there and it had been for a whole year. Then, all of the plans that I had had to honor the first anniversary of his passing and the seventieth anniversary of Grandma Rose's passing on December 22nd were dashed. I had a memorial mass set on that day for both of them, but a severe snowstorm crippled everything and I was unable to attend. I did not get to visit their graves either, as they were buried in snow, their Christmas blankets obscured from view.

On Christmas Eve, I went with Victoria to see Mom, Dad and Robert. At first, we had decided that we would leave one another's Christmas gifts on the stoop. We were so incredibly afraid of the spread of Covid-19 to my parents. Then, Dad said that he would rather be dead by next Christmas than to miss seeing us for this one, so we went in and social distanced in the living room as we stood among the piles of Christmas gifts and the familiar sound of the electric trains zooming around the track around the base of the Christmas tree. The familiar ornaments that I have known as well as my family my whole life were a welcoming sight. Mom was sitting in her reclining chair and beaming, as Dad and Robert handed us bags of gifts and we handed them theirs. Once again, as we shared our love with our voices and our eyes and the gifts we exchanged, we just had to be grateful to be together at all.

Vanessa had gotten her Covid vaccine on that Christmas Eve and spend most of Christmas Day laying down from the effects from the vaccine. I talked with Mom and Dad on the phone that day, as we both had a quiet day at home, as Victoria played with all of her new presents with the glee and delight of an eight-year-old on Christmas morning.

A week later, on New Year's Eve, I had had my Covid vaccine two days before and had just had a few hours of feeling very weak and out of sorts, but otherwise came through it fine. Vanessa was at work, and we were all full of concern because Mom's sister, Aunt Sue, was hospitalized. When I called that evening to speak with Mom on her house phone, she had Aunt Sue on speaker phone on her cell phone. At the same time, Dad had Eric and his wife on Facetime on his cell phone. With every one of us on speaker phone, in Deer Park and North Babylon, and North Carolina and Florida, we all talked and laughed as we celebrated all apart and completely together at the same time. As always, as the clock struck midnight and ushered in 2021, we were all on the phone with each other to say Happy

New Year and thanking God that we had all rung in another year together. After losing Grandpa Pat only a few days before New Year's last year, we were even more keenly aware that nothing can be taken for granted. I had come so close to losing my life in 2020, as had Mom and both of Vanessa's parents. We were all blessed to still be here and fighting the good fight.

Eric had not only become my best friend and older brother, but he had become a vital member of the family for all of us. As everyone enjoyed the company of each other so incredibly much, his wife had devised the plan that we should all do a Zoom call together. In spite of technical difficulties, everyone talking at the same time, and the constant laughter, all of us were reunited on Facetime. Mom and Dad would be on, Eric and his wife, Aunt Sue and Don, Eric's sister and brother-in-law, Mo and George, and Vanessa, Victoria, and I. We had a steady appointment to meet at 7 p.m. on Saturdays and everyone looked forward to it all week long. On February 20th, we had our usual call except that Mom said she really wasn't up to the call and wouldn't be coming on. I was shocked because I knew how much she had been looking forward to it all week, right up to that morning. When the call began at 7 p.m., Dad was on with everyone, but not Mom. He said she wasn't feeling well and wouldn't be on. In the meantime, Mo and George had their granddaughters over the house for a sleepover and the sound of the voices of the little girls perked Mom up a bit. Although she had not planned to participate at all that night, she wanted to see Mo's girls. Dad handed her his tablet, and all of us were in shock at how incredibly ill Mom looked. She stayed on for only a few minutes, but every one of us who saw her felt unsettled that she was nothing like her usual, jovial, and fun-loving self. We got off the call around 8:30 p.m. and were texting privately how concerned we all were.

I was saying the rosary while sitting at my roll top desk in my second-floor book room at home when my brother, Robert, called me at 8 a.m. the next morning, Sunday, February 21, 2021. My mother was currently in an ambulance on her way to Good Samaritan Hospital. Mom had spent the night sleeping in her reclining chair. At the same time, Dad was sitting in his reclining chair, when all of the sudden, she tumbled to the floor. Dad sprung to his feet immediately and was overcome with fear that she had died. She had not made any sound as she fell to the floor. When Mom's face made contact with the hardwood floor, she said that she must not have been conscious because she didn't even know she was falling until she hit the floor. When efforts to get her up proved futile, the Deer Park Fire Department was called, and Mom forlornly looked up at Dad and said, "I guess we're going to be separated again." When Mom had been felled ill in September and had left the house for the rehab, it had been the longest that my parents had ever been separated in the fifty years that they knew one another. Now, knowing this was happening again, they were both filled with dread that this was going to be a major possibility once again.

When the police and ambulance arrived at the house, because she was on blood thinners and had had such a hard blow to her head and body to the floor, they said that she should be evaluated at the hospital. Dad followed in his car as the ambulance headed for West Islip.

At first glance, everything seemed to be that Mom was going to be quickly evaluated and discharged once that it was proved she had not sustained any serious injury or suffering from internal bleeding. Due to the fact that it was a Sunday and that the physical therapy department were not going to be there to evaluate her, it seemed that she would be at least spending the night. When I spoke with her, she mentioned that they had given her a pamphlet to choose a rehab facility to be transferred to in the event that she needed to go to one.

I visited Mom in the emergency room after I got out of work at 10 p.m., and although she was uncomfortable in the hospital bed, which I had addressed with the doctor on the floor, she was just talking about choosing a rehab to go to with me. I left there after 11 and felt this was just a very temporary setback and everything would be fine.

The next morning, Mom called me in a pretty cheery mood around 5 a.m. that she was going to be going to a room and they were going to evaluate her, as planned. She wanted Dad to bring her stuff so she would have it to take with her when she was transferred to a rehab.

The transfer was postponed because Mom started to have difficulty with her oxygen levels and was put on a nasal canular…then to a full-face oxygen mask…and then to what is referred to as a "non-rebreather." In the meantime, the phone calls continued Monday, Tuesday, and Wednesday. By Thursday, the phone calls from her had ceased. Once Mom went into a room in the hospital, we were not able to visit her due to Covid restrictions. Everything seemed OK until the calls stopped completely. I was informed by nurses that she was "lethargic." I asked them if she had her cell phone and they told me that it was in her hand. I asked them if the phone battery had died. It had not. Why wasn't she answering the phone?

By the second day that she was not answering the phone, I demanded that someone on the floor go to her bed and tell her to answer her phone. A hospital staffer answered the phone for her and when they gave her the phone, she was unable to have a conversation with me. She sounded like she had been woken from a deep sleep and was barely able to communicate. I got frantic on the phone and then was told that I could come to the hospital to see her between the hours of 3 and 6. I picked up Victoria and her friend, Ethan, from school and dropped them off with Kristen, Ethan's mom, and rushed to the hospital. When I approached my mother's bed, I felt all the blood go to my feet. I was grief-stricken and enraged. She wasn't lethargic!!! She was unconscious!!! And why? What was happening to my mother? I would shake her and she would look at me, her eyebrows would go up in recognition and she would say, "Oh, hi!" and then I would lose her back into slumber. A nurse did the same and the nurse asked her, "Who is this?" Mom replied, "That's my son," and then went back to sleep. I frantically called my father, then my aunt, my wife, and then a friend. I was in shock. I was frantic. I didn't know what to do. Apparently, she was having trouble getting rid of her carbon dioxide and it was causing her to not be able to stay awake. I began to wonder if this was the reason that she had toppled out of the recliner chair in the first place. I went home that night extremely agitated and never fell asleep that night as I walked the floors and silently said my Our Father's, Hail Mary's, and Glory Be's, as my rosary beads slid through my fingers. How could this be happening now?

When I got out of work on Saturday, February 27th, I went directly to the hospital. Only one family member was allowed to visit per day between the hours of 3 and 6. I got there just after 4 p.m., and when I was coming out of the elevator, I saw a light going off above my mother's room and nurses and staff running for her room. I felt myself get weak as I unsuccessfully was bracing myself for the worst. A rapid response had been called and I was asked to go to the waiting room as they stabilized her. Mom's oxygen levels had plummeted and they had to get her stabilized. I sat in that little, dark room down the hall and just stared at the door, as I called Vanessa, Dad and Robert, Aunt Sue, and Eric and his wife. In the meantime, my rosary beads were once again going through my fingers. Once she was finally stabilized, I went back in there. The room was dark and she was breathing, but unconscious. I just sat there and watched her breathe in disbelief. Feeling I was going to lose my mind after a while, I stepped out into the hallway and called Eric again because he has the ability to always keep me calm and sustain me with strength. I didn't want to upset my family as I became unglued. As we were talking, once again, the staff started running for my mother's room. She had had a rapid decline in her oxygen levels again. They informed me that she would have to be transferred to the Intensive Care Unit. What was happening? Was I going to lose my mother this time? It felt like an eternity as I waited for them to transfer her. For the better part of an hour, if not an hour, I stared at the door as I prayed. Then, finally, I went out into the hallway as I saw my mother being wheeled by. She saw me and we squeezed each other's hands as she yelled, "There's my handsome son!" Then they took her behind closed doors. I was told that they would come to get me when she was stable.

For hours I sat in that room, feeling weak and absolutely helpless, as I wondered what was happening to my mother. What could be happening to her? Why was this happening? What happened during those five days when I wasn't allowed to see her? When I couldn't take waiting anymore, after three hours, I said that I had been patient long

PASQUALE

enough and demanded to know what was happening to my mother. A nurse came out from the ICU doors and said that he was shocked because no one had notified them that my mother had any family members waiting in the waiting room. He took me to her bedside, where she was not awake, but was resting comfortably and stable on 100 percent oxygen on a Bi-Pap machine for the time being. The ICU nurse, who was incredibly kind, told me that they were going to do their very best to avoid Mom having to go on a ventilator. At that point, everything seemed to be calm, but he insisted on the fact that I should call any time if I was concerned about her status.

I went home that night so incredibly exhausted and feeling ill from the anxiety, but sleep would not come. I walked the floors all night, I went upstairs in my book room, and I cried while everyone slept. I couldn't believe this was happening to my mother…to us.

The following day, Sunday, February 28th, a week after the fall, I went to the hospital when I got out at 4 p.m. From being a funeral director, all of the staff know me on a first name basis, and I could see the sympathy in their eyes, as I gave my mother's name and room number, my information, as my temperature was taken and a visitor's sticker was issued to me. Before boarding the elevator, I would always go into the hospital's chapel, where there is one side altar to The Sacred Heart and another to The Blessed Mother. I lit candles in front of both of them and prayed for my mother.

When I got upstairs, my heart was so full, I felt like it would burst. All was good with the world! Mom was fully awake and in really cheery spirits. I couldn't believe how much better she seemed with the Bi-pap. While I had to put my ear to the mask to understand her at times, her expressive eyes were bright and her eyebrows were arching high when she made her points. I felt so grateful and so hopeful. I immediately called my Dad and Robert and they talked for a while. Then I called Vanessa and Victoria, followed by Aunt Sue, then Eric and his wife, and lastly, Eric's sister, Mo. Everyone was so excited to hear her voice. I felt that we must be turning the corner and soon she would be back home with us. When I reluctantly left her when visiting ended at 6 p.m., I left feeling peace and slept that night for the first time since the fall. When I was getting ready to leave, there was a *Star Wars* marathon on her television. When the nurse asked her if she wanted her to change it, my mother said, "No, leave it on. It makes me feel like my kids are here. We're a Star Wars family."

When I got out of work on Monday, March 1st, I didn't find everything as positive as I had the day before. Mom was now in kidney failure and they had to start administering dialysis from her neck. She also needed a blood transfusion because her hemoglobin levels were low. In the meantime, they were trying to wean Mom off of the Bi-Pap and tried alternating it with a high oxygen cannula in her nostrils. When I walked in the room, she was in the middle of receiving a dialysis treatment and was in a great deal of discomfort. The exuberance was gone and her face was filled with anguish and defeat. She didn't want to really talk on the phone to anyone, but I insisted that she talk to Dad and Robert. She spoke very briefly with them. Her eyes hurt from the Bi-Pap machine, she had a terrible headache, and she felt altogether unwell. I left the hospital feeling very upset again.

On Tuesday, March 2nd, Mom was feeling even worse than she did the day before. She said that she couldn't take the pain and that she had the worst headache of her life. The temperature that day was in the single digits outside and my hands were like blocks of ice from having spent a long time directing a funeral at Calverton National Cemetery. I held one of her hands and the other I placed on her forehead to give her some relief. She looked the most unhappy and uncomfortable and miserable that I had probably ever seen her. I felt sick when she looked me in the face and with dark, intense eyes said to me, "I don't know if I'm going to make it. They keep telling me more and more bad news."

I couldn't take hearing or even considering those words. I told her that she just had to keep fighting and that everything would be OK. Although she really didn't want to talk on the phone, I insisted on three short phone calls. The first one was to my Dad and Robert. Dad told her how much he missed her and that he had her birthday present. He had bought her a Baby Yoda charm for her Pandora Bracelet. She said that she looked forward to seeing it. I then called

Vanessa and Victoria. When Victoria heard my mother's weak voice, she was taken aback. After they hung up, Victoria asked Vanessa, "Is Nanny going to die?"

The last phone call I made was to Aunt Sue. They too had a short conversation. It was a real struggle for her to do this, but I just felt that it was too important and had to be done, no matter how she was feeling. We didn't speak too much, as I let her rest with my cold hand on her forehead. I told her that Msgr. Greg Wielunski was offering his masses up for her in Miami, and that brought her a lot of peace and comfort. In fact, she even told her nurse about it.

About twenty minutes before six, the sciatica that shot from my lower back and down my left leg became so excruciating that I had to go home. When I told Mom that I was leaving, she opened her eyes and looked at the clock. Then she looked into my eyes with her brows furrowed and said, "But it's only twenty to six." I told her how much pain that I was in and that I would be there tomorrow as soon as I got out of work. I kissed her on the forehead and said goodnight, stopping by the nurse's station to thank them as I did every night, and went home.

The next morning, Wednesday, March 3, 2021, I was riding in the hearse in a funeral procession to Our Lady of Perpetual Help Church in Lindenhurst to direct the funeral for the grandfather of Brian LaPersonerie, a friend of mine, when my phone was going off. The hospital had to speak to me. It was the greatest comfort in the world to me that if I had to receive difficult news on the job that one of my friends was right there. How ironic that my job was to console him on that morning, when it was Brian consoling me.

When I finally spoke to the doctor, he informed me that there was no alternative but to place my mother on the ventilator. He said that he had discussed it with her, and even knowing the great risk that they may not be able to wean her off of it, she said that she was willing to take that risk. "Tell my son to give me the chance," was what the doctor told me she said. Robert had driven my father to Patchogue to receive the first dose of his Covid-19 vaccine and Vanessa was there to be one of the nurses administering them. I was in the middle of a funeral. None of us were able to be there, since the doctor said that we would have to be there in the next ten minutes if we wanted to see her before intubation. With none of that possible for all of us, my mother would have to be placed under sedation with the knowledge that she may never wake up again without the ability to see any of us.

Following the burial, I went back to work and let them know what had taken place, and finding myself unable to stop crying, I left work and headed for the hospital.

When I walked in, I was overcome with grief as I saw my mother on a ventilator for the second time in my life. My mother may never wake up again. I may never hear her voice again or see those dark, expressive eyes. She was receiving a dialysis treatment at the time. I sat in a chair and wept bitterly, but got permission for my father and Robert to be able to see her, in spite of the fact that there was only one visitor allowed at a time. The three of us stood together at the foot of her bed, Annie's three boys. We were all there. We just wanted her to fight. I was racked with an intense grief like I had never felt before, but my father had full faith that all was going to be well. She was going to come out of it just like she had in 2006. After they had left, Vanessa too came up directly from work, and she looked over everything and spoke with the medical staff.

When I was bracing myself to go to see Mom for the second day under sedation, I was losing courage fast. Eric "talked me off the ledge," as we say to one another, and recommended that I grabbed my Bible on the way to the hospital and read the Book of Job to myself for solace and inspiration. I would just sit there and watch her and pray, read from the Bible, say a rosary and a Chaplet of Divine Mercy, call my family to give them updates, and just keep hoping for a miracle. And when I wasn't doing any of those things, I would just cry.

In spite of the darkness that I was engulfed in, one nurse in particular who took care of my mother was a bright light in my life. Gerry Connolly, Mom's nurse, was a comforting presence on so many different levels. His expertise in the field of nursing and his ability to explain everything happening with my mother on the level of a veteran, like Vanessa, or a novice like me, earned him the deepest of respect from me and the highest of praise from my wife. In addition to this, the attention to detail and overall attentiveness to my mother, in spite of the fact that my mother was not conscious, was extremely touching to me as well. On top of all of this, I truly believe that Gerry is the most compassionate medical professional that I have ever met. In spite of the bleak situation that my mother was now in, I slept better at night knowing when she was in Gerry's care.

On Wednesday, March 10, 2021, I was in my cubicle at work when my cell phone went off and I recognized the number to be coming from Good Samaritan Hospital. The person from the hospital said that they would like to speak to me about end-of-life care for my mother. My mind just went blank. We were really here. There was no hope. In spite of the fact that nothing had happened regarding my mother that showed any improvement, I wasn't ready to accept the fact that my mother was truly dying. I told the person on the phone that I was only about three miles away and could I speak with them in person. How could I talk about these decisions just sitting in my cubicle? I left work and went to my father's house to pick him up, while Vanessa came from work to meet us at Good Samaritan Hospital. We lit candles in the chapel and waited in the lobby to be met by the palliative care team.

Eventually, we were called upstairs to a waiting area, where we sat with the palliative care doctor. She said that there was no hope for my mother to be returning to us, and that now it was a matter of time as to when we wanted to put her on comfort care to help ease her transition. My attitude was that she had only been like this for a week now. It was two weeks before a person had to be put on a trach. While we were all in agreement that a trach would be totally against her wishes, I thought that we could buy as much time as possible. That would bring us to March 17th, but given the fact how much she loved Saint Patrick's Day, I asked for a delay until March 19th, the Feast Day of Saint Joseph, patron saint of a happy death. That was also the day that her Grandpa Carrano passed away in 1964. At that point, I felt that we still had nine days for which prayers could be answered and this would have time to turn around.

After the meeting, I just sat and cried and cried at my mother's bedside. My mother was going to die. How could we cope with this trial? How could we possibly go on without her? Vanessa and a doctor that she worked with in the past comforted me as I sobbed at my mother's bedside. He gently explained to me that my mother was never going to recover, that she was never going to open her eyes or speak to me again. My mother was gone from me and was not coming back. Aunt Sue booked her flight to come to New York to be with her sister at the end, in spite of Covid restrictions and having just gotten over a bad bout of ill health.

When I got to my mother's bedside the following day and saw that there was still no hope and that the end was nearing, I called my dear friend, Father David Atanasio, to administer last rites to my mother. The sight of Father Dave walking down the corridor toward my mother's room brought such a comfort and peace, as I felt him bringing God right to her bedside. In the dark room, as she breathed on the respirator, Father Dave spoke to her so gently and warmly as he performed the Last Rites of the Catholic Church. As he had done for Grandpa Pat only fifteen months before, my mother was now ready for when the time came for her to go home to God.

The following day, Friday, March 12, 2021, Dad and I drove out to the Shrine of Our Lady of the Island in Eastport, Long Island, because we were having a mass said for Mom's healing. We both got peace and serenity with the knowledge that Mom was surrounded by love and prayers.

As we headed back home, Vanessa called to say that Mom's condition had deteriorated and that she had developed a fever. In the meantime, Aunt Sue's flight was in the air headed from North Carolina to New York to be at my mother's bedside. I brought my father to his house and told him that as soon as Aunt Sue arrived, she should jump into his car and head directly to the hospital. As I was my mother's health care proxy, I went ahead of everyone. Driving the few miles ride down Deer Park Avenue to Montauk Highway, I was both sickened and driven by the weight of the enormity of the moment. The time had come. My mother was dying.

PASQUALE

When I got to my mother's bedside, the nurse had told me that Mom's temperature was now over 104. Sepsis had taken over and this was the end. I called Vanessa, Robert, and my father that everyone should assemble. It was very clear by what the nurse was saying, and seeing my mother's terrible struggle, in spite of being unconscious and on the ventilator, that the end was fast approaching. I pulled out my rosary beads and began to pray the rosary and then the Chaplet of Divine Mercy. All of those years ago, Mom had asked me to say the Chaplet when she was going into the coma. Now I said it as she prepared to go home to the Lord. I just couldn't believe it, no matter how much I tried to wrap my mind around it. My mother was dying.

Aunt Sue's plane had landed and she rushed to the hospital immediately with Dad. It had always been my fear when the pandemic hit that her and Mom would never see one another again. While Mom was slipping away, she was still here, and Aunt Sue got to talk with her for an hour about everything she had wanted to say. Vanessa arrived, as my sister-in-law, Vicki, had taken Victoria for the night. And then, Robert arrived. We were all around her bed. The last time that we would all be together. The room was dimly lit and quiet. The door was shut to close out what was happening in the intensive care unit. Only fifteen months before, I had been at Grandpa Pat's death bed. And now, here I was, at my mother's.

I laid my head on my mother's shoulder and cried. I held her hand, which was warm and so alive, as she was getting good oxygenation from the vent. And yet, I knew, very soon, that was going to change. I thought to myself that I wanted my mother to hear beautiful things as the last things she heard on Earth. Taking out my cellphone, I laid it on her pillow and played Andrea Boccelli's *Con Te Partiro*, her favorite song that she and I shared together since 1998. As Boccelli belted out those Italian words that brought my mother such delight, the tears rolled down my cheeks and my shoulders wracked with sobs. Her breathing was starting to slow, so I was inspired to play one more song for her. It was a World War I ballad that her family sang every time they got together for decades. It was called *Till We Meet Again*. The recording that I had on my phone was sung by none other than her parents, Nana Nettie and Grandpa

Bob, and her Aunt Rosie Carrano. Through the tears, we sang along with our family who were long gone, a song that brought my mother comfort. Then, just as the song was about to end, Dad saw one single tear release from the corner of my mother's eye and roll down her cheek. Then, the room got quiet, and Mom breathed her last. At 7:33 p.m. on Friday, March 12, 2021, my mother, AnnMarie Boniface Franzese, went home to God. She was sixty-eight years old.

As my mother let go, Dad asked Mom to please tell his mother, Rose, that he loved her, and say hello to his father, Pat, her buddy. His mother who he never knew was the first person who came to my father's mind as he said goodbye. The love of his life was about to meet the woman who had loved him first, who had not held him in over seventy years. I just stared at Mom's face in disbelief. As a funeral professional who looks into the face of the recently deceased on a daily basis, nothing prepared me for the agonizing emotion of seeing my mother laying there lifeless in the hospital bed. I cried like I never cried before. I thought back to the line of a song Aunt Rosie used to sing to me as a child, "My mother is in heaven, above the skies so blue."

It took nearly a week for me to get through all of the preparations for my mother's funeral. She would wear the salmon-colored gown that she wore to my wedding and Vanessa had given her one of her shawls. She died wearing a yarn bracelet that Victoria had made for Mom to wear because they couldn't be together in those final days. All of the things that my mother loved throughout her life would be put on display. Thousands of photos had to be gone through to put together in the video. Her wedding gown had to come down from the attic and the box opened for the first time since 1973. Victoria requested that a photograph of my mother taken on Victoria's First Holy Communion day in July be used for her prayer card. My mother was going to have a funeral for a queen like she always was for us.

I was full of angst all of those days following Mom's passing because perfection for her funeral became my obsession. I did not truly begin to calm down until Wednesday, March 17, 2021. It was Saint Patrick's Day. I was standing in front of my house when Eric and his wife had flown in from Florida and their rental car pulled into my driveway. Just like when I was at my worst during the pandemic, Eric had come to help and be the rock for me as I sustained the greatest sorrow of my life. While nothing could make this heartbreak better, I was now feeling peace that everything was going to be OK. My best friend, who I had dubbed "Superman without the cape" in the *Florida Today* newspaper article the year before, had come to see me through this great catastrophe.

That night, Eric and his wife and Vanessa and I went out to dinner at Fancy Li in Babylon Village, and then the wives went back to my house, while Eric and I headed for Boyd-Spencer Funeral Home to bring all of the stuff needed for my mother's wake the next day. I felt paralyzed for a fleeting moment as I sat in my car in the back of the building with Eric. My mother was in that chapel. I was going to be seeing my mother in a casket for the first time. This moment was going to change me for the rest of my life. I was not doing this alone though. Eric was with me every step of the way.

The first time that I had seen Grandpa Pat and Mom in their caskets had been here. This place had become part of the Franzese family's story. Eric went in with me, while my coworker, Anthony Estremo, assisted and was getting her wedding gown ready to be displayed. As I stood with Eric at her casket, I was awestruck by how amazing my mother looked. Everything was flawless. She looked so good that it felt surreal. There was that element that felt like it was a dream. This couldn't be happening, but I knew that it was. As Eric stood beside me, it occurred to me that one of the last things Mom had done before she died was to send Eric a Saint Patrick's Day card. And here he was, standing at her casket on that Saint Patrick's Day.

Due to Covid restrictions, everyone who attended my mother's wake had to wear a mask and social distance as best as they could. In spite of this, my mother's wake was very well attended. Although there were concerns, it warmed my heart that so many had turned out to celebrate her, from her Greenpoint, Brooklyn days, her Richmond Hill days, and her Deer Park days.

Friday, March 19, 2021, Saint Joseph's Day, my mother was laid to rest one week after her passing. Vanessa, Victoria, Dad, Robert, Aunt Sue, Eric and his wife and I all met at my house in the morning and had bagels together, before the limousine arrived to pick everyone up. As I approached my mother's casket that morning, I knelt on the kneeler and cried as I rested my head on her shoulder. This was really and truly goodbye. I would never again see my mother's face in this life. How much I would miss her face. Her voice. That twinkle in her eyes and her expressive eyebrows, arched highly in excitement and furrowed in disapproval. Both brought a smile to my face. We all loved to imitate her, and she would feign insult, but we all knew that she loved the attention. Victoria grew to love imitating her most of all.

I remember standing in front of the room when it was time for us to say goodbye, but I do not remember so much. I do not remember the closing of my mother's casket, but that is probably for the best. Her silver casket, tinged with pink, was led to the waiting hearse. I had Eric ride with my mother. After all, he was my archangel on Earth and who better than he to be with my mother on her final Earthly journey. James Bizzaro, who had driven the hearse for Grandpa Pat and his best friend, Johnny Morena, both in 2019, would now drive my mother. I joined my family in the limousine, which held Vanessa, Victoria, Dad, Robert, Aunt Sue, and Eric's wife.

Her last ride down Deer Park Avenue. Her last trip to the church she loved so much, Ss. Cyril & Methodius Church in Deer Park, her parish for the past thirty-two years. As my mother wanted, the pastor, Fr. Gius Garcia, would say her funeral mass. She loved his singing voice. And, at her request, her favorite singer, Peggy, had come back to Saint Cyril's just for her.

As the pall bearers led my mother's casket down the center aisle of St. Cyril's, Eric and I walked behind with Victoria between us. We each held one of her hands, as my father, Robert, Vanessa, Aunt Sue, Uncle Paul and Vicki, and many other relatives and friends walked behind in procession. At the altar, Eric and I picked Victoria up after the pall was placed on top of the casket, so she could put the crucifix on top of Mom's casket. I had used the same crucifix for my mother that had been used for her mother, Nana Nettie Boniface, for her funeral back in 1989.

PASQUALE

At the conclusion of mass, Victoria joined Eric and I, along with the pall bearers, as we bowed at the altar and got into position. She once again held our hands during that heavy moment of my mother leaving St. Cyril's for the last time. It gave me that hollow feeling just like it did when my Nana Nettie left St. Cecilia's in Brooklyn for the last time all of those years ago. It was final. As we processed out of the church, my mind went back to seeing my mother sitting in her wheelchair at the back of the church on July 21, 2020, where she proudly sat watching Victoria make her First Holy Communion. Today, it was her life that was being celebrated and remembered, as we took her to her final place of rest.

On the way to the cemetery, the funeral procession went down Nicolls Road for my mother's last ride. I got a hard lump in my throat as I watched Eric walk solemnly up my mother's front stoop and gently lay roses from her casket spray on the top step.

We pulled through the gates of St. Charles Cemetery from Wellwood Avenue in Farmingdale on that frigid Friday just after noon. The bitter cold stung my face and paralyzed my hands, but the emptiness inside of me left me unaware of the pain. We were a small assembly crowded around her grave, which included members of the Franzese family, Uncle Paul and Vicki, and Cousin Joni Pisano Roderka, the great-granddaughter of Grandpa Pete Franzese's sister, Virginia. Grandma Rose's only living brother, Uncle Stevie Porti, and his wife, Aunt Diana, were there, as were his son, Karl, and his wife, Abby. Some of my mother's cousins were there as well, including a few friends. My childhood friend from kindergarten, Mike Zumpano, who was also a funeral director with me and had been an invaluable source of strength for me in that week was also there. Eric stood beside me in front of the mourners in case I was unable to speak, as Father Mickey Bancroft conducted the graveside service.

I had been unable to undo the paralysis of my mind to write a eulogy for my mother. I had done it for so many others, but the adequate words failed me, until now. As Father Mickey finished his service, I stood before all of those assembled and shared with them who my mother was and who they had each been to her. They had all been a part of her journey. She had been AnnMarie Boniface from

Kingsland Avenue, a member of the Carrano family who had settled in Greenpoint in 1896. She had been a St. Cecilia's girl. She was a proud member of the Franzese family for 50 years and was much loved by every member of the extended tribe. She was loved by them all, mourned deeply by each, and would be forgotten by none. A few rows behind her, Mom's lifelong best friend and childhood next door neighbor, Joann Panarelli Corvino, had been buried nearly five years before. Joann's daughter, Angela, and granddaughter, Giovanna, were present to celebrate her life. All of the pieces of the mosaic that made up her life story were represented, and truth be told, although she had not been well for fifteen years, she had a wonderful life and left a legacy that would live on. She instilled the legacy of the Franzeses, the Portis, the Bonifaces and the Carranos in her family, and now, a certain eight-year-old little girl, Victoria Rose Franzese, would carry it on to future generations.

As I stood alone watching my mother's casket being lowered into her grave, I saw the history of my whole life being buried with her. To understand me, to know me, was in the casket being laid to rest in that grave like buried treasure. Grandma Rose's sister, Theresa, had said to me in 1991, to know my Grandma Rose was to love her. What was truer than the same words about my mother?

After all of the mourners had departed, my father's only brother, Uncle Paul, and his wife, Vicki, joined us as we sat for a little while to let my father rest and be bolstered in the greatest tragedy of his life. Mom was now at rest with Grandpa Pat and Grandma Rose and Nana Nettie and Grandpa Bob and countless others, but Dad was getting a great deal of comfort being with his brother. Robert, Aunt Sue, Vanessa, Victoria, Uncle Paul, Vicki, Eric and his wife, and I sat that afternoon together as we reflected on Mom's story, and not this time with tears, but with laughter about the things that she used to say and do that never failed to make us smile and laugh. Aunt Sue and Eric and his wife would all be flying home. Robert, Vanessa and I would be going back to work. Victoria would be going back to school. Life would once again have to resume somehow, forever changed.

Peter on the day of AnnMarie's funeral with Peter Michael, Victoria, and Peter's brother, Paul, and sister-in-law, Vicki

Peter on the day of AnnMarie's funeral with Robert, Eric Daniels, and Peter Michael

In the weeks following my mother's death, we faced the milestones of her sixty-ninth birthday on April 23rd and my parents' forty-eighth wedding anniversary on May 5th without her. On Mother's Day, we all assembled as a family at her grave, where the marker was yet to be installed and the soft earth covering her grave had yet to spring forth with grass. A month after my mother's death, I needed to retreat and heal for a few days and was welcomed to spend a few days in Florida with Eric to heal and renew my strength. And although Eric's encouragement and support always makes me feel stronger, the silence of my mother's daily calls and absence of her strong presence was still very daunting. Over the course of fifteen months, I had lost the two legends of my living family tree.

On Sunday, June 6, 2021, Dad and I returned to Greenpoint for the first time following Mom's passing. Margie Keller Formato, the wife of Grandpa Pat's childhood friend, Rocky Formato, and the daughter of his first boss from Brooklyn Box Toe, Frank Keller, had passed away at the age of ninety-five. Coming down the Meeker Morgan ramp, rolling past my mother's home on Kingsland Avenue, down Frost Street past the two houses where Grandpa Pete had lived, past the churches of St. Cecilia's and St. Francis de Paola, and Richardson Street where Rose had lived, made us realize that no matter where we went in life, or how far away, this little area would always be where the story began. For Pete and Lorenzina, for Pat and Rose, for Peter and AnnMarie, for me.

I parked along McGuinness Boulevard on the side of Evergreen Funeral Home and Dad and I saw that it was still too early to enter the funeral home. He suggested that we go for a walk. Dad and I walked down Nassau Avenue to Manhattan Avenue. One by one, he told me what each storefront had once been when he was growing up there on Calyer Street. The doors of his old parish, Saint Anthony of Padua Church were locked, much to his disappointment. We walked and he talked and I listened, just like I had done with his father up and down Graham Avenue only a few years before. We stopped in front of the old Meserole movie theater. Although the building had been a drug store for many years afterward, the boards in front of the structure gave us that uneasy feeling that, just like the loss of the icons of our childhood, the historic movie theater too was going to be reduced to rubble. While he mourned his wife, he mourned the loss of his father and so many of the Franzeses, and he mourned the loss of the past, my father, Peter Franzese, at the age of seventy, stood there with his fedora and walking stick, staring at the old building in disbelief to say goodbye.

"I really enjoyed this walk with you," my father said to me, "just like you used to do with my father."

We will have to do this walk again and soon. We must continue the story. The story that began when Pietro Franzese first got off that boat onto Ellis Island and went to go live with his Uncle Joseph Iovino in this little neighborhood of Greenpoint-Williamsburg, Brooklyn, back in 1903. I will continue the story when my father and I walk with my daughter, Victoria, down Humboldt Street and my father will begin with the story, "My Grandpa Pete owned a grocery store that stood right here where that Johnny pump is, and my father, Pa Pat, was born inside the store. They knocked it down to build this bridge, the BQE. Pa Pat was born and grew up here as The Brooklyn Grocer's Son."

Peter & Peter Michael, June 5, 2021

Peter and Victoria Rose at AnnMarie's grave in September 2021

Peter Michael at the grave of Pat and Grace, March 2022

PASQUALE

Franzese Family Plot in Calvary Cemetery

389

CPSIA information can be obtained
at www.ICGtesting.com
Printed in the USA
LVHW021941301122
733368LV00001B/3